Black Folk: Then and Now

THE OXFORD W. E. B. DU BOIS

Henry Louis Gates, Jr., Editor

The Suppression of the African Slave-Trade to the United States
of America: 1638–1870
  Introduction: Saidiya Hartman

The Philadelphia Negro: A Social Study
  Introduction: Lawrence Bobo

The Souls of Black Folk
  Introduction: Arnold Rampersad

John Brown
  Introduction: Paul Finkelman

Africa, Its Geography, People and Products
Africa—Its Place in Modern History
  Introductions: Emmanuel Akyeampong

Black Reconstruction in America
  Introduction: David Levering Lewis

Black Folk: Then and Now
  Introduction: Wilson J. Moses

Dusk of Dawn
  Introduction: Kwame Anthony Appiah

The World and Africa
Color and Democracy: Colonies and Peace
  Introductions: Mahmood Mamdani and Gerald Horne

In Battle for Peace: The Story of My Eighty-third Birthday
  Introduction: Manning Marable

The Black Flame Trilogy: Book One
The Ordeal of Mansart
  Introduction: Brent Edwards
  Afterword: Mark Sanders

The Black Flame Trilogy: Book Two
Mansart Builds a School
Introduction: Brent Edwards
Afterword: Mark Sanders

The Black Flame Trilogy: Book Three
Worlds of Color
Introduction: Brent Edwards
Afterword: Mark Sanders

Autobiography of W. E. B. Du Bois
Introduction: Werner Sollors

The Quest of the Silver Fleece
Introduction: William L. Andrews

The Negro
Introduction: John K. Thornton

Darkwater: Voices from Within the Veil
Introduction: Evelyn Brooks Higginbotham

Gift of Black Folk: The Negroes in the Making of America
Introduction: Glenda Carpio

Dark Princess: A Romance
Introduction: Homi K. Bhabha

BLACK FOLK
Then and Now

An Essay in the History and Sociology
of the Negro Race

W. E. B. Du Bois

Series Editor, Henry Louis Gates, Jr.

Introduction by Wilson Moses

OXFORD
UNIVERSITY PRESS

For Cornel West

OXFORD
UNIVERSITY PRESS

Oxford University Press, Inc., publishes works that further
Oxford University's objective of excellence in research,
scholarship, and education.

Oxford   New York
Auckland   Cape Town   Dar es Salaam   Hong Kong   Karachi
Kuala Lumpur   Madrid   Melbourne   Mexico City   Nairobi
New Delhi   Shanghai   Taipei   Toronto

With offices in
Argentina   Austria   Brazil   Chile   Czech Republic   France   Greece
Guatemala   Hungary   Italy   Japan   Poland   Portugal   Singapore
South Korea   Switzerland   Thailand   Turkey   Ukraine   Vietnam

Copyright © 2007 by Oxford University Press

Published by Oxford University Press, Inc.
198 Madison Avenue, New York, NY 10016
www.oup.com

Library of Congress Cataloging-in-Publication Data is available.

ISBN: 978-0-19-938322-1

THIS BOOK
IS DEDICATED TO
MY GRANDDAUGHTER
DU BOIS WILLIAMS
ON HER SIXTH BIRTHDAY IN
THE HOPE THAT HER BRIGHT
EYES MAY ONE DAY SEE
SOME OF THE THINGS
I DREAM

Contents

The Black Letters on the Sign: W. E. B. Du Bois and the Canon

". . . the slave master had a direct interest in discrediting the personality of those he held as property. Every man who had a thousand dollars so invested had a thousand reasons for painting the black man as fit only for slavery. Having made him the companion of horses and mules, he naturally sought to justify himself by assuming that the negro was not much better than a mule. The holders of twenty hundred million dollars' worth of property in human chattels procured the means of influencing press, pulpit, and politician, and through these instrumentalities they belittled our virtues and magnified our vices, and have made us odious in the eyes of the world. Slavery had the power at one time to make and unmake Presidents, to construe the law, and dictate the policy, set the fashion in national manners and customs, interpret the Bible, and control the church; and, naturally enough, the old masters set themselves up as much too high as they set the manhood of the negro too low. Out of the depths of slavery has come this prejudice and this color line. It is broad enough and black enough to explain all the malign influences which assail the newly emancipated millions to-day. . . . The office of color in the color line is a very plain and subordinate one. It simply advertises the objects of oppression, insult, and persecution. It is not the maddening liquor, but the black letters on the sign telling the world where it may be had . . . Slavery, stupidity, servility, poverty, dependence, are undesirable conditions. When these shall cease to be coupled with color, there will be no color line drawn."

—FREDERICK DOUGLASS, "The Color Line," 1881.

William Edward Burghardt Du Bois (1868–1963) was the most prolific and, arguably, the most influential African American writer of his generation. The novelist and poet James Weldon Johnson (1871–1938) once noted the no single work had informed the shape of the African American literary tradition, except perhaps *Uncle Tom's Cabin*, than had Du Bois's seminal collection of essays *The Souls of Black Folk* (1903). While trained as a sociologist at Berlin and as a historian at Harvard, Du Bois was fearless in the face of genre—even when some of the genres that he sought to embrace did not fully embrace him in return. Du Bois published twenty-two single-author works, twenty-one in his lifetime (his *Autobiography*, edited by his friend and literary executor, Herbert Aptheker, would not be published until

1968). A selection of his greatest works, *An ABC of Color: Selections from over a Half Century of the Writings of W. E. B. Du Bois*, appeared in 1963, the year he died. And while these books reflect a wide variety of genres—including three widely heralded and magisterial books of essays published in 1903, 1920, and 1940 (*The Souls of Black Folk*, *Darkwater: Voices from within the Veil*, and *Dusk of Dawn: An Essay toward an Autobiography of a Race Concept*), one biography, five novels, a pioneering sociological study of a black community, five books devoted to the history of Africa, three historical studies of African American people, among others—Du Bois was, in the end, an essayist, an essayist of the first order, one of the masters of that protean form that so attracted Du Bois's only true antecedent, Frederick Douglass (1818–1895) as well as Du Bois's heir in the history of the form, James Baldwin (1924–1987). (Baldwin, like Du Bois, would turn repeatedly to fiction, only to render the form as an essay.)

Du Bois, clearly, saw himself as a man of action, but a man of action who luxuriated within a verdant and fecund tropical rainforest of words. It is not Du Bois's intoxication with words that marks his place in the history of great black public intellectuals—persons of letters for whom words are a vehicle for political action and their own participation in political movements. After all, one need only recall Du Bois's predecessor, Frederick Douglass, or another of his disciples, Martin Luther King Jr. for models in the African American tradition of leaders for whom acting and speaking were so inextricably intertwined as to be virtually coterminous; no, the novelty of Du Bois's place in the black tradition is that he wrote himself to a power, rather than spoke himself to power. Both Douglass and King, for all their considerable literary talents, will be remembered always for the power of their oratory, a breathtaking power exhibited by both. Du Bois, on the other hand, was not a great orator; he wrote like he talked, and he talked like an extraordinarily well-educated late Anglo-American Victorian, just as James Weldon Johnson did; no deep "black" stentorian resonances are to be found in the public speaking voices of either of these two marvelous writers. Booker T. Washington (1856–1915) spoke in a similar public voice.

First and last, W. E. B. Du Bois was a writer, a writer deeply concerned and involved with politics, just as James Baldwin was; as much as they loved to write, Douglass and King were orators, figures fundamentally endowed with a genius for the spoken word. Even Du Bois's colleague, William Ferris, commented upon this anomaly in Du Bois's place in the tradition, at a time (1913) when he had published only five books: "Du Bois," Ferris wrote, "is one of the few men in history who was hurled on the throne of leadership by the dynamic force of the written word. He is one of the few writers who leaped to the front as a leader and became the head of a popular movement through impressing his personality upon men by means of a book" ("The African Abroad," 1913). Despite the fact that Du Bois by this time had published his Harvard doctoral dissertation in history, *The Suppression of the African Slave-Trade* (1896), his sociological study, *The Philadelphia Negro* (1899), *The Souls of Black Folk* (1903), the sole biography that he would publish, *John Brown* (1909), and his first of five novels, *The Quest of the Silver Fleece* (1911), Ferris attributed Du Bois's catapult to leadership to one book and one book alone, *The Souls of Black Folk*. Indeed, it is probably true that had Du Bois published this book alone, his place in the canon of African American literature would have been secure, if perhaps not as fascinating!

The Souls of Black Folk, in other words, is the one book that Du Bois wrote which most of us have read in its entirety. It is through *The Souls of Black Folk* that we center Du Bois's place in the literary canon; it is through *Souls* that we structure the arc of his seven decade career as a man of letters. There are many good reasons for the centrality of this magical book to Du Bois's literary career, but it is also the case that the other works that comprise Du Bois's canon deserve fresh attention as a whole. And it is for this reason that my colleagues and I have embarked upon this project with Oxford University Press to reprint Du Bois's single-authored texts, and make them available to a new generation of readers in a uniform edition. The only other attempt to do so—Herbert Aptheker's pioneering edition of Du Bois's complete works, published in 1973—is, unfortunately, long out of print.

The Souls of Black Folk is such a brilliant work that it merits all of the attention that it has been given in the century since it was published. In April 1903, a thirty-five-year-old scholar and budding political activist published a 265 page book subtitled "Essays and Sketches," consisting of thirteen essays and one short story, addressing a wide range of topics, including the story of the freed slaves during Reconstruction, the political ascendancy of Booker T. Washington, the sublimity of the spirituals, the death of Du Bois's only son Burghardt, and lynching. Hailed as a classic even by his contemporaries, the book has been republished in no fewer than 120 editions since 1903. In fact, it is something of a rite of passage for younger scholars and writers to publish their take on Du Bois's book in new editions aimed at the book's considerable classroom market.

Despite its fragmentary structure, the book's disparate parts contribute to the sense of a whole, like movements in a symphony. Each chapter is pointedly "bicultural," prefaced by both an excerpt from a white poet and a bar of what Du Bois names "The Sorrow Songs" ("some echo of haunting melody from the only American music which welled up from black souls in the dark past.") Du Bois's subject was, in no small part, the largely unarticulated beliefs and practices of American Negroes, who were impatient to burst out of the cotton fields and take their rightful place as Americans. As he saw it, African American culture in 1903 was at once vibrant and disjointed, rooted in an almost medieval agrarian past and yet fiercely restive. Born in the chaos of slavery, the culture had begun to generate a richly variegated body of plots, stories, melodies, and rhythms. In *The Souls of Black Folk*, Du Bois peered closely at the culture of his kind, and saw the face of black America. Actually, he saw two faces. "One ever feels his two-ness—an American, a Negro," Du Bois wrote. "Two souls, two thoughts, two unreconciled strivings; two warring ideals in one dark body, whose dogged strength alone keeps it from being torn asunder." He described this condition as "double consciousness," and his emphasis on a fractured psyche made *Souls* a harbinger of the modernist movement that would begin to flower a decade or so later in Europe and in America.

Scholars, including Arnold Rampersad, Werner Sollors, Dickson Bruce, and David Levering Lewis, have debated the origins of Du Bois's use of the concept of "double consciousness," but what's clear is that its roots are multiple, which is appropriate enough, just as it is clear that the source of one of Du Bois's other signal metaphors—"the problem of the twentieth-century is the problem of the color line"—came to him directly from Frederick Douglass's essay of that title. Du Bois had studied in Berlin during a Hegel revival, and Hegel, famously, had written on the relationship between master and bondsman, whereby each defines himself through the recognition of the other. But the concept comes up, too, in Emerson, who wrote in 1842 of the split between our reflective self, which wanders through the realm of ideas, and the active self, which dwells in the here and how, a tension that recurs throughout the Du Bois oeuvre: "The worst feature of this double consciousness is that the two lives, of the understanding and of the soul, which we lead, really show very little relation to each other."

Even closer to hand was the term's appearance in late-nineteenth-century psychology. The French psychologist, Alfred Binet, writing in his 1896 book, *On Double Consciousness*, discusses what he calls "bipartititon," or "the duplication of consciousness": "Each of the consciousnesses occupies a more narrow and more limited field than if there existed one single consciousness containing all the ideas of the subject." William James, who taught Du Bois at Harvard, talked about a "second personality" that characterized "the hypnotic trance." When Du Bois transposed this concept from the realm of the psyche to the social predicament of the American Negro, he did not leave it unchanged. But he shared with the psychologists the notion that double consciousness was essentially an affliction. "This American world," he complained, yields the Negro "no true self-consciousness, but only lets him see himself through the revelation of the other world. It is a peculiar sensation, this double-consciousness, this sense of always looking at one's self through the eyes of others, of measuring one's soul by the tape of a world that looks on in amused contempt and pity." Sadly, "the double life every American Negro must live, as a Negro and as an American," leads inevitably to "a painful self-consciousness, an almost morbid sense of personality and a moral hesitancy which is fatal to self-confidence." The result is "a double life, with double thoughts, double duties and double social classes," and worse, "double words and double ideas," which "tempt the mind to pretense or revolt, hypocrisy or to radicalism." Accordingly, Du Bois wanted to make the American Negro whole; and he believed that only desegregation and full equality could make this psychic integration possible.

And yet for subsequent generations of writers, what Du Bois cast as a problem was taken to be the defining condition of modernity itself. The diagnosis, one might say, outlasted the disease. Although Du Bois would publish twenty-two books, and thousands of essays and reviews, no work of his has done more to shape an African American literary history than *The Souls of Black Folk*, and no metaphor in this intricately layered book has proved more enduring than that of double consciousness, including Du Bois's other powerfully resonating metaphors, that of "the veil" that separates black America from white America, and his poignant revision of Frederick Douglass's metaphor of "the color line," which Du Bois employed in that oft-repeated sentence, "The problem of the twentieth-century is the problem of the color line"—certainly his most prophetic utterance of many.

Like all powerful metaphors, Du Bois's metaphor of double consciousness came to have a life of its own. For Carl Jung, who visited the United States in the heyday of the "separate but equal" doctrine, the shocking thing wasn't that black culture was not equal, the shocking thing was that is was not separate! "The naïve European," Jung wrote, "thinks of America as a white nation. It is not wholly white, if you please; it is partly colored," and this explained, Jung continued, "the slightly Negroid mannerisms of the American." "Since the Negro lives within your cities and even within your houses," Jung continued, "he also lives within your skin, subconsciously." It wasn't just that the Negro was an American, as Du Bois would note, again and again, but that the American was, inevitably and inescapably, a Negro. The bondsman and the slave find their identity in each other's gaze: "two-ness" wasn't just a black thing any longer. As James Baldwin would put it, "Each of us, helplessly and forever, contains the other—male in female, female in male, white in black, black in white."

Today, talk about the fragmentation of culture and consciousness is a commonplace. We know all about the vigorous intermixing of black culture and white, high culture and low—from the Jazz Age freneticism of what the scholar Ann Douglass calls "mongrel Manhattan" to Hip Hop's hegemony over American youth in the late-twentieth and early-twenty-first centuries. Du Bois yearned to make the American Negro one, and lamented that he was two. Today, the ideal of wholeness has largely been retired. And cultural multiplicity is no longer seen as the problem, but as a solution—a solution to the confines of identity itself. Double consciousness, once a disorder, is now the cure. Indeed, the only complaint we moderns have is that Du Bois was too cautious in his accounting. He'd conjured "two souls, two thoughts two unreconciled strivings." Just two, Dr. Du Bois, we are forced to ask today? Keep counting.

And, in a manner of speaking, Du Bois did keep counting, throughout the twenty two books that comprise the formal canon of his most cogent thinking. The hallmark of Du Bois's literary career is that he coined the metaphors of double-consciousness and the veil—reappropriating Frederick Douglass's seminal definition of the semi-permeable barrier that separates and defines black-white racial relations in America as "the color line"—to define the place of the African American within modernity. The paradox of his career, however, is that the older Du Bois became, the more deeply he immersed himself in the struggle for Pan-Africanism and decolonization against the European colonial powers, and an emergent postcolonial "African" or "Pan-Negro" social and political identity—culminating in his own life in his assumption of Ghanaian citizenship in 1963. And the "blacker" that his stand against colonialism became, the less "black," in a very real sense, his analysis of what he famously called "The Negro Problem" simultaneously became. The more "African" Du Bois became, in other words, the more cosmopolitan his analysis of the root causes of anti-black and -brown and -yellow racism and colonialism became, seeing the status of the American Negro as part and parcel of a larger problem of international economic domination, precisely in the same way that Frederick Douglass rightly saw the construction of the American color line as a function of, and a metaphor for, deeper, structural, economic relations—"not the maddening liquor, but the black letters on the sign telling the world where it may be had," as Douglass so thoughtfully put it. The Negro's being-in-the-world, we might say, became ever more complex for Du Bois the older he grew, especially as the Cold War heated up and the anti-colonial movement took root throughout Africa and the Third World.

Ironically, Du Bois himself foretold this trajectory in a letter he wrote in 1896, reflecting on the import of his years as a graduate student at Friedrich Wilhelm University in Berlin: "Of the greatest importance was the opportunity which my *Wanderjahre* [wander years] in Europe gave of looking at the world as a man and not simply from a narrow racial and provincial outlook." How does the greatest black intellectual in the twentieth century—"America's most conspicuously educated Negro," as Werner Sollors puts it in his introduction to Du Bois's *Autobiography* in this series—make the rhetorical turn from defining the Negro American as a metaphor for modernity, at the turn of the century, to defining the Negro—at mid-century—as a metonym of a much larger historical pattern of social deviance and social dominance that had long been central to the fabric of world order, to the fabric of European and American domination of such a vast portion of the world of color? If, in other words, the Negro is America's metaphor for Du Bois in 1903, how does America's history of black-white relations become the metaphor of a nefarious pattern of economic exploitation and dominance by the end of Du Bois's life, in 1963? Make no mistake about it: either through hubris or an uncanny degree of empathy, or a mixture of both, throughout his life, W. E. B. Du Bois saw his most naked and public ambitions as well as his most private and intimate anxieties as representative of those of his countrymen, the American Negro people. Nevertheless, as he grew older, the closer he approached the end of his life, Du Bois saw the American Negro as a metaphor for class relations within the wider world order.

In order to help a new generation of readers to understand the arc of this trajectory in Du Bois's thinking, and because such a large part of this major thinker's oeuvre remains unread, Oxford University Press and I decided to publish in a uniform edition the twenty-one books that make up Du Bois's canon and invited a group of scholars to reconsider their importance as works of literature, history, sociology, and political philosophy. With the publication of this series, Du Bois's books are once again in print, with new introductions that analyze the shape of his career as a writer, scholar, and activist.

Reading the canon of Du Bois's work in chronological order, a certain allegorical pattern emerges, as Saidiya Hartman suggests in her introduction to *The Suppression of the African Slave-Trade*. Du Bois certainly responded immediately and directly to large historical events through fierce and biting essays that spoke adamantly and passionately to the occasion. But he also used the themes of his books to speak to the larger import of those events in sometimes highly mediated ways. His first book, for example, proffers as its thesis, as Hartman puts it, a certain paradox: "the slave trade flourished under the guise of its suppression," functioning legally for twenty years following the Compromise of the Federal Convention of 1787 and "illegally for another half century." Moreover, Du Bois tackles this topic at precisely the point in American history when Jim Crow segregation is becoming formalized through American law in the 1890s, culminating in 1896 (the year of the publication of his first book) with the infamous *Plessy v. Ferguson* "separate but equal" decision of the Supreme Court—exactly twenty years following the end of Reconstruction. Three years later, as Lawrence Bobo shows, Du Bois publishes *The Philadelphia Negro* in part to detail the effects of the "separate but equal" doctrine on the black community.

Similarly, Du Bois's biography of John Brown appeared in the same year as a pioneering band of blacks and whites joined together to form the National Association for the Advancement of Colored People (NAACP), the organization that would plot the demise of legal segregation through what would come to be called the Civil Rights Movement, culminating in its victory over de jure segregation in the Supreme Court's *Brown v. Board of Education* decision, which effectively reversed the *Plessy* decision, and in the Civil Rights Act of 1964 and the Voting Rights Act of 1965. John Brown, for Du Bois, would remain the' emblem of this movement.

Likewise, Du Bois's first novel, *The Quest of the Silver Fleece*, published just two years following his biography of John Brown, served as a subtle critique both of an unreflective assimilationist ideology of the early NAACP through its advocacy of "a black-owned farming cooperative in the heart of the deep South," as William Andrews puts it, just as it surely serves as a critique of Booker T. Washington's apparently radical notion that economic development for the newly freed slaves could very well insure political equality in a manner both irresistible and inevitable, an argument, mind you, frequently made today under vastly different circumstances about the role of capitalism in Du Bois's beloved Communist China.

Du Bois registers his critique of the primitivism of the Harlem Renaissance in *The Gift of Black Folk*, as Glenda Carpio cogently argues, by walking "a tightrope between a patriotic embrace of an America in which African American culture has become an inextricable part and an exhortation of the rebellion and struggle out of which that culture arose." In response to the voyeurism and faddishness of Renaissance Harlem, Du Bois harshly reminds us that culture is a form of labor, too, a commodity infinitely exploitable, and that the size of America's unprecedented middle class can be traced directly to its slave past: "It was black labor that established the modern world commerce which began first as a commerce in the bodies of the slaves themselves and was the primary cause of the prosperity of the first great commercial cities of our day"—cities such as New York, the heart of the cultural movement that some black intellectuals passionately argued could very well augur the end of racial segregation throughout American society, or at least segregation between equal classes across the color line.

Paul Finkelman, in his introduction to *John Brown*, quotes the book's first line: "The mystic spell of Africa is and ever was over all America." If that is true, it was also most certainly the case for Du Bois himself, as John Thornton, Emmanuel Akyeampong, Wilson J. Moses, and Mahmood Mamdani show us in their introductions to five books that Du Bois published about Africa, in 1915, 1930, 1939, and 1947. Africa, too, was a recurring metaphor in the Duboisian canon, serving variously as an allegory of the intellectual potential of persons of African descent; as John K. Thornton puts it, "What counted was that African history had movement and Africans were seen as historical actors and not simply as stolid recipients of foreign techniques and knowledge," carefully "integrating ancient Egypt into *The Negro* as part of that race's history, without having to go to the extreme measure of asserting that somehow the Egyptians were biologically identical to Africans from further south or west." The history of African civilization, in other words, was Du Bois's ultimate argument for the equality of Americans white and black.

Similarly, establishing his scholarly mastery of the literature of African history also served Du Bois well against ideological rivals such as Marcus Garvey, who attacked Du Bois for being "too assimilated," and "not black enough." Du Bois's various studies of African history also served as a collective text for the revolutions being formulated in the forties and fifties by Pan-African nationalists such as Kwame Nkrumah and Jomo Kenyatta, who would lead their nations to independence against the European colonial powers. Du Bois was writing for them, first as an exemplar of the American Negro, the supposed vanguard of the African peoples, and later, and more humbly, as a follower of the African's lead. As Wilson J. Moses notes, Du Bois once wrote that "American Negroes of former generations had always calculated that when Africa was ready for freedom, American Negroes would be ready to lead them. But the event was quite opposite." In fact, writing in 1925 in an essay entitled "Worlds of Color," an important essay reprinted as "The Negro Mind Reaches Out" in Alain Locke's germinal anthology *The New Negro* (as Brent Staples points out in his introduction to Du Bois's fifth novel, *Worlds of Color*, published just two years before he died), Du Bois had declared that "led by American Negroes, the Negroes of the world are reaching out hands toward each other to know, to sympathize, to inquire." And, indeed, Du Bois himself confessed at his ninety-first birthday celebration in Beijing, as Moses notes, that "once I thought of you Africans as children, whom we educated Afro-Americans would lead to liberty. I was wrong." Nevertheless, Du Bois's various books on Africa, as well as his role as an early theorist and organizer of the several Pan-African Congresses between 1900 and 1945, increasingly underscored his role throughout the first half of the century as the father of Pan-Africanism, precisely as his presence and authority within such civil rights organizations as the NAACP began to wane.

Du Bois's ultimate allegory, however, is to be found in *The Black Flame Trilogy*, the three novels that Du Bois published just before repatriating to Ghana, in 1957, 1959, and 1961. The trilogy is the ultimate allegory in Du Bois's canon because, as Brent Edwards shows us in his introductions to the novels, it is a fictional representation of the trajectory of Du Bois's career, complete with several characters who stand for aspects of Du Bois's personality and professional life, including Sebastian Doyle, who "not only studied the Negro problem, he embodied the Negro problem. It was bone of his bone and flesh of his flesh. It made his world and filled his thought," as well as Professor James Burghardt, trained as a historian at Yale and who taught, as Du Bois had, at Atlanta University, and who believed that "the Negro problem must no longer be regarded emotionally. It must be faced scientifically and solved by long, accurate and intense investigation. Moreover, it was not one problem, but a series of problems interrelated with the social problems of the world. He laid down a program of study covering a hundred years."

But even more important than these allegorical representations of himself, or early, emerging versions of himself, Du Bois used *The Black Flame* novels to underscore the economic foundation of anti-black racism. As Edwards notes, "The real villain," for Du Bois, "is not an individual Southern aristocrat or racist white laborer, but instead capitalism itself, especially in the corporate form that has dominated the economic and social landscape of the world for more than a century," which underscores Du Bois's ideological transformations from an integrationist of sorts to an emergent mode of African American, first, and then Pan-Africanist cultural nationalism, through socialism, landing squarely in the embrace of the Communist Party just two years before his death.

Despite this evolution in ideology, Mansart, Du Bois's protagonist in the triology, ends his series of intellectual transformations precisely where Du Bois himself began as he embarked upon his career as a professor just a year after receiving his Harvard PhD in 1895. In language strikingly familiar to his statement that the time he spent in Berlin enabled him to look "at the world as a man and not simply from a narrow racial and provincial outlook," Du Bois tells us in the final volume of the trilogy that Mansart "began to have a conception of the world as one unified dwelling place. He was escaping from his racial provincialism. He began to think of himself as part of humanity and not simply as an American Negro over against a white world." For all of his ideological permutations and combinations, in other words, W. E. B. Du Bois—formidable and intimidating ideologue and ferocious foe of racism and colonialism—quite probably never veered very far from the path that he charted for himself as a student, when he fell so deeply in love with the written word that he found himself, inevitably and inescapably, drawn into a life-long love affair with language, an affair of the heart to which he remained faithful throughout an eighty-year career as a student and scholar, from the time he entered Fisk University in 1885 to his death as the Editor of "The Encyclopedia Africana" in 1963. And now, with the publication of the Oxford W. E. B. Du Bois, a new generation of readers can experience his passion for words, Du Bois's love of language purely for its own sake, as well as a conduit for advocacy and debate about the topic that consumed him his entire professional life, the freedom and the dignity of the Negro.

✦ ✦ ✦

The first volume in the series is Du Bois's revised dissertation, and his first publication, entitled *The Suppression of the African Slave-Trade to the United States of America*. A model of contemporary historiography that favored empiricism over universal proclamation, *Suppression* reveals the government's slow movement toward abolition as what the literary scholar Saidiya Hartman calls in her introduction "a litany of failures, missed opportunities, and belated acts," in which a market sensibility took precedence over moral outrage, the combination of which led to the continuation of the Atlantic slave trade to the United States until it was no longer economically beneficial.

Lawrence D. Bobo, one of the foremost urban sociologists working today, argues in his introduction to *The Philadelphia Negro: A Social Study* (1899), that Du Bois was not only an innovative historian, as Hartman properly identifies him, but also a groundbreaking social scientist whose study of Philadelphia displays "the most rigorous and sophisticated social science of its era by employing a systematic community social survey method." Although it was well reviewed at its publication—which coincided with the advent of the field of urban sociology—*The Philadelphia Negro* did not become the subject of significant scholarly attention until the 1940s, and has become, since then, a model for the study of black communities.

The distinguished scholar of black literature and culture, Arnold Rampersad, calls *The Souls of Black Folk* "possibly the most important book ever penned by a black American"—an assertion with which I heartily agree. A composite of various essays, subjects, and tones, *Souls* is both very much of its time, and timeless. It contributed to the American lexicon two terms that have been crucial for more than a century in understanding the African American experience: the "color line" and "double consciousness." For Rampersad, that we have learned so much about both issues since Du Bois first wrote, but have not made either irrelevant to our twenty-first century experience is, in a real way, our scholarly blessing and burden.

Abandoning the scholarly and empirical prowess so vividly on display in *Suppression* and *Philadelphia Negro*, Du Bois meant his biography of John Brown to be not a work of scholarship but rather one "about activism, social consciousness, and the politics of race," argues the legal historian Paul Finkelman in his introduction to *John Brown* (1909). The only biography in Du Bois's vast oeuvre, the book grew out of his participation in the Niagara Movement's meeting at Harpers Ferry in 1906 (an event the centenary of which I had the good fortune to celebrate), and—with the myth of John Brown taking precedence at times over the facts of his life—marks Du Bois's transition from professional academic to full-time activist.

There was not a genre that Du Bois did not attempt in his long career as a writer. After the John Brown biography, Du Bois turned to the novel. In his introduction to *The Quest of the Silver Fleece* (1911), Du Bois's first novel, the literary historian William Andrews looks beyond the Victorian diction and sometimes purple prose to see a work that is the "most noteworthy Great *African* American Novel of its time." *Quest* is a "Southern problem" novel writ large on a national and even mythic canvas, and one that is ultimately radical in its endorsement of strong black womanhood, equality and comradeship between the sexes, and, in Du Bois's words, "a bold regeneration of the land," which for Andrews means a hitherto-unheard-of proposed economic alliance between poor blacks and poor whites in the rural South.

Moving from a national to an international canvas, Du Bois published *The Negro* (1915), more than half of which is devoted to African history. In this way, John K. Thornton argues in his introduction, Du Bois firmly grounded for an educated lay readership the history of African Americans in the history of Africa. Drawing on the emergent disciplines of anthropology and linguistics and including, even sketchily, accounts of what would now be called Diaspora communities in the Caribbean and Latin America, *The Negro* is important in that it presents, in Thornton's words, "African history [as having] movement and Africans . . . as historical actors and not simply as stolid recipients of foreign techniques and knowledge."

Dismissed by some critics and lauded by others as the "militant sequel" to *The Souls of Black Folk*, *Darkwater: Voices from Within the Veil* (1920) appeared in a world radically transformed by the ravages of World War I. In addition to these international upheavals, and to the "crossing and re-crossing" of the color line engendered by the war, the historian Evelyn Brooks Higginbotham tells us in her magisterial introduction to this volume that blacks at home in the U.S. faced major changes and relocations. The Great Migration was in full swing when Du Bois wrote *Darkwater*, and the change in the center of black life is reflected in the change of scene to the North, a far, urban cry from the rural setting of most of *Souls*. If *Souls* saw the American landscape in black and white, Higginbotham finds that *Darkwater* is like chiaroscuro, the painting technique developed by artists of the Italian Renaissance: "Du Bois, like these Renaissance painters, moves beyond the contouring line of the two-dimensional and introduces depth and volume through his representation of color—through his contrast and shading of white and various darker peoples." Higginbotham goes on to say that "Du Bois continually undermines the fixedness of racial boundaries and subverts the visual coherence of racial identities to an extent that cannot be accidental." The Du Bois who emerges in *Darkwater* is increasingly a citizen of the world, whose gaze may be fixed on his native land but whose understanding of that land is inextricably bound to the larger world around him.

The Gift of Black Folk (1924) had an odd genesis as part of the Knights of Columbus's series on "Racial Contributions to the United States." In her introduction, Glenda Carpio notes that Du Bois's celebration of black accomplishments did not turn away from the bitter history of slavery that spawned them: these were not gifts always rendered freely, Carpio points out. Though less substantial than many of his other works, and primarily a catalog of black accomplishments across different fields, *Gift* is notable for the complex ways Du Bois links African American contributions in the arenas of labor, war, church and social life, fraternal organizations, and especially the arts, by both women and men, to the bitter history of slavery.

Homi Bhabha sees *The Dark Princess* (1928) as another odd work, a "Bollywood-style Bildungsroman," in which the race-man Mathew Towns teams with Kautilya, the "dark Princess of the Tibetan Kingdom of Bwodpur," to combat international colonialism in the struggle for global emancipation. But in this somewhat messy novel, which renders the international scenes with a Zolaesque precision, Bhabha detects a serious philosophical purpose: to elaborate on the "rule of juxtaposition" (first defined in *Darkwater*), which "creat[es] an enforced intimacy, an antagonistic proximity, that defines the color-line as it runs across the uncivil society of the nation."

Du Bois moved from the esoteric exercise of *The Dark Princess* to a more accessible form for his next publications, *Africa, Its Geography, People and Products*, and

Africa—Its Place in Modern History (1930). Published as Blue Books for the educated lay reader by E. Haldeman-Julius of Girard, Kansas, the two volumes are,
for the African historian and African Emmanuel Akyeampong, remarkably useful and trenchant. The first volume is a relatively straightforward analysis of
Africa's geography, climate, and environment, and the impact these physical factors have had on the development of African civilization. The second volume,
which seeks "to place the continent at the very center of ancient and modern history," is more polemical, with economics cited as the central motivating factor
behind modern colonialism and the slave trade.

The anger that was evident in the second of the two Blue Books came to full
flower in *Black Reconstruction* (1935), a sweeping corrective to contemporary histories of the Reconstruction era, which (white) historians had shaped with the
view of blacks as inadequate to the task of capitalizing on the freedom that emancipation had given them, and black history as "separate, unequal, and irrelevant,"
in the words of Du Bois's Pulitzer Prize-winning biographer, David Levering
Lewis. Inspired by *The Gift of Black Folk* and from Du Bois's own withdrawal of his
article on the Negro in the *Encyclopedia Britannica*, which demanded an excision of
"a paragraph on the positive Reconstruction role of black people," *Black Reconstruction* provided original interpretations of black labor's relation to industrial
wealth and, most radically, of the *agency* of black people in determining their lives
after the Civil War. In his introduction, Lewis contends, rightly, that the books
marks a progression in Du Bois's thought, from his early faith in academic knowledge and empiricism as a cure-all for the nation's problems, to the "more effective
strategy of militant journalism informed by uncompromising principles and vital
social science."

Wilson J. Moses presents *Black Folk Then and Now* (1939) as a midway point
between *The Negro* (1915) and *The World and Africa* (1946). While all three volumes
sought to address the entire span of black history, the special mandate of *Black
Folk* was to "correct the omissions, misinterpretations, and deliberate lies that
[Du Bois] detected in previous depictions of the Negro's past." In this volume, he
went back to the original Herodotus and provided his own translation, which led
him to affirm, with other black writers, that the Egyptians were, indeed, black (a
conclusion he had resisted earlier in his career). But even in this work, with such
evidence of his intellectual background on display, Du Bois is less interested in
intellectual history than in social history. Even as he tracks developments in the
United States, the Caribbean, Latin America, Du Bois neglects the Pan-African
movement and his own involvement in it.

Du Bois's autobiography, on the other hand, shows a man far more interested
in writing about his intellectual journey than his personal or social life. The
philosopher Anthony Appiah, in his subtle introduction to *Dusk of Dawn*, tells us
that Du Bois was famous for nothing so much as his accomplishments as an intellectual and a writer; his institutional affiliations (with the NAACP, with the Pan-
African Congress) were fleeting, and his internal contradictions were vexing (he
was both a committed Socialist and a committed elitist). The aim of this account,
like so much of Du Bois's other work, was to address the problem of the color line,
and he presents his distinguished, singular life as emblematic of that problem,
and himself as hopeful for its solution.

At the time he rejoined the NAACP to oversee its global programming in 1944, Du Bois was prepared to dedicate himself completely to the abolition of colonialism, which he saw as the driving force behind all global conflicts. What was remarkable about his anti-colonialism was, as Gerald Horne rightly points out in his introduction to *Color and Democracy* (1946), Du Bois's inclusion of Asia, and particularly Japan, in the discussion. As fertile ground for colonial enterprises, Asia yielded still more evidence of the "inviolate link between color and democracy."

Color continued to preoccupy Du Bois, and in The World and Africa, he attempted to correct the ways in which color (black) had affected history. Mahmood Mamdani tells us in his introduction that Du Bois's motivation in writing this somewhat hasty volume was to tell the story of "those left out of recorded history" and to challenge, in effect, "an entire tradition of history-writing . . . modern European historiography." Du Bois was aware that this was just a beginning to a much larger project, to connect the history of Europe that dominated the academic discipline of history to events and progress in the world at large, including Africa.

In Battle for Peace: The Story of My 83rd Birthday features an embattled Du Bois enduring prosecution by (and eventually winning acquittal from) the federal government whose indictment of him as an unregistered agent for the Soviet Union was, according to Manning Marable, a trumped-up means by which to discredit the great black leader and frighten his fellow supporters of international peace into silence. It worked, at least in part: while Du Bois drew support from many international associations, the NAACP essentially abandoned him. Ten years later, in 1961, Du Bois would permanently leave the United States for Ghana.

Brent Hayes Edwards in his introduction calls the *Black Flame* trilogy of novels Du Bois's most neglected work. Written in the last few years of life, *The Ordeal of Mansart* (1957), *Mansart Builds a School* (1959), and *Worlds of Color* (1961) follow the life of Manuel Mansart from his birth in 1876 (the last year of Reconstruction) to his death in 1956, a period which spans his rise from a noted but provincial Southern educator to a self-educating citizen of the world of color. With its alternating apocalyptic and utopian tone, its depiction of real historical figures and events, and its thoughtful "animation of economic history and especially labor history," the Black Flame trilogy offers, according to Edwards, "the clearest articulation of Du Bois's perspective at the end of his life, and his reflections on an unparalleled career that had stretched from Reconstruction through the Cold War."

Du Bois was a largely marginalized figure in the last decade of his life, and his work published at that time, most notably the *Black Flame* trilogy, went into the critical and cultural abyss. Mark Sanders suggests that the "invisibility" of the trilogy, then and now, can be explained by an evolution in literary "taste" in the 1950s, wrought by new trends in literary criticism and magazine culture, the emergence of the Civil Rights Movement, and Du Bois's own development. Even if we have rejected in many real ways the ethos of the 1950s, for Sanders, our prescriptions for taste still owe a great deal to that decade.

Werner Sollors finds "four major narrative strains" in the posthumously published *Autobiography of W. E. B. Du Bois* (1968): the personal (including "startling" sexual revelations from the famously staid Du Bois); the academic, editorial, and organizational, in which his work is fully explored, and the political is always personal even while science and reason are held to be the solution to the race problem; the Communist, first as interested onlooker and then as Party member; and the elderly, in which an old man takes stock of contemporary youth culture with something of a jaundiced eye. Sollors suggests that far from being disjointed, the various strands of the *Autobiography* are united by Du Bois's ongoing quest for recognition. I would argue that there is nothing pathetic in this quest; it is simply the desire for respect from the society (black and white) that Du Bois spent his long life trying to understand.

Henry Louis Gates, Jr.
Cambridge, Massachusetts
December 7, 2006

Introduction

Wilson Moses, Pennsylvania State University

All history is "revisionism," as W. E. B. Du Bois well knew when he turned to the Greek historian Herodotus, from the fifth century B.C.E., for both a model and a source for reconstructing the role of black folk in ancient history. Herodotus, known as "the father of history," has also, since antiquity, been called "the father of lies."[1] Such pejorative terms are, alas, the fate of all historians, ancient and modern, for no author has ever been without detractors. Nor has any author ever set out to write history purely for the purpose of telling the truth. Everyone who has ever undertaken the writing of history has done so in order to correct the mistaken opinions of predecessors or in order to bring to the fore those facts that previous writers have neglected, whether through honest incompetence or through malicious intent. Thus it was that Du Bois entered on his project of correcting the omissions, misinterpretations, and deliberate lies that he detected in previous depictions of the Negro's past. But like all revisionists, Du Bois accepted certain orthodoxies. Thus he cited numerous authors, both ancient and modern, in support of his thesis that the African peoples possessed a noble heritage, and that they had made seminal contributions to the march of humanity from barbarism to civilization.[2]

Black Folk Then and Now (1939) represented the intermediate stage in a project destined to occupy Du Bois for the entirety of his professional life. *Black Folk Then and Now* reiterated—and with greater assurance—ideas that Du Bois had pondered in his 1896 pamphlet, *The Conservation of Races*, and it borrowed copiously from another previous work, *The Negro* (1915).[3] The first of these efforts, *The Conservation of Races*, originated in a paper that Du Bois delivered at the inaugural meeting of an institution known as the American Negro Academy when he was twenty-nine years old; he spoke before a gathering of senior "race men" convened by the venerable Episcopalian minister Alexander Crummell. In this paper Du Bois had been markedly circumspect in his vindication of the Negro's claims relating to the civilization of ancient Egypt. He was either unaware of or unconvinced by Frederick Douglass's confident assertion in "The Claims of the Negro Ethnologically Considered" (1854) that the peoples of sub-Saharan Africa were racially and culturally linked to the kingdoms of the pharaohs.

Following Herodotus's reasoning, Douglass argued that the people of Colchis, who were said to be black, were a colony of Egypt, from which it might be deduced that both they and the Egyptians were black. Douglass read Herodotus as saying, "there was one fact strongly in favor of this opinion—the Colchians were black and wooly haired." To this Douglass added another snippet of interpretive mythology:

> The Pigeon said to have fled to Dodona, and to have founded the Oracle, was declared to be *black*, and that the meaning of the story was this: The Oracle was, in reality, founded by a female captive from the Thebiad; she was *black*, being an Egyptian. Other Greek writers . . . have expressed themselves in similar terms.[4]

Where Douglass had relied on both the legend of the priestess at Dodona and the authority of professors at the University of Rochester, who recommended translations of Herodotus's works, Du Bois relied on his own reading and reproduced the original Greek of Herodotus, who described the Egyptians as μελάγχοές εἰσι καὶ οὐλότριχες. Du Bois translated the word μελάγχροές (melangchroes) as "black," whereas others had translated it as "dark." Most Victorian translators into English had preferred to view the Egyptians as "dark skinned and curly haired." Although Du Bois neglected both Douglass and Herodotus in 1896, he mentioned Herodotus in *The Negro* and again in *Black Folk Then and Now*, and he marched into territory that the redoubtable Douglass had previously explored. Du Bois deviated slightly from Douglass by translating the key words as "black and curly-haired," and he abbreviated Douglass's treatment of Herodotus considerably, omitting Herodotus's snippet of interpretative mythology concerning the Pigeon of Dodona.

Du Bois made many superficial references to the intellectual traditions of African and African American writers and speakers, but he offered no critical analysis of previous treatments of Egyptian ethnology by black authors. He overlooked the perceptive comment of Alexander Crummell that the peoples of the ancient world were "cosmopolitan thieves" who promiscuously appropriated one another's cultural treasures and benefited from the appropriating.[5] The bibliography of *The Negro* included *Christianity, Islam, and the Negro Race* (1887), a work by Edward Wilmot Blyden, a Liberian nationalist born in West India, who asserted that the Negro was descended from the builders of the pyramids. Joseph Ephraim Casely Hayford, in his *Ethiopia Unbound* (1911)—a work mildly critical of Du Bois[6]—had insisted that the Sphinx was the creation of black architects. Thus when Du Bois published *The Negro*, he was reinforcing positions that had existed among past and present generations of black intellectuals in the cultural triangle of Africa, America, and the West Indies. The historian Mia Bay, among others, has written on this antebellum tradition among black intellectuals and its survival into the Harlem Renaissance of the 1920s.[7]

Du Bois's lack of interest in relating his ideas to a preexisting Pan-African intellectual tradition is conspicuous. His works contain only the vaguest and most cursory allusions to black intellectual history or biography, but at no place in his voluminous works is there any systematic treatment of those literary and intellectual giants on whose shoulders he stood. It is true that he occasionally alluded to the existence of these traditions, but Du Bois was committed primarily to social history—not to intellectual history. In this respect, he may be contrasted to St. Clair Drake, whose work *Black Folk Here and There* (1987) was "an obvious variation" on Du Bois's title, and Drake saw it as an extension of the project of the American Negro Academy "to defend the Negro against vicious assaults." Thus when Drake deployed the term "vindicationist tradition," he assigned a place of honor within it to Du Bois.[8] Martin Bernal, in his *Black Athena* (New Brunswick, N.J.: Rutgers University Press, 1987, vol. 1, p. 437), likewise placed Du Bois honorably within the intellectual tradition that Du Bois inherited and advanced.

The historical content of *Black Folk Then and Now* was by no means restricted to ancient Africa. Du Bois addressed, as he had in *The Negro*, more recent developments in Africa, the United States, Latin America, and the Caribbean. These histories are, of necessity, because of the brevity of the work, sketchily rendered. The outline history of the Negro in the United States from the inauguration of the slave trade to the Emancipation Proclamation is of great interest because it reflects Du Bois's pioneering interpretation of social and economic history, which he had formulated in his *Black Reconstruction*, published in 1934. Du Bois viewed the postslavery history of Africans in the United States as a frustrated experiment in populist democratic government. The core of this interpretation had appeared in a chapter titled "Of the Dawn of Freedom," a history of the Freedmen's Bureau, in *The Souls of Black Folk* (1903).[9]

With respect to indexing, we reluctantly observe the deficiencies of *Black Folk Then and Now* and its two revisions. Names and topics that are responsibly treated in the body of the work are difficult to retrieve because the indexes do not mention them. Thus the casual reader, one who simply tastes the works, may easily miss Du Bois's discussions of or remarks on Melville Herskovits, Constantin Volney, Alexander Crummell, and Arthur de Gobineau. The bibliographies are also surprisingly shoddy, as well as incomplete. The entries are by category, but they are not alphabetized, and the full names and publication details are not given. The bibliographies are nonetheless useful as a guide to what Du Bois found interesting or important, and they can assist the reader in discovering what to look for, in the absence of adequate indexes.[10]

Neither Booker T. Washington nor Marcus Garvey was overlooked in the index, but neither was discussed in the text with any degree of complexity or detail. Washington was described as the author of a misguided attempt "to develop a Negro bourgeoisie who would hire black labor and cooperate with white capital."[11] Garvey was dismissed with the curious description, "a leader of the Jamaican peasants." There is a certain clarity in Du Bois's perception of Washington and Garvey as figures who made abortive attempts to address the problems of the black world with economic programs. Nonetheless, each man had, in his way, some legitimacy as a Pan-Africanist—as one who, like Du Bois, sought to reshape images of Africa, to develop an African historical worldview, and to encourage a universal sense of black political consciousness. Pan-Africanism did not, however, capture Du Bois's attention in *Black Folk Then and Now*. His decision not to address the Pan-African movement, or even his own involvement in it, is more clear evidence of Du Bois's surprising lack of interest in intellectual history as a discipline.

Chapter 11 of *Negro Folk Then and Now*, which has the misleading name of "Black Europe," introduces a survey of colonialism in Africa, which was the predominant concern of the book's second half. In terms that were both economic and moral, Du Bois called for the economic liberation of Africa. He was not entirely negative in his description of the effects of colonialism, and he acknowledged the limited efforts that Belgium, France, and Great Britain had made in the areas of health, education, and welfare. Nonetheless, he presented an agenda for democratic home rule. The final chapter of *Negro Folk Then and Now* is entitled "The Future of World Democracy," and as its title implies, it was concerned with integrating the movement for African liberation with a cosmopolitan worldview.

"The problem of the twentieth century is the problem of the color line" is the final sentence of *Black Folk Then and Now*. Du Bois was reiterating what he called this "pert and ringing phrase," a phrase that he had coined at the turn of the century and recycled in 1919. There is no question that the color line was one of the problems of the twentieth century, but calling it the central problem may have been premature. Du Bois delivered the corrected page proofs of the manuscript of *Black Folk Then and Now* to his publisher on May 2, 1939, and had copies in his possession by May 29. Within four months Hitler had invaded Poland, and for several months before that Jewish victims of Kristallnacht had already been shipped to the concentration camp at Dachau. The ensuing five years led Du Bois to reevaluate many of his perspectives on world history.

The final revision of *Black Folk Then and Now* appeared in 1946, under the title *The World and Africa*, and in it, Du Bois still viewed the world in terms of color. But some of the walls seemed to be tumbling down, and he noted laconically that several African American scientists had contributed to the "development of the atomic bomb."[12] In a posthumous new edition of *The World and Africa*, we see a Du Bois who was well on the way to his conversion to communism. The views he expressed in that work, like those expressed in the captivating pastiche referred to as *The Autobiography of W. E. B. Du Bois*, represented the culmination of the idea that he had once referred to as "Pan-Negroism"—the idea that the heritage and goals of black folk transcended geographical limits.

NOTES

1. For "father of lies," see Cicero, De Legibus, 1.1.5.
2. Arthur A. Schomburg—in his essay "The Negro Digs Up His Past," in Alain Locke, editor, *The New Negro* (New York: Boni, 1925), p. 231—speaks of "vindicating evidences" of black capacity, as found in the work of Abbe Henri Grégoire, *De la littérature des Nègres* (1808). St. Clair Drake, in volume 1 of *Black Folk Here and There: An Essay in History and Anthropology* (Los Angeles: Center for Afro-American Studies, University of California, Los Angeles, 1987), refers to the works of Grégoire, Schomburg, and others in the copious index entries for "vindicationist scholarship."

3. For a detailed scholarly introduction to the three works, see Herbert Aptheker's introductions to the Kraus-Thompson Organization's reprint editions of the published works of W. E. B. Du Bois. Also indispensable is George Shepperson's introduction to the 1970 Oxford University Press edition of Du Bois's *The Negro*.

4. Frederick Douglass, "The Claims of the Negro Ethnologically Considered: An Address Delivered in Hudson, Ohio, on 12 July 1854," in John W. Blassingame, editor, *The Frederick Douglass Papers* (New Haven, Conn.: Yale University Press, 1979–1992), vol. 2, pp. 497-525.

5. Alexander Crummell, "The Destined Superiority of the Negro," in *The Greatness of Christ, and Other Sermons* (New York: Thomas Whittaker, 1882), pp. 332–352, reprinted in Alexander Crummell, *Destiny and Race: Selected Writings, 1840–1898*, edited by Wilson J. Moses (Amherst: University of Massachusetts Press, 1992), p. 196.

6. Du Bois apparently took no umbrage at Hayford's criticisms, considering that he cited Hayford's work admiringly in his 1919 publication *Darkwater*.

7. Bay, Mia *The White Image in the Black Mind: African-American Ideas about White People*. New York: Oxford, 2000. Bruce, Dickson D. *Black American Writing from the Nadir: The Evolution of a Literary Tradition*. (Baton Rouge: Louisiana State University Press, 1989). Patrick Rael *Black Identity and Black Protest in the Antebellum North*. Chapel Hill: The University of North Carolina Press, 2002; Wilson J. Moses, *Afrotopia: Roots of African-American Popular History*. New York and Cambridge: Cambridge University Press, 1998.

8. Drake discusses vindicationism in *Black Folk Here and There*, p. xviii, note 339; also see the index entries for "vindicationist" and "vindicationist scholarship."

9. This chapter had been published earlier as an article, "The Freedman's Bureau," in *Atlantic Monthly*, March 1901.

10. According to Aptheker, Du Bois compiled the index.

11. W. E. B. Du Bois, *Black Folk Then and Now* (New York: Holt, 1939), p. 179.

12. W. E. B. Du Bois, *The World and Africa* (New York: Macmillan, 1946), p. 260. Kenneth R. Manning writes, "Blacks who worked together with whites on the atomic bomb included physicists Edwin R. Russell and George W. Reed, as well as the chemists Moddie D. Taylor and the brothers William J. and Lawrence H. Knox" ("Essays on Science and Society: Science and Opportunity," http://www.math.buffalo.edu/mad/special/science-culture.html).

Preface

This is not a work of exact scholarship; far too few studies in history and sociology are. But certainly those who write of human experience and social action today have a better ideal than yesterday for the careful establishing of fact and limitation of wish and conjecture. The kernel of this work is, I believe, a body of fairly well-ascertained truth; but there are also areas here of conjecture and even of guesswork which under other circumstances I should have hesitated to publish.

But we face a curious situation in the world attitude toward the Negro race today. On the one hand there is increasing curiosity as to the place of black men in future social development; in their relation to work, art and democracy; and judgment as to the future must depend upon the past. Yet this past lies shrouded not simply by widespread lack of knowledge but by a certain irritating silence. Few today are interested in Negro history because they feel the matter already settled: the Negro has no history.

This dictum seems neither reasonable nor probable. I remember my own rather sudden awakening from the paralysis of this judgment taught me in high school and in two of the world's great universities. Franz Boas came to Atlanta University where I was teaching history in 1906 and said to a graduating class: You need not be ashamed of your African past; and then he recounted the history of the black kingdoms south of the Sahara for a thousand years. I was too astonished to speak. All of this I had never heard and I came then and afterwards to realize how the silence and neglect of science can let truth utterly disappear or even be unconsciously distorted.

For instance, I am no Egyptologist. That goes without saying. And yet I have written something in this volume on the Negro in Egypt, because in recent years, despite the work of exploration and interpretation in Egypt and Ethiopia, almost nothing is said of the Negro race. Yet that race was always prominent in the Valley of the Nile. The fact, however, today has apparently no scientific interest. Or again, writers like Lugard and Reisner tell us that the Nigerians and Ethiopians were not "Negroes." The statement seems inexplicable, until we learn that in their view most of the black folk in Africa are not Negroes. The whole argument becomes merely a matter of words and definitions. Yet upon this easily misunderstood interpretation, millions of black and brown folk today, not to speak of most educated whites, have no conception of any role that black folk have played in history, or any hope in the past for present aspiration, or any apparent justification in demanding equal rights and opportunity for Negroes as average human beings.

Because of this situation I have for the last six years interested myself in trying to promote an Encyclopaedia of the Negro; an effort to ascertain and publish the verifiable history and social condition of the Negro race, according to the best scholarship of the world, regardless of race, nation or color. I believe the time over-ripe for such encyclopaedic treatment. The trustees of the Phelps-Stokes Fund and the many men, white and black, native and foreign, who are working with me in the project have not yet been able to secure the necessary funds for its collection and publication; but we are still not without hope.

Meantime it has seemed to me not out of place to do again, and I hope somewhat more thoroughly, the task which I attempted twenty-three years ago in a little volume of the Home University Library, called *The Negro*. This book incorporates some of that former essay, but for the most part is an entirely new production and seeks to bring to notice the facts concerning the Negro, if not entirely according to the results of thorough scholarship, at least with scholarship as good as I am able to command with the time and money at my disposal.

The larger difficulties of this work are manifest: the breadth of the field which one mind can scarcely cover; the obstacles to securing data. Color was not important in the ancient world but it is of great economic and social significance today. Convincing proof of Negro blood in the Pharaohs was immaterial in 1900 B.C. and an almost revolutionary fact in 1900 A.D. Significant facts today are obscured by the personalities and prejudices of observers; the objects of industrial enterprise and colonial governments; the profit in caste; the assumed necessity of bolstering the *amour-propre* of Europe by excusing the slave trade and degrading the African.

I do not for a moment doubt that my Negro descent and narrow group culture have in many cases predisposed me to interpret my facts too favorably for my race; but there is little danger of long misleading here, for the champions of white folk are legion. The Negro has long been the clown of history; the football of anthropology; and the slave of industry. I am trying to show here why these attitudes can no longer be maintained. I realize that the truth of history lies not in the mouths of partisans but rather in the calm Science that sits between. Her cause I seek to serve, and wherever I fail, I am at least paying Truth the respect of earnest effort.

W. E. BURGHARDT DU BOIS
ATLANTA UNIVERSITY
May, 1939

Black Folk: Then and Now

CHAPTER I

◆

Negroes and Negroids

It is generally recognized today that no scientific definition of race is possible. Differences, and striking differences, there are between men and groups of men, but so far as these differences are physical and measurable they fade into each other so insensibly that we can only indicate the main divisions in broad outline. Of the psychological and mental differences which exist between individuals and groups, we have as yet only tentative measurements and limited studies; these are not sufficient to divide mankind into definite groups nor to indicate the connection between physical and mental traits. Especially is it difficult to say how far race is determined by a group of inherited characteristics and how far by environment and amalgamation.

Race would seem to be a dynamic and not a static conception, and the typical races are continually changing and developing, amalgamating and differentiating. In this book, then, we are studying the history of the darker part of the human family, which is separated from the rest of mankind by no absolute physical line and no definite mental characteristics, but which nevertheless forms, as a mass, a series of social groups more or less distinct in history, appearance, and in cultural gift and accomplishment.

Skin color in the past has been the conventional criterion by which we divided the main masses of mankind. To this is usually added hair form, although the two criteria do not entirely correspond. If we add to these two criteria any third measurement we are more at sea: long-headed people may be found among white, black and brown; and broad-headed people are of all colors and sorts of hair. Facial measurements are not only difficult to standardize but even more difficult to co-ordinate with other human characteristics.

Moreover, many of these physical distinctions depend obviously on climate, diet and environment, and are of no intrinsic significance unless they indicate lines of evolution and deeper physical, mental and social differences. Whatever men may believe concerning this—and there is a mass of passionate and dogmatic belief—there is no clear scientific proof. The most we can say today is that there appear to be three types or stocks of man, judging mainly by color and hair: the Caucasian with light skin and straight or wavy hair; the Negroid with dark skin and more or less close-curled hair; and the Mongoloid with sallow or yellow skin and straight hair.

1

It is not possible absolutely to delimit these three stocks of men. They fade gradually into each other and of course we might so subdivide men as to make five or more main stocks. Assuming three main stocks, we have Africa as the main home of the Negroids, although they are also represented in southern Asia and the Melanesian Islands. They are characterized by dark skins and more or less closely curled hair. Many of them are broad-headed but perhaps most of them are long-headed. They vary in height from the tallest of men in certain parts of the Sudan to the shortest among the Pygmies. They show prognathism to an undetermined extent.

There has been a tendency to try to pick out among the different stocks some ideal which characterizes the stock in its purest form. Two methods are prevalent: one, to characterize as the "pure" representative of the stock, that which varies most widely from the other ideal stocks; that is, the pure Caucasic would be represented by blond and blue-eyed Scandinavians; the pure Mongoloids by yellow, slant-eyed, straight-haired Chinese; and the pure Negro by those of darkest skin and crispest hair, together with certain extreme facial and cranial forms. There is no reason to believe that these extreme variations from the normal examples of the stocks of men represent anything racially pure or indeed anything more than local variation due primarily to climate, environment and social factors. Another method would seem much more rational and that is to regard the average representatives of the stocks as normal.

What relation is there between the black natives of Australia, India and the Melanesian Islands and those of Africa? We do not know. Perhaps there is no relation at all; simply the fact that they have been exposed to similar climatic and environmental influences. On the other hand, there may have been a continent like Lemuria between Africa and Australia from which the Negroids dispersed to both the continents and to Asia; or beginning in Asia black peoples may have wandered west; or beginning in Africa they may have migrated east. All this is pure guesswork.

A reasonable but of course unproven and perhaps unprovable thesis is that humankind in Africa started from the Great Lakes, developed down the Nile Valley and spread around the shores of the Mediterranean, forming thus the basis of both African and European peoples.

The Grimaldi Negroids, discovered in the Principality of Monaco on the French-Italian frontier in 1901, have been regarded as the earliest representatives of *homo sapiens* yet found in Europe. Creditable opinion is that they belong to a race of emigrants from Africa and that it was they who first established the great Aurignacian culture in Europe. It is possible to believe that the type which they represent may have been ancestral to the famous Cro-Magnon Race—a race marked in many instances by definite Negroid characters and which dominated Europe during the later phase of the Aurignacian Age.

Perhaps, too, if we think of Africa as the center of all human development, another branch went into Asia, developing into the Mongoloid peoples and the Negroid peoples of southern Asia and Oceanica. The basic Indian culture, once attributed to conquering and invading "Aryans," is now considered by most students as the product of the dark substratum of the Indian stock.

There is evidence of ancient Negro blood on the shores of the Mediterranean, along the Tigris-Euphrates and the Ganges. These earliest of cultures were crude and primitive, but they represented the highest attainment of mankind after tens of thousands of years in unawakened savagery.

It is reasonable, according to fact and historic usage, to include under the word "Negro" the darker peoples of Africa characterized by a brown skin, curled hair, some tendency to a development of the maxillary parts of the face, and a dolichocephalic head. This type is not fixed nor definite. The color varies widely; it is never black, as some say, and it becomes often light brown or yellow. The hair varies from curly to a crisp mass, and the facial angle and cranial form show wide variation.

The color of this variety of man, as the color of other varieties, is due to climate. Conditions of heat, cold, and moisture, working for thousands of years through the skin and other organs, have given men their differences of color. This color pigment is a protection against sunlight and consequently varies with the intensity of the sunlight. Thus in Africa we find the blackest of men in the fierce sunlight of the desert, red Pygmies in the forest, and yellow Bushmen on the cooler southern plateau.

Next to the color, the hair is the most distinguishing characteristic of the Negro, but the two characteristics do not vary with each other. Some of the blackest of the Negroes have curly rather than woolly hair, while the crispest, most closely curled hair is found among the yellow Hottentots and the Bushmen. The difference between the hair of the lighter and darker races is mainly one of degree, not of kind, and can easily be measured. The elliptical cross-section of the Negro's hair causes it to curl more or less tightly.

It is impossible in Africa as elsewhere to fix with any certainty the limits of racial variation due to heredity, to climate and to intermingling. In the past, when scientists assumed one distinct Negro type, every variation from that type was interpreted as meaning mixture of blood. Today we recognize a broader normal African type which, as Palgrave says, may best be studied "among the statues of the Egyptian rooms of the British Museum; the large gentle eye, the full but not over-protruding lips, the rounded contour, and the good-natured, easy, sensuous expression. This is the genuine African model." To this race Africa in the main and parts of Asia have belonged since prehistoric times.

Assuming prehistoric man, whether of African or Asiatic genesis, as having developed in historic times into three main stocks, we find all these stocks represented in Africa and for the most part inextricably intermingled. The intercourse of Africa with Arabia and other parts of Asia has been so close and long-continued that it is impossible today entirely to disentangle the blood relationships. Semites in early and later times came to Africa across the Red Sea. The Phoenicians came along the northern coasts a thousand years before Christ and began settlements which culminated in Carthage and extended down the Atlantic shores of North Africa nearly to the Gulf of Guinea. Negro blood certainly appears in strong strain among the Semites; and the obvious mulatto groups in Africa, arising from ancient and modern mingling of Semite and Negro, have given rise to the term "Hamite," under cover of which millions

ANCIENT DISTRIBUTION OF NEGRO AND NEGROID RACES IN THE OLD WORLD

of Negroids, some of them the blackest of men, have been characteristically transferred to the "white" race by some eager scientists. A "Hamite" is simply a mulatto of ancient Negro and Semitic blood.

Today we have Negroid populations in Africa which we may study under certain types. It would be impossible in limited space to name all of the at least five hundred main tribal units, which could be expanded almost indefinitely. Grouping of these tribes by physical, social or psychological measurement is impossible for lack of scientific data on any adequate or dependable scale. Cultural division is more important and possible.

One grouping follows Herskovits and is geographical and cultural: *One,* the Hottentot area in Southwest Africa. The Hottentots are perhaps the result of a mixture between the Bushmen and taller northern Negro tribes. There are comparatively few of them left; most of them have been absorbed into the Dutch and East Indian population. They are herdsmen originally clothed in skins and originally polygamous.

Two, the Bushmen in South Central Africa; here is a poor material culture with flowering of art and folklore, representing a very early stratum of African cultural life, with hunting as the chief occupation. The Bushman is short but not a Pygmy; his skin is yellow or yellowish-brown; his hair, sparse and closely curled; he is a hunter and lives in small bands of fifty to a hundred people; he is characterized by his rock paintings; he wears little clothing and is usually monogamous. There are also in Central Africa, the Pygmies, an interesting remains of a human group of which we know little. They are hunters and trappers and live in the thick forest. They perhaps represent the earliest African population and were known to the ancient world. They are reddish or brown in color with crisp hair.

Three, the East African cattle area, extending from the Nile Valley along the Great Lakes into South Africa; cattle occupy the most important place in the life of the people, but with this is an agricultural culture; the area of the tsetse fly breaks this culture in the center near the Great Lakes; ironworking and woodworking are pursued; the Bantu tongues are spoken in the south and the Nilotic tongues north of the lakes. A branch of this culture is found on the southwest coast.

Four, the Congo area, noted by the absence of cattle on account of the tsetse fly. It is predominantly agricultural; the secret society is important; political organization and markets occur, together with craft guilds. A branch of this Congo area can be found on the coast north of the Gulf of Guinea, in Liberia and Sierra Leone. Here is more complex political and social organization, distinctive art and larger domestic animals. These West African and Congo Negroes furnished the main mass of American Negroes.

Five, the East Horn includes such tribes as the Galla and Somali and modern Abyssinians. They are Negroids with more or less Semitic blood.

Six, the Eastern Sudan from Lake Chad to the Nile Valley and between the Sahara and the Congo. The people are mainly Negro nomads converted to Islam and organized about their live stock.

Seven, the Western Sudan, the battle ground of Mohammedanism and aboriginal religions. This is the area of great kingdoms and the flowering of political organization not unlike that of the Middle Ages in Europe. The economic life consists of herding, agriculture, manufacture and trade; the art is famous.

Eight, this section includes the desert with Mohammedan, Berber and Negroid nomads engaged in trade, camel and horse breeding.

Nine, Egypt with Arabian and some Negro blood and the Negroid Sudan.

Coming now to specific African tribes, we may attempt some general description of the various inhabitants of Africa, although the available knowledge for some regions is vague. A line drawn from the mouth of the Senegal River to Khartoum and through Abyssinia divides the Negroids of Africa into two closely related but fairly discernible parts; north of the line are peoples of mixed Negroid, Caucasic and Asiatic elements. In the extreme north Caucasians predominate among the Berbers, but fade decidedly into the Negroids after leaving the coast. Negroids are found east of Tripoli between the Sahara and the Mediterranean and evidently have lived there for a long time. Some of them resemble the ancient Egyptian stock: short, dark, long-headed people; and the same type can be found along the northern shores of the Mediterranean. The veiled Tuareg are of mixed blood but very largely Negroid. The Tibu merge into the Negroids of the central Sudan. The Fulani, spread over the western Sudan and Upper Senegal, are red-brown Negroids in part and in part Berber mulattoes. Their language is Negro.

Throughout Africa are many Arabs, but usually they are dark-skinned, if not black and Negroid, with close-curled hair. The term is applied to any person professing Islam with little reference to his blood. The conquest of Egypt by the Arabs in the seventh century brought few actual Arabian invaders to the Nile Valley. On the other hand, the invasion of the eleventh century brought a considerable number to the Sudan. There are numbers of Arabian tribes now: those to the north and east have predominant Caucasic blood and those to the west and south predominant Negro blood. In modern Egypt there is considerable Negro as well as Arab blood.

South of the Senegal-Khartoum line, we find to the west, the Sudanic and Guinea Negroes whom we can divide today only by language. They are tall and black with close-curled hair, often with broad noses and sometimes with prognathism. They build gable-roofed huts, use drums and the West African harp and are clothed in bark clothing and palm fiber. They organize secret societies and use masks, carve wood and make baskets. They are agriculturists but do not use cattle except north of the forest. They are especially the artists of Africa, working in ivory, wood and bronze. Their secret societies are primarily mutual benefit groups sometimes based on occupational guilds.

Among these people may be differentiated the Wolofs and the Serer between the Senegal and Gambia Rivers; then the Tukolors and the Mandingoes. The Wolofs are tall and black and divided into castes; the Mandingoes are tall and slender and lighter in color. All are agriculturists and many of them Mohammedans. The Songhai are tall, long-headed and brown. Perhaps there are two million of them today. The Mossi are widespread in West Africa and untouched by Mohammedanism. Their government is intricate and they are agriculturists.

In the central Sudan, east of the Niger, nearly all the tribes are Mohammedans and their political systems have been disintegrated by state building and conquest. They are the people of Kanem and of Bornu and the Bagirmi around Lake Chad. They are tall, broad-nosed and long-headed black people.

Farther south and along the coast, are found the Kru, numbering about 40,000 and noted as seamen. On the Guinea coast are the Ashanti and allied peoples; the Ewe-speaking peoples and those of Dahomey, and especially the notable Yoruba. They have an advanced political organization and highly organized states such as Ashanti, Benin, Dahomey and Oyo. The Ashanti are of moderate stature and long-headed, numbering perhaps a quarter of a million people. Dahomey long had human sacrifice and a corps of women soldiers. They are tall and long-headed people, some of them the tallest in the world. Many are noted for their high social organization.

Across the Sudan from the Niger to the Nile stretch millions of black hillmen, some pagan and some Mohammedan, with a history of a succession of great states. The Hausa form a mixture of various tribes, united by language, and number more than five million. They are united in the Mohammedan emirates of Sokoto, Katsina, Kano, Zaria and others. They are farmers, traders and artisans and in the Middle Ages were divided into seven powerful states. They are tall, black and long-headed but usually not prognathic nor broad-nosed.

In this part of Africa are large numbers of pagan groups like the Nupe and the Jukur whose king is regarded as semi-divine. Farther to the east are the tall Nuba in the hills of southern Kordofan and the peoples of Darfur whose sultanate ended only with the World War. East of Kordofan are the Fung and other tribes, some of whom have mixtures of Asiatic blood.

In this Nile Valley are the Beja, the Nubians, the Galla, the Somali and the Abyssinians. The early Egyptians up the Nile Valley are probably represented today by the Beja. The shorter and more delicate pre-dynastic Egyptians were eventually mixed with stronger, taller and darker people from the upper Nile Valley and it was this sort of Egyptian that developed the highest civilization; from these, modern Egyptians have descended with dark color and a considerable proportion of broad noses and crisp hair.

Nubians are the descendants of those whom the Egyptians regarded as pure Negroes and whom they endeavored to keep above the first cataract. The Nubians are of medium height and long-headed. They have a long history going back two or three thousand years before Christ and closely intertwined with that of Egypt. Between the Sudan and Kenya are Eritrea, Abyssinia and Somaliland. The Negroids here have been mixed more or less with Semitic blood, especially toward the east and in Abyssinia, where Asiatic and Negroid languages are spoken. In Abyssinia the main mass are Semitic mulattoes; beside these are the black Jews known as Falashas; the Galla, tall brown people; the Somali, tall black people; and the Danakil, thin black curly-haired folk. All through this part of Africa are many small, unclassified tribes representing various kinds of artisans with some relationships to the Pygmies and Bushmen.

The peoples of East Africa and East Central Africa have often been given the name of Hamites. They represent the successive invasions from southern Arabia and the Horn of Africa spreading among various African peoples. Among them are the Masai and Nandi, the Suk and others. They are tall, slender and long-headed and brown or black in color. Many of them are nomadic herdsmen. Their cattle have exaggerated importance and are the center of their life and social organization. The medicine man plays a large part. There are also the Bari- and the Lotuko-speaking people, divided into totemic clans.

Between the Nile and the Congo are numbers of people often called Nilotic, like the Bongo, the Azande and the Mangbettu. The Azande are a confederation of tribes forming something like a nation. This confederation was pushing east and west at the time of the forming of the Belgian Congo. They are of varied physical characteristics and are organized in clans.

The so-called Nilotic peoples extend from some two hundred miles south of Khartoum to Lake Kiogo in the Anglo-Egyptian Sudan. Among them are the Shilluk, the Dinka and the Nuer. They are all tall, black, long-headed people. Cannibalism and human sacrifice are unknown and they are herdsmen and hunters with varied social organization. The Shilluk are united into a strong nation with a king and have a long cultural history.

The Bantu are a mingled mass of tribes in central and southern Africa, united by the type of language which they speak. They probably originated near the Great Lakes. East and south there is some infiltration of Asiatic blood. They may be divided into southern, western and eastern Bantu. The southern Bantu are south of the Zambesi River, covering Southern Rhodesia, the southern half of Portuguese East Africa, the Union of South Africa, Southwest Africa and Bechuanaland. The eastern Bantu stretch through Kenya, Tanganyika, Northern Rhodesia, Nyasaland and Portuguese East Africa north of the Zambesi. The western Bantu stretch from the Great Lakes to the Atlantic and up to French West Africa.

The southern Bantu form the largest group, divided into numbers of tribes. It includes the Shona people toward the north and toward the east the Zulu-Xosa which include the Xosa, the Tembu, the Pondo, etc., the Matabele and others. In the center are the Bechuana, the Bamangwato and the Basuto. Toward the west are the Herero-Ovambo. They are tall graceful people with Negro hair and dark chocolate tinge.

The Basutos consist of various tribes welded together by Moshesh into a nation. The Zulus consist of a hundred small separate tribes united by Chaka at the end of the eighteenth century. The history of Southeast Africa is one of wars, separations, migrations, etc., out of which various tribes emerged. The tribes vary in size from a few hundred to a couple of thousand and in some cases larger. The Bakwena number 11,000; the Bamangwato 60,000; the Ovambo 65,000; the Swazi 110,000 and the Basuto nearly a half million. They live in small households which unite into villages of some five to fifty households. The southern Bantus are patrilineal; the western largely matrilineal. They keep cattle and raise crops. Ancestor worship is strong.

The western Bantu include French Equatorial Africa and the Congo Free State together with Portuguese East Africa north of Zambesi. This is the tropical rain forest of Africa and has had many highly organized kingdoms like the

Kingdom of the Kongo, Balunda and later the Bushongo Empire. There are some one hundred and fifty tribes in this territory. Among these are the Barotse, the Luba-Wenda tribes, the Basongo; the Bakongo and Bushongo groups who are noted for their wood carving; the Bateke; and farther north the Pangwe or Fang. The eastern Bantu include the peoples of Uganda who formed at one time the Kitwara empire. The Baganda have a semi-feudal organization. They form a part of Uganda, where there is evidence of invading warriors among agricultural people. The Baganda are tall stout men dark in color with Negroid hair. Other lake tribes include the Wanyamwezi.

The eastern Bantu fall into two main parts: the Akamba and Kikuyu toward the north and numbers of tribes with totemic clans and age groups. The Kikuyu have large plantations, cattle and goats. In the east, among the eastern Bantu, the Swahili are important because their language has become the chief medium of communication over all East Africa. It is a Bantu language with Arabic and Portuguese words. The tribe itself is mixed with many elements.

The general physical contour of Africa has been likened to an inverted plate with one or more rows of mountains at the edge and a low coastal belt. In the south the central plateau is three thousand or more feet above the sea, while in the north it is a little over one thousand feet. Thus two main divisions of the continent are easily distinguished: the broad northern rectangle, reaching down as far as the Gulf of Guinea and Cape Guardafui, with seven million square miles; and the peninsula which tapers toward the south, with five million square miles. More than any other land, Africa lies in the tropics, with a warm, dry climate, save in the central Congo region, where rain at all seasons brings tropical luxuriance.

If the history of Africa is unusual, its strangeness is due in no small degree to the physical peculiarities of the continent. With three times the area of Europe it has a coast line a fifth shorter. Like Europe it is a peninsula of Asia, curving southwestward around the Indian Sea. It has few gulfs, bays, capes, or islands. Even the rivers, though large and long, are not means of communication with the outer world, because from the central high plateau they plunge in rapids and cataracts to the narrow coastlands and the sea.

Two physical facts underlie all African history: the peculiar in accessibility of the continent to peoples from without, which made it so easily possible for the great human drama played here to hide itself from the ears and eyes of other worlds; and, on the other hand, the absence of interior barriers—the great stretch of that central plateau which placed practically every budding center of culture at the mercy of barbarism, sweeping a thousand miles, with no Alps or Himalayas or Appalachians to hinder, although the Congo forest was a partial barrier.

With this peculiarly uninviting coast line and the difficulties of interior segregation must be considered the climate of Africa. While there is much diversity and many salubrious tracts along with vast barren wastes, yet, as Sir Harry Johnston well remarks, "Africa is the chief stronghold of the real Devil—the reactionary forces of Nature hostile to the uprise of Humanity. Here Beelzebub, King of the Flies, marshals his vermiform and arthropod hosts—insects, ticks, and nematode worms—which more than in other continents (excepting Negroid Asia) convey to the skin, veins, intestines, and spinal marrow of men and other vertebrates, the micro-organisms which cause deadly, disfiguring, or debilitating diseases, or themselves create the morbid condition of the persecuted human being, beast, bird, reptile, frog, or fish."[1] The inhabitants of this land have had a sheer fight for physical survival comparable with that in no other great continent, and this must not be forgotten when we consider their history.

Four great rivers and many lesser streams water the continent. The greatest is the Congo in the center, with its vast curving and endless branches; then the Nile, draining the cluster of the Great Lakes and flowing northward "like some grave, mighty thought, threading a dream"; the Niger in the northwest, watering the Sudan below the Sahara; and, finally, the Zambesi, with its greater Niagara in the southeast. Even these waters leave room for deserts both south and north, but the greater ones are the three million square miles of sand wastes in the north.

It may well be that Africa rather than Asia was the birthplace of the human family and ancient Negro blood the basis of the blood of all men. Negro races were among the first who made and used tools, developed systematic religion, pursued art, domesticated animals and smelted metal, especially iron. The subsequent development of the Negro race was affected by physical changes in Africa: the Sahara and Lybian deserts, once fertile plains, were desiccated, forcing Negroes to migrate. Many of the peoples and much of the culture of ancient Egypt originated in Equatorial Africa. In the mythology of ancient Greece many Negroes play parts—Memnon, Eurybates, Cephus, Cassiopeia and Andromeda. During the Middle Ages in the western Sudan, Negro kingdoms and empires were organized with as high culture as many of the contemporary states in Europe. The increasing desiccation of north and south Africa, the introduction of Christianity and Mohammedanism and the establishment of the Arab and European slave trade overthrew these Negro states and largely ruined their culture.

Africa is at once the most romantic and the most tragic of continents. Its very names reveal its mystery and wide-reaching influence. It is the "Ethiopia" of the Greek, the "Kush" and "Punt" of the Egyptian, and the Arabian "Land of the Blacks." To modern Europe it is the "Dark Continent" and "Land of Contrasts"; in literature it is the seat of the Sphinx and the lotus eaters, the home of the dwarfs, gnomes, and pixies, and the refuge of the gods; in commerce it is the slave mart and the source of ivory, ebony, rubber, gold, and diamonds. What other continent can rival in interest this Ancient of Days?

NOTE

1. *Negro in the New World*, pp. 14–15.

CHAPTER II

◆

The Valley of the Nile

The Nile Valley has been called "one continuous cemetery of buried civilizations." From prehistoric time, it has been regarded as the home of Black Folk, and its southern portions, above the First Cataract, were known to the Greeks and Romans as Ethiopia, the "Land of Burnt Faces." The term occurs in the writings of Homer, dating about the 9th century B.C., and some think it had currency before that. Black people were present in the Aegaean world in the Pre-Homeric period. The early Greeks of Homeric and pre-Homeric times included in the term "Ethiopia" lands and peoples in both Africa and Asia.

In the very dawn of Greek literature we hear in the *Iliad* (i. 423–5) how Zeus and other gods went each year to feast for twelve days among "the blameless Ethiopians," while the *Odyssey* (i. 22–6) represents Poseïdon as doing the same upon his own account. Here, too, among "the Ocean streams" the cranes made their winter home, carrying "death and destruction" to the Pygmies. Black Memnon, King of Ethiopia, was one of Homer's heroes. Homer sings of a black man, a "reverend herald":

> Of visage solemn, sad, but sable hue,
> Short, woolly curls, o'erfleeced his bending head, . . .
> Eurybates, in whose large soul alone,
> Ulysses viewed an image of his own.[1]

Homer, Herodotus, Strabo, Diodorus, Pliny and others frequently mentioned Ethiopia. Homer speaks of eastern and western Ethiopia. Herodotus places Ethiopia southwest of Egypt as the last inhabited land in that direction. There is gold there, elephants, ebony and the men are tall, handsome and long-lived.

The term "Ethiopia" was employed mainly by Greeks and Romans; the Egyptians, the Ethiopians, Assyrians and Hebrews had other names for Ethiopia. The Ethiopians designated the country or a large part of it as "Ques" or "Kesh," which the Egyptians translated into "Kush." Parts of Ethiopia near Egypt were called "Land of the Kupar" or "Korti." Below that came various districts: Mam, Mash, Napata, etc. Further south were Yesbe, Meroe, and Thabre. The Egyptians called part of Ethiopia nearest them "the Land of Nehesi"; that is, the land of the blacks. Beyond that was Khent, the borderland; and Ta Sti, "the Land of the Bow." During the Middle and New Kingdoms, the Egyptians called Ethiopia "Kash" or "Kush." In the farthest confines of Kush lay Punt, the cradle of their race.

There has been much dispute as to the location of Punt. Many think it was on the shores of the Red Sea or even in Arabia or perhaps in Somaliland; but the sort of goods which Egypt brought from Punt, gold and tropical products, point rather to the region of the Great Lakes. Semitic writers called the country by the name which its own people gave to it, Cashi, and Kush. It will be noted that nearly all these writers merged Kush and Egypt as forming essentially one people.

After the fifth and fourth centuries before Christ, the term Ethiopia was used by the Greeks usually to designate only regions situated in Africa. These regions corresponded roughly to the territory which we now know as the Anglo-Egyptian Sudan. The Arabic name Sudan or Bilad-es-Sudan was applied to the country of the blacks stretching from the Nile west to the Atlantic. The part around Dongola eventually received the name of Nubia, meaning land of gold, and it is known by that name today.

"The Ethiopians conceived themselves," says Diodorus Siculus (Lib. III), "to be of greater antiquity than any other nation; and it is probable that, born under the sun's path, its warmth may have ripened them earlier than other men. They supposed themselves also to be the inventors of worship, of festivals, of solemn assemblies, of sacrifices, and every religious practice." Pliny says that Ethiopia was a vigorous and powerful country at the time of the Trojan War when Memnon was its king. Strabo, Diodorus and Pliny conceived Ethiopia as the kingdoms of Meroe and Napata.

Our knowledge of the history of Ethiopia comes from Ethiopian documents and from Egyptian, Assyrian and Hebrew sources. The Egyptian records of Ethiopian history are preserved on their monuments and in manuscripts. The Ethiopian records are preserved mainly on sandstone steles, and inscriptions on monuments. All those which have been recovered date from the eighth century B.C. to the fourth century A.D. There are many Greek and Roman accounts, including Homer, ninth century B.C.; Hesiod, eighth century B.C.; Herodotus, fifth century B.C.; Diodorus Siculus, first century B.C.; Strabo, first century B.C.; Pliny, first century A.D.; Ptolemy, second century A.D. and Dion Cassius, second century A.D. There are a number of other references by literary writers, more or less authentic, as for instance, Callisthenes and Josephus. Fragments of still other writers, writing in the classical age, are often referred to. It is interesting to remember that most of the accounts of these authors refer to the ancient Ethiopians in exalted terms, and consider them as the oldest, the wisest and most just of men.

The racial identity of the Ethiopians has often been disputed. There is no question but that they were dark brown or black people. If, however, scientists go beyond that and, like Reisner, apparently confine the designation "Negro" to black people with close-curled hair, flat noses, thick lips and prognathism, many of the Ethiopians were not Negroes; although there is distinct evidence of the wide prevalence of precisely this type of Negro among the blacks of Ethiopia; but according to such definition, most black people of Africa and the world are not Negroes and never were, leaving the number of "pure" Negroes too small to form a race.[2]

Lepsius declared the Ethiopians were of the same stock as the modern Nubians or, as he concluded later, the Beja. Sayce and Reisner admit that there was Negro blood in Ethiopia but declare that the ruling classes were "Lybians." Randall-MacIver declares that the Ethiopians were Negroes and that the century 741 to 663 B.C. was the heyday of the Negro.

All this seems much like fruitless quibbling and comes from the fact that there is no agreement among anthropologists as to what a race is and particularly who are Negroes; and finally as to just what could possibly be expected in human culture of the Negro race. As Montesquieu once wrote ironically of the arguments of the eighteenth century, "It is almost unthinkable that God, who is goodness itself, could have determined to place a soul, much less a good soul, in a body so black and repulsive as that of the Negro."

Written Ethiopian records go back many centuries. They are in the form of inscriptions carved on stone walls, or on slabs of stone, and a few records have been found written in ink or painted on plaster. Ethiopians had no limestone, marble or alabaster, such as were common in Egypt, and were forced to use soft sandstone or sedimentary rock. Their inscriptions, therefore, have not been as well preserved.

They fall into three general groups: those using the Egyptian hieroglyphs; those using the Meroitic hieroglyphs, and those using the Meroitic script. The Egyptian hierology dates from the eighth and seventh centuries before Christ, when the political and cultural relations between Ethiopia and Egypt were strong. By the fifth century B.C. the language had become distinct, and an Ethiopian hieroglyphic was used with distinctive innovations. Finally, came the script which had an alphabet of twenty-three characters, and which is not yet altogether translatable. It is possible that the script was invented before the hieroglyphics. Diodorus says that whereas in Egypt the priests alone knew the hieroglyphic writing, in Ethiopia all writers used it.

"The oldest and most important source of Ethiopian history is the Stele of Piankhy, erected at Gebel Barkal about 720 B.C. Its wealth of historical detail, its picturesqueness and fervor of language, and above all the incidental manner in which it reveals the ability, character, and magnanimity of a great personality, have led scholars to place this celebrated inscription among the most valuable of primary historical documents that have come down to the present from the ancient world."[3]

The territory formerly occupied by Ethiopia has today, in the northern part, a rainless desert; in the central part, a steppe country, fading off toward the south into a savannah country. In the southern part it is a region of rain and forests. In Ethiopia is situated the greater part of one of the large river systems of the world, the Nile and its tributaries. In the east are two smaller river systems, both of which are drying up. In the west, are three dead rivers which once flowed into the Nile, but are now nearly dry. There are numbers of other indications of ancient

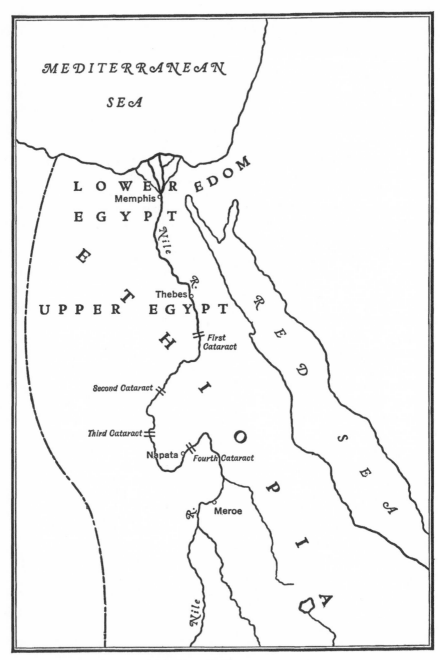

ETHIOPIA ABOUT 750 B.C.

rivers. There are no lakes in the territory but traces of ancient lakes now represented by salt beds and small oases.

Today, Ethiopia is divided into the following districts:
1. Nubia
2. The Eastern Desert
3. The Western Desert
4. The Island of Meroe
5. Abyssinia

Nubia roughly includes the Nile Valley from the First Cataract down to the junction of the Atbara and the Blue Nile. From Alexandria to the First Cataract and from the First Cataract to the junction of the rivers, is each a section of about five hundred miles. Throughout Nubia, the Nile River does not overflow, even in flood. Here and there it fertilizes a narrow stretch on the banks, but that is exceptional. For the most part the desert comes down to the banks. Thus, the Nile Valley in Nubia today has very limited economic value, and its inhabitants are scarce and poor. On the other hand, in ancient times, this region was occupied by a large prosperous population, with many towns and cities. There is no doubt that once the Nile at its flood rose at least twenty feet higher than today and irrigated an extensive area. There were well-wooded regions where now the Valley is practically without forests.

At the junction of the Atbara and the Blue Nile begins "the Island of Meroe." It is almost completely surrounded by the waters of the Nile and its branches, which reach up into the mountains of Abyssinia to Lake Tsana. This island resembles Ireland in shape and size.

The northern part today is a desert; south of this there is tall grass with bushes and trees, which shrivel during the dry season. At the southern end is a zone fairly well watered with much fertile soil.

Here again there is much evidence that in ancient times the island was much more fertile and densely populated. It formed the heart of the Ethiopian empire. Here was the capital city, Meroe, the largest, most powerful, and probably the second oldest Ethiopian city. Meroe is mentioned by Herodotus and tradition today says that the people in ancient times "were powerful and wise, and of great wealth, but God grew angry with them and stopped the rain."

The Eastern Desert extends from the southern boundaries of Egypt to the northern boundary of Abyssinia, and from the Nile to the Red Sea. It is a hilly plateau, mostly desert, but with some arable tracts. In this Eastern Desert dwell the Beja tribes who may represent descendants of those who in ancient times populated Ethiopia and Egypt. They are black and brown with curly or frizzly hair, and present many of the same types as American Negroes do today.

The Western Desert includes the whole western side of the Nile Valley until it merges with the Sahara. On the north, it begins with the Mediterranean Sea, and sweeps down 1,500 miles to Equatorial Africa. It is one of the most desolate parts of the earth, without animal or vegetable life. "For miles and miles there is but a vast ocean with flat sand without feature or hill, mound, rock or stone."

In the far southern section, the sand gives way to stony ground, and there are ranges, which support a small nomad population. Again much of this desert was probably well-watered in ancient times, but today for a stretch of 1,800 miles the Nile receives no western tributary, although in earlier times it received several rivers. Ruins of ancient settlements and petrified trees dot the banks of these dry streams.

Research in the Nile Valley and study of the records establish the fact that ancient Ethiopia in what is now the Anglo-Egyptian Sudan was the seat of one of the oldest and greatest of the world's civilizations. The golden age of this culture dates from the middle of the eighth century before Christ to the middle of the fourth century after Christ. But its beginnings go back to the dawn of history, four or five thousand years before Christ, and in a way Ethiopian history parallels that of ancient Egypt.

A reasonable interpretation of historical evidence would show that the history of the Nile Valley was something as follows: Negro tribes migrated down the Nile, slowly penetrating what is now modern Egypt. They there gradually came in contact and mingled with whites from the north and Semites from the east. Stimulated to an unusual degree by this contact of the three primitive stocks of mankind, the resulting culture of Egypt was gradually developed.

Of what race, then, were the Egyptians? They certainly were not white in any sense of the modern use of that word—neither in color nor physical measurement; in hair nor countenance; in language nor social customs. They seem to have stood in relationship nearest the Negro race in earliest times, and then gradually through the infiltration of Mediterranean and Semitic elements became what would be described in America as a light mulatto stock of octoroons or quadroons. This stock was varied continually; now by new infiltration of Negro blood from the south, now by Semitic blood from the east, now by Caucasic types from the north and west.

Herodotus, who knew and saw Egyptians four hundred and fifty years before Christ, in an incontrovertible passage alludes to the Egyptians as "black and curly-haired"[4]—a peculiarly significant statement from one used to the brunette Mediterranean type; nor was this a mere slip of the pen, for again, in his second book (Chapters 55–57), he tells of the legend of the two black doves, who flew from Egypt and became soothsayers at Dodona. He explains that the women were called doves because they were foreigners, and their words sounded like the noise of birds; and then he says: "Lastly, by calling the dove black, the Dodonaeans indicated the woman was an Egyptian." Further, he says, "There can be no doubt that the Colchians are an Egyptian race. Before I heard any mention of the fact from others, I had remarked it myself. My own conjectures were founded first, on the fact that they are black-skinned and have woolly hair, which certainly amounts to but little, since several other nations are so too; but further and more especially, on the circumstance that the Colchians, the Egyptians, and the Ethiopians, are the only nations who have practised circumcision from the earliest times."[5] Aeschylus, mentioning a boat seen from the shore, declares that its crew are Egyptians, because of their black complexions.

Diodorus says that the Ethiopians declared that the Egyptians were settlers from Ethiopia. "That Egypt itself is a land built up by the slime and mud which the Nile brought down from Ethiopia. Most of the Egyptian laws and customs are of Ethiopian origin."

The Egyptians themselves, in later days, affirmed that they and their civilization came from the south and from the tribes of Punt; and certainly "at the earliest period in which human remains have been recovered Egypt and Lower Nubia appear to have formed culturally and racially one land."[6] Modern archaeological and anthropological research lends some confirmation to the tradition that the original homeland of many of the people of Egypt and of their culture was Equatorial Africa. Many evidences of Negro descent are revealed by the bones and statues of Egypt's ancient dead.

"The more we learn of Nubia and the Sudan," writes Dr. D. Randall-MacIver, "the more evident does it appear that what was most characteristic in the predynastic culture of Egypt is due to intercourse with the interior of Africa and the immediate influence of that permanent Negro element which has been present in the population of Southern Egypt from remotest times to our own day."

Sir Flinders Petrie, in the same vein, writes that it is remarkable how renewed vitality came to Egypt from the south. The First Dynasty appears to have moved up from Punt. The Third Dynasty which led to the Fourth shows a strongly Ethiopian face in Sa Nekht; the Twelfth Dynasty we can trace to a Galla origin; the Eighteenth Dynasty was an Ethiopian race paled by marrying a Libyan princess; the Twenty-fifth Dynasty was from distant Meroe.

Volney in the eighteenth century expressed the belief that the ancient Egyptians were Negroes, or at any rate, strongly Negroid. Recently, Ripley, in his *Races of Europe*, agrees with this fact. Dr. Randall-MacIver, and Dr. Arthur Thompson, after an extensive survey of skeletons of ancient Egypt, said that of the Egyptians studied from the early predynastic to the Fifth Dynasty, twenty-four per cent of the males and nineteen per cent of the females must be classified as Negro. In every character they conform to the Negro type. From the Sixth to the Eighteenth Dynasty, twenty per cent of the males and fifteen per cent of the females were Negroes. There were in all these cases a number of intermediate types with Negroid traits, but the Negro features were not sufficiently distinct to class these skeletons with Negroes.

Others have shown Negro individuals with woolly or frizzly hair, thick noses, and thick lips, portrayed in the predynastic period of Egypt. Griffith says that more than one Nubian can be traced as holding a high position in Egypt during the Fourth and Fifth Dynasties. The famous Stele of Yna shows that in the Sixth Dynasty, Asiatics in Palestine were annihilated by an army of many tens of thousands made up of soldiers recruited from among various groups of Negroes. In the fourth, third, second and first millenniums before Christ, there were repeated migrations and invasions of African peoples into Northern Ethiopia and Egypt.

Among the Pharaohs of the earlier dynasties whose statues or recovered bones show them to have been deeply tinged with Negro blood are King Den of the First Dynasty, King Khasekhemui of the Third Dynasty, and King Sa-Nekht of the

Third Dynasty. Sir Harry Johnston writes: "The Dynastic Egyptians were not far distant in physical type from the Galla of today, but they had perhaps some element of the proto-Semite; and their language, which is still rather a puzzle to classifiers, though mainly Kushite in its features, exhibited early in its history the influence of Semitic speech, and no doubt absorbed into itself elements of the Libyan sister, which it perhaps found already extending to the valley of the Nile. The Dynastic Egyptians evidently concentrated themselves in the narrow strip of fertility along the banks of the Nile, not colonizing very markedly the Red Sea coast-lands. By about 8,000 years ago they had become the conquerors and rulers of Lower and Upper Egypt. The inhabitants of Egypt were thenceforth a people in which Hamitic (Libyan-Kushite), Semitic, Nilotic and even Sudanese-Negro elements were fused."

In Egyptian sculpture and painting, the Negro type appears as a slave and captive, as a tribute-bearer and also as ruler and official. The great Sphinx at Gizeh, so familiar to all the world; the Sphinxes of Tanis, the statue from Fayum; the statue of the Esquiline at Rome; and the Colossi of Bubastis, all represent Negroid types. They are described by Petrie as "having high cheek bones, flat cheeks, both in one plane, a massive nose, firm projecting lips, and thick hair, with an austere and almost savage expression of power."[7]

Blyden, the modern black leader of West Africa, said of the Sphinx at Gizeh: "Her features are decidedly of the African or Negro type, with 'expanded nostrils.' If, then, the Sphinx was placed here—looking out in majestic and mysterious silence over the empty plain where once stood the great city of Memphis in all its pride and glory, as an 'emblematic representation of the king'—is not the inference clear as to the peculiar type of race to which that king belonged?"[8]

Chamberlain says of the Negro in Egypt: "Ancient Egypt knew him, both bond and free, and his blood flowed in the veins of not a few of the mighty Pharaohs." Besides these marked individual instances, "there is the fact that the Egyptian race itself in general had a considerable element of Negro blood, and one of the prime reasons why no civilization of the type of that of the Nile arose in other parts of the continent, if such a thing were at all possible, was that Egypt acted as a sort of channel by which the genius of Negroland was drafted off into the service of Mediterranean and Asiatic culture."[9]

To one familiar with the striking and beautiful types arising from the mingling of Negro with Latin and Germanic types in America, the puzzle of the Egyptian type is easily solved. It was unlike any of its neighbors and a unique type until one views the modern mulatto; then the faces of Rahotep and Nefert, of Khafra and Amenemhat I, of Aahmes and Nefertari, and even of the great Ramessu II, become curiously familiar. The Egyptian treatment and arrangement of the hair and beard indicate strongly their Negroid affinity and similar coiffures suitable to crisp hair can be seen in modern Africa.

Of course, the number of those who deny the presence of Negro blood to any great extent in Egypt is large. One must remember that Egyptology, starting in 1821, grew up during the African slave trade, the Sugar Empire and the Cotton Kingdom. Few scientists during that period dared to associate the Negro race with humanity, much less with civilization. A curious incident of the World War throws interesting light on Egyptian blood today: When the "Anzacs" from New Zealand and Australia came to be quartered in Egypt, they stared at the fellahin and cried: "My god! We didn't know Egyptians was niggers!"

The history of Egypt is a science in itself and must not detain us. Before the reign of the first recorded king, five thousand years or more before Christ, there had already existed in Egypt a culture and art arising by long evolution from the days of paleolithic man, among a people with certainly some Negroid characteristics. At the end of the period the empire fell apart into Egyptian and Ethiopian halves, and a silence of three centuries ensued.

The middle empire arose 3064 B.C. and lasted nearly twenty-four centuries. The ancient glories of Egypt were restored and surpassed. At the same time there is strong continuous pressure from unruly Negro tribes of the upper Nile Valley, and we get some idea of the fear which they inspired throughout Egypt when we read of the great national rejoicing which followed the triumph of Usertesen III (*circa* 2660–2622 B.C.), over these hordes. He drove them back and attempted to confine them to the edge of the Nubian Desert above the Second Cataract. Hemmed in here, they set up a state about this time and founded Napata.

Notwithstanding this repulse of black men, less than one hundred years later a full-blooded Negro from the south, Ra Nehesi, was seated on the throne of the Pharaohs and was called "The king's eldest son." This may mean that an incursion from the far south had placed a black conqueror on the throne. At any rate, the whole empire was in some way shaken, and two hundred years later the invasion of the Hyksos began, whose domination lasted for five hundred years.

The redemption of Egypt from these barbarians came from Upper Egypt, led by Aahmes. He founded in 1703 B.C. the new empire, which lasted fifteen hundred years. His Queen, Nefertari, "the most venerated figure of Egyptian history,"[10] was a woman of royal Ethiopian lineage and Negroid characteristics. She was represented on the Egyptian monument with "a complexion of ebony-blackness," and as Chamberlain says was "a Negress of great beauty, strong personality, and remarkable administrative ability." She was for years associated in the government with her son, Amenhotep I, who succeeded his father. Queen Nefertari was highly venerated and many monuments were erected in her honor; she was venerated as "ancestress and founder of the Eighteenth Dynasty" and styled "the wife of the god Ammon." In addition to being the wife of Aahmes, the founder of the Eighteenth Dynasty, she was also the mother of Amenhotep I, and according to some authorities, the grandmother of Thothmes I, and the great-grandmother of Hathshepsut and Thothmes III—two of the greatest sovereigns that ever sat on an Egyptian throne.[11]

Another strain of Negro blood came into the line of the Pharaohs with Mut-em-ua, wife of Thothmes IV, whose son, Amenhotep III, had a Negroid physiognomy. Amenhotep III was famous as a builder and his reign (*circa* 1400 B.C.) is distinguished by a marked improvement in Egyptian art and architecture. He it was who built the great temple of Ammon at Luxor and the colossi of Memnon.

The whole of the period in a sense culminated in the great Ramessu II, the oppressor of the Hebrews, who with his Egyptian, Libyan and Negro armies fought half the world. His reign, however, was the beginning of decline, and foes began to press Egypt from the white north and the black south. The priests transferred their power to Thebes, while the Assyrians under Nimrod overran lower Egypt. The center of interest is now transferred to Ethiopia. From records and reports of expeditions, the history of Ethiopia can be reconstructed as follows:

1. A pre-historic period, extending down to 3500 B.C.
2. A proto-historic period, from 3500 B.C. to 723 B.C. This includes two periods corresponding with the Old and Middle Kingdoms of Egypt, and a third period corresponding with the New Egyptian empire.
3. An historic period, from 1723 B.C. to 355 A.D. This includes:
   A. The Napatan Period—1723 to 308 B.C.
   B. The Middle-Meroitic Period—308 B.C. to 10 A.D.
   C. The Late Meroitic Period, 10 A.D. to 355 A.D.

In prehistoric times, Ethiopians traded gold, ivory and skins with the Egyptians for food. Caravans from Ethiopia and even from places south visited Egypt. Egyptians and Ethiopians were friendly during the First and Second Dynasties but, at the beginning of the Fourth Dynasty, an Egyptian Pharaoh raided Ethiopia and returned with black prisoners and live stock. He probably went south as far as the Fourth Cataract or even to Khartoum. During the Fifth Dynasty, when the Egyptians made war on the people in the eastern desert, the Egyptian soldiers were joined by Ethiopian soldiers, including blacks from five provinces. This led to a conference between the Pharaoh and the chiefs of the blacks and some Egyptian control over Ethiopia.

As social order was overthrown after the Sixth Dynasty, Egyptian control over Ethiopia ceased and tribute was no longer paid. In the Ninth and Tenth Dynasties there were punitive expeditions against Ethiopia and also widespread trade. Blacks came north into Egypt both as free settlers and as slaves. The Pharaohs of the Eleventh Dynasty extended their influence south beyond Thebes and Ethiopians had probably moved north and invaded Egyptian territory as far as Thebes. Kings of the Twelfth Dynasty made raids into Nubia and pushed the borders of Egypt to the Third Cataract. They opened gold mines and Ethiopian forced labor resulted. The Pharaoh Usertesen I conquered a number of tribes and districts and extended the power of Egypt; but it was Usertesen III who took Egyptian power to the Second Cataract and built two forts. He used Ethiopian soldiers with Egyptian officers.

Thus we see that as soon as the civilization below the Second Cataract reached a height noticeably above that of Ethiopia, there was continued effort to protect that civilization against the incursion of barbarians. Hundreds of campaigns through thousands of years repeatedly subdued or checked the blacks and brought them in as captives to mingle their blood with the Egyptian nation; but the Egyptian frontier was not advanced.

A separate and independent Ethiopian culture finally began to rise during the middle empire of Egypt and centered at Napata and Meroe. Widespread trade in gold, ivory, precious stones, skins, wood and works of handicraft arose. The Negro began to be the great trader of Egypt. This new wealth of Ethiopia excited the cupidity of the Pharaohs and led to aggression and larger intercourse, until at last, when the dread Hyksos appeared, Ethiopia became both a physical and cultural refuge for conquered Egypt.

During the Hyksos invasion, i.e., in the Fourteenth, Fifteenth, Sixteenth and Seventeenth Dynasties, many noble Egyptian families migrated to Ethiopia and intermarried with the ruling houses of Ethiopia. Later one of these Egypto-Ethiopian families, ruling under the Hyksos at Thebes, revolted, and through the aid of Ethiopian soldiers, expelled the invaders and established the great Eighteenth Dynasty.

The ensuing New Empire witnessed the gradual incorporation of Ethiopia into Egypt, although the darker kingdom continued to resist. Both Aahmes and Amenhotep I sent expeditions into Ethiopia, and in the latter's day sons of the reigning Pharaoh began to assume the title of "Royal Son of Kush" in some such way as the son of the King of England becomes the Prince of Wales. Trade relations were renewed with Punt under circumstances which lead us to place that land in the region of the African lakes. The Sudanese tribes were aroused by these and other incursions, until the revolts became formidable in the fourteenth century B.C.

Egyptian culture, however, gradually conquered Ethiopia where her armies could not, and Egyptian religion and civil rule began to center in the darker kingdom. When, therefore, Sheshang I, the Libyan, usurped the throne of the Pharaohs in the tenth century B.C., the Egyptian legitimate dynasty went to Napata as king-priests and established a theocratic monarchy. Gathering strength, the Ethiopian kingdom under this dynasty expanded north about 750 B.C. and for a century ruled all Egypt.

At present, we have the names of forty-nine kings and queens of Ethiopia, from 750 B.C. to 355 A.D., and records of twenty-seven others, whose names are not known, making seventy-six rulers in all. During the early Napata period, extending from 750 to 308 B.C., there were twenty-six kings, of whom the most noted were Piankhy, 744–710; Shabaka, 710–700; Taharka, 688–663; and Nastasen, 328–308 B.C. The first king, Piankhy, was Egyptian bred and a mulatto type; but his successors showed more and more evidence of Negro blood—Kashta the Kushite, Shabaka, Taharka, and Tanutamen.

Piankhy ascended the throne of Ethiopia about 744 B.C., and ruled thirty-four years. He inherited from his father, Kashta, dominion over Egypt as far northward as Thebes, and perhaps for 200 or 300 miles farther, and he served as governor or viceroy over Egypt under the Ethiopian crown before the conquest. Piankhy was religious and peaceful, but he was also a practical statesman, with a river navy and trained soldiers.

In 732 B.C. Piankhy was informed by courier that a Libyan prince from the Delta was marching south. Piankhy waited for the Libyan to get as far as possible from his base. When he reached Hermophlis, 400 miles south of the Mediterranean, Piankhy started the attack, assembling an army at Napata, and ordering them to march northward to Thebes. Finally, he himself joined his armies, swept through Egypt, and received the submission of sixteen princes. The Libyan leader himself wrote: "So now, through fear of thee, I have fled to the uttermost swamps, down by the great green sea."

Egypt thus became a tribute-paying dependency upon Ethiopia, with rulers whose titles were confirmed by the Kings of Ethiopia. Eventually, in 710 B.C., when Piankhy died, the Ethiopian council at Napata chose Shabaka as king of the two lands. He kept peace and was a good administrator. The influence of Egypt was restored and he tried to stem the power of Assyria by negotiation. Diodorus says that Shabaka "went beyond all his predecessors in his worship of the Gods and his kindness to his subjects." Herodotus says that he abolished capital punishment in Egypt.

During Ethiopian rule, a royal son was appointed to rule Egypt, just as formerly a royal Egyptian had ruled Kush. This Ethiopian kingdom showed its Negro peculiarities: first, in its worship of Sudanese gods; secondly, in the custom of female succession to the throne; and thirdly, by the election of the kings from among the claimants to the throne. "It was the heyday of the Negro. For the greater part of the century . . . Egypt itself was subject to the blacks, just as, in the New Empire, the Sudan, had been subject to Egypt."

Shabaka attempted to restore Egyptian art. He began works at Karnak, and preserved historical documents. Finally, however, the Assyrians defeated the forces of Egypt and Ethiopia at the battle of Eltekeh in Assyria. Shabaka abdicated, and Shabataka succeeded him. At last, 688 to 663 B.C, came the greatest of the Ethiopian kings, Taharka. His reign, with all its wars, was an era of prosperity and cultural advancement. Weigall calls his reign: "That astonishing epoch of nigger domination"; and Randall-MacIver says: "It seems amazing that an African Negro should have been able with any sort of justification to style himself Emperor of the World." Taharka ascended the throne 688 B.C. at the age of about forty-two. For fifteen years Taharka fostered the economic, cultural, and religious life of Ethiopia and Egypt. The trade of the country increased and there was money to repair the ancient temples and build new ones. Taharka established friendly alliances with western Asia and with Assyria, and the Assyrian expedition against Egypt and Ethiopia was stopped. The Hebrew Bible chronicles this as the downfall of Sennacherib, and notes Ethiopia's trade.[12]

Taharka's building at Karnak, although never finished, was planned as one of the most striking in the ancient world. The temple built at Thebes has a relief representing the four courts of the four quarters of the Nilotic world: Dedun the great God of Ethiopia, represents the South; Sopd, the Eastern Desert; Sedek, the West Desert; while Horus represents the North. Petrie says: "This shows how Southern was the center of thought, when the whole of Egypt was recorded as the North." Some writers say that Taharka traveled beyond his domains, and Strabo even declares that, with four other kings, Taharka led expeditions as far as the Straits of Gibraltar.

Eventually the Assyrians were too strong for Taharka and he had to give up Egypt and retire into Ethiopia and the "night of death." Tanutamen, his successor, held back the Assyrian storm for a while (*Nahum*, iii, 1–19), but Ethiopian and Egyptian strength were eventually dashed to pieces. Egyptian temples were wrecked, and the conqueror, Ashurbanipal, declared: "I captured Thebes like a flood."

The Assyrians conquered Northern Egypt, but the dynasty was continued in Southern Egypt by Ethiopian kings. Egyptian rule was revived briefly in Northern Egypt but this was followed by two invasions from Persia, 525–415 B.C. and 342–332 B.C., and finally by the domination of Egypt by Greece after 332 B.C.

Aspeluta, whose mother and sister are represented as full-blooded Negroes, ruled probably from 593–567 B.C. Horsiatef (c. 372–61 B.C.) made nine expeditions against the war-like tribes south of Meroe, and his successor was Nastasen (c. 328–308 B.C.) who removed the capital from Napata to Meroe, although Napata continued to be the religious capital and the Ethiopian kings were still crowned on its golden throne. In 525 or 524 B.C. Cambyses, the Persian, tried to invade Nubia, but was either defeated or his army died from starvation.

During the middle period, 308–225 B.C., there were ten rulers, five reigning at Napata and five at Meroe. Then the kingdoms became united again under Ergamenes, 225–200 B.C., and six kings reigned over the whole of Ethiopia; then came nine kings, of whom four reigned at Meroe, and five at Napata. These were succeeded by three kings ruling over Ethiopia until 15 A.D. From that time to 355 A.D. there ruled twenty-two kings over a united Ethiopia. The Ptolemies did not invade Nubia but tried to obtain trade by peaceful inroads. Ergamenes was brought up at the court of Ptolemy II and the "nine nations" of Ethiopia were brought under complete control of Egypt without war.

Meroe, between the Atabara and the Blue Nile, was founded later than Napata, and probably not earlier than the eighth century B.C. Kings reigned at Meroe in all for about six hundred years. It stands on the banks of the Nile, midway between the Fifth and Sixth Cataracts, and is accessible to caravans coming across the Atabara from the Red Sea. It was, therefore, the natural outlet to the Nile of the desert route from the east. It was said to have had a standing army of two hundred thousand and four thousand artisans. The people adopted the Egyptian hieroglyphic system of writing which they modified somewhat. Excavations so far have not discovered anything in Meroe older than the first century. It may not have been a flourishing city in early times, but was probably always an important trading center. It developed greatly after the downfall of Napata. It was the center of a network of roads leading in all directions. It had palaces and baths, temples and pyramids, and was widely famous.

It was here that the Candaces reigned as queens—the designation being a title rather than a given name. Pliny tells us that one Candace of the time of Nero had had forty-four predecessors on the throne. The prestige of Ethiopia at this time was considerable throughout the world. Pseudo-Callisthenes tells of a visit of Alexander the Great to Candace, Queen of Meroe, fabulous perhaps but showing her fame: Candace will not let him enter Ethiopia and says he is not to scorn her people because they are black, for they are whiter in soul than his white folk. She sent him gold, maidens, parrots, sphinxes, and a crown of emeralds and pearls. She ruled eighty tribes, who were ready to punish those who attacked her.

On the death of Cleopatra, Egypt became a province of the Roman Empire and Augustus sent a prefect there. The power of Ethiopia declined before black invaders from the west. The Prefect Gallus summoned these chiefs and granted them their independence under the power of Rome in 29 A.D. After his death, the blacks revolted and advanced northward into the Thebaid. The Romans sent a great army of 10,000 infantry and 800 cavalry to suppress 30,000 rebels. The Romans were victorious and advanced on the Ethiopians at Napata, where a Candace, a masculine woman with one eye, was reigning. She is probably the "Candace" mentioned in Acts viii, 27. Petronius captured Napata, and 1,000 prisoners were sent to Caesar as slaves and many sold at auction. Nevertheless as soon as Petronius left Candace attacked the Roman garrison at Premis where the Pharaohs had formerly had a fort. The Ethiopians demanded the right to lay their case before Caesar, which was granted, and Caesar remitted the tribute.

The Roman Emperor Nero, A.D. 64–68, planned to invade Ethiopia and sent some scouts to report. They penetrated as far as the region of the Sadd. For the next 200 years the Nubians and other desert tribes did as they pleased, while the power of Ethiopia continued to decline. From the beginning of the third century, tribes from the eastern desert called the Blemmyes, probably the modern Beja, invaded Egypt and plundered; becoming masters of Southern Egypt during the reign of Aurelian. The Romans continued to have so much trouble with their Ethiopian frontier that finally, when the Abyssinian Semitic mulattoes appeared in the east, the Emperor Diocletian invited the Nubians (Nobadae) from the west to repel them. These Nubians eventually embraced Christianity, and Northern Ethiopia came to be known in time as Nubia. The Roman garrisons were withdrawn and the Romans depended upon the Nubians from the western desert, Darfur and Kordofan, to protect their interests. Diocletian gave these Nubians land and a yearly subsidy and also subsidized the Beja. In this way, playing off tribe against tribe, he secured peace. Nevertheless during the reigns of Theodosius and Justinian the tribes broke into revolt again and again.

The Negro and Negroid populations of eastern Africa received, from time to time, Semitic immigration from the east and an Abyssinian empire was built up. These Semitic mulattoes lived on the highlands bordering the Red Sea and Asia. On both sides of this sea Negro blood is strongly in evidence, predominant in Africa and influential in Asia. Ludolphus, writing in the seventeenth century, says that the Abyssinians "are generally black, which [color] they most admire." Trade and war united the two shores, and merchants have passed to and fro for thirty centuries.

In this way Arabian, Jewish, Egyptian, Greek, and Roman influences spread slowly upon the Negro foundation. Early legendary history declared that a queen, Maqueda, or Nikaula of Sheba, a state of central Abyssinia, visited the Jewish Solomon in 1050 B.C. and had her son Menelik educated in Jerusalem. This was the supposed beginning of the Axumite kingdom, the capital of which, Axum, was a flourishing center of trade. Ptolemy Evergetes and his successors did much to open Abyssinia to the world, but most of the population of that day was nomadic. In the fourth century, Byzantine influences began to be felt, and in 330, St. Athanasius of Alexandria consecrated Fromentius as Bishop of Ethiopia. He tutored the heir to the Abyssinian kingdom and began its gradual Christianization. By the early part of the sixth century, Abyssinia was trading with India and Byzantium, and was so far recognized as a Christian country that the Emperor Justinian appealed to its King Kaleb to protect the Christians in southwestern Arabia. Kaleb conquered Yemen in 525 and held it fifty years, and sent 40,000 men against Mecca.

Eventually a Jewish princess, Judith, usurped the Axumite throne; the Abyssinians were expelled from Arabia, and a long period begins when, as Gibbon says, "encompassed by the enemies of their religion, the Ethiopians (i.e., the Abyssinians) slept for nearly a thousand years, forgetful of the world by whom they were forgotten." Throughout the middle ages, however, the legend of a great Christian kingdom hidden away in Africa persisted, and the search for Prester John became one of the world quests.

It was the expanding power of Abyssinia that led Rome to call in the Nubians from the western desert. The Nubians had formed a strong league of tribes, and as the ancient kingdom of Ethiopia declined, they drove back the Abyssinians, who had already established themselves at Meroe.

About 450 A.D. the Nubians under Silco, king of the Beja, had embraced Christianity and made Old Dongola their capital. The new capital replaced Napata and Meroe, and by the twelfth century, churches and brick dwellings had appeared. As the Mohammedan flood pressed up the Nile Valley it was the Nubians who held it back for two centuries. Omar, second of the Mohammedan Caliphs, invaded Egypt in 641. He sent twenty thousand men into Nubia but the Nubians in turn invaded Upper Egypt.

The Arabs attacked Dongola but finally the matter was arranged by the Nubians paying tribute, which they did for six hundred years. This history of revolt and defeat was kept up until 1225, when Saladin crushed the Nubians and the Arabs annexed Nubia in 1275. Between 1311 and 1412 fighting went on between Arabians and Nubians and finally the Christian kingdom of the Nubians fell in the sixteenth century.

Farther south other wild tribes pushed out of the Sudan. Chief among these were the Fung, who fixed their capital at Senaar, at the junction of the White and Blue Nile. The first king of the Fung was Amar Dunkas, who began to reign in 1515. When Selim conquered and invaded Egypt in 1617, the Fung embraced Islam and arranged to divide Ethiopia between themselves and the Arabs, so that the Fung ruled from the Third Cataract to Senaar from 1515 to 1789. Islam then swept on south in a great circle, skirted the Great Lakes, and then curled back to Somaliland, completely isolating Abyssinia. In the latter part of the seventeenth century a king of the Fung conquered the Shilluks. He was a patron of learning and built a mosque at Senaar. Another in the eighteenth century defeated the Abyssinians who had invaded Ethiopia. East of Wadai and nearer the Nile lay the kindred state of Darfur, a Nubian nation whose sultans reigned over two hundred years and which reached great prosperity in the early seventeenth century under Soliman Solon.

Before the Mohammedan power reached Abyssinia, the Portuguese pioneers had entered the country from the east and begun to open it again to European knowledge. Without doubt, in the centuries of silence, a civilization of some height had flourished in Abyssinia, but all authentic records were destroyed by fire in the tenth century. When the Portuguese came, the older Axumite kingdom had fallen and had been succeeded by a number of petty states.

The Sudanese kingdoms of the Sudan resisted the power of the Mameluke Beys in Egypt, and later the power of the Turks, until the nineteenth century, when the Sudan was made nominally a part of Egypt. Continuous upheaval, war, and conquest had by this time done their work and little of ancient Ethiopian culture survived the new and increasing slave trade.

From 1789 to 1821 there were a number of kings but a general state of anarchy. During this time the Fung tried to annex northern Ethiopia but were driven back with slaughter. In 1820, Mohammed Ali sent his son with Turks and Arabs to conquer Nubia. He defeated the Mameluke Beys at Dongola and then marched through Ethiopia, but was killed in 1822 just after he had founded Khartoum. Mohammed Ali avenged this terribly and eventually in 1839 determined to exploit the Sudan for gold and slaves. He stirred up strife among the chiefs and took their land and destroyed their people. About 1840, Mohammed Ali's Sudan included all the territory formerly belonging to Napata and Meroe and from then until 1880 Ethiopia was reduced to a state of ruin and misery by the Arab masters of the Egyptians. .

The entrance of England into Egypt, after the building of the Suez Canal, eventually stirred up revolt in the Sudan by loosing the hold of the Arab taskmasters on the natives. Led by a Sudanese Negro, Mohammed Ahmad, who claimed to be the Messiah (Mahdi), the Sudan arose in revolt in 1881, determined to resist a hated religion and Egyptian oppression. The Sudan was soon aflame, and the able mulatto general, Osman Digna, aided by revolt among the heathen Dinka, drove both Egypt and England out of the Sudan for sixteen years.

The Mahdi was a black Kushite born in the Dongola Province, the son of a boat builder. The Mohammedans expected the Saviour to appear in 1882. Mohammed Ahmad announced publicly that he was the Mahdi in 1881. The authorities tried to capture him, but he escaped, defeating the governor of Fashoda in the mountains of southern Kordofan and then seized Kordofan in 1883. He massacred the army of the Englishman Hicks Pasha, 10,000 strong, at Chekan in November, 1883. The Egyptian governor of Darfur and the Bahr-el-Ghazal surrendered in 1884. Only Emin Pasha in Equatoria and the governor of Dongola held out. In 1885 the Mahdi seized Omdurman, a suburb of Khartoum, and later entered Khartoum over the mud of the dammed river and killed Chinese Gordon. He was now master of four-fifths of the Egyptian Sudan, but died of typhoid fever the same year. His successor, the Khalifa Abdullah, belonged to the Baggara tribe of Arabian Negroes. He displaced the Nubian relatives of the Mahdi with Darfur people, attacked Abyssinia and killed the Negus John. Emin Pasha abandoned Equatoria in 1889 and the Khalifa Abdullah established himself there in 1892.

Meantime this Mahdist revolt had delayed England's designs on Abyssinia, and the Italians, encouraged by England, attempted a protectorate. Menelik of Shoa, one of the smaller kingdoms of Abyssinia, was a shrewd man of predominantly Negro blood, and had been induced to make a treaty with the Italians after King John had been killed by the Mahdists. The exact terms of the treaty were disputed, but undoubtedly the Italians tried by this means to reduce Menelik to vassalage. Menelik stoutly resisted, and at the great battle of Adua, one of the decisive battles of the modern world, the Abyssinians, on March 1, 1896, inflicted a crushing defeat on the Italians, killing four thousand of them and capturing two thousand prisoners. The empress, Taitou, a full-blooded Negress,[13] led some of the charges. By this battle Abyssinia became independent until 1936.

England was startled and her colonial policy was stampeded into a new and vaster policy of economic imperialism. Her dream of Cape to Cairo was threatened by two black men: one in Abyssinia and one in the Sudan; and by the French in alliance with Abyssinia. No sooner did England hear of the battle of Adua, than Kitchener started to Egypt with machine guns and modern military equipment. He recaptured Khartoum in 1898, killing and wounding 27,000 natives at a cost of less than 500 casualties among his troops; the Khalifa was defeated and killed, Osman Digna captured and the tomb of the Mahdi desecrated. The road to the gold and diamonds of Cape Town lay open.

Such in general outline is the strange story of the Valley of the Nile. Strange, not so much because of the facts, but because of the extraordinary interpretation put upon them. By general consent modern historians have cut the history of the Nile Valley entirely away from the history of Africa and most of them deny any connection between the two. This is directly against the known evidence. Egypt was by blood and by cultural development a part of the history of Africa and Negro Africa must be explained certainly in part by the history and development of Egypt. Further than that, in Ethiopia and in what is known as the Anglo-Egyptian Sudan, we have pre-eminently a land of the black race from prehistoric times; and yet today by a narrow and indefensible definition the connection even of Ethiopia with Negro history is denied; while the Sudan is left as a sort of historical no man's land, and is regarded now as Arabian, now as Egyptian, now as "Hamitic," and always as not worth careful investigation and study. Its events have been misinterpreted and its heroes, like the Mahdi, maligned and written down as the cause of that very misery and turmoil against which they rebelled and fought. Such at the hands of modern science has been the fate of

That starr'd Ethiop Queen that strove
To set her beauty's praise above
The Sea nymphs.

NOTES

1. "Γυρὸς ἐν ὤμοισιν, μελανόχροος οὐλοκάρηνος." *Odyssey* XIX, 246.
2. *Cf.* Ratzel, *History of Mankind* (Butler trans.), Vol. II, p. 313.
3. "Sources for Study of Ethiopian History," Hansberry, *Howard University Studies in History*, p. 32.
4. "Αὐτός δὲ εἴκασα τῆδε καὶ ὅτε μελάγχροές εἰσι καὶ οὐλότριχες." Liber II, Cap. 104.
5. *History of Herodotus*, translated by George Rawlinson, pp. 163, 164.

6. Reisner, *Archeological Survey of Nubia*, Vol. I, p. 319.
7. *History of Egypt*, Vol. I, p. 237.
8. *West Africa to Palestine*, p. 114.
9. *The Contribution of the Negro*, pp. 483, 484.
10. Petrie, *History of Egypt*, Vol. II, p. 337.
11. Chamberlain, *Journal of Race Development*, April, 1911.
12. *Isaiah* xviii, 37.
13. At least, according to her alleged photographs.

CHAPTER III

$\blacklozenge$

The Niger and the Desert

The Arabian expression "Bilad es Sudan" (Land of the Blacks) was applied to the whole region south of the Sahara, from the Atlantic to the Nile. It is a territory some thirty-five hundred miles by six hundred miles, containing two million square miles, and has today a population of perhaps eighty million. It is thus two-thirds the size of the United States and about as thickly settled. In the western Sudan the Niger plays the same role as the Nile in the east. In this chapter we follow the history of the Niger.

The history of this part of Africa was probably something as follows: primitive man from the Great Lakes spread in the Nile Valley, and wandered westward to the Niger. Herodotus tells of certain youths who penetrated the desert to the Niger and found there a city of black dwarfs. Succeeding migrations of Negroes pushed the dwarfs gradually into the inhospitable forests and occupied the Sudan, pushing on to the Atlantic. Here the newcomers, curling northward, came in contact with Europeans or Berbers, or actually crossed into Europe; while to the southward the Negro came to the Gulf of Guinea and the thick forests of the Congo Valley. Indigenous civilizations arose on the west coast in Yoruba and Benin, and contacts of these with the Berbers in the desert, and Semites from Arabia and from the east gave rise to centers of Negro culture in the Sudan, at Ghana and Melle and in Songhay; in Nupe, the Hausa states, and Bornu.

We know that Egyptian Pharaohs in several cases ventured into the western Sudan and Egyptian influences are distinctly traceable. Greek and Byzantine culture and Phoenician and Carthaginian trade also penetrated, while Islam had wide influence. Behind all these influences, however, stood from the first an indigenous Negro culture. The stone figures of Sherbro, the megaliths of Gambia, the art and industry of the West Coast are all too deep and original evidences of civilization to be merely importations from abroad.

Nor was the Sudan the inert recipient of foreign influence when it came. According to credible legend, the "Great King" at Byzantium imported glass, tin, silver, bronze, cut stones, and other treasure from the Sudan. Embassies were sent and states like Nupe recognized the suzerainty of the Byzantine emperor. The people of Nupe especially were filled with pride when the Byzantine people learned certain kinds of work in bronze and glass from them, and this intercourse was only interrupted by the Mohammedan invasion.

To this ancient culture, modified somewhat by Byzantine and Christian influences, came Islam and the Arabs. They swept in as a conquering army in the seventh century but were comparatively few in actual numbers until the eleventh century, when there was a large Arab immigration. In the seventh century the Arabs conquered North Africa from the Red Sea to the Atlantic. The Berber Mohammedans, led by the Arabs, entered Spain in the eighth century and overthrew the Visigoths. In 718 A.D. they crossed the Pyrenees and met Charles Martel at Poitiers. The invaders, repulsed, turned back and settled in Spain, occupying it without much attempt to proselyte. But in time the conflict for the control of the Mohammedan world left Spain in anarchy.

In 758 there arrived in Spain a Prince of Omayyads, Abdurrahman, who after thirty years of fighting founded an independent government which in the tenth century became the Caliphate of Kordova. The power was based on his army of Negro and Slavonian Christian slaves. Abdurrahman III, 912–961, established a magnificent court and restored order. His son gave protection to writers and thinkers. His power passed into the hands of a mulatto known as Almansur, who kept order with his army of Berbers and Negroes, making fifty invasions into Christian territory. He died in 1002 and in a few years through the revolt of the army the Caliphate declined and the Christians began to reconquer the country. The Mohammedans began to look to Africa for rescue.

"When the conquest of the West [by the Arabs] was completed, and merchants began to penetrate into the interior, they saw no nation of the Blacks so mighty as Ghanah, the dominions of which extended westward as far as the ocean." In the eleventh century there was a large Arab immigration. The Berbers by that time had adopted the Arab tongue and the Mohammedan religion, and Mohammedanism had spread slowly southward across the Sahara; while in east Africa, Arabs, Persians and Indians had planted commercial colonies on the coast.

About 1000–1200 A.D. the situation was this: Ghana was on the edge of the desert in the north; Mandingoland was between the Niger and the Senegal in the south and the western Sahara, the Wolofs were in the west on the Senegal; and the Songhay on the Niger in the center. The Mohammedans came chiefly as traders and found a trade already established. Here and there in the great cities were districts set aside for these new merchants, and the Mohammedans gave frequent evidence of their respect for these black nations.

Islam did not found new states, but modified and united Negro states already ancient; it did not initiate new commerce, but developed a widespread trade already established. It is, as Frobenius says, "easily proved from chronicles written in Arabic that Islam was effective in fact only as a fertilizer and stimulant. The essential point is the resuscitative and invigorative concentration of Negro power in the service of a new era and a Moslem propaganda, as well as the reaction thereby produced."[1] Later in the eleventh century Arabs penetrated the Sudan and Central Africa from the east, filtering through the Negro tribes of Darfur, Kanem, and neighboring regions.

In the twelfth century a learned Negro poet resided at Seville, and Sidjilmessa, the last town in Lower Morocco toward the desert, was founded in 757 by a

Negro who ruled over the Berber inhabitants. Indeed, many towns in the Sudan and the desert were thus ruled, and felt no incongruity in this arrangement. They say, to be sure, that the Moors destroyed Audoghast because it paid tribute to the black town of Ghana, but this was because the town was heathen and not because it was black. On the other hand, there is a story that a Berber king overthrew one of the cities of the Sudan and all the black women committed suicide, being too proud to allow themselves to fall into the hands of white men.

In the west the Moslems first came into touch with the Negro kingdom of Ghana. Here large quantities of gold were gathered in early days. The history of Ghana goes back at least to the fourth century. It was probably founded by Berbers but eventually passed into the control of the black Sarakolle peoples. In the ninth and tenth centuries it was flourishing but fell before the proselyting Almoravides and eventually passed under the control of Melle. Its chief city was Kumbi-Kumbi, the ruins of which have been identified. It had prosperous agriculture and its later decline was due in part to the encroachment of the desert. The surrounding country was inhabited by the Bafur Negroes, who formed the Songhay toward the east, and Serers and the Wangara in the center. To the Wangara belong the Mandingoes who founded Melle. West of Ghana a mixture of Serers and Berbers formed the mulatto Fulani peoples. The black kings of Ghana eventually extended their rule over the Berber city of Audhoghast and the veiled tribes of the desert.

At Ghana we are told that there were forty-four white rulers, half coming before the Hegira and half after it. Then the power passed to black Sarakolles who were Negroes with some Semitic blood. By the middle of the eleventh century Ghana was the principal kingdom in the western Sudan. Already the town had a native and a Mussulman quarter, and was built of wood and stone with surrounding gardens. The king had an army of two hundred thousand and the wealth of the country was great. A century later the king had become Mohammedan in faith and had a palace with sculptures and glass windows. The great reason for this development was the desert trade. Gold, skins, ivory, kola nuts, gums, honey, wheat, and cotton were exported, and the whole Mediterranean coast traded with the Sudan.

Meantime, led by Yassine, three Berber tribes, inflamed with religious zeal, began to spread, starting from the lower Senegal and converting the black natives over a considerable territory. Audhoghast was recaptured from Ghana in the eleventh century, and reinforced by black converts, the movement spread until eventually it went into Morocco and then into Spain. Composed now of Berbers and Negroes, these fanatics shaped their course northward, and, united under the name of Al Morabitun, or Champions of the Faith, they subjugated the fertile countries on both sides of the southern Atlas, and founded, in 1073, the empire and city of Morocco.

The Al Morabitun, or Morabites, subsequently extended their plan into Spain, in the history of which country they figure under the name of Almoravides. "But long before they carried their arms into Europe, they corresponded intimately with the polished courts of Mohammedan Spain; and while they had not yet quite relinquished the desert, nor forgotten their acquaintance with the frontiers of

ANCIENT KINGDOMS OF THE SUDAN, 800–1591 A.D.

Map labels:

SONGHAY
1355–1591 A.D.

MELLESTINE
1285–1468 A.D.

GHANA
800–1076 A.D.

TIBESTI
BORKU
DARFUR
KANEM
BORNU
Lake Chad
Shari R.
Congo R.
Agades
Katsena
Kano
HAUSA
BENIN
MOSSI
Niger R.
JENNE
Timbuktu
MANDINGOLAND
Senegal R.
GAMBIA R.
Cape Verde
CAPE VERDE ISLANDS
CANARY ISLANDS
SHERBORO I.
GULF OF GUINEA
ATLANTIC OCEAN

Negro-land, they communicated their information to the inquisitive, and, for that age, well-instructed Spanish Arabs."[2] This movement invaded Spain and inflicted a decisive defeat on Alphonso VI and Zilaca in 1086 under the leadership of Yusuf. The Almoravides held the conquest until 1120 when they suffered defeat at Kutanda at the hands of the Almohades, a more bigoted religious sect, who were victorious in 1195 and held Mohammedan Spain until 1212. By 1238, however, Mohammedan Spain was reduced to the ports between Granada and Cadiz.

The spread of Islam in Africa was slow. Timbuktu founded, in the eleventh century, did not become Mohammedan until 1591. The Congo forest kept back the Arabs from expanding westward from the east coast, just as the Sahara kept them from expanding southward in North Africa. At the end of the eleventh century the Almoravides carried their proselyting down toward the Gulf of Guinea, attracted by the abundance of kola nuts, and founded a city on the Volta River. This city, Bego, became an important metropolis and center of commerce and propaganda. Later its inhabitants spread along the Ivory Coast, enriching themselves with commerce and intellectual development, which has continued up to the present.

In the early part of the thirteenth century the prestige of Ghana began to fall before the rising Mandingan kingdom to the west. Melle, as it was called, was founded in 1235 and formed an open door for Moslem and Moorish traders. The new kingdom, helped by its expanding trade, began to grow, and Islam slowly surrounded the older Negro culture west, north, and east. However, a compact mass of that older heathen culture, pushing itself upward from the Guinea coast, stood firmly against Islam down to the nineteenth century.

Steadily Mohammedanism triumphed in the growing states which almost encircled the protagonists of ancient Atlantic culture. Mandingan Melle eventually supplanted Ghana in prestige and power, after Ghana had been overthrown by the Soso in 1203. The territory of Melle lay southeast of Ghana and some five hundred miles north of the Gulf of Guinea. Its kings were known by the title of Mansa, and from the middle of the thirteenth century to the middle of the fourteenth, the Mellestine, as its dominion was called, was the leading power in the land of the blacks.

Melle began on the left bank of the Upper Niger, under Negro kings who reigned without interruption, save for fifteen years, from 600 to the present, and are probably the oldest reigning dynasty in the world. The Mansa, or kings of Melle, were obscure rulers until about 1050, when they were converted to Mohammedanism.

"As to the people of Mali [Melle], they surpassed the other Blacks in these countries in wealth and numbers. They extended their dominions, and conquered the Susu, as well as the kingdom of Ghanah in the vicinity of the Ocean towards the west. The Mohammedans say that the first King of Mali was Baramindanah. He performed the pilgrimage to Mekkah, and enjoined his successors to do the same."[3]

Melle secured control of the trade in gold dust which Ghana had formerly monopolized. It was annexed by the Soso in 1224, but Sundiata Keita made the country independent and allied himself with neighboring Mandingo chiefs. He took Ghana and destroyed it in 1240 and developed agriculture, also the raising and wearing of cotton. Under his successor, various southern territories, including the valley of the Gambia River, were added to Melle; and from 1307 to 1332, Gongo-Mussa brought the kingdom of Melle to its highest prosperity. He made a pilgrimage to Mecca in 1324 which aroused great interest, and brought back with him an Arab who began a new style of architecture in the black Sudan.

"The number of people employed to carry his baggage and provisions amounted to 12,000, all dressed in tunics of figured cotton, or the silk called El-Yemeni. The Haji Tunis, interpreter of this nation in Kahirah [Cairo], said that Mansa [Gongo] Mussa brought with him to Egypt no less than 80 loads of Tibar [gold dust], each weighing 300 pounds."[4]

On his return from Mecca, Gongo-Mussa found that Timbuktu had been sacked by the Mossi, but he rebuilt the town and filled the new mosque with learned blacks from the University of Fez. Gongo-Mussa reigned twenty-five years and "was distinguished by his ability and by the holiness of his life. The justice of his administration was such that the memory of it still lives."

"Ibn Said, a writer of the thirteenth century, has enumerated thirteen nations of Blacks, extending across Africa, from Ghanah in the west, to the Boja [Beja] on the shores of the Red Sea in the east."

The Mandingan empire at this time occupied nearly the whole of what is now French West Africa, including part of British West Africa. The rulers had close relations with the rulers of Morocco and interchanged visits. Ibn Batuta visited Melle in 1352 and testified to the excellent administration of the city, and its courtesy, prosperity and discipline. Its finances were in good condition and there was luxury and ceremony. In fine the culture of Melle at this time compared favorably with the culture of Europe. The Mellestine preserved its pre-eminence until the beginning of the fifteenth century, when the rod of Sudanese empire passed to Songhay, the largest and most famous of the black empires.

This Negro kingdom centered at Gao, where a dynasty called the Dia, or Za, remained in power on the western Niger from 690 to 1335. The known history of Songhay covers a thousand years and three dynasties, and centers in the great bend of the Niger. There were thirty kings of the First Dynasty. During the reign of one of these, the Songhay kingdom became the vassal kingdom of Melle, then at the height of its glory. In addition to this, the Mossi crossed the valley, plundered Timbuktu in 1339, and separated Jenne, the original seat of the Songhay, from the main empire. The sixteenth Songhay king was converted to Mohammedanism in 1009, and after that all the Songhay princes were Mohammedans.

Gongo-Mussa, on his capture of Timbuktu, had taken two young Songhay princes to the court of Melle to be educated in 1326. These boys when grown ran away and founded a new dynasty in Songhay, that of the Sonnis, in 1355. Seventeen of these kings reigned, the last and greatest being Sonni Ali, who ascended the throne in 1464. Melle was at this time declining, and other cities like Jenne, with its seven thousand villages, were rising, and the Tuaregs (Berbers with Negro blood) had captured Timbuktu.

Sonni Ali was a soldier and began his career with the conquest of Timbuktu in 1469. He also succeeded in capturing Jenne and attacked the Mossi and other enemies on all sides. Finally he concentrated his forces for the destruction of Melle and subdued nearly the whole empire on the west bend of the Niger. In summing up Sonni Ali's military career the chronicle says of him, "He surpassed all his predecessors in the number and valor of his soldiery. His conquests were many and his renown extended from the rising to the setting of the sun. If it is the will of God, he will be long spoken of."

After the death of Sonni Ali, the dynasty of the Askias ruled in Songhay from 1493 to 1591. The first one, Askia Mohammed, ruled from 1493 to 1529. Sonni Ali was a Songhay, whose mother was black and whose father, a Berber. He was succeeded by a full-blooded black, Mohammed Abou Bekr, who had been his prime minister. Mohammed was hailed as "Askia" (usurper) and is best known as Mohammed Askia. He was strictly orthodox where Ali was rather a scoffer, and an organizer where Ali was a warrior. On his pilgrimage to Mecca in 1497 there was nothing of the barbaric splendor of Gongo-Mussa, but a brilliant group of scholars and officials with a small escort of fifteen hundred soldiers and nine hundred thousand dollars in gold. He stopped and consulted with scholars and politicians, and studied matters of taxation, weights and measures, trade, religious tolerance and manners. Eventually he was made by the authorities of Mecca, Caliph of the Sudan. He returned to the Sudan in 1497.

He had a genius for selecting collaborators, and instead of forcing the peasants into the army, he recruited a professional army and encouraged farmers, artisans and merchants. He undertook a holy war against the indomitable Mossi, and finally marched against the Hausa. He subdued these cities and even imposed the rule of black men on the Berber town of Agades, a rich city of merchants and artificers with stately mansions. In fine, Askia, during his reign, conquered and consolidated an empire two thousand miles long by one thousand wide at its greatest extent—a territory as large as all Europe. The territory was divided into four vice-royalties, and the system of Melle, with its semi-independent native dynasties, was carried out. His empire extended from the Atlantic to Lake Chad and from the salt mines of Tegazza and the town of Augila in the north to the tenth degree of north latitude toward the south.

It was a six months' journey across the empire and, it is said, "he was obeyed with as much docility on the farthest limits of the empire as he was in his own palace, and there reigned everywhere great plenty and absolute peace." Leo Africanus described his state about 1507. He made intellectual centers at cities like Gao, Timbuktu and Jenne, where there were writers and where students from North Africa came to study. A literature developed in Timbuktu in the sixteenth and seventeenth centuries. The University of Sankore became a center of learning in correspondence with Egypt and North Africa and had a swarm of black Sudanese students. Law, literature, grammar, geography, and surgery were studied. Askia the Great reigned thirty-six years, and his dynasty continued on the throne until after the Moorish invasion of 1591.

Before continuing the history of the Songhay, we may note some smaller, contemporary states. There were the Bambara south of Timbuktu, who flourished from 1660 to 1862; there were the various Fulani kingdoms from the sixteenth to the eighteenth centuries, and the Tukolor conquest of 1776. West of Ghana, the long dwelling of Berbers with the black Serers formed eventually the Fulani people who sent forth groups to the southwest, east and southeast. In the early sixteenth century the Fulani attacked Songhay but were repulsed and took refuge northwest of the Futa-Jalon. Eventually they founded a kingdom under the so-called Deninake who maintained power from 1559 to 1776. In the Futa-Jalon, inland from French Guinea, the Soso and Fulani, together with other Negro tribes, formed a nation called the Fula, speaking the Fulani language and for the most part Mohammedans, who built up a theocratic state.

Many smaller states were involved in this history; there was the kingdom of Diara southwest of Ghana, which lasted from the thirteenth to the sixteenth century with more or less independence, and was finally incorporated into the Songhay empire. The kingdom of the Soso southwest of Timbuktu was at first dependent upon Ghana. Then Sumangura in 1203 overwhelmed Ghana and held it for a few years, but the Soso were finally overcome by Sundiata of Melle and the state annexed. Far to the west came a revolt of Tukolor Negroes late in the eighteenth century. They triumphed over the Fulani, and under Omar extended their conquest considerably. Omar made a pilgrimage to Mecca. He was finally put to flight by the French in 1859 with the help of the mulatto French commander Paul Holle. His entire territory was annexed by the French in 1890.

The Mossi had two kingdoms founded in the eleventh and twelfth centuries among the Negroes inland from the Gulf of Guinea. They are of interest because of the type of state which they invented, and which was widely copied over Negro Africa and still persists. The main Mossi empire had four vassal kingdoms besides the kingdom of the ruler. In the ruler's kingdom there were five provinces whose governors made up the imperial council and were the chief officers of state. Associated with the council were eleven ministers ruling the army, religion, musicians and collecting taxes. The Mossi empires were peculiar in having little or no Berber or white influence. They did not make extensive conquests, but at one time attacked Timbuktu and later resisted Sonni Ali.

Askia Mohammed of the Songhay was succeeded by descendants who nearly ruined his great country by civil wars, massacres and unfortunate military expeditions. One successor, Daoud, who reigned from 1549 to 1583, renewed agriculture and science and was closely associated with the Sultan of Morocco, but already the empire was on the decline.

Meantime great things were happening in the world beyond the desert, the ocean, and the Nile; Arabian Mohammedanism succumbed to the wild fanaticism of the Seljukian Turks. These new conquerors were not only firmly planted at the gates of Vienna, but had swept the shores of the Mediterranean and sent all Europe scouring the seas for their lost trade connections with the riches of Asia. Religious zeal, fear of conquest, and commercial greed inflamed Europe against the Mohammedans and led to the discovery of a new world, the riches of which poured first on Spain and then on England.

Oppression of the Berbers and Moors in Spain followed and in 1502 they were driven back into Africa, despoiled and humbled. Here the Spaniards followed and harassed them; and here the Turks, fighting them and the Christians, captured the Mediterranean ports and cut the Moors off permanently from Europe.

The Moors in Morocco had come to look upon the Sudan as a gold mine, and knew that the Sudan was especially dependent upon salt. In 1545 Morocco claimed the principal salt mines at Tegazza, but the reigning Askia refused to recognize the claim. When the Sultan Almansur came to the throne of Morocco, he increased the efficiency of his army by supplying it with firearms and cannon. Almansur determined to attack the Sudan. A company of 3,000 Spanish renegades with muskets, led by Judar, finally attacked the Songhay in 1590. They overthrew the Askias at the battle of Tondibi in 1591 and thereafter ruled at Timbuktu.

Askia Ishak, the king, offered terms, and Judar Pasha referred them to Morocco. The Sultan, angry with his general's delay, deposed him and sent another who crushed and treacherously murdered the king and set up a puppet. Thereafter there were two Askias, one at Timbuktu and one who maintained himself in the Hausa states to the east, which the invaders could not subdue. Anarchy reigned in Songhay. The soldiers tried to put down disorder with a high hand, drove out and murdered distinguished men of Timbuktu, and as a result let loose a riot of robbery and decadence throughout the Sudan. Pasha now succeeded pasha with revolt and misrule, until in 1612 the soldiers elected their own pasha and deliberately shut themselves up in the Sudan by cutting off approach from Morocco and the north.

Hausaland and Bornu were still open to Turkish and Mohammedan influence from the east, and the Gulf of Guinea to the slave trade from the west; but the face of the finest Negro civilization the modern world had produced, was veiled from Europe and given to the defilement of a wild horde, which Delafosse calls the "Scum of Europe." In 1623 it is written "excesses of every kind are now committed unchecked by the soldiery," and "the country is profoundly convulsed and oppressed."

The Tuaregs marched down from the desert and deprived the invaders of many of the principal towns. The rest of the empire of the Songhay was by the end of the eighteenth century divided among separate chiefs, who bought supplies from the Negro peasantry and were "at once the vainest, proudest, and perhaps the most bigoted, ferocious, and intolerant of all the nations of the south." They lived a nomadic life, plundering the Negroes. To such depths did the mighty Songhay fall.

After 1660 these Pashas, now of mixed Spanish and Negro blood, ruled at Timbuktu for 120 years. They preserved a pretense of authority by paying tribute to the black Bambara kings of Segu and also by bribing the Tuaregs. After 1780 the title of Pasha disappeared and "mayors" of Timbuktu were chosen sometimes by the Bambara, sometimes by the Tuareg, and sometimes by the Fulani. In 1894 the city was taken by Joffre, later Marshal of France.

Meanwhile, to the eastward, two powerful states had appeared. They never disputed the military supremacy of Songhay, but their industrial development was marvelous. The Hausa states were formed by seven original cities, of which Kano was the oldest and Katsina the most famous. Gober was celebrated after the sixteenth century for its cotton and leather manufacture. Kano was populous in the sixteenth century. Katsina was the center of agriculture and had military power, and Zaria was a center of commerce. In the fifteenth century these states were united under the kings of Kebbi. In 1513 the Hausa states made alliance with Askia Mohammed of Songhay, but afterward regained their independence.

Their greatest leaders, Mohammed Rimpa and Ahmadu Kesoke, arose in the fifteenth and early sixteenth centuries. The land was subject to the Songhay, but the cities became industrious centers of smelting, weaving, and dyeing. Katsina especially, in the middle of the sixteenth century, is described as a place thirteen or fourteen miles in circumference, divided into quarters for strangers, for visitors from various states, and for the different trades and industries, as saddlers, shoemakers, dyers, etc.

The Hausa were converted to Mohammedanism about the beginning of the nineteenth century. This was accomplished by the Sheik Ousman, who extended his rule over the Hausa kingdom and Kebbi, and even invaded Bornu early in the nineteenth century. He was succeeded by Mohammed Bello, who reigned from 1815 to 1837. Mohammed Bello was a noted man of letters who composed poems and prose works in Arabic. He was succeeded by his brother and then by his son, who were harassed by continual revolts. Finally the pieces of the empire fell apart in 1904, and the capital Sokoto was occupied by the British under Lugard.

To the east of the Hausa, on both sides of Lake Chad, is a domain called Bornu in the west and Kanem in the east. The population is dispersed across immense territories and divided into a great number of tribes, some frankly Negroes and others more or less mixed with white blood. The first ruler of Bornu-Kanem was Saefe and was certainly Negro, although we do not know exactly when he lived. Toward the eleventh century under one of his successors, Mohammedanism made its first appearance. The dynasty of Saefe was overthrown by Mohammedans, whose kings took the title of Mai. The first king, ruling from 1220 to 1259, had to contend with continual revolts from the subdued peoples, so that two centuries passed in anarchy. Mai Idris I, 1352 to 1376, came to the throne when the Arab traveler, Ibn Batuta, was visiting near. At that time copper mines were in full operation and many Negro customs were evident, like the concealment of the king behind a curtain, and the use of drums with different rhythms to send messages. Under Idris III, 1573 to 1603, the empire of Bornu was at its height. It ruled over Kano and the Air, over Kanem and land south of Lake Chad. The Tunjur Negroes were in the ascendancy. Rabah attacked and conquered the country in 1893, but after his death the English made Bornu a British protectorate.

Southwest of Lake Chad, arose in 1520 a sultanate of Bagirmi, which reached its highest power in the seventeenth century. This dynasty was overthrown by the Negroid Mabas, who established Wadai to the eastward about 1640. After struggling with Bornu it was attacked by Rabah in 1893 and annexed by the French in 1896. Wadai and a number of other tribes with Arabian and Negro blood ruled in the eastern Sudan in the seventeenth century.

Darfur and Kordofan in the eastern Sudan arose to power in the sixteenth and seventeenth centuries. A ruler of Kordofan was in touch with Napoleon in his Egyptian campaign late in the eighteenth century. Kordofan was occupied by the Egyptians in the nineteenth century and extended to the Nile. The southern or mountainous part of Kordofan was called Nubia, although that name is also used for the region about Dongola. The central figure of the eastern Sudan in the nineteenth century is Rabah. Rabah was the son of a Negro woman and the principal lieutenant in the army of Zobir Pasha, who was governor of the Bahr-el-Ghazal in 1875. When Zobir's son was overthrown, Rabah took the army and began conquest northwest of the Bahr-el-Ghazal in 1878. He brought a considerable part of north central Africa under control, overthrowing the Bagirmi, Bornu, Gober and many other states around Lake Chad. In 1900 he was conquered and killed by the French after an adventure of twenty-two years.

These complicated and not yet thoroughly known phases of history have almost been forgotten in modern times. Many long regarded it as Arabian and Mohammedan history because Arabic was the *lingua franca* of most of these peoples. Lately, however, a clearer knowledge of the meaning and development in this part of Africa has been attained. These peoples were not Arabs. They were Negroes with some infiltration of Arabian blood. They were not all Mohammedans, but their history is that of a more or less fierce clash of Moslem religion and ancient African beliefs.

The chief difficulty here was the impossibility of self-defense on the part of various centers of culture and rising nations, and the overwhelming force that entered from time to time both from Europe and Asia. The proximity of these rising and falling empires and centers of culture to the cheap labor of the south led increasingly to the slave trade, which became a cause of demoralization and weakness, especially when encouraged and carried on by alien merchants. On the other hand the pressure of Sudanese kingdoms upon the ancient peoples of the West Coast not only weakened this indigenous African culture, cut it off from Europe, but left it a prey to the Christian slave trade. Thus the black civilization of the Sudan in a sense fell before the onslaught of two of the world's great religions.

NOTES

1. *Voice of Africa*, Vol. II, pp. 359–360.
2. Cooley, *The Negro Land of the Arabs*, p. 3.
3. Cooley, *The Negro Land of the Arabs*, pp. 61, 62.
4. Cooley, *The Negro Land of the Arabs*, pp. 61, 62.

CHAPTER IV

◆

Congo and Guinea

One of the great cities of the Sudan was Jenne. The chronicle says that "its markets are held every day of the week and its populations are very enormous. Its seven thousand villages are so near to one another that the chief of Jenne has no need of messengers. If he wished to send a note to Lake Dibo, for instance, it is cried from the gate of the town and repeated from village to village, by which means it reaches its destination almost instantly."[1]

From the name of this city we get the modern name Guinea, which is used today to designate the country contiguous to the great gulf of that name—a territory often referred to in general as West Africa. Here, reaching from the mouth of the Gambia to the mouth of the Niger, is a coast of six hundred miles, where a marvelous drama of world history has been enacted. The coast and its hinterland comprehend many well-known names. First comes ancient Guinea, then modern Sierra Leone and Liberia; then follow the various "coasts" of former traffic—the grain, ivory, gold, and slave coasts—with the adjoining territories of Ashanti, Dahomey, Lagos, and Benin; and farther back, such tribal and territorial names as those of the Mandingoes, Yorubas, the Mossi, Nupe, Borgu, and others.

If ever a people exhibited unanswerable evidence of indigenous civilization, it is the west-coast Africans. Undoubtedly they adapted much that came to them, utilized new ideas, and grew from contact. But their art and culture are Negro. Recent investigation makes it certain that an ancient civilization existed on this coast, which may have gone back as far as three thousand years before Christ. Frobenius, perhaps fancifully, identified this African coast with the Atlantis of the Greeks and as a part of that great western movement in human culture, "beyond the pillars of Hercules," which thirteen centuries before Christ strove with Egypt and the East.

It is, at any rate, clear that ancient commerce reached down the west coast. The Phoenicians, 600 B.C., and the Carthaginians, a century or more later, record voyages, and these may have been attempted revivals of still more ancient intercourse. These coasts at some unknown prehistoric period were peopled from the Niger plateau toward the north and west by the black West African type of Negro, while along the west end of the desert these Negroes mingled with the Berbers, forming various Negroid types.

We have already noted in the main the history of black men along the wonderful Niger and seen how, pushing up from the Gulf of Guinea, a powerful wedge of ancient culture held back Islam for a thousand years, now victorious, now stubbornly disputing every inch of retreat. The center of this culture lay probably, in oldest time, above the Bight of Benin, along the Slave Coast, and reached west and north. We trace it today not only in the remarkable tradition of the natives, but in stone monuments, architecture, industrial and social organizations, and works of art in bronze, glass and terra cotta.

Down the west coast of Africa, south of the Senegal, came first the Wolofs and then the Serer, remarkable for their organization. Beyond that were similar groups and a flourishing agriculture. Further along between the Gambia River and French Guinea we come to a number of backward half savage tribes, who are the remains of populations overthrown and driven back by the Mandingo and Fulani. Sometimes they have taken refuge on islands and up the branches of rivers. From these, their more powerful neighbors drew thousands of slaves who crossed the Atlantic to the American colonies.

From French Guinea toward Liberia, the Mandingoes and allied tribes like the Susu pushed toward the sea. With them were the Vai, who invented a written language with an alphabet toward the end of the eighteenth century. In the hinterland behind Liberia and Sierra Leone there were a series of primitive people, sometimes cannibals, who cultivated the kola nut. Near them in the dense forests were other primitive people, who on the coast were known as the Kru men and who for five centuries have been sailors and workers on ships.

East of the Kru, from the Bambara River to the Volta, are a group of people with striking intellectual development, later debased by imported liquor. They include the Agni, the Abron, who have a well-organized state dating from the fifteenth century; and the Ashanti and Fanti. The Ashanti organized a well-constituted kingdom with its capital at Kumasi, which lasted from 1700 to 1895. Beyond the Volta River are peoples with intellectual and artistic gifts and excellent political organization. Among them are the Ewe, the Yoruba, and people of Benin, Dahomey and Nupe.

The kingdom of Yoruba can be traced back to the early eighteenth century when it invaded Dahomey twice but finally made peace in 1847, at which time the king of Dahomey undertook to pay annual tribute. The kings of Yoruba, Egba, Ketu and Jebu were closely allied, the title of the first being Alafin, and the king of the Egba being known as the Alake. About 1800 the Yoruba kingdom began to break up. The Fulani and others had entered the territory of the Hausa, and they, driven southward, pressed upon Yoruba.

The Yoruba, moving southward because of this and because of the rebellion of the Mohammedan party in their own territory, came to their present capital Oyo; and the Egbas, declaring independence, moved to their present capital Abeokuto. Ibadan in the old province of Egba declared its independence, and other secessions took place, making seven independent states; while the former Yoruba province was inhabited by Fulani and people of Bornu and Hausa.

Meantime Lagos and the coast had been colonized by Yoruba at the beginning of the eighteenth century and was noted as a slave market; and the captives in these wars were sent down there and sold to the slave traders.

West of Yoruba on the lower courses of the Niger is Benin, a state which in 1897 traced its twenty-three kings back a thousand years; some legends even named a line of sixty kings. It seems probable that Benin developed the imperial idea and once extended its rule into the Congo Valley.

Benin was one of the most carefully organized of the Negro states on the West Coast with a rare native culture. The Portuguese discovered the country about 1585 and traded with it in slaves and other produce. Lagos and other coast towns were first established by the Beni. It was a small country but its influence extended from Sierra Leone to the mouth of the Congo because of the widespread belief in the power of its Juju or chief spirit. The king was in the hands of the priesthood and the worship of the Juju demanded human sacrifice by crucifixion. Nevertheless the deaths were mercifully inflicted and the Beni had a high culture. They were noted for their work in brass and ivory. The British came in contact with Benin in 1553 and dealt in ivory, palm oil and other goods. The Dutch established factories near and engaged in the slave trade.

The slave trade long centered here and, after its abolition, explorers like Mungo Park and the Lander Brothers penetrated the interior. Between 1840 and 1860 European merchants of several nations were trading up these rivers and after the pause that followed the Indian mutiny and the Franco-Prussian War, British companies began to be formed.

The British attacked Lagos and after severe losses drove out one king and proclaimed another. Traders and missionaries flocked in. Finally in 1861 by force and bribes the king was induced to cede the territory to the protection of Great Britain. Benin still resisted.

Later and also to the west of Yoruba come two states showing a fiercer and ruder culture, Dahomey and Ashanti. Dahomey was probably founded before the sixteenth century and is mentioned by Leo Africanus. The kings at the capital, Abomey, were warriors and slave traders and celebrated for human sacrifice, but had an extraordinary well-organized state and were good farmers and artisans with high intellectual capacity.

The known history of Dahomey begins with the seventeenth century when the three sons of a Negro monarch established states of which one, Dahomey, in 1724–28, conquered the other two. King Gezo from 1818 to 1858 raised the power of Dahomey to the highest point and made a treaty with the French. There had been a widespread custom of human sacrifice based on filial piety and loyalty to the chief. These sacrifices Gezo greatly reduced. When England annexed Lagos in 1861, France began to intrigue for Dahomey and German agents also appeared. Finally in 1889 the French and the English agreed, and the French claimed Dahomey. There was severe fighting in which the Amazons took part. Peace was made in 1890, but war broke out again in 1892 when the mulatto General Dodds with French and Senegalese soldiers finally defeated the Dahomey troops and the king set fire to his capital. The country was divided and the royal family restored. Gradually the hinterland toward the north was added.

In the interior and to the north between these people and the bend of the Niger are a large number of tribes, primitive and chaotic in organization, sometimes included in the empire-building states and at other times repelling them by their wild independence. They are chiefly notable for their excellent farming. Further up on the Volta, near the beginning of the great forest, are little states founded by the Sunufo, noted for the iron industry, pottery, agriculture and the art of music.

The Akan people formed one tribe and lived originally further to the north toward the great bend of the Niger. The expanding imperialism there drove them south and divided them into various tribes. The first known king of Ashanti, a part of the Akans, reigned about 1600. He had been preceded by at least two kings. Gold was then unknown and iron was currency. Osai Tutu came to the throne in 1697 and founded Kumasi. The Ashanti were at war with the Denkara early in the eighteenth century and overcame them, thus coming in contact with the Dutch at Elmina on the coast. The next important king, Osai Kwesi, came to the throne in 1742 and kept up conquest and the putting down of revolts. Osai Tutu Kwamina was the first Ashanti king who came in contact with the English. By this time the Ashanti ruled over a vast extent of country with many tribes, calling for great activity in order to put down various rebellions.

The Portuguese arrived on the Guinea coast in the middle of the sixteenth century and were expelled by the Dutch in the seventeenth century. The Dutch quarreled with the English and eventually the English took possession of the coast and the slave trade. There ensued between 1803 and 1874 six Ashanti wars with the English. Ostensibly they were aimed at the customs of human sacrifice in Ashanti and to put down aggression upon the Fanti tribes who owed allegiance to Ashanti, but became allied with the English. In reality these wars all aimed at trade monopoly and economic empire for the English.

The records of the action of the English on the Gold Coast, "the earliest beginnings of which had their inception in the dark days of the slave trade, cannot but hold many things that modern Englishmen must recall with mingled shame and horror. The reader will find much to deplore in the public and private acts of many of the white men, who, in their time, made history on the Coast; and some deeds were done which must forever remain among the most bitter and humiliating memories of every Britisher who loves his country and is jealous of its fair fame."[2]

When the first Ashanti war took place under King Osai Tutu Kwamina between 1803 and 1807 it began characteristically with the theft of gold and valuables from a grave—a blasphemy of death and eternal life. The King of Ashanti demanded redress, but his messengers to the accused Fanti were killed. This led to a war between the Ashanti and the Fanti in which the English governor promised to defend some of the allies of the Fanti. The Ashanti advanced toward the sea and captured a fort belonging to the Dutch. The English governor tried to defend the allies of the Fanti and as a result his supporters were shut up in the fort and besieged by the Ashanti. Although the fort made a brilliant defense, 10,000 or more of the Fanti were killed. The governor sent for English ships to support him, but the officer in charge insisted on coming to terms with the Ashanti king. Eventually hostages from the Fanti allies were delivered to the Ashanti and a peace was planned, in which it was acknowledged that the coast and the territory of the Fanti belonged exclusively to the empire of the Ashanti, and that while the whites might have judicial authority in the forts, nevertheless the Ashanti were the rulers of the country.

This treaty was never actually signed, but the Ashanti withdrew, and the British trade on the Gold Coast was safe. The second Ashanti war was really a continuation of the first and lasted from 1808 to 1813. The Ashanti army had withdrawn after the proposed peace in 1807 because of the outbreak of smallpox and scarcity of supplies. Thereupon the Fanti began another rebellion, and peoples of the Gold Coast were warned by the English governor to take no part. Nevertheless they did, and attacked the Elminas who were allies of the Ashanti. The Ashanti king sent messengers declaring that he desired peace and trade, which were being interfered with by the Fanti. Nothing was done and the Ashanti after two weeks came to the support of the Elminas with a large army. Eventually they were victorious but lived up to their promise not to harm Europeans. Their allies, however, the Elminas, killed the Dutch governor, and the Fanti murdered the mulatto commandant of one of the forts and eventually killed an Englishman. As a result English ships destroyed the fort.

Certain of the tributaries of the Ashanti rebelled in 1811, and in 1814 the King of Ashanti determined to crush them. He especially demanded the surrender of three recalcitrant chiefs and came down to the coast to find them. The English governor sent to inquire the reason and promised that if he could find the rebels he would return them. The Ashanti, on the other hand, promised not to molest any of the people living under the protection of the forts. Eventually the chiefs were found and killed. In this way peace was restored between the Ashanti and the Fanti and great numbers of the Ashanti came down to Cape Coast and there was a brisk trade.

The English, thereupon, began to make efforts to extend their jurisdiction on the coast. On the conclusion of peace in 1816, the English felt that a regular treaty with the Ashanti ought to be made. They, therefore, sent an embassy to Kumasi under Bowdich. It was received in state with an assembling of 30,000 Ashanti soldiers and chiefs under gorgeous silk umbrellas. The description of the Ashanti court is worth quoting:

"The sun was reflected, with a glare scarcely more supportable than the heat, from the massy gold ornaments, which glistened in every direction. . . . The Caboceers, as did their superior captains and attendants, wore Ashantee cloths of extravagant price from the costly foreign silks which had been unravelled to weave them, . . . and massy gold necklaces intricately wrought. . . . Some wore necklaces reaching to the navel, entirely of aggry beads; a band of gold and beads encircled the knee, from which several strings of the same depended; small circles of gold like guineas, rings, and casts of animals, were strung round their ankles . . . and rude lumps of rock gold hung from their left wrists, which were so heavily laden as to be supported on the head of one of their handsomest boys. Gold and silver pipes and canes dazzled the eye in every direction. Wolves' and rams' heads as large as life, cast in gold, were suspended from their gold-handled swords, which were held around them in great numbers."[3]

The king showed his readiness to come to understanding with the English, but the question of the payments for the occupation of forts came up. For more than a century the kings of Ashanti had received payment for Elmina Castle, and lately for the English and Dutch forts of Accra and the Danish fort. The king, however, showed that he had been cheated in these payments and most of the rentals had been retained by local chiefs. Bowdich, however, reassured the king, and the governor was communicated with and the payments were readjusted.

As a result a treaty was signed in 1817 in ten articles, promising peace between the British and Ashanti, security for the people of Cape Coast, and redress by the governor for any case of aggression on the part of the natives under British protection. A British officer was to reside at Kumasi as a means of communication with the governor. Trade was to be encouraged and the governor was to have the right to punish subjects of Ashanti for secondary offenses but not serious crimes. Two children of the king were to be sent to Cape Coast for education.

Here was a chance for peace and civilization on the Gold Coast through the alliance of one of the leading white civilized nations of Europe and a powerful black kingdom of Africa, independent and self-assertive, but eager to know the new white world. Inevitably war and blood sacrifice must have in the end succumbed to normal industry and philanthropic effort. The Ashanti king of the day was a man of unusual ability and high character, honorable and desiring peace. He never broke his word to the English. Claridge says:

"Osai Tutu Kwamina is, of all the Ashanti monarchs, the one on whom the Englishman should look with the most interest, for he was the first of the line who came into contact with Europeans, and by observing the attitude which he adopted towards them before the occurrence of those hostilities by which the relations of the two powers were subsequently embittered, we may learn what was the position that the Ashantis would have spontaneously adopted towards the white men."[4]

The English did not understand Negro customs nor did their changing officials know or try to know what promises their government had made. As a result, the Fanti and other tribes, although the sworn vassals of the king of Ashanti, were struggling for freedom. They tried to gain their independence of Ashanti by putting themselves under the protection of the English, and thus led the English to interfere with the Ashanti power in ways which they had specifically promised not to use.

The fourth and fifth Ashanti wars were due entirely to such action on the part of the Fanti, and to the English breaking the treaty which they signed. The English went into the fourth war without right and without appreciating the power of Ashanti. The result was that at the battle of Insamankow, in 1824, the English Governor McCarthy was killed and his army beaten, on the same day that the Ashanti king himself died a natural death at Kumasi. This defeat was partially retrieved by a later English success and the withdrawal of the Ashanti. It was a double disaster.

The English were now disposed to give up efforts on the Gold Coast. The war had cost a large sum; the slave trade had been forbidden, and while not stopped it was ceasing to be profitable to the English. The English merchants on the coast, however, saw further possibilities. They, therefore, got permission to carry on, and under a far-seeing governor, George Maclean, a new start was made, although trade had been nearly annihilated and the Ashanti were sullen. Nevertheless a peace was signed in 1831 and trade reopened. Two princes of the Ashanti royal family were sent to England to be educated. A serious attempt was made to introduce Christianity by sending missionaries in 1827, 1835, and 1843.

Maclean also tried to get at the root of the trouble by signing with the Fanti chiefs, who were at the bottom of so much of the trouble, the celebrated Bond of 1844. This bond acknowledged the power and jurisdiction exercised hitherto "for and on behalf of Her Majesty the Queen of Great Britain" and was signed by the chiefs and the governor. This bond really conferred no territorial rights but legalized and defined jurisdiction in criminal matters. The Fanti then took another interesting step. Their chiefs met and formed a legislative body which proposed a poll tax to be used for education and public improvements. It looked as though a new start for peace and advancement was being made on the Gold Coast through the chiefs who had been longest working in alliance with the English.

But two difficulties overthrew this: first, the English complicated the poll tax collection by establishing municipal corporations and local taxation; and, secondly, the Ashanti still considered that their jurisdiction over the Fanti had been interfered with. The Ashanti finally went to war again in 1860, capturing a number of Fanti prisoners, and the English gave up the attempt to punish them. The home agitation to withdraw from the Gold Coast was renewed.

In the meantime the Dutch and English had come to an understanding on the coast and had arranged an exchange of territory; but this meant that Elmina, which under the Dutch had always been the acknowledged property of the Ashanti, was now to be turned over to the English, and trouble between the Ashanti and Elminas broke out.

The Fanti as has been noted organized a confederation which if recognized by the English would have consolidated their power and made an organized center of defense against the power of Ashanti; but the English at that time in charge upon the coast were short-sighted and alarmed. The chiefs and educated Fanti natives had adopted a constitution to promote friendly intercourse between the kings and chiefs; to improve the country with roads and schools; and to have a representative assembly for preparing laws. The governor promptly arrested some of the leaders, although they were afterwards released by the home secretary of state. But the Confederation failed, leaving a great deal of bad feeling. All this irritated the Ashanti, and the war which had apparently stopped in 1863 broke out into new hostilities in 1873, when Elmina was occupied by the English. The Ashanti army began to march in 1873, and fought two hard battles which led to the retirement of the British. The British bombarded Elmina and brought in reinforcements.

This finally led the British to appoint Sir Garnet Wolseley to take charge. He came and demanded the withdrawal of the Ashanti. The Ashanti complained that their vassals refused to serve the king and ran away to the English, and that the Fanti plundered the agents of the Ashanti when they came down to the coast. "They fought with me six times and I drove them away and they escaped to be under you," said the king. Nevertheless the Ashanti retreated and Wolseley slowly followed; but he did not have European troops and the Fanti allies did not respond. Some indecisive battles took place and the Ashanti finally withdrew, but lost a large number of men and chiefs.

The English now determined to reduce Ashanti to complete submission. The whole European situation had changed: the Franco-Prussian war had been fought; Germany was a great power and England was consolidating her economic empire. Wolseley imported a well-equipped modern army from England and invaded Ashanti in 1873. In February he was at Kumasi and burned the town. The king of Ashanti renounced all his rights over subject tribes and over Elmina and promised heavy indemnities.

Between 1875 and 1880 the power of Ashanti partially revived but the English now were determined on domination. The Ashanti sent an embassy representing the king direct to England in 1894, but the colonial officials refused to receive it and recognized the head of the Ashanti state only as "King of Kumasi." Against him at last an expeditionary force was sent and he was surrounded in his capital.

"The scene was a most striking one. The heavy masses of foliage, that solid square of red coats and glistening bayonets, the artillery drawn up ready for any emergency, the black bodies of the Native levies, resting on their long guns in the background, while inside the square the Ashantis sat as if turned to stone, as Mother and Son, whose word was a matter of life and death, and whose slightest move constituted a command which all obeyed, were thus forced to humble themselves in sight of the assembled thousands."[5]

Not only was King Prempeh arrested and deported and the Ashanti humiliated, but the English governor even demanded the Golden Stool upon which kings of Ashanti always sat and which represented the "soul of the nation." To secure it they besieged Kumasi after a revolt in 1900, captured the city and overthrew the government; but the Golden Stool had disappeared. Years later when the King was brought back from exile the Golden Stool was found and surrendered.

In these states, and in later years, the whole character of West Coast culture had changed. In place of the Yoruban culture, with its city democracy, its elevated religious ideas, its finely organized industry, and its noble art, came cruder exhibitions of force and fetish in Ashanti and Dahomey. What was it that thus changed the character of the West Coast from developing culture to increased war and blood sacrifice, such as we read of later in these lands? There can be but one answer: the slave trade. Not simply the sale of men, but an organized effort to turn the attention and energies of men from nearly all other industries; to encourage war and all the cruelest passions of war; and to concentrate this traffic in precisely that part of Africa farthest from the ancient Mediterranean lines of contact.

We need not assume that the cultural change was sudden or absolute. Ancient Yoruba had the cruelty of a semi-civilized land, but it was neither aggressive nor tyrannical. Modern Benin and Dahomey showed traces of art, skill, and industry along with cruelty and insensibility to suffering. But it was the slave trade that turned the balance and set these lands backward. Dahomey was the last word in a series of human disasters in Africa which began with the defeat of the Askias at Tondibi.

From the middle of the fifteenth to the last half of the nineteenth centuries the American slave trade centered in Guinea and devastated the coast morally, socially, and physically. European rum and fire-arms were traded for human beings, and it was not until 1787 that any measures were taken to counteract this terrible scourge. In that year the idea arose of repatriating stolen Negroes on the coast and establishing civilized centers to supplant the slave trade. About four hundred Negroes from England were sent to Sierra Leone, to whom the promoters considerately added sixty white prostitutes as wives. The climate on the low coast, however, was so deadly that new recruits were soon needed.

An American Negro, Thomas Peters, who had served as sergeant under Sir Henry Clinton in the British army in America, went to England seeking an allotment of land for his fellows. The Sierra Leone Company welcomed him and offered free passage and land in Sierra Leone to the Negroes of Nova Scotia. As a result fifteen vessels sailed with eleven hundred and ninety Negroes in 1792. Arriving in Africa, they found the chief white man in control there so drunk that he soon died of delirium tremens. John Clarkson, the abolitionist, eventually assumed the lead, founded Freetown, and the colony began its checkered career. Later the colony was saved from insurrection by the exiled maroon Negroes from Jamaica. After 1833, when emancipation in English colonies began, severe measures against the slave trade were possible and the colony began to grow. Today its imports and exports amount to fifteen million dollars a year.

Liberia was a similar American experiment. In 1816 American philanthropists decided that whether slavery persisted or died out, the main problem lay in getting rid of the freed Negroes, of which there were then two hundred thousand in the United States. Accordingly the American Colonization Society was proposed this year and founded January 1, 1817, with Bushrod Washington as president. It was first thought to encourage migration to Sierra Leone, and eighty-eight Negroes were sent, but they were not welcomed. As a result territory was bought in the present confines of Liberia, December 15, 1821, and colonists began to arrive. A little later an African depot for recaptured slaves taken in the contraband slave trade, provided for in the Act of 1819, was established and an agent sent to Africa to form a settlement. Gradually this settlement was merged with the settlement of the Colonization Society, and from this union Liberia was finally evolved.

The last white governor of Liberia died in 1841 and was succeeded by the first colored governor, Joseph J. Roberts, a Virginian. The total population in 1843 was about twenty-eight hundred and with this as a beginning in 1847 Governor Roberts declared the independence of the state. The recognition of Liberian independence by all countries, except the United States, followed in 1849. The United States, not wishing to receive a Negro minister, did not recognize Liberia until the Civil War.

No sooner was the independence of Liberia announced than England and France began a long series of aggressions to limit her territory and sovereignty. A new conception of the role of Africa in European economy was emerging and an independent Negro republic did not fit into it. The English implied promise of independence for Sierra Leone was lost sight of, and the difficulties which Liberia has since encountered are not due to the American Negro immigrant and his ability, as much as to the fact that a free Negro state and European industrial imperialism clashed here in West Africa; and the little Negro state was almost overthrown. Only the intrusion of American capital after the World

War saved Liberia from English, French, and German determination to dominate this rich remnant of the continent.

Considerable territory was lost by treaty, and in the effort to get capital in
England to develop the rest, Liberia was saddled with a debt of four hundred
thousand dollars, of which she received less than one hundred thousand dollars
in actual cash. A second effort to redeem the first failure was equally unsuccessful, and international market control and monopoly freight rates brought the
Liberians near despair. Finally, the Liberians turned to the United States for capital and protection. As a result the Liberian customs were put under international control and Charles Young, the ranking Negro officer in the United States
army, with several colored assistants, was put in charge of the making of roads
and drilling a constabulary to keep order in the interior, where "incidents" of
tribal disorder, often deliberately incited, were continual excuses for foreign
aggression. The debt was consolidated and control of customs was vested in a
general receiver appointed by the United States.

Turning now from Guinea we pass down the West Coast. In 1482 Diego Cam
of Portugal, sailing this coast, set a stone at the mouth of a great river which he
called "The Mighty," but which eventually came to be known by the name of
the powerful Negro kingdom through which it flowed—the Congo.

We must think of the valley of the Congo, with its intricate interlacing of water
route and jungle of forest, as a vast caldron shut away at first from the African
world by known and unknown physical hindrances. It was first penetrated by the
tiny red drawfs and afterward horde after horde of tall black men swirled into the
valley like a maelstrom, moving usually from north to east and from south to
west. The Congo Valley became, therefore, the center of the making of what we
know today as the Bantu nations. They are not a unified people, but a congeries
of tribes of considerable physical diversity, united by the compelling bond of language and other customs imposed on the conquered by invading conquerors.

The history of these invasions we must today largely imagine. Between two
and three thousand years ago the wilder tribes of Negroes began to move out of
the region south or southeast of Lake Chad. This was always a land of shadows
and legends, where fearful cannibals dwelt and where no Egyptian, Ethiopian or
Sudanese armies dared to go. It is possible, however, that pressure from civilization in the Nile Valley and rising culture around Lake Chad was at this time reinforced by expansion of the Yoruba-Benin culture on the West Coast. Perhaps, too,
developing culture around the Great Lakes in the east beckoned, or the riotous
fertility of the Congo valleys became known. At any rate the movement commenced, now by slow stages, now in wild forays.

There may have been a preliminary movement from east to west to the Gulf of
Guinea. The main movement later, however, was eastward, skirting the Congo
forests and passing down by the Victoria Nyanza and Lake Tanganyika. Here two
paths beckoned: the lakes and the sea to the east, the Congo to the west. A great
stream of men swept toward the ocean and, dividing, turned northward and
fought its way down the Nile Valley and into the Abyssinian highlands; another
branch turned south and approached the Zambesi, where we shall meet it again.
Another horde of invaders turned westward and entered the valley of the Congo

in three columns. The northern column moved along the Lualaba and Congo Rivers to the Cameroons; the second column became the industrial and state-building Luba and Lunda peoples in the southern Congo Valley and Angola; while the third column moved into Damaraland and mingled with Bushman and Hottentot.

The kingdom of Loango lay between Cape Lopez and the mouth of the Congo River. East of Loango and northwest of the Congo was the kingdom of Ansika, whose inhabitants were the Bateke. The kingdom of Lunda extended into the valley of the Kasai and the Zambesi. This kingdom was the realm of Mwata-Yanvo. Between this kingdom and the Monomotapa on the middle Zambesi were the Barotse; and north of that, the Katanga. The Ba-Luba were found northwest of Lake Tanganyika and east of that lake was the realm of the Wanyamwezi. North of Lake Victoria was Uganda. Most of these kingdoms have been preserved even to our day.

These beginnings of human culture were, however, peculiarly vulnerable to invading hosts of later comers. There were no natural protecting barriers like the narrow Nile Valley or the Kong Mountains or the forests below Lake Chad. Once the pathways to the valley were open, for hundreds of years the newcomers kept arriving, especially from the welter of tribes south of the Sudan and west of the Nile, which rising culture beyond kept in unrest and turmoil.

Against these intruders there was but one defense, the State. State building was thus forced on the Congo Valley. How early it started we cannot say, but when the Portuguese arrived in the fifteenth century there had existed for centuries a large state among the Ba-Congo, with its capital at the city now known as San Salvador. This Kingdom of Congo dates back to the fourteenth century and extended over modern Angola as far east as the Kasai and Upper Zambesi Rivers.

The Negro Mfumu, or emperor, was eventually induced to accept Christianity. His sons and many young Negroes of high birth were taken to Portugal to be educated. There several were raised to the Catholic priesthood and one became bishop; others distinguished themselves at the universities. Thus suddenly there arose a Catholic kingdom south of the valley of the Congo, which lasted three centuries, but was partially overthrown by invading barbarians from the interior in the seventeenth century. A king of Congo still reigns as pensioner of Portugal, and on the coast today are the remains of the kingdom in the civilized blacks and mulattoes, who are intelligent traders and boat builders.[6]

The original Bushongo stock belongs to the Ba-Luba family, which extends from the Kasai River to Lake Nyasa and from the Sankuro River to Lake Bangweulu. A race of roving warriors or hunters came from the north and established a domination over the Ba-Luba. These Sudanese conquerors gave political security under which artistic gifts were encouraged and allowed to develop. One of their greatest kings, Shamba Bolongongo (about 1600), before his accession traveled for years in the west and visited among other places the kingdom of Congo where Ntotila, king of Congo, was reigning. The pomp and ceremonial of this country greatly impressed Shamba either because of this actual visit or from reports of embassies. Long before 1700 the greatest of Congo kingdoms was thus reflected in central Africa.

One of the remarkable characteristics of the Bushongo is the organization of its national council, which contains representatives of various arts and crafts. Trade representation is not usual among the Bantu. Torday thinks that this representation of trades and crafts comes from the Kingdom of Congo. There originally every clan had its special crafts, such as weavers, palm wine-makers, potters, smiths. In common they had only agriculture, the women's share; and hunting and fishing, the men's. Every chief of a clan who lived was not only the representative of a territorial division, but also voiced the wishes of some particular art or craft in the council of the king.

The Bushongo learned the use of the loom, as well as the arts of damask weaving, embroidery, and pile-cloth making from the Bapende. The use of the loom in Africa reached the coast after its use inland had become general. Velvets, brocades, satins, taffetas, and damasks were imported to Congo by those great traders, the Bateke.

"It seems to be fairly well established that peaceful penetration of Central Africa from the West Coast, particularly from the Kingdom of Congo, had begun quite early in the seventeenth century. As far as Bushongo is concerned, somewhere between 1600 and 1614, it must have fallen under the spell of Congo."[7]

The Luba-Lunda people to the eastward had founded Katanga and other states, and in the sixteenth century the larger and more ambitious realm of the Mwata Yanvo. The last of the fourteen rulers of this line was feudal lord of about three hundred chiefs, who paid him tribute in ivory, skins, corn, cloth and salt. This included about one hundred thousand square miles and two million or more inhabitants. Eventually this state became torn by internal strife and revolt, especially by attacks from the south across the Congo-Zambesi divide. Farther north, among the Ba-Lolo and the Ba-Songo, the village policy persisted but the cannibals of the northeast pressed down on the more settled tribes. The result was a curious blending of war and industry, artistic tastes and savage customs.

The organized slave trade of the Arabs penetrated the Congo Valley in the sixteenth century and soon was aiding all the forces of unrest and turmoil. Industry was deranged and many tribes forced to take refuge in caves and other hiding places. Here, as on the West Coast, disintegration and retrogression followed, for as the American traffic lessened, the Arabian traffic increased.

In following the history of human development on the Guinea Coast and in the Congo Valley one cannot but feel, as elsewhere in Africa, that the outcome was not simply a matter of racial ability or natural human development; on the other hand, it is clear that the impact of a great movement which initiated the Industrial Revolution in Europe and started the hegemony of the white race over the world was accomplished at the expense of human culture in West Africa. Further, in the Congo Valley efforts at integration, civilization and state building crowded upon each other. There seemed no lack of human ability and ingenuity but there was rivalry and conquest and the intrusion of elements from other parts of Africa pouring in like waves, started by upheavals in the Sudan and on the West Coast. Finally there came to the Congo not simply a slave trade quite as destructive as the American traffic, but also the new economic imperialism of Africa built on American slavery and destined to build a new agricultural and industrial slavery in Africa.

NOTES

1. Quoted in Du Bois: *Timbuktu*.
2. Claridge, *History of the Gold Coast and Ashanti*, Vol. I, p. ix.
3. Claridge, *A History of the Gold Coast and Ashanti*, Vol. I, p. 289.
4. Claridge, *A History of the Gold Coast and Ashanti*, Vol. I, p. 360.
5. Claridge, *A History of the Gold Coast and Ashanti*, Vol. II, p. 413.
6. Torday, "The Kingdom of Kongo," *Africa*, April, 1928.
7. *Africa*, April, 1928, pp. 168, 169.

CHAPTER V

◆

From the Great Lakes to the Cape

The earliest inhabitants of the land around the Great Lakes were apparently of the Bushman or Hottentot type of Negro. These were gradually pushed southward and westward by the intrusion of the Nilotic Negroes. The Nilotic Negroes early became great traders in ivory, gold, leopard skins, gums, beasts, birds, and slaves, and they opened up systematic trade between Egypt and the Great Lakes. From these and Sudanese tribes were gradually formed the Bantu.

The migration of the Bantu is the first clearly defined Negro mass movement of modern times. As we have shown, they began to move southward at least a thousand years before Christ, skirting the Congo forests and wandering along the Great Lakes and down to the Zambesi. Inland among the Bantu arose before the tenth century the line of rulers called the Monomotapa, among the Makalanga, Matabele and Mashona. Their state was very extensive. Map makers of the seventeenth century outlined it as stretching from the Zambesi to the Fish River. Its territory ran seven hundred and fifty miles inland along the south bank of the Zambesi and was approximately the size of Mexico. It was strongly organized, with feudatory allied states, and carried on an extensive commerce by means of the traders on the coast. The kings were converted to nominal Christianity by the Portuguese.

"Monomotapa," said Professor Frobenius, "was undoubtedly a very great kingdom, and from documents which are now in our possession it is apparent that its rulers wielded great power. . . . The Kings and Emperors of Monomotapa used to observe very curious customs. The King was very powerful, and conducted courts of justice and sacrifice in the spring and at harvest time. Every seventh year, however, he was killed by the people, and a new King was crowned. This is a very old custom, which was observed on the borders of the Indian Ocean. . . . The name itself means 'Prince of the Mine,' for the area was a great mineral center, from which much gold and many rubies and diamonds were apparently extracted long before man had learned to use stones and metals."

The history of the social development here is not known certainly, but from what we do know we may reconstruct the situation in this way: the primitive culture of the Hottentots had been replaced by other stronger Negro stocks like the Makalanga until it reached a highly developed stage. Widespread agriculture and mining of gold, silver, and precious stones started a trade that penetrated to Asia and North Africa. This may have been the source of the gold of the Ophir. Doubtless Asiatic elements from Arabia or India penetrated the land and influenced and quickened the Negroes.

The state that thus arose became in time strongly organized; it employed slave labor in crushing the hard quartz, sinking pits, and carrying underground galleries; it carried out a system of irrigation and built stone buildings and fortifications. There exist today many remains of these building operations in the Kalahari desert and in Northern Rhodesia. Five hundred groups, covering an area of over one hundred and fifty thousand square miles, lie between the Limpopo and Zambesi Rivers. Mining operations have been carried on in these plains for generations, and one estimate is that at least three hundred and seventy-five million dollars' worth of gold had been extracted. Some have thought that the older workings must date back to one or even three thousand years before the Christian era.

"There are other mines," writes De Barros[1] in the seventeenth century, "in a district called Toroa, which is otherwise known as the kingdom of Batua, whose ruler is a prince, by name Burrow, a vassal of Benomotapa. This land is near the other which we said consisted of extensive plains, and those ruins are the oldest that are known in that region. They are all in a plain, in the middle of which stands a square fortress, all of dressed stones within and without, well wrought and of marvelous size, without any lime showing the joinings, the walls of which are over twenty-five hands thick, but the height is not so great compared to the thickness. And above the gateway of that edifice is an inscription which some Moorish [Arab] traders who were there could not read, nor say what writing it was. All these structures the people of this country call Symbabwe [Zymbabwe], which with them means a court, for every place where Benomotapa stays is so called."

Later investigation has shown that these buildings were in many cases carefully planned and built fortifications. At Niekerk, for instance, nine or ten hills are fortified on concentric walls thirty to fifty feet in number, with a place for the village at the top. The buildings are forts, miniature citadels, and also workshops and cattle kraals. Iron implements and handsome pottery were found here, and close to the Zambesi there are extraordinary fortifications. Farther south at Inyanya there is less strong defense, and at Umtali there are no fortifications, showing that builders feared invasion from the north.

These people worked in gold, silver, tin, copper, and bronze and made beautiful pottery. There is evidence of religious significance in the buildings, and what is called the temple was the royal residence and served as a sort of acropolis. The surrounding residences in the valley were evidently occupied by wealthy traders and were not fortified. Here the gold was received from surrounding districts and bartered with traders.

As usual there have been repeated attempts to find an external and especially an Asiatic origin for this culture. There is no proof of this. How far back this civilization dates it is difficult to say, a great deal depending upon the dating of the Iron Age in South Africa. If it was the same as in the Mediterranean regions, the earliest limit was 1000 B.C.; it might, however, have been earlier, especially if, as seems probable, the use of iron originated in Africa. On the other hand, the culmination of this culture has been placed by some as late as the late Middle Ages.

The balance of authority today leans toward the Bantu origin of these buildings and mines, although it is probable that trade and contact with Asia brought Mongoloid influences and perhaps an Asiatic migration.

What was it that overthrew this civilization? Undoubtedly the same sort of raids of barbarous warriors that we have known in our day. For instance, in 1570 there came upon the country of Mozambique, farther up the coast, "Such an inundation of pagans that they could not be numbered. They came from that part of Monomotapa where is the great lake from which spring these great rivers. They left no other signs of the towns they passed but the heaps of ruins and the bones of inhabitants." So, too, it is told how the Wa-Zimba came, "a strange people never seen before there, who, leaving their own country, traversed a great part of this Ethiopia like a scourge of God, destroying every living thing they came across. They were twenty thousand strong and marched without children or women," just as four hundred years later the Zulu impi marched. Again in 1602 a horde of people came from the interior called the Cabires, or Cannibals. They entered the kingdom of Monomotapa, and the reigning king, being weak, was in great terror. Thus gradually the Monomotapa fell, and its power was scattered until the Kafir-Zulu raids of our day.

The Arab writer, Macoudi, in the tenth century, visited the East African coast somewhere north of the equator. He found the Indian Sea at that time frequented by Arab and Persian vessels, but there were no Asiatic settlements on the African shore. The Bantu, or as he calls them, Zenji, inhabited the country as far south as Sofala, where they bordered upon the Bushmen. These Bantus were under a ruler with the dynastic title of Waklimi. He was paramount over all the other tribes of the north and could put three hundred thousand men in the field. They used oxen as beasts of burden and the country produced gold in abundance, while panther skins were largely used for clothing. Ivory was sold to Asia and the Bantu used iron for personal adornment instead of gold or silver. They rode on their oxen, which ran with great speed, and they ate millet and honey and the flesh of animals.

There are indications of trade between Nupe in West Africa and Sofala on the east coast, and certainly trade between Asia and East Africa is earlier than the beginning of the Christian era. The Asiatic traders settled on the coast and by means of mulatto and Negro merchants brought Central Africa into contact with Arabia, India, China and Malaysia.

The coming of the Asiatics was in this wise: Zaide, great-grandson of Ali, nephew and son-in-law of Mohammed, was banished from Arabia as a heretic. He passed over to Africa and formed temporary settlements. His people mingled with the blacks, and the resulting mulatto traders, known as the Emoxaidi, seem to have wandered as far south as the equator. Soon other Arabian families came over on account of oppression and founded the towns of Magadosho and Brava, both not far north of the equator. The first town became a place of importance and other settlements were made. The Emoxaidi, whom the later immigrants regarded as heretics, were driven inland and became the interpreting traders between the coast and the Bantu. Some wanderers from Magadosho came into the port of Sofala and there learned that gold could be obtained. This led to a small Arab settlement at that place.

Seventy years later, and about fifty years before the Norman conquest of England, certain Persians settled at Kilwa in East Africa, led by Ali, who had been despised in his land because he was the son of a black Abyssinian slave mother. Kilwa, because of this, eventually became the most important commercial station on the East African coast, and in this and all these settlements a very large mulatto population grew up, so that very soon the whole settlement was indistinguishable in color from the Bantu. From 975 until its capture by the Portuguese in the fifteenth century, forty sovereigns ruled here.

A Semitic trading empire was thus built up by the fourteenth century, composed mainly of people of mixed Negro and Semitic blood. There was much fighting between Persians, Arabs and Kafir and Bantu. Trade went by sea to Asia and India, usually carried by mulattoes.

In 1330 Ibn Batuta visited Kilwa. He found an abundance of ivory and some gold and heard that the inhabitants of Kilwa had gained victories over the Zenji, or Bantu. Kilwa had at that time three hundred mosques and was "built of handsome houses of stone and lime, and very lofty with their windows like those of the Christians; in the same way it has streets, and these houses have terraces, and the wood worked in with the masonry, with plenty of gardens, in which there are many fruit trees and much water."[2]

Kilwa after a time captured Sofala, seizing it from Magadosho. Eventually Kilwa became mistress of the island of Zanzibar, of Mozambique, and of much other territory. The forty-third ruler of Kilwa after Ali was named Abraham, and he was ruling when the Portuguese arrived. The latter reported that these people cultivated rice and cocoa, built ships, and had considerable commerce with Asia. All the people, of whatever color, were Mohammedans, and the richer were clothed in gorgeous robes of silk and velvet. They traded with the inland Bantus and met numerous tribes, receiving gold, ivory, millet, rice, cattle, poultry, and honey. On the islands, the Asiatics were independent, but on the mainland south of Kilwa the sheiks ruled only their own people, under the overlordship of the Bantus, to whom they were compelled to pay large tribute each year.

The sultans of Sofala and Zanzibar became in time independent of Kilwa. These sultans were not governors of states, but heads of Mohammedan colonies with natives living near. Their principal occupation came at last to be trade in slaves with Negro chiefs. They sent the slaves to the Persian Gulf or sold them to the Portuguese. All the Negro tribes scattered along the east coast were known as the Zendi, hence the name Zanzibar. Vasco da Gama doubled the Cape of Good Hope in 1497 and went north on the east coast as far as India. In the next ten years the Portuguese occupied the Coast and both here and on the West Coast widely intermarried with the natives.

Thus civilization waxed and waned in East Africa among prehistoric Negroes, Arab and Persian mulattoes on the coast, in the Zend or Zeng empire of East African Negroes, and in the Negro rule of the Monomotapa. And thus, too, among later throngs of the fiercer, warlike Bantu, the ancient culture of the land largely died. Yet something survived, and in the modern Bantu state, language, and industry can be found links that suggest the identity of the absorbed peoples with the builders of Zymbabwe.

So far we have traced the history of the lands into which the southward stream of invading Bantus turned, and have followed them to the Limpopo River. We turn now to the lands north from Lake Nyasa. The aboriginal Negroes sustained in prehistoric time, invasion from the northeast by Negroids of a type like the ancient Egyptians and like the modern Gallas, Masai, and Somalis. To these migrations were added attacks from the Nile Negroes to the north and the Bantu invaders from the south. This has led to great differences among the groups of the population and their customs. Some are fierce mountaineers, occupying hilly plateaus six thousand feet above the sea level; others, like the Wa-Swahili, are traders on the coast. There are the Masai, chocolate-colored and frizzly-haired, organized for war and cattle lifting; and Negroids like the Gallas, who, blending with the Bantus, have produced the race of modern Uganda.

It was in this region that the kingdom of Kitwara was founded by the Galla chief, Kintu. About the beginning of the nineteenth century the empire was dismembered, the largest share falling to Uganda. The ensuing history of Uganda is of great interest. When King Mutesa came to the throne in 1862, he found Mohammedan influences in his land and was induced to admit Protestants and Catholics. The Protestants, representing British imperialism, tried to convert the King, and the Catholics, representing French imperialism, tried to make him a Catholic. In the midst of this more Mohammedans appeared, seeking also to convert Mutesa. He refused all these faiths and died a rugged pagan.

He was succeeded by his son Mwanga, who distrusted the whites. He ordered the eastern frontier closed against Europeans and when the Protestant Bishop Hannington attempted to cross in 1885, he had him killed. The Protestants organized against Mwanga and he ordered both Protestants and Catholics away, and the Mohammedans became the power behind the throne. The Protestants withdrew from Buganda into Angola and organized a united front of Christians against Mohammedans and Mwanga. They captured Mwanga's capital and divided it between Protestants and Catholics. The Mohammedans began to fight back and finally the Protestants appealed to the British East Africa Company. In 1889 the company dispatched a military mission to Uganda which was later joined by Lugard. Open civil war ensued between Catholics and Protestants.

"At the head of a considerable military force, Captain Lugard, of the Imperial British East Africa Company (Ibea), penetrated as far as Mengo, the residence of King Mwanga, and forced upon him a treaty of protectorate: then turning against the Catholics, he attacked them on some futile pretext, and drove them into a big island on Lake Victoria. There, around the king and the French missionaries, had gathered for refuge a considerable multitude of men, women, and children. Against this harmless and defenseless population Captain Lugard turned his guns and maxims. He exterminated a large number, and then, continuing his work of destruction, he gave full rein to his troops and adherents, who burnt all the villages and stations of the White Fathers, their churches and their crops."[3]

The British Sudanese troops, who under Lugard had carried on the war, afterwards rebelled and had to be disbanded. The Imperial British East Africa Company administered its holdings in Uganda, Kenya and along the East African Coast until 1896, when it withdrew as a governing institution. In 1897 the king, Mwanga, returned from German East Africa with Mohammedan natives and drove out the British garrison from one of their forts. Mwanga was finally defeated in 1899, taken prisoner and deported. Uganda became a British protectorate in 1899.

German East Africa was annexed in 1889 and declared a protectorate. The Germans met revolt after revolt, especially among the southern tribes who resented the hut tax and forced labor. These revolts culminated in a national Maji-Maji in 1905, in which many whites were killed and 12,000 natives were massacred or died of famine.

Primitive man in Africa is found in the interior jungles and down at Land's End in South Africa. The Pygmy people in the jungles represent today a small survival from the past, but a survival of curious interest, pushed aside by the torrent of conquest. Also, pushed on by these waves of Bantu conquest, moved the ancient Abatwa or Bushmen. They are small in stature, yellow in color, with crisp-curled hair. The traditions of the Bushmen say that they came southward from the regions of the Great Lakes, and indeed the king and queen of Punt, as depicted by the Egyptians, were Bushmen or Hottentots.

Their tribes may be divided, in accordance with their noticeable artistic talents, into the painters and sculptors. The sculptors entered South Africa by moving southward through the more central portions of the country, crossing the Zambesi, and coming down to the Cape. The painters, on the other hand, came through Damaraland on the west coast; when they came to the great mountain regions, they turned eastward and can be traced as far as the mountain regions, they turned eastward and can be traced as far as the mountains opposite Delagoa Bay. The mass of them settled down in the lower part of the Cape and in the Kalahari Desert. The painters were true cave dwellers, but the sculptors lived in large communities on the stony hills, which they marked with their carvings.

These Bushmen believed in an ancient race of people who preceded them in South Africa. They attributed magic power to these unknown folk, and said that some of them had been translated as stars to the sky. Before their groups were dispersed, the Bushmen had regular government. Tribes with their chiefs occupied well-defined tracts of country and were subdivided into branch tribes under subsidiary chiefs. The great cave represented the dignity and glory of the entire nation.

The Bushmen suffered most cruelly in the succeeding migrations and conquest of South Africa. They fought desperately in self-defense; they saw their women and children carried into bondage and they themselves hunted like wild beasts. Both savage and civilized men appropriated their land. Still they were brave people. "In this struggle for existence, their bitterest enemies, of whatever shade of color they might be, were forced to make an unqualified acknowledgement of the courage and daring they so invariably exhibited."[4]

Here, to a remote corner of the world, where, as one of their number said, they had supposed that the only beings in the world were Bushmen and lions, came a series of invaders. It was the outer ripples of civilization starting far away, the indigenous and external civilizations of Africa beating with great impulse among the Ethiopians, the Egyptian mulattoes, the Sudanese Negroes and West Africans; and driving many tribes southward, the migrants absorbed the settlers of Zymbabwe and later were in turn pushed down upon the primitive Bushmen; possibly an earlier mingling of the Bushmen and the Nilotic Negroes gave rise to the Hottentots.

The Hottentots, or as they called themselves, Khoi Khoin (Men of Men), were physically a stronger race than the Abatwa and gave many evidences of degeneration from a high culture, especially in the "phenomenal perfection" of a language which "is so highly developed, both in its rich phonetic system, as represented by a very delicate graduated series of vowels and diphthongs, and in its varied grammatical structure, that Lepsius sought for its affinities in the Egyptian at the other end of the continent."

When South Africa was first discovered there were two distinct types of Hottentots. The more savage Hottentots were simply large, strong Bushmen, using weapons superior to the Bushmen, without domestic cattle or sheep. Other tribes, nearer the center of South Africa, were handsomer in appearance and raised an Egyptian breed of cattle which they rode.

In general the Hottentots were yellow, with close-curled hair, high cheekbones, and somewhat oblique eyes. Their migration commenced about the end of the fourteenth century and was, as is usual in such cases, a scattered, straggling movement. The traditions of the Hottentots point to the lake country of Central Africa as their place of origin, whence they were driven by the Bechuana tribes of the Bantu. They fled westward to the ocean, skirting the realm of the Monomotapa, and then turned south and came upon the Bushmen, whom they had only partially subdued when the Dutch arrived.

The Dutch were fighting Spain in the sixteenth century and began to trade with the East even before they were independent. The East India Company received a charter in 1602 and established themselves at the Cape of Good Hope in 1652. They found there, toward the west, Bushmen still hunters in the Stone Age; the Hottentots toward the east and Bantu toward the north; but with them they did not come in contact for some time. There was raiding and fighting between the Bushmen and Dutch and the Dutch and the Hottentots. In 1658 came the first of the Hottentot Wars, arising from runaway slaves and cattle raiding. Some West African slaves had been introduced. By 1664 there was much racial intermingling, with resulting mulatto children. Slavery was well established by 1770.

The Bantu[5] gradually moved into South Africa by way of the Great Lakes. The Makalanga began to press upon the coastland behind Sofala as early as the ninth century and later established the empire of the Monomotapa, mingling possibly with earlier settlers. Late in the sixteenth the Abambo and the Amazimba rushed down upon the Monomotapa and poured into what is now Natal. They were followed by the Barotse and in the first half of the eighteenth century by the Bavenda and Bakwena, who conquered what is now the Transvaal and the Free State and as far south as the Caledon River. The Batlapin and the Barolong drove the Leghoia into the northeastern Free State and before that the Leghoia had driven other tribes into the Kalihara Desert. Then about 1775 the Ovaherero and the Damaras came into southeast Africa. South of the empire of the Congo and along the ocean arose the state of Mataman, composed of the Herero, Damaras and the Hottentots.

The Dutch "Boers" began by purchasing land from the Hottentots and then, as they grew more powerful, they dispossessed the dark men and tried to enslave them. There grew up a large Dutch-Hottentot class. Indeed infiltration of Negro blood noticeable in modern Boers accounts for much curious history. Soon after the advent of the Dutch, some of the Hottentots, of whom there were not more than thirty or forty thousand, led by the Korana clans, began slowly to retreat northward, followed by the invading Dutch, and fighting the Dutch, each other, and the wretched Bushmen. In the latter part of the eighteenth century the Hottentots had reached the great interior plain and met the oncoming outposts of the Bantu nations.

The Bechuana, whom the Hottentots first met, were the most advanced of the Negro tribes of Central Africa. They had crossed the Zambesi in the fourteenth or fifteenth century; their government was a sort of feudal system with hereditary chiefs and vassals; they were careful agriculturists, laid out large towns with great regularity, and were the most skilled smiths. They used stone in building, carved on wood, and many of them, too, were keen traders. They seemed to echo the builders of Zymbabwe. These tribes, coming southward, occupied the east central part of South Africa, comprising modern Bechuanaland. Apparently they had started from the central lake country somewhere late in the fifteenth century, and by the middle of the eighteenth one of their great chiefs, Tao, met the oncoming Hottentots.

The Hottentots compelled Tao to retreat, but the mulatto Gricquas arrived from the south, and, allying themselves with the Bechuana, stopped the rout. The Gricquas sprang from and took their name from an old Hottentot tribe. They were led by Kok and Barends, and by adding other elements they became, partly through their own efforts and partly through the efforts of the missionaries, a community of fairly well-civilized people. In Gricqualand West, the mulatto Gricquas, under their chiefs Kok and Waterboer, lived until the discovery of diamonds on their land.

The Gricquas and Bechuana tribes were thus gradually checking the Hottentots when, in the nineteenth century, there came two new developments: first, the English took possession of Cape Colony, and the Dutch began to move in larger numbers toward the interior; secondly, a newer and fiercer element of the Bantu tribes, the Xosa, appeared. The "Kafirs," or as they called themselves, the Ama Xosas, claimed descent from Zuide, a great chief of the fifteenth century in the lake country. They are among the tallest people in the world, averaging five feet ten inches, and are slim, well proportioned, and muscular. The more warlike tribes were usually clothed in leopard or ox skins. Cattle formed their chief wealth, stock-breeding, hunting and fighting their main pursuits. Mentally they were men of tact and intelligence, with a national religion based upon ancestor worship, while their government was a patriarchal monarchy limited by an aristocracy and almost feudal in character. The common law which had grown up from the decisions of the chiefs made the head of the family responsible for the conduct of its branches, a village for all its residents, and the clan for all its villages. Finally there was a paramount chief, who was the civil and military father of his people. These people laid waste to the coast regions and in 1779 came in contact with the Dutch. A series of Dutch-Kafir wars ensued between 1779 and 1795 in which the Dutch were hard pressed.

Thus in the latter part of the eighteenth century there were three main groups of Bantu in the hinterland of Cape Colony. To the north were the plateau tribes: Ovaherero and Damaras, blacker and smaller than the rest; and behind them the Ovambo, Batlapin mixed with Bakalahari and Balala and also with Hottentots and Bushmen; Bechuana and Bataung. To the northeast were the highlanders, Barotse, Bavenda and Bakwena, copper-colored to black, with crisp hair and beards, some with flat noses, others with aquiline noses. To the east were the coast tribes who came in contact with the Europeans at the Fish River.[6]

The Abambo, and perhaps other tribes, came to be known after their chiefs, Ama-Xosa, Ama-Tembu, Ama-Pondo, Ama-Swazi, etc. They began to push down the coast toward the colony. They chased away the Bushmen and mixed with the Hottentots. The Xosa crossed the Kei River in 1702 and came in contact with the Dutch in cattle barter. About 1775 the Xosa crossed the Fish River. The Bantu were organized into tribes with paramount chiefs and much depended upon the chief and his counselors. There soon rose the inevitable conflict of ideas concerning the ownership of land; the Kafirs had no conception of individual landowning, but simply of crop raising; the Dutch wished individual holding of the land. The land became a problem of frontiers between white and black cattle farmers. A Bantu or "Kafir" war broke out on the eastern frontier in 1779, arising from charges of cattle stealing, shooting, etc. The colonists won in this first war and drove the Xosas back across the Fish River, seizing over 5,000 cattle.

Another Kafir war broke out in 1791, arising again over cattle; the Hottentots fought beside the whites. In 1795, at the beginning of the Napoleonic Wars, nine British warships with troops landed in South Africa and after some fighting took possession. By this time the Hottentots were regarded as free men. Their tribal system had been broken up and most of them had been deprived of their lands. Others together with half breeds were leaving the colony and settling in various localities to the north. The Koks were on the middle Orange Valley and the Namaquas moving south. Thus the Orange Valley swarmed with mulattoes, Hottentots, run-away slaves and white outlaws.

Northeast of them were the oncoming Bantu. There was continual bickering and rebellion among these various groups. In 1795 there were in the colony 16,000 Europeans, 17,000 slaves and an unknown number of Hottentots and Bushmen. The Dutch East Indian Company came to an end in 1798 and the Cape Colony was handed back to the new Batavian Republic in 1802 by the English, according to the Treaty of Amiens. The new governor pacified the Hottentots and made them allies against the Xosas.

In 1805 the British came again with sixty-one ships and seized the Cape. At that time there were twenty-five thousand Boers, twenty-five thousand pure and mixed Hottentots, and twenty-five thousand slaves. British settlers began to come. The Xosas were now across the Fish and claiming land. The English began to push them back and establish block houses.

Between 1811 and 1877 there were six Kafir-English wars. One of these in 1818 grew out of the ignorant interference of the English with the Kafir tribal system; then there came a terrible war between 1834 and 1835, followed by the annexation of all the country as far as the Kei River. Intra-tribal fighting began among the Xosa concerning the paramount chieftainship. The English began to offer land for new settlers and Parliament voted money. Some 5,000 British came between 1820 and 1821. From 1823 to 1837 Great Britain took more interest in the colony. The Reform Bill became the law in England in 1832 and slave emancipation was decreed in 1833 by Parliament. The Hottentots and colored persons had been given civil rights in 1828 and the freeing of the slaves was now imminent. Hottentots, Bushmen and other colored persons were given rights to own land in 1828. Rules for the care and education of slaves had been passed in 1823 and there was much negotiation from 1826 to 1834 as to methods of emancipation. Some of the Dutch farmers threatened rebellion. It was arranged that the ex-slaves were to be apprenticed to their former masters for four years after 1834 and compensation was paid, although it was less than had been expected.

Meantime between 1824 and 1834 trouble continued among the Bantu. Chaka had succeeded Dingiswayo. This great Zulu chieftain armed his unmarried warriors with great ox-hide shields and assagais, and arranged them in formation; discipline was stiffened and captains of the regiments chosen arbitrarily. McDonald says, "There has probably never been a more perfect system of discipline than that by which Chaka ruled his army and kingdom. At a review, an order might be given in the most unexpected manner, which meant death to hundreds. If the regiment hesitated or dared to remonstrate, so perfect was the discipline and so great the jealousy that another was ready to cut them down. A warrior returning unsuccessful in the main purpose of his expedition shared the same fate. Whoever displeased the king was immediately executed. The traditional courts practically ceased to exist so far as the will and the action of the tyrant was concerned."

With this army Chaka fell on tribe after tribe. He drove some tribes northward through the eastern coastland as far as Lake Nyasa and then rushed down through Natal. Umsilikazi, leader of one of Chaka's regiments, laid waste to the southwestern Transvaal. The Bechuanas fled to the Kalihara Desert, having already suffered under other tribes flying from Chaka. By the time the English came to Port Natal, Chaka was ruling over the whole southeastern seaboard, from the Limpopo River to Cape Colony, including the Orange and Transvaal States and the whole of Natal. Chaka was killed in 1828 and was eventually succeeded by his brother, Dingaan, who reigned twelve years.

The Portuguese in East Africa began to lose power in the eighteenth and the first quarter of the nineteenth century and were indulging in the slave trade with the English and American slavers. There were raids and counter raids with the Bantu between 1823 and 1834. The Xosa became restless because of the pressure of the Zulu and of the tribes that were pushing before them. The Tembus moved into Cape Colony and were driven back. There was trouble over cattle in 1834 and the Xosa warriors poured into the colony and ravaged the country for two weeks from Algoa Bay to Somerset East. War ensued, leaving 7,000 white farmers destitute; 455 farms were burnt and many people both white and Hottentots had been killed. Colonial losses were put at 300,000 pounds sterling.

There was a great deal of dissatisfaction and finally, in 1837, numbers of Boer farmers sold their farms and some 2,000 of them crossed the Orange River on the Great Trek. This was a quickening of a steady drift of Europeans and mulattoes beyond the frontiers which the colony had tried to proclaim. The Kafirs had stopped migration across the Fish River in 1779 but in 1832 new generations of Boers were demanding land. The Boers regarded the colony as too small and were seeking expansion. The Kafir war cut across the projected trek and when the fighting was finished, the first two organized parties of Boers crossed the Orange in 1835. Then came a severe drought and the Great Trek got into full movement in 1836. The trek was a demand for land and the control of labor.

Dingaan was alarmed at this invasion and killed the main Dutch leader, Retief, and his companions, including his Hottentot retainers, in February, 1838. He allowed the English missionaries to get away but attacked the Boer settlement; but was attacked in turn in December, 1838, and defeated. The river where 3,000 dead were left on the field has since been known as Blood River, and Dingaan's Day is the great Boer holiday. The Boers were now established in Natal and began to push northward into Zululand. They set the Zulus fighting against each other and this ended in the flight and death of Dingaan in 1840. On the border of the colony and between them and the new settlement were two native powers: the Griquas, mulattoes under the Koks, and the Basutos.

In 1846 the War of the Ax broke out on the eastern frontier between the English and the Kafirs, which lasted two or three months but cost a million pounds. In December, 1856, despairing of resistance to the whites, a black prophet arose among the Ama Xosa who advised the wholesale destruction of all Kafir property except weapons, in order that this faith might bring back their dead heroes. The result was that almost a third of the nation perished from hunger. In British Kaffraria alone the Bantu decreased from 105,000 to 37,000 souls.

A demand arose in 1856 for labor in Natal. The Bantu refused to leave their reserves in spite of the hut tax, and imported labor was demanded. England refused to send out convicts or destitute children and finally arrangements were made for East Indians, and at the same time the hut tax for natives was increased and forced labor on the roads required. By 1865, 6,500 Indians were at work in Natal.

There were continued hostilities between the Basutos and the Boers. The Basutos fought with the Zulus, but before Chaka died Moshesh founded the Basuto nation high up in his mountain fastness. He was hard beset by both Boers and English and by other Bantu at various times and his own warriors often made forays for cattle. Frequently he appealed to the English authorities at the Cape. Sometimes they aided him, sometimes they did not. At one time the

Boers accused his people of stealing cattle, and the English demanded as penalty 10,000 head of cattle and 1,000 horses within three days. Moshesh surrendered only about one-third of this number, which was probably as much as he could do. The English troops started against him and were repulsed at Berea in 1852. The Basuto's chances for thoroughly thrashing the English were good, but at midnight, December 20, 1852, Moshesh wrote to the English governor, "As the object for which you have come is to have a compensation for the Boers, I beg that you will be satisfied with what you have taken. I entreat peace from you." The governor was wise. He marched back home and did not renew the attack. After the British withdrew, the Basutos defended themselves against the Boers, and in 1854 the Boer States and Basutoland were given up by the British.

However, the Indian Mutiny of 1857 began to influence Great Britain's colonial policy. The Boers declared war on the Basutos in 1858 and annexed much of their territory and live stock. In 1859 the British interfered and the boundaries of Basutoland were defined. British aggression led to the Gun War in 1880 and again the British withdrew. Again the Boers and the Basutos fought, but the British drove the Boers away and declared Basutoland a protectorate in 1884. Gold and diamonds began to be discovered in 1886. The famous diamond, the Star of Ethiopia, was found in Griqualand in 1869 and changed hands first for 11,000 pounds sterling and then for 25,000. The English arranged to have Griqualand declared part of Cape Colony.

Dingaan was succeeded by Panda. Under this chief there was something like repose for sixteen years, but in 1856 civil war broke out between his sons, one of whom, Cetewayo, succeeded his father in 1862. He fell into border disputes with the English, and the result was one of the fiercest clashes of Europe and Africa in modern days. The Zulus fought desperately, annihilating at one time a whole detachment and killing the young prince Napoleon. But after all, it was assagais against guns, and the Zulus were finally defeated at Ulundi, July 4, 1879. Thereupon Zululand was divided among thirteen semi-independent chiefs and became a British protectorate. Meantime in Portuguese territory south of the Zambesi there arose Gaza, a contemporary and rival of Chaka. His son, Manikus, was deputed by Dingaan, Chaka's successor, to drive out the Portuguese. This Manikus failed to do, and to escape vengeance he migrated north of the Limpopo. Here he established his military kraal in a district thirty-six hundred and fifty feet above the sea and one hundred and twenty miles inland from Sofala. From this place his soldiery nearly succeeded in driving the Portuguese out of East Africa.

North of the Zambesi, in British territory, the chief role in recent times was played by the Bechuana, the first of the Bantu to return northward after the South African migration. Livingstone found there the Makololo, who with other tribes had moved northward on account of the pressure of the Dutch and Zulus below, and by conquering various tribes in the Zambesi region, had established a strong power. This kingdom was nearly overthrown by the rebellion of the Barotse, and in 1875, the Barotse kingdom comprised a large territory. Today their king rules directly and indirectly fifty thousand square miles, with a population between one and two and a half million. They form a reserve area in Northern Rhodesia.

The result of all these movements was to break the inhabitants of Bechuanaland into numerous fragments. There were small numbers of mulatto Gricquas in the southwest and similar Bastaards in the northwest. The Hottentots and Bushmen were dispersed into groups and seemed doomed to extinction, the last Hottentot chief being deposed in 1810 and replaced by an English magistrate. Partially civilized Hottentots still live grouped together in their kraals and are members of Christian churches. The Bechuana hold their own in several centers; one is in Basutoland, west of Natal, where a number of tribes were welded together under the far-sighted Moshesh into a modern and fairly civilized nation. In the north part of Bechuanaland are the self-governing Bamangwato and the Batwana, the former long ruled by Khama, one of the canniest of modern rulers in Africa.

The Boers helped by the Swazi were fighting Bantu tribes again in 1879, when the Ama-Xosa confederacy was finally broken up, and gradually these tribes passed from independence to vassalage to the British. Toward the north, Umsilikatsi, who had been driven into Matabeleland by the terrible Chaka in 1828 and defeated by the Dutch in 1837, had finally re-established his head-quarters in Rhodesia in 1838. Here he introduced the Zulu military system and terrorized the peaceful and industrious Bechuana populations. Lobengula suc-ceeded Umsilikatsi in 1870 and, realizing that his power was waning, began to retreat northward toward the Zambesi. Warren seized Bechuanaland in time for the Conference at Berlin. Boers and natives fighting together took up arms in 1880 and compelled the British to withdraw after the defeat at Majuba in 1881.

The independence of the Transvaal was guaranteed at the Pretoria Convention, but the British entered the Transvaal again in 1884 on account of gold. In 1889 a charter was issued to the British South Africa Company. The Boer War broke out in September, 1899. The natives gave the English their sympathy and co-operation during the war, but in 1906 there was a revolt against the poll tax on the part of the natives in Natal and a serious rebellion in Zululand under Dinizulu, son of Cetewayo.

In Southwest Africa, Hottentot mulattoes crossing from the Cape caused widespread change. They were strong men and daring fighters and soon became dominant in what is now German Southwest Africa, where they fought fiercely with the Bantu Ova-Hereros. Armed with firearms, these Namakwa Hottentots threatened Portuguese West Africa; but Germany intervened, ostensibly to pro-tect missionaries. By spending millions of dollars Germany exterminated thou-sands of natives. Berlin made an annual grant of five million dollars to the colony of Southwest Africa and equipped it with railways, roads and arms. There were 12,000 white inhabitants and among them three thousand soldiers and police.

After the South African war Botha became Prime Minister of the Transvaal and, with Smuts, was prominent in the Convention of 1909 which formed the Union of South Africa. The native was practically unmentioned in the constitu-tion of the new state. Imperial safeguards as to his treatment were not reaf-firmed, his right to hold office was denied, and his disfranchisement in all provinces except the Cape was confirmed.

Botha became Prime Minister of the Union in 1910 and 1913. His first duty was to seek to unite the Dutch and English into one nation, and the next to attack the difficult native problem. However, the World War intervened and Botha found himself facing a rebellion among the Dutch, who favored the Germans. Some 12,000 rebels were in arms, when finally the revolt was quelled. The last leader to surrender was Martiz, who declared that he did not want South Africa ruled "by Englishmen, Niggers and Jews."

In 1915 a diversion was created by the conquest of German Southwest Africa, which was accomplished under Botha's leadership. Nevertheless in the fall, his majority in Parliament was seriously reduced and the Dutch threatened a further uprising. Botha died in 1919. His colleague Hertzog, who had been in Botha's first cabinet in 1910 but was left out of the cabinet in 1913, had formed the National Party. The National Party sent a delegation to the peace conference asking independence for South Africa. Smuts tried to incorporate Southern Rhodesia so as to increase his political power against Boer nationalism and labor demands, but the Rhodesians feared the trends in the Union: the possible influx of poor whites, and the drawing off of their native labor; in 1922, Southern Rhodesia refused to enter the union. Smuts was overthrown in the election of 1924, and Hertzog came to power.

Thus we have, between the years 1400 and 1900, successive waves when Bushmen, Hottentot, Bantu, Dutch and English appear in succession at Land's End. In the latter part of the eighteenth century we have the clash of the Hottentots and Bechuana, followed in the nineteenth century by the terrible wars of Chaka, the Kafirs, and Matabele. All of this history is complicated and obscured by lack of exact knowledge of tribal relations and movements. Finally, in the latter half of the nineteenth century, we see the gradual subjection of the Kafir-Zulus and the Bechuana under the English and the subjugation of the Dutch. Later the Dutch became the paramount element in the English colony and achieved political independence under the economic overlordship of English investors. The resulting racial and social problems in South Africa are of great intricacy. With significant symbolism, the ship of the Flying Dutchman still beats back and forth about the Cape on its endless quest.

NOTES

1. Quoted in Bent, *Ruined Cities of Mashonaland*, pp. 238 ff.
2. Barbosa, quoted in Keane, Vol. II, p. 482.
3. Darcy, quoted in Woolf, *Empire and Commerce in Africa*, p. 288.
4. Stow, *Native Races of South Africa*, pp. 215–216.
5. I.e., the peoples now known as Bantu, but composed originally of widely differing elements.
6. Walker, *History of South Africa*, p. 115.

CHAPTER VI

---◆---

The Culture of Africa

The new anthropology is beginning to give us a rational and scientific picture of primitive man and so-called backward peoples, to replace the legends and assumptions of other days. If we could have a scientific study of mankind in Africa without economic axes to grind, without the necessity of proving race superiority, without religious conversion or compulsions of any kind or exaggerated consciousness of color; if we could have the known facts of history set down without bias and the unknown studied without propaganda, we might come to know much better not only Africa but Europe and America and human nature in general. No attempt has been made to summarize adequately the rich material concerning primitive Africa recently gathered. Its wide extent, intricacy of detail and inevitable gaps and contradictions call for time, thought and much further study. But the beginnings made are of great value.

It is, of course, easy to exaggerate the cultural gifts of any particular people; or, as is more common in the case of Africa, to underrate plain evidence and interpret all difference as inferiority. Even backwardness in a human group is a purely relative term with no absolute significance. The "backward" races of the Age of Pericles included most of the world's leading peoples today; and the cultural space between West Africa and England is nothing compared with that between the New Empire of Egypt and Rome. There is no scientific explanation of the rate and distribution of human progress. What the facts concerning the culture of Africa begin to tell us is simply that here we have a normal human stock whose development has been conditioned by certain physical and social factors.

The physical factors are of great importance: the comparative inaccessibility of the continent from without, contrasted with the ease of communication within, except the barriers of the deserts and the jungles. Three principal zones of habitation appear: first, the steppes and deserts around the Sahara in the north and the Kalahari Desert in the south; second, the grassy highlands bordering the Great Lakes and connecting these two regions; third, the forests and rivers of Central and West Africa. In the deserts are the nomads, and the Pygmies are in the forest fastnesses. Herdsmen and their cattle cover the steppes and highlands, save where the tsetse fly prevents. In the open forests and grassy highlands are the agriculturists.

Among the forest farmers the village is the center of life, while in the open steppes political life tends to spread into larger political units. Political integration is, however, hindered by an ease of internal communication almost as great as the difficulty of reaching outer worlds beyond the continent. The narrow Nile Valley alone presented physical barriers formidable enough to keep back the invading barbarians of the south or let them but slowly filter through, and even then with difficulty. Elsewhere communication was all too easy. For a while the Congo forests fended away the restless, but this was only temporarily.

On the whole, Africa from the Sahara to the Cape offered no physical barrier to the invader, and we continually have whirlwinds of invading hosts rushing now southward, now northward, from the interior to the coast and from the coast inland, and hurling their force against states, kingdoms, and cities. Some resisted for a generation, some for centuries, some but a few years. It is, then, this sudden change and the fear of it that marks African culture, particularly in its political aspects, and which make it so difficult to trace this changing past. Nevertheless, beneath all change rests the strong substructure of custom, religion, industry, and these are well worth the attention of students.

Starting with agriculture, we learn that "among all the great groups of the 'natural' races, the Negroes are the best and keenest tillers of the ground. A minority despise agriculture and breed cattle; many combine both occupations. Among the genuine tillers the whole life of the family is taken up in agriculture, and hence the months are by preference called after the operations which they demand. Constant clearing changes forests to fields, and the ground is manured with the ashes of the burnt thicket. In the middle of the field rise the light watch-towers, from which a watchman scares grain-eating birds and other thieves. An African cultivated landscape is incomplete without barns. The rapidity with which, when newly imported, the most varied forms of cultivation spread in Africa, says much for the attention which is devoted to this branch of economy. Industries, again, which may be called agricultural, like the preparation of meal from millet and other crops, also from cassava, the fabrication of fermented drinks from grain, or the manufacture of cotton, are widely known and sedulously fostered."[1]

Bücher reminds us of the deep impression made upon travelers when they sight suddenly the well-attended fields of the natives on emerging from the primeval forests: "In the more thickly populated parts of Africa these fields often stretch for many a mile, and the assiduous care of the Negro women shines in all the brighter light when we consider the insecurity of life, the constant feuds and pillages, in which no one knows whether he will in the end be able to harvest what he has sown. Livingstone gives somewhere a graphic description of the devastations wrought by slave hunts; the people lying about slain, the dwellings demolished; in the fields, however, the grain was ripening and there was none to harvest it."[2]

Sheep, goats, and chickens are domestic animals all over Africa, and Von Franzius considers Africa the home of the house cattle and the Negro as the original tamer. Northeastern Africa especially is noted for agriculture, cattle raising and fruit culture. In the eastern Sudan and among the great Bantu tribes, extending from the Sudan down toward the south, cattle are evidences of wealth; one tribe, for instance, having so many oxen that each village had ten or twelve thousand head. Lenz (1884), Bouet-Williamez (1848), Hecquard (1854), and Baker (1868) all bear witness to this, and Schweinfurth (1878) tells us of great cattle parks and of numerous agricultural and cattle-raising tribes. Von der Decken (1859–61) described the paradise of the dwellers about Kilimanjaro—the bananas, fruit, beans and peas, cattle raising with stall feed, the fertilizing of the fields, and irrigation. The Negroid Gallas have seven or eight cattle to each inhabitant. Livingstone bears witness to the busy cattle raising of the Bantus and Kafirs. Hulub (1881) and Chapman (1868) tell of agriculture and fruit raising in South Africa. Shutt (1884) found the tribes in the southwestern basin of the Congo with sheep, swine, goats, and cattle. On this agricultural and cattle-raising economic foundation has arisen the organized industry of the artisan, the trader, and the manufacturer.

While the Pygmies, still living in the age of wood, make no iron or stone implements, they seem to know how to make bark cloth and fiber baskets and simple outfits for hunting and fishing. Among the Bushmen the art of making weapons and working in hides is quite common. The Hottentots are further advanced in the industrial arts, being well versed in the manufacture of clothing, weapons, and utensils. In the dressing of skins and furs, as well as in the plaiting of cords and the weaving of mats, we find evidences of their workmanship. In addition they are good workers in iron and copper, using the sheepskin bellows for this purpose. The Ashantis of the Gold Coast know how to make "cotton fabrics, turn and glaze earthenware, forge iron, fabricate instruments and arms, embroider rugs and carpets, and set gold and precious stones."[3]

Among the people of the banana zone we find rough basket work, coarse pottery, grass cloth, and spoons made of wood and ivory. The people of the millet zone, because of uncertain agricultural resources, quite generally turn to manufacturing. Charcoal is prepared by the smiths, iron is smelted, and numerous implements are manufactured. Among them we find axes, hatchets, hoes, knives, nails, scythes, and other hardware. Cloaks, shoes, sandals, shields, and water and oil vessels are made from leather which the natives have dressed. Soap is manufactured in the Bautschi district, glass is made, formed, and colored by the people of Nupeland, and in almost every city, cotton is spun and woven and dyed. Barth tells us that the weaving of cotton was known in the Sudan as early as the eleventh century. There was also extensive manufacture of wooden ware, tools, implements, and utensils.

In describing particular tribes, Baker and Felkin tell of smiths of wonderful adroitness; goatskins prepared better than a European tanner could do; drinking cups and kegs of remarkable symmetry; and polished clay floors. Schweinfurth says, "The arrow and the spear heads are of the finest and most artistic work; their bristle-like barbs and points are baffling when one knows how few tools these smiths have." Excellent wood carving is found among the Bongo, Ovambo, and Makalolo. Pottery and basketry and careful hut-building distinguish many tribes. Cameron (1877) tells of villages so clean, with huts so artistic, that save in book knowledge, the people occupied no low plane of civilization. The Mangbettu work both iron and copper. "The masterpieces of the Monbutto

(Mangbettu) smiths are the fine chains worn as ornaments, and which in perfection of form and fineness compare well with our best steel chains." Shubotz in 1911 called the Mangbettu "a highly cultivated people" in architecture and handicraft. Barth found copper exported from Central Africa in competition with European copper at Kano.

Nor is the iron industry confined to the Sudan. About the Great Lakes and other parts of Central Africa it is widely distributed. Thornton says, "This iron industry proves that the East Africans stand by no means on so low a plane of culture as many travelers would have us think. It is unnecessary to be reminded what a people without instruction, and with the rudest tools to do such skilled work, could do if furnished with steel tools." Arrows made east of Lake Nyanza were found to be nearly as good as the best Swedish iron in Birmingham. From Egypt to the Cape, Livingstone assures us that the mortar and pestle, the long-handled ax, the goatskin bellows, etc., have the same form, size, etc., pointing to a migration southwards. Holub (1879), on the Zambesi, found fine workers in iron and bronze. The Bantu huts contain spoons, wooden dishes, milk pails, calabashes, handmills, and axes.

In the Congo Valley the invaders settled in villages, absorbed such indigenous inhabitants as they found or drove them deeper into the forest; and immediately began to develop industry and political organization. They became skilled agriculturists, raising in some localities a profusion of cereals, fruit, and vegetables such as manioc, maize, yams, sweet potatoes, ground nuts, sorghum, gourds, beans, peas, bananas, and plantains. Everywhere they showed skill in mining and the welding of iron, copper, and other metals. They made weapons, wire and ingots, cloth, and pottery. A widespread system of trade arose. Some tribes extracted rubber from the talamba root; others had remarkable breeds of fowl and cattle, and still others divided their people by crafts into farmers, smiths, boatbuilders, warriors, cabinet-makers and armorers. Women here and there took part in public assemblies and were rulers in some cases. Large towns were built, some of which required hours to traverse from end to end. Many tribes developed intelligence of a high order. Wissmann called the Ba-Luba, "a nation of thinkers." Bateman found them "thoroughly and unimpeachably honest, brave to foolhardiness, and faithful to each other and to their superiors."[4]

Kafirs and Zulus, in the extreme south, are good smiths, and the latter melt copper and tin together and draw wire from it, according to Kranz (1880). West of the Great Lakes, Stanley (1871) found wonderful examples of smith work: figures worked out of brass and much work in copper. Cameron (1878) saw vases made near Lake Tanganyika which reminded him of the amphorae in the villa of Diomedes, Pompeii. Horn (1882) praises tribes here for iron and copper work. Livingstone (1871) passed thirty smelting houses in one journey, and Cameron came across bellows with valves, and tribes who used knives in eating. He found tribes which no Europeans had ever visited, who made ingots of copper in the form of the St. Andrew's cross, which circulated even to the coast.

In the southern Congo basin, iron and copper are worked; also wood and ivory carving and pottery making are pursued. In equatorial West Africa, Lenz and Du Chaillu (1861) found ironworkers with charcoal, and also carvers of bone and ivory. Near Cape Lopez, Hübbe-Schleiden found tribes making ivory needles inlaid with ebony. Wilson (1856) found natives in West Africa who could repair American watches.

Gold Coast Negroes make gold rings and chains, forming the metal into all kinds of forms. Soyaux says, "The works in relief which natives of Lower Guinea carve with their own knives out of ivory and hippopotamus teeth, are really entitled to be called works of art; and many wooden figures of fetishes in the Ethnographical Museum of Berlin show some understanding of the proportions of the human body." Great Bassam is called by Hecquard the "Fatherland of Smiths." The Mandingo in the northwest are remarkable workers in iron, silver, and gold, we are told by Mungo Park (1800); while there is a mass of testimony as to the work in the northwest of Africa in gold, tin, weaving, and dyeing. Caille found the Negroes in Bambana manufacturing gunpowder (1824–28), and the Hausa make soap; so, too, Negroes in Uganda and other parts made guns after seeing European models.

Benin art has been practiced without interruption for centuries, and Von Luschan says that it is "of extraordinary significance that by the sixteenth and seventeenth centuries a local and monumental art had been learned in Benin which in many respects equaled European art and developed a technique of the very highest accomplishment."

"The native arts and crafts of Benin, in comparison with those of the Yoruba towns, are still in a highly flourishing condition; the wood-carvers in particular were fully occupied. Again and again I came across altars for ancestor worship, images, carved doors, etc., which have been made during the last few score years. They show a wealth of pagan artistic skill of high order which is most impressive, especially in contrast with the stagnation at such places as Ibadan and Ife; and is even more astonishing, as Benin was overwhelmed by a catastrophe from which one might have expected that it would never recover. A British punitive expedition conquered the city and dethroned the king in 1897 and an extensive fire burnt down the whole place. At this time most of the Benin bronze work came to Europe; of the older products only a few were left in their original home. Consequently, the art of new Benin has been built up again on a *tabula rasa*. But the work of these forty years is plentiful enough. One has the impression that Benin is determined to make good the colossal damage that was done to it."[5]

"The *ars atrium*, however, of Negro Africa is the use of iron. The question of the origin of the art of iron-smelting is now being treated in detail by ethnologists, and, while general agreement has not been reached, the mass of evidence so far disclosed has convinced eminent men of science like Boas and Von Luschan that the smelting of iron was first discovered by the African Negroes, from whom, by way of Egypt and Asia Minor, this art made its way into Europe and the rest of the Old World."[6]

Gabriel de Mortillet (1883) declared Negroes the only iron users among primitive people. Some would, therefore, argue that the Negro learned it from other folk, but Andrée declares that the Negro developed his own "Iron Kingdom."

Boas says, "It seems likely that at a time when the European was still satisfied with rude stone tools, the African had invented or adopted the art of smelting iron. Consider for a moment what this invention has meant for the advance of the human race. As long as the hammer, knife, saw, drill, the spade, and the hoe had to be chipped out of stone, or had to be made of shell or hard wood, effective industrial work was not impossible, but difficult. A great progress was made when copper found in large nuggets was hammered out into tools and later on shaped by melting; and when bronze was introduced; but the true advancement of industrial life did not begin until the hard iron was discovered. It seems not unlikely that the people who made the marvelous discovery of reducing iron ores by smelting were the African Negroes. Neither ancient Europe, nor ancient western Asia, nor ancient China knew iron, and everything points to its introduction from Africa. At the time of the great African discoveries toward the end of the past century, the trade of the blacksmiths was found all over Africa, from north to south and from east to west. With his simple bellows and a charcoal fire he reduced the ore that is found in many parts of the continent and forged implements of great usefulness and beauty."[7]

Torday has argued, "I feel convinced by certain arguments that seem to prove to my satisfaction that we are indebted to the Negro for the very keystone of our modern civilization and that we owe him the discovery of iron. That iron could be discovered by accident in Africa seems beyond doubt: if this is so in other parts of the world, I am not competent to say. I will only remind you that Schweinfurth and Petherick record the fact that in the northern part of East Africa smelting furnaces are worked without artificial air current and, on the other hand, Stuhlmann and Kollmann found near Victoria Nyanza that the natives simply mixed powdered ore with charcoal and by introduction of air currents obtained the metal. These simple processes make it clear that iron could have been discovered in East or Central Africa. No bronze implements have ever been found in black Africa; had the Africans received iron from the Egyptians, bronze would have preceded this metal and all traces of it would not have disappeared. Black Africa was for a long time an exporter of iron, and even in the twelfth century exports to India and Java are recorded by Idrisi."[8]

Much of the industry, arts and skills thus described by travelers in the eighteenth and nineteenth centuries have changed and disappeared today: agriculture has retrograded among many tribes; cattle raising has led to erosion and lean and ill-fed herds; the work of native artisans has been replaced by cheap European manufactures in iron, earthenware and fiber. Sometimes new skills and methods borrowed from the white invaders or imitated have come in to replace the old, sometimes there has been nothing but retrogression; and, on the other hand, in many cases there is entire adaptation of European arts and methods, or of such portions of them as natives are permitted to learn.

The Negro is a born trader. Lenz says, "Our sharpest European merchants, even Jews and Armenians, can learn much of the cunning and trade of the Negroes." We know that the trade between Central Africa and Egypt was in the hands of Negroes for thousands of years, and in the early days the cities of the Sudan and North Africa grew rich through Negro trade. Leo Africanus, writing of Timbuktu in the sixteenth century, said, "It is a wonder to see what plentie of Merchandize is daily brought hither and how costly and sumptuous all things be. . . . Here are many shops of artificers and merchants and especially of such as weave linnen and cloth."

Long before cotton weaving was a British industry, West Africa and the Sudan were supplying a considerable part of the world with cotton cloth. Even today cities like Kuku on the west shore of Lake Chad and Sokoto are manufacturing centers where cotton is spun and woven, skins tanned, implements and iron ornaments made.

"Travelers," says Bücher, "have often observed this tribal or local development of industrial technique." "The native villages," relates a Belgian observer of the Lower Congo, "are often situated in groups. Their activities are based upon reciprocality, and they are to a certain extent the complements of one another. Each group has its more or less strongly defined specialty. One carries on fishing; another produces palm wine; a third devotes itself to trade and is broker for the others, supplying the community with all products from outside; another has reserved to itself work in iron and copper, making weapons for war and hunting, various utensils, etc. None may, however, pass beyond the sphere of its own specialty without exposing itself to the risk of being universally proscribed."

From the Loango coast, Bastian tells of a great number of centers for special products of domestic industry. "Loango excels in mats and fishing baskets, while the carving of elephants' tusks is specially followed in Chilungo. The so-called Mafooka hats with raised patterns are drawn chiefly from the bordering country of Kakongo and Mayyume. In Bakunya are made potter's wares, which are in great demand; in Basanza, excellent swords; in Basundi, especially beautiful ornamented copper rings; on the Congo, clever wood and tablet carvings; in Loango, ornamented clothes and intricately designed mats; in Mayumbe, clothing of finely woven matwork; in Kakongo, embroidered hats and also burnt clay pitchers; and among the Bayakas and Mantetjes, stuffs of woven grass."[9]

A native Negro student tells of the development of trade among the Ashanti. "It was a part of the state system of Ashanti to encourage trade. The king once in every forty days, at the Adai custom, distributed among a number of chiefs various sums of gold dust with a charge to turn the same to good account. These chiefs then sent down to the coast caravans of tradesmen, some of whom would be their slaves, sometimes some two or three hundred strong, to barter ivory for European goods, or buy such goods with gold dust, which the king obtained from the royal alluvial workings. Down to 1873, a constant stream of Ashanti traders might be seen daily wending their way to the merchants of the coast and back again, yielding more certain wealth and prosperity to the merchants of the Gold Coast and Great Britain than may be expected for some time yet to come from the mining industry and railway development put together. The trade chiefs would, in due time, render a faithful account to the king's stewards, being allowed to retain a fair portion of the profit. In the king's household, too, he would have special men who directly traded for him. Important chiefs carried on the same system of trading with the coast as did the king. Thus every member of the state, from the king downward, took an active interest in the promotion of trade and in the keeping open of trade routes into the interior."[10]

The trade thus encouraged and carried on in various parts of West Africa reached wide areas. From the Fish River to Kuka, and from Lagos to Zanzibar, the markets have become great centers of trade, the leading implement of civilization. Permanent markets are found in places like Ujiji and Nyangwe, where everything can be bought and sold from earthenware to wives; from one to three thousand traders flocked here.

"How like is the market traffic, with all its uproar and sound of human voices, to one of our own markets. There is the same rivalry in praising the goods, the violent, brisk movements, the expressive gesture, the inquiring, searching glance, the changing looks of depreciation or triumph, of apprehension, delight, approbation." So says Stanley. Trade customs are not everywhere alike. "If when negotiating with the Bangalas of Angola you do not quickly give them what they want, they go away and do not come back. Then perhaps they try to get possession of the coveted object by means of theft. It is otherwise with the Songos and Kiokos, who let you deal with them in the usual way. To buy even a small article you must go to the market; people avoid trading anywhere else. If a man says to another: 'Sell me this hen' or 'that fruit,' the answer as a rule will be, 'Come to the market place.' The crowd gives confidence to individuals and the inviolability of the visitor to the market, and of the market itself, looks like an idea of justice consecrated by long practice. Does not this remind us of the old Germanic 'market place'?"[11]

Of the social organization of Negroes, we are just beginning to have scientific study, and no adequate summary of the studies already made and making is available; but some observations of travelers and observers may be quoted for what they are worth. Beginning with the Negro family and social life, we find, as among all primitive peoples, polygamy and marriage by actual or simulated purchase. Out of the family develops the typical African village organization, which is thus described in Ashanti by a native Gold Coast writer: "The headman, as his name implies, is the head of a village community, a ward in a township, or of a family. His position is important inasmuch as he has directly to deal with the composite elements of the general bulk of the people.

"It is the duty of the head of a family to bring up the members thereof in the way they should go; and by 'family' you must understand the entire lineal descendants of a materfamilias, if I may coin a convenient phrase. It is expected of him by the state to bring up his charge in the knowledge of matters political and traditional. It is his work to train up his wards in the ways of loyalty and obedience to the powers that be. He is held responsible for the freaks of recalcitrant members of his family, and he is looked to keep them within bounds and to insist upon conformity on their part with the customs, laws, and traditional observances of the community. In early times he could send off to exile by sale a troublesome relative who would not observe the laws of the community.

"It is a difficult task that he is set to, but in this matter he has all-powerful helpers in the female members of the family, who will be either the aunts, or the sisters, or the cousins, or the nieces of the headman; and as their interests are identical with his in every particular, the good women spontaneously train up their children to implicit obedience to the headman, whose rule in the family thus becomes a simple and easy matter. 'The hand that rocks the cradle rules the world.' What a power for good in the native state system would the mothers of the Gold Coast and Ashanti become by judicious training upon native lines.

"The headman is par excellence the judge of his family or ward. Not only is he called upon to settle domestic squabbles, but frequently he sits judge over more serious matters arising between one member of the ward and another; and where he is a man of ability and influence, men from other wards bring him their disputes to settle. When he so settles disputes, he is entitled to a hearing fee, which, however, is not so much as would be payable in the regular court of the king or chief.

"The headman is naturally an important member of his company and often is a captain thereof. When he combines the two offices of headman and captain, he renders to the community a very important service. For in times of war, where the members of the ward would not serve cordially under a stranger, they would in all cases face any danger with their own kinsman as their leader. The headman is always succeeded by his uterine brother, cousin, or nephew—the line of succession, that is to say, following the customary law."[12]

We may contrast this picture with the more warlike Bantus of Southeast Africa. Each tribe lived by itself in a town with from five to fifteen thousand inhabitants, surrounded by gardens of millet, beans, and watermelon. Beyond these roamed their cattle, sheep, and goats. Their religion was ancestor worship with sacrifice to spirits and the dead, and some of the tribes made mummies of the corpses and clothed them for burial. They wove cloth of cotton and bark, they carved wood and built walls of unhewn stone. They had a standing military organization, and the tribes had their various totems, so that they were known as the Men of Iron, the Men of the Sun, the Men of the Serpents, Sons of the Corn Cleaners, and the like. Their system of common law was well conceived and there were organized tribunals of justice. In difficult cases precedents were sought and learned antiquaries consulted. At the age of fifteen or sixteen the boys were circumcised and formed into guilds. The land was owned by the tribe and apportioned to the chief by each family, and the main wealth of the tribe was in its cattle.

In general, among the African clans, the idea of private property was but imperfectly developed and never included land. The main mass of visible wealth belonged to the family and clan rather than to the individual; only in the matter of weapons and ornaments was exclusive private ownership generally recognized.

The government, vested in fathers and chiefs, varied in different tribes from absolute despotism to limited monarchies, almost republican. Viewing the Basuto National Assembly or Pitso in South Africa, Lord Bryce wrote, "The resemblance to the primary assemblies of the early peoples of Europe is close enough to add another to the arguments which discredit the theory that there is any such thing as an Aryan type of institution."[13]

Of the larger political developments of the Negro, much has already been said on the history of Ethiopia, the Sudanese kingdoms and the central and southern African tribes. A word may be added on the development of cities. Yoruba forms one of the three city groups of West Africa; another is around Timbuktu, and a third in the Hausa states. The Sudanese cities have from five to fifteen hundred towns, while the Yoruba cities have one hundred and fifty thousand inhabitants and more. The Hausa cities are many of them important, but few are as large as the Yoruba cities and they lie farther apart. All three centers, however, are connected with the Niger, and the group nearest the coast—that is, the Yoruba cities—has the greatest number of towns, the most developed architectural styles, and the oldest institutions.

The Yoruba cities are not only different from the Sudanese in population, but in their social relations. The Sudanese cities were influenced from the desert and the Mediterranean, and form nuclei of larger surrounding monarchial states. The Yoruba cities, on the other hand, remained comparatively autonomous organizations down to modern times, and their relative importance changed from time to time, without the group developing an imperialistic idea or subordinating the group to one overpowering city.

While women are sold into marriage throughout Africa, nevertheless their status is far removed from slavery. In the first place, the tracing of relationships through the female line, which is all but universal in Africa, gives the mother great influence. Parental affection is very strong, and throughout Negro Africa the mother is the most influential councilor, even in cases of tyrants like Chaka or Mutesa.

"No mother can love more tenderly or be more deeply beloved than the Negro mother. 'Everywhere in Africa,' writes Mungo Park, 'I have noticed that no greater affront can be offered a Negro than insulting his mother.' 'Strike me,' cried a Mandingo to his enemy, 'but revile not my mother.' The Herero swears 'By my mother's tears.' The Angola Negroes have a saying, 'As a mist lingers on the swamps, so lingers the love of father and mother.' "[14]

Black queens have often ruled African tribes. Among the Ba-Lolo, we were told, women take part in public assemblies where all-important questions are discussed.

Close knit with the family and social organization comes the religious life of the Negro. The religion of Africa is the universal animism or fetishism of primitive peoples, rising to polytheism and approaching monotheism chiefly, but not wholly, as a result of Christian and Islamic missions. Of fetishism there is much misapprehension. It is not mere senseless degradation. It is a philosophy of life. Among primitive Negroes there can be, as Miss Kingsley reminds us, no such divorce of religion from practical life as is common in civilized lands. Religion is life, and fetish an expression of the practical recognition of the dominant natural forces which surround the Negro. To him all the world is spirit. Miss Kingsley says, "If you want, for example, to understand the position of man in nature according to fetish, there is, as far as I know, no clearer statement of it made than is made by Goethe in his superb 'Prometheus.'[15] Fetish is a severely logical way of accounting for the world in terms of good and malignant spirits.

"It is this power of being able logically to account for everything that is, I believe, at the back of the tremendous permanency of fetish in Africa, and the cause of many of the relapses into it by Africans converted to other religions; it is also the explanation of the fact that white men who live in the districts where death and danger are everyday affairs, under a grim pall of boredom, are liable to believe in fetish, though ashamed of so doing. For the African, whose mind has been soaked in fetish during his early and most impressionable years, the voice of fetish is almost irresistible when affliction comes to him."[16]

Ellis tells us of the Ewe people, who believe that men and all nature have the indwelling "Kra," which is immortal; that the man himself after death may exist as a ghost, which is often conceived of as departed from the "Kra," a shadowy continuing of the man. Bryce, speaking of the Kafirs of South Africa, says, "To the Kafirs, as to the most savage races, the world was full of spirits—spirits of the rivers, the mountains, and the woods. Most important were the ghosts of the dead, who had power to injure or help the living, and who were, therefore, propitiated by offerings at stated periods, as well as on occasions when their aid was especially desired. This kind of worship, the worship once most generally diffused throughout the world, and which held its ground among the Greeks and Italians in the most flourishing period of ancient civilization, as it does in China and Japan today, was, and is, virtually the religion of the Kafirs."[17]

African religion does not, however, stop with fetish, but, as in the case of other peoples, tends toward polytheism and monotheism. Among the Yoruba, for instance, Frobenius shows that religion and city-state go hand in hand.

"The first experienced glance will here detect the fact that this nation originally possessed a clear and definite organization so duly ordered and so logical that we but seldom meet with its like among all the peoples of the earth. And the basic idea of every clan's progeniture is a powerful God; the legitimate order in which the descendants of a particular clan unite in marriage to found new families, the essential origin of every new-born babe's descent in the founder of its race and its consideration as a part of the God in Chief; the security with which the newly wedded wife not only may, but should, minister to her own God in an unfamiliar home." "This people . . . give evidence of a generalized system; a theocratic scheme, a well-conceived perceptible organization, reared in a rhythmically proportioned manner."

In the religious mythology of black West Africa, Shango, the Yoruba God of Thunder, is another legend of a dying divinity. He was the mightiest man born of the All-Mother in Ife and soars above the legend of Thor and Jahveh. "He is the Hurler of thunderbolts, the Lord of the Storm, the God who burns down compounds and cities, the Render of trees and the Slayer of men; cruel and savage, yet splendid and beneficent in his unbridled action. For the floods which he pours from the lowering welkin give life to the soil that is parched and gladden the fields with fertility. And, therefore, mankind fear him, yet love him."

The basis of Egyptian religion was "of a purely Nigritian character,"[18] and, in its developed form, Sudanese tribal gods were invoked and venerated by the priest. In Upper Egypt, near the confines of Ethiopia, paintings repeatedly represent black priests conferring on red Egyptian priests the instruments and symbols of priesthood. In the Sudan today, Frobenius distinguishes four principal religions: first, earthly ancestor worship; next, the social cosmogony of the Atlantic races; third, the religion of the Bori, and fourth, Islam. The Bori religion spreads from Nubia as far as the Hausa, and from Lake Chad in the Niger as far as the Yoruba. It is the religion of possession and has been connected by some with Asiatic influences.

From without have come two great religious influences: Islam and Christianity. Islam came by conquest, trade, and proselytism. As a conqueror it reached Egypt in the seventh century and had by the end of the fourteenth century firm footing in the Egyptian Sudan. It overran the central Sudan by the close of the seventeenth century, and at the beginning of the nineteenth century had swept over Senegambia and the whole valley of the Niger down to the Gulf of Guinea. On the east, Islam approached as a trader in the eighth century; it spread into Somaliland and overran Nubia in the fourteenth century. Today Islam dominates Africa north of ten degrees north latitude and is strong between five and ten degrees north latitude. In the east it reaches below the Victoria Nyanza.

Christianity early entered Africa; indeed, as Mommsen says, "It was through Africa that Christianity became the religion of the world. Tertullian and Cyprian were from Carthage, Arnobius from Sicca Veneria; Lactantius, and probably in like manner, Minucius Felix, in spite of their Latin names, were natives of Africa, and not less so Augustine. In Africa the Church found its most zealous confessors of the faith and its most gifted defenders."[19]

The Africa referred to here, however, was not Negroland, but for the most part Africa above the desert, where Negro blood was represented in the ancient Mediterranean race and by intercourse across the desert. On the other hand, Christianity was early represented in the Valley of the Nile under "the most holy pope and patriarch of the great city of Alexandria and of all the land of Egypt, of Jerusalem, the holy city, of Nubia, Abyssinia, and Pentapolis, and all the preaching of St. Mark." This patriarchate had a hundred bishoprics in the fourth century and included thousands of black Christians. Through it the Cross preceded the Cresent in some of the remotest parts of black Africa.

All these beginnings were gradually overthrown by Islam except among the Copts in Egypt, and in Abyssinia. The Portuguese in the sixteenth century began to replant the Christian religion and for a while had great success, both on the east and west coasts. Roman Catholic enterprise halted in the eighteenth century and the Protestants began. Today the West Coast is studded with English and German missions, South Africa is largely Christian through Dutch and English influence, and the region about the Great Lakes is becoming Christianized. The Roman Catholics have lately increased their activities, and the Negroes of America have entered with their own churches and with the curiously significant "Ethiopian" movement.

On the other hand and in connection with religious customs, there can be no question as to the outcropping of cruelty and oppression in Africa. Slavery was widespread in Africa and domestic slavery still persists to some extent. Whether or not slavery was more common in Africa than elsewhere cannot be stated dogmatically and may be doubted; but it certainly was common and widespread. The slave trade which supplied domestic slaves was an outcome of intertribal wars, until a foreign demand arose which raised an unusual economic problem and led to stupendous results which we shall treat in another chapter.

Out of fetish and witchcraft, out of pestilence, conquest and political change grew, especially in the jungle and the fever coast of West Africa, many terrible customs: human sacrifice, in some cases and times on a large scale; witch-hunting, cannibalism and cruel punishments. Compared with European and Asiatic civilization these occurrences are not altogether unusual. "It has been estimated that in England between 1170 and 1783 at least 50,000 persons suffered death at Tyburn alone. English criminals during that time were branded, hanged, drawn and quartered and burned alive." Nevertheless the persistence of these customs in some parts of Africa and especially often among otherwise gifted and progressive folk, argues for some special reasons.

The widespread system of human sacrifice on the West Coast of Africa was an arresting and sinister phenomenon. It was not, however, deliberate cruelty, but part of an age-old belief in the spirit world and the eternity of royal power. It provided the king after death not only with wives but servants in the spirit world, and renewed these servants from time to time. With this also went appeasement of evil spirits and punishment of crime.

There is no doubt that this custom waxed and waned with various influences. The foreign slave trade increased ruthless cruelty and provided victims, while on the other hand strong kings like Gezo of Dahomey limited the custom, if they could not wholly do away with it. Had Ashanti been allowed to consolidate the power of the state, and the slave trade had not interfered with the normal economy, there is no reason to doubt that the artistic sense and industrial technique of the West Coast would gradually have abated these customs. Instead of this, there came the Europeans with distaste for many Negro customs and horror at blood sacrifice, but nevertheless with no purely philanthropic motives; as former Governor Hugh Clifford says:

"There can be no reasonable doubt that, if the British had not interfered, the Ashantis would have extended their empire over all the nations of the Gold Coast; but our disapproval of their invasions were due, in the beginning, not so much to any feeling of pity for their victims, as to resentment at the disturbance to trade which they occasioned. Thus the role of protector of the defenseless was more or less inexorably thrust upon us in the interests of our own commerce."[20] It may be that the difficult fight which man in certain areas of Africa has had for physical survival against disease, the fear of wild beast and wilder men, the gloom of the jungle, made human sacrifice and cannibalism a more lasting phenomenon than in cases of most other peoples.

There is general agreement as to the main groups of African languages. They are Bushmen, Bantu, Sudanic and Semitic, and what is probably a combination of the last two, and usually called Hamitic. There is as yet no certainty as to the unity of Sudanic languages and the relation between the Sudanic and the Bantu tongues, nor are we sure just what is meant by the Hamitic languages. We recognize today, in world speech, three kinds of languages: the isolating languages such as the Chinese, where most words are mono-syllables and meaning is conveyed in part by intonation; next the agglutinating languages where formative elements are attached to the roots of words as separable parts; and finally inflectional languages where the formative elements are added to the roots and cannot be separated.

Covering the southern half of Africa are about one hundred and eighty-two Bantu languages in a closely united family. They are agglutinating, and the dominating factor in their structure is inflection by prefixes, the genitive following the governing nouns and the verb with many derivative forms. The Bantu is divided into eleven groups, which include Swahili, Zulu, Herero and Congo. Their "intricacy combined with regularity of structure is found in very few languages." They have sometimes been called Italian in their clarity, and exhibit "a beauty and harmony of euphonic sound hardly to be equaled."

There are about two hundred and sixty-four Sudanic languages, used in a stretch across the continent from the Atlantic to Abyssinia. They are not as unified as the Bantu tongues, as a result of past movements and shiftings of population. Some tongues have perished and others grown up. These languages have, however, certain common likenesses. They are isolating tongues and depend on intonation, have monosyllabic stems, and no grammatic sex distinctions. The genitive precedes the thing possessed and the verbal stem is not changed in conjugation. The Sudanic languages are divided into eastern, central and western groups. In the eastern group the largest divisions are the Shilluk, Dinka and Nuer; the central group comprises the Nile-Congo languages, the Ubangi, the Shari and the Niger Cameroons; the western Sudanic group includes various languages of the coast of the Gulf of Guinea like the Ewe, Yoruba, Nube and others, and also the west Atlantic languages, the Mandingo and others.

The inflectional Semitic languages are Arabic, spoken in North Africa and the eastern Sudan, and some of the languages of Abyssinia. There are perhaps in all ten Semitic dialects. There are forty-two languages in Africa which would seem to lie between the Semitic and the other African languages. They include probably ancient Egyptian and today languages spoken by the Galla, the Nandi, the Suk, etc., and also the Berber dialects and perhaps the Hausa. They are called "Hamitic" languages. The Hottentot language of South Africa resembles the Hamitic family. The Bushmen tribes speak languages which can be divided into three groups: southern, central and northern. They are remarkable for the so-called "clicks." No Pygmy language seems to be known.

In general the Negro languages of Africa have a common linguistic substratum in etymology and in many formative elements. Of the languages of Africa, many are spoken over a small area by a few people. Twelve are spoken by a million or more people. "Many Bantu languages and dialects, especially those of the Zulu-Xosa groups, have a quality of music which makes them a delight to listen to, as they roll forth with their trochaic lilt on the smooth, round baritone of the male voices. Nor is the music confined to language. The Bantu obviously share with the Negroes a very marked general musical flair." Other languages like the Swahili may be placed among the more important languages of the world. "Hausa, Ibo, Yoruba, Mossi-Dagomba, Mandingo, Lulua are spoken by millions of people. There are many other purely tribal languages, such as Zulu, Xosa, Suto, Ganda, Nyamwezi, Ruanda, Luo, Zande, Banda, Efik, the Akan stock, Ewe,

Mende, each comprising hundreds of thousands of speakers and some of them with a definite expansive tendency. There is no inherent reason why such languages should not evolve a literature."[21]

Language was reduced to writing among the Egyptians and Ethiopians and to some extent elsewhere in Africa. Over one hundred manuscripts of Ethiopian and Ethiopic-Arabian literature are extant, including a version of the Bible and historical chronicles. The Arabic was used as the written tongue of the Sudan, and Negroland has given us in this tongue many chronicles and other works of black authors.[22] The greatest of these is the Epic of the Sudan (Tarik-es-Soudan). Another is the Tarikh-al-Fettach. In other parts of Africa there were no written languages, but there was, on the other hand, an unusual perfection of oral tradition through bards, and extraordinary efficiency in telegraphy by drum and horn.

The folklore and proverbs of the African tribes are exceedingly rich. Some of these have been made familiar to English writers through the work of "Uncle Remus" and the Annancy tales. Others have been collected by Johnston, Ellis and Theal.

African art has doubtless received many stimuli from abroad. It has felt the influence of the Arabian, Indian and Persian; a streak of culture has probably come from the South Seas as well as from Europe and the Near East. Nevertheless, African art is as original as any art, and is in the main indigenous, authentic and beautiful. There can be no doubt of the Negro's deep and delicate sense of beauty in form, color, and sound. Soyaux says of African industry, "Whoever denies to them independent invention and individual taste in their work, either shuts his eyes intentionally before perfectly evident facts, or lack of knowledge renders him an incompetent judge."[23] M. Rutot has lately told us how the Negro race brought art and sculpture to prehistoric Europe. The bones of the European Negroids are almost without exception found in company with drawings and sculpture in high and low relief; some of their sculptures, like the Wellendorff "Venus," are unusually well finished for primitive man. So, too, the painting and carving of the Bushmen and their forerunners in South Africa have drawn the admiration of students.

Schweinfurth, who has preserved for us much of the industrial art of the Negro, speaks of their delight in the production of works of art for the embellishment and convenience of life. Frobenius expressed his astonishment at the originality of the African in the Yoruba temple which he visited. The lofty veranda was divided from the passageway by fantastically carved and colored pillars. On the pillars were sculptured knights, men climbing trees, women, gods, and mythical beings. The dark chamber lying beyond showed a splendid red room with stone hatchets, wooden figures, cowry beads, and jars. The whole picture, the columns carved in colors in front of the colored altar, the old man sitting in the circle of those who reverenced him, the open scaffolding of ninety rafters, made a magnificent impression.[24]

To sum up Yoruban civilization, it has been said that "the technical summit of that civilization was reached in the terra-cotta industry, and that the most important achievements in art were not expressed in stone, but in fine clay baked in the furnace; that hollow casting was thoroughly known, too, and practiced by these people; that iron was mainly used for decoration; that, whatever their purpose, they kept their glass beads in stoneware urns within their own locality, and that they manufactured both earthen and glass ware; that the art of weaving was highly developed among them; that the stone monuments, it is true, show some dexterity in handling and are so far instructive, but in other respects evidence a cultural condition insufficiently matured to grasp the utility of stone monumental material; and, above all, that the then great and significant idea of the universe as imaged in the temple was current in those days."[25]

The Germans have found, in Kamerun, towns built, castellated, and fortified in a manner that reminds one of the prehistoric cities of Crete. The buildings and fortifications of Zymbabwe have already been described and something has been said of the art of Benin, with its brass and bronze and ivory. All the work of Benin in bronze and brass was executed by casting, and by methods so complicated that it would be no easy task for a modern European craftsman to imitate them.

Frobenius has recently directed the world's attention to art in West Africa. Quartz and granite he found treated with great dexterity. But more magnificent than the stone monument is the proof that at some remote era glass was made and molded in Yorubaland and that the people here were brilliant in the production of terra-cotta images. The great mass of potsherds, lumps of glass, heaps of slag, etc., "proves, at all events, that the glass industry flourished in this locality in ages past. It is plain that the glass beads found to have been so very common in Africa, were not only not imported, but were actually manufactured in great quantities at home."

The terra-cotta pieces are "remains of another ancient and fine type of art" and are "eloquent of a symmetry, a vitality, a delicacy of form, and practically a reminiscence of the ancient Greeks." An antique bronze head, Frobenius describes as "a head of marvelous beauty, wonderfully cast," and "almost equal in beauty and, at least, no less noble in form than, and as ancient as, the terra-cotta heads."

In a park of monuments, Frobenius saw the celebrated forge and hammer: a mighty mass of iron, like a falling drop in shape, and a block of quartz fashioned like a drum. Frobenius thinks these were relics dating from past ages of culture, when the manipulation of quartz and granite was thoroughly understood and when iron manipulation gave evidence of a skill not met with today.

"Today the art of Negro Africa has its place of respect among the esthetic traditions of the world. . . . For us its psychological content must always remain in greater part obscure. But, because its qualities have a basic plastic integrity and because we have learned to look at Negro art from this viewpoint, it has finally come within the scope of our enjoyment, even as the art expressions of such other alien cultures as the Mayan, the Chaldaean, and the Chinese."[26]

"It is the vitality of the forms of Negro art that should speak to us, the simplification without impoverishment, the unerring emphasis on the essential, the consistent, three-dimensional organization of structural planes in architectonic sequences, the uncompromising truth to material with a seemingly intuitive adaptation of it, and the tension achieved between the idea or emotion expressed through representation and the abstract principles of sculpture. The art of Negro Africa is a sculptor's art: As a sculptural tradition in the last century it has had no rival."[27]

"The general distinction between native African and European music is this: that European music (since about A.D. 1600) is built on harmony; all other music on pure melody. In fact it is non-European music which has made us remember what pure melody really is."[28]

"In African music, three features stand out and have been stressed by all those who have heard Negroes sing: antiphony (the alternate singing of solo and chorus), part-singing, and highly developed rhythm."[29]

"The African Negroes are uncommonly gifted for music—probably, on an average, more so, than the white race. This is clear not only from the high development of African music, especially as regards polyphony and rhythm, but a very curious fact, unparalleled, perhaps, in history, makes it even more evident; namely, the fact that Negro slaves in America and their descendants, abandoning their original musical style, have adapted themselves to that of their white masters and produced a new kind of folk-music in that style. Presumably no other people would have accomplished this."[30]

In the life of primitive man, and especially among African Negroes, music and dance have a greater significance than with whites. They do not come under the general headings of Art or Games and serve neither as pastimes nor recreations.

"A short analysis of an African dance will show that its structure is quite different from modern European dancing. Thus when the dance is only a small one, and much more so when several hundreds of persons are taking part in it, it requires a stereotyped form, a prescribed mode of performance, concerted activities, recognized leadership and elaborate organization and regulation."[31]

The Negro has been prolific in the invention of musical instruments and has given a new and original music to the western world, not only in the spirituals, but in the "blues" and "rag-time" which have launched modern dance music. These are the only kinds of music brought forth in America by immigrants.

Even when we contemplate such revolting survivals of savagery as cannibalism, we cannot jump too quickly at conclusions. Cannibalism is spread over many parts of Negro Africa, yet the very tribes who practice cannibalism show often other traits of industry and power. "These cannibal Bassonga were, according to the types we met with, one of those rare nations of the African interior which can be classed with the most esthetic and skilled, most discreet and intelligent of all those generally known to us as the so-called natural races. Before the Arabic and European invasion they did not dwell in 'hamlets,' but in towns with twenty or thirty thousand inhabitants, in towns whose highways were shaded by avenues of splendid palms planted at regular intervals and laid out with the symmetry of colonnades. Their pottery would be fertile in suggestion to every art craftsman in Europe. Their weapons of iron were so perfectly fashioned that no industrial art from abroad could improve upon their workmanship. The iron blades were cunningly ornamented with damascened copper, and the hilts artistically inlaid with the same metal. Moreover, they were most industrious and capable husbandmen, whose careful tillage of the suburbs made them able competitors of any gardener in Europe.

"Their sexual and parental relations evidenced an amount of tact and delicacy of feelings unsurpassed among ourselves, either in the simplicity of the country or the refinements of the town. Originally their political and municipal system was organized on the lines of a representative republic. True, it is on record that these well-governed towns often waged an internecine warfare; but in spite of this it had been their invariable custom from time immemorial, even in times of strife, to keep the trade routes open and to allow their own and foreign merchants to go their ways unharmed. And the commerce of these nations ebbed and flowed along a road of unknown age, running from Itimbiri to Batubenge, about six hundred miles in length. This highway was destroyed by the 'missionaries of civilization' from Arabia, only toward the close of the eighteenth century. But even in my own time there were still smiths who knew the names of places along that wonderful trade route driven through the heart of the 'impenetrable forests of the Congo.' For every scrap of imported iron was carried over it."[32]

In disposition the Negro is among the most lovable of men. Practically all the great travelers, who have spent any considerable time in Africa testify to this, and pay deep tribute to the kindness with which they were received. One has but to remember the classic story of Mungo Park, the strong expressions of Livingstone, the words of Stanley, and hundreds of others to realize this.

Ceremony and courtesy mark Negro life. Livingstone again and again reminds us of "true African dignity." "When Ilifian men or women salute each other, be it with a plain and easy curtsey (which is here the simplest form adopted), or kneeling down, or throwing oneself upon the ground, or kissing the dust with one's forehead, no matter which, there is yet a deliberateness, a majesty, a dignity, a devoted earnestness in the manner of its doing, which brings to light with every gesture, with every fold of clothing, the deep significance and essential import of every single action. Everyone may, without too greatly straining his attention, notice the very striking precision and weight with which the upper and lower native classes observe these niceties of intercourse."[33]

Let it therefore be said, once for all, that racial inferiority is not the cause of anti-Negro prejudice. Boas, the anthropologist, says, "An unbiased estimate of the anthropological evidence so far brought forward does not permit us to countenance the belief in a racial inferiority which would unfit an individual of the Negro race to take his part in modern civilization. We do not know of any demand made on the human body or mind in modern life that anatomical or ethnological evidence would prove to be beyond the powers of the Negro.

"We have every reason to suppose that all races are capable, under proper guidance, of being fitted into the complex scheme of our modern civilization, and the policy of artificially excluding them from its benefits is as unjustifiable scientifically as it is ethically abhorrent." What is, then, this so-called "instinctive" modern prejudice against black folk?

Undoubtedly color prejudice in the modern world is the child of the American slave trade and the Cotton Kingdom. Before American slavery became the foundation of a new and world-wide economic development, the trend of human thought was toward recognizing the essential equality of all men, despite obvious differences. Beginning, however, with the second quarter of the nineteenth century and with the recognition of the value of black slave labor, came a determined, even though partially unconscious, effort to prove scientifically the essential inferiority of Africans.

There had been attempts to reduce racial differences to scientific measurement in the eighteenth century. It was at first anthropological and emphasized differences in physical development; and then it leaped to conclusions concerning mental and social achievement. By the middle of the nineteenth century, however, the new theory of evolution led to studies in comparative anatomy, brain capacity and brain weights; and finally in the twentieth century came the psychological intelligence tests. Today little scientific weight is given to the older anthropological and anatomical studies as determining racial differences or racial superiority, but effort has been centered upon attempts to measure intelligence.

Most of the efforts to measure differences in human intelligence between black and white have been carried out in the United States, which is in some respects unfortunate, because of the natural bias of most of the investigators, due to the history of the Negro problem. Psychological studies and measurements in Africa where the bulk of the Negro race lives have hardly begun. A review of intelligence tests in the United States shows that, first, in most of these investigations the fundamental conditions of measurement and experimentation have not been observed; and, secondly, the tests used have been standardized upon whites in the northern part of the United States while most of the Negroes measured have been from the South where Negro slavery disappeared only two generations ago. The sampling has been faulty either because the groups have been too small or unlike in social status, school training and cultural background.

A questionnaire sent out in 1929–30 and answered by over one hundred and fifty leading psychologists, educationists, sociologists and anthropologists in the United States, who had been in the closest contact with the field of measuring racial differences for twenty years or more, showed that over three-fourths of them believed that a fair interpretation of the intelligence tests hitherto made was either inconclusive as to the inherent mental ability of the Negro or showed him to be equal to the whites.[34]

Moreover, the fundamental and logical difficulty with all racial comparison is that there is no way of determining just what a race is; how far the characteristics of a given group are inherited; how far they are due to social and physical environment and what biological mixtures have taken place.

"We find, according to Dixon and others, that due to wholesale amalgamation in extremely early times, there are no longer any primary races; for these, if there were such, have been and are now in a state of flux. According to Hooton, the most common of the human races are of the secondary sort and primary races are decidedly rare. Finally, if fertility of inter-breeding is to be considered a criterion, all 'breeds of man must be assigned to one group.' In fact one anthropologist, Haddon, regards racial types as an artificial concept."[35]

The mulatto hypothesis which assumes that the intermingling of white and black blood produces an offspring of intermediate intelligence has not been sustained. As Herskovits has shown, the result of such unions depends entirely upon the individuals mated and not upon the "race."

Lord Bryce says of the intermingling of blacks and whites in South America, "The ease with which the Spaniards have intermingled by marriage with the Indian tribes—and the Portuguese have done the like, not only with the Indians, but with the more physically dissimilar Negroes—shows that race repugnance is no such constant and permanent factor in human affairs as members of the Teutonic peoples are apt to assume. Instead of being, as we Teutons suppose, the the rule in the matter, we are rather the exception, for in the ancient world there seems to have been little race repulsion."

The average social scientist today is born with so firm and unconscious a belief in the inferiority of darker races that unbiased investigation is difficult. Take for instance the study of recruits in the American army during the World War. A larger proportion of Negroes in the South were found fit for service in the army than of whites; and at the same time they were found of inferior mental ability. But the first conclusion was certainly influenced by a desire to send Negroes to the front and a reluctance of white men to go; while the second conclusion was influenced by the desire to keep Negroes from being selected as officers or even put into the fighting ranks but rather relegated as largely as possible to the regiments of stevedores.

The measurements for the most part were done by or under the direction of American army officers whose anti-Negro attitude is well known. The conclusions from these measurements were foregone, and despite the fact that the "Negroes" measured included mulattoes of all degrees, the results were attributed to the "Negro" race. While it was found that Negroes in northern units were inferior in mental ability to whites, it was also found that northern Negroes were in many cases superior to southern whites. Nevertheless, this was not allowed to alter the general conclusion.

The question of individual accomplishment and genius as exhibited by the Negro race is not easy to judge. Not only is our general estimate of what great men have done colored largely by selected facts and unconscious propaganda, but in the case of foreigners and members of alien races their work is quite apt to be forgotten or distorted. Especially in the case of the Negro the fact is that his color is easily forgotten after the deed, and last and always, what is a "Negro"? It is impossible, therefore, to answer the question as to how far genius or unusual ability has appeared in the Negro race, until we are able to determine scientifically just what a "Negro" is, and to prove historically in what degree particular examples of genius belonged to this race.

What we can say, however, today is this: there is no color line in genius; exceptional ability has occurred repeatedly among the darkest of mankind; and we are justified in asserting that if the world of men be divided into three great types by measurable physical and cultural differences, the darkest section has repeatedly given birth to exceptional men in art, religion and government. This we can assert, despite the fact that with the modern emphasis put upon the accomplishment of white folk, much that black folk have done has been forgotten or ignored.

If we speak first of black men in whom there is no clear evidence of Caucasic or Mongoloid blood, we have not only the more or less legendary black men of the ancient world like Memnon, Clitus and Eurybates; and writers like Lokman and Aesop himself; but also the fact that the Buddha throughout India, China and Japan is represented often as black with closely curled hair and a large number of his proselyting disciples are shown as black. In Japanese history there is the black Sakanouye Tamuramaro, who subdued the Ainus.

Passing by for the moment the Negroids of Egypt, we cannot forget the unquestioned black folk of distinction: Nefertari, "the most venerated figure in Egyptian history," Queen Mut-em-ua, and the Pharaoh, Ra-Nehesi, with many other blacks in high station.

In ancient Ethiopia there are the black kings of Ethiopia like Taharka, the queens called Candace, and that succession of powerful Negroes who led the world in the seventh and sixth centuries before Christ.

In Arabian and Mohammedan history there are Bilal, the friend of Mohammed; writers like Nosseyeb, the black poet in the Court of Haroun al Raschid; and Al Kenemi at the Court of Almansur in Spain and Ahmed Baba, Sudanese savant. As rulers and warriors, we may remember black rulers of the Sudan like the great Mohammed Askia; Bafur, viceroy of Egypt in the tenth century; Abu'l Hasan Ali, the Black Sultan of Morocco; Mohammed Ahmad, the Madhi; and the black rajahs of India.

In modern days we have Toussaint L'Ouverture and Christophe in Haiti, Chaka and Moshesh in South Africa; Tutu Kwamina and Blyden in West Africa; Tippoo Tip in the Congo; Calemba, one of the kings of the Ba-Luba, "a really princely prince," who, Batemar says, would "amongst any people be a remarkable and indeed in many respects a magnificent man."[36] In Europe we may note Latino, and Amo who taught in the University of Wittenberg; and Hannibal, once commander-in-chief of the Russian army under the Empress Elizabeth.

In the church we have black saints like Saint Benedict, Blessed Martin of Porres and Benoit of Palermo in the Catholic Church, not to mention reputed black popes and church fathers; Bishop Crowther in the English Church and Alexander Crummell in America.

In Mexico there was Dorantes, the discoverer of the southwestern United States. In the United States Phyllis Wheatley, the poet; Paul Cuffe, Robert Brown Elliot, the politician; Paul Lawrence Dunbar, the poet; Roland Hayes and Paul Robeson.

The list of distinguished black folk with more or less admixture of other types would include in the ancient world great pharaohs like Amen-hotep I and Amen-hotep III, the builder of Luxor; Tahutmes III and many others; and all the mulatto rulers of Ethiopia like Pianky, conqueror and redeemer of Egypt, and Shabaka. The kings and emperors of Abyssinia would come in this list, including Theodore, Menelik II and Haile Selassie; the founders of the Songhay, especially Es-Sadi. There are Tarik ben Zaid, who captured Gibraltar, Almansur the conqueror of North Africa and southern Europe, Yusuf I, the Almoravide, and the rulers of Morocco like Mulai Ismail. Most such mulattoes in ancient and medieval times escaped notice because their color and racial descent was not thought of sufficient importance to emphasize.

Since the African slave trade, while many West Indians and Americans of Negro descent are not so recorded, many others are. There are Dario and Placido, West Indian poets; Bridgewater, the friend of Beethoven; Chevalier Sainte-Georges, knighted by Louis XVI; Gomez, the Spanish painter, and Lislet Geoffroy, a corresponding member of the French Academy; Coleridge-Taylor in England. We have Petion in Haiti; Pushkin, the father of Russian literature; Alexander Dumas, the father of romance; Maceo, the martyr to Cuban independence; several presidents of Brazil, like Pecanha, and Patrocinio, the emancipator; McCoy and Matseliger, distinguished American inventors. In America too we have had Benjamin Banneker, Frederick Douglass; Henry O. Tanner, the painter, and Ira Aldridge, the actor, both of whom had an European reputation; Rillieux, inventor of the sugar vacuum pan; and the Lamberts, Burleigh, Rosamond Johnson and Dett, musicians; Booker T. Washington, who was known the world over.

In some cases cited here there has been dispute as to whether the person was really a "Negro" or was really great. Impartial judgment, based on such facts and testimony as are available, seems, however, to confirm the partial catalog given above. Much that is known and proven about persons of this sort has been curiously slurred over and forgotten in modern days. We know, for instance, the *Arabian Nights,* but almost nothing of the *Romance of Antar,* a cycle of poems published in Cairo in thirty-two volumes and first introduced to European readers in 1802. The romance is a companion piece to the *Arabian Nights* and a standard work of Arabia, and is founded on the career of the mulatto son of Sheik Shedad and a black woman. One of Antar's poems was hung in the temple at Mecca among the greatest poems written, that all pilgrims might know and do obeisance to them. Many white men of the highest distinction in Europe and America had Negro blood, but to this day prejudice is too bitter even to mention the fact, while documentary proof is usually impossible. But this was not always so.

Black faces are repeatedly represented in medieval art; among the three kings at the birth of Christ; by the black Virgin Mary and by travelers' stories; by the multitude of brown and black saints pictured in cathedrals like Chartres; especially is Shakespeare's Othello a peculiar case in point. Coleridge says that Shakespeare could not have been so utterly ignorant as to make a barbarian Negro plead royal birth; and Brandes regards it quite unreasonable to suppose that Shakespeare thought of Othello as a Negro. But Alice Werner, the great English student of Africa, says: "There are sufficient indications in the play that Shakespeare had the Negro and not the Arab type in mind; the "thick lips," and the repeated reference to blackness, which cannot be understood of anything but the real African tint. Still more conclusive is Shakespeare's conception of Othello's character: 'There is a great-hearted simplicity, a boundless capacity for affection and reverence, in the African character, of which Coleridge would not seem to have had the faintest suspicion.'" Miss Werner reminds us that, "in 1486, the King of Benin sent an Embassy to the King of Portugal, requesting the latter to send Christian priests to instruct his people. The Kings of Congo were potentates recognized and treated with by Portugal in Shakespeare's day." "Certainly, Othello on the stage should be black, or rather—for absolutely black people are in a minority, even in Africa—some shade of dark brown, like Khama, or Dinuzulu, or Lewanika, or Daudi Chwa of Uganda."

Europe during the Middle Ages had some knowledge of the Sudan and Africa. Melle and Songhay appear on medieval maps. In literature we have many allusions: the mulatto king, Feirifis, was one of Wolfram von Eschenbach's heroes; Prester John furnished endless lore; all show more or less legendary knowledge of what African civilization was at that time doing. A stream of travelers, like Leo Africanus, Ibn Batuta, Idrisi and others, brought continuous reports at least to Mediterranean lands.

We must, then, look for the origin of modern color prejudice not to physical or cultural causes, but to historic facts. And we shall find the answer in modern Negro slavery and the slave trade.

A word should be added on the scientific study of culture in Africa. Recent trends of investigation have emphasized the study of primitive culture and have led to a wide realization of the essential likenesses in the development of early human culture and emphasis on the fact that difference, in time or method, is no proof of race inferiority or cultural limitations. On the other hand there has been little effort on the part of sociology to follow the lead of anthropology and study Negro groups past and present which have emerged from primitive conditions and achieved a more or less civilized status. The development then of the Negro in the Nile Valley and the Sudan, in West and South Africa is left in strange silence or still surrendered to the unproven assumptions of nineteenth century philosophical history. Administration, on the other hand, assuming that science thus proves Africa has been and is now simply primitive, proceeds to rule on this assumption, to ignore fact and present progress and to pour its contempt on educated and presumptuous "niggers" aping white folk. The call here to scientific sociology and history is loud and imperative.

NOTES

1. Ratzel, *History of Mankind*, Vol. II, pp. 280 ff.
2. *Industrial Evolution*, p. 47.
3. These and other references in this chapter are from Schneider: *Cultur-fähigkeit des Negers*.
4. Keane, *Africa*, Vol. II, pp. 117–118.
5. *Africa*, January, 1938, Vol. XI, p. 55.
6. Chamberlain, *The Contribution of the Negro*, p. 494.
7. *Atlanta University Publications*, No. 20, p. 83.
8. *Journal of the Royal Anthropological Institute*, Vol. XLIII, pp. 414, 415. *Cf.* also *The Crisis*, Vol. IX, p. 234.
9. Karl Bücher, *Industrial Evolution* (tr. by Wickett), pp. 57–58.
10. Hayford, *Native Institutions*, pp. 95–96.
11. Ratzel, *History of Mankind*, Vol. II, p. 376.
12. Hayford, *Native Institutions*, pp. 76 ff.
13. *Impressions of South Africa*, third ed., p. 352.
14. Wilhelm Schneider, *op. cit.*
15. *West African Studies*, Chap. V.
16. *West African Studies*, Chap. V.

17. *Impressions of South Africa.*
18. *Encyclopaedia Britannica,* 9th ed., Vol. XX, p. 362.
19. *The African Provinces,* Vol. II, p. 345.
20. Claridge, *A History of the Gold Coast and Ashanti,* Vol. I, p. x.
21. Westermann, *The African To-day,* p. 254.
22. Words from Ethiopian, Coptic and other Negro languages appear in the Koran. *Cf.* Bell's *Mutawakkili of As-siyuti.*
23. Quoted in Schneider, *op. cit.*
24. Frobenius, *Voice of Africa,* Vol. I, p. 47.
25. Von Luschan, *Verhandlungen der berliner Gesellschaft für Anthropologie,* etc., 1898.
26. Sweeney (Ed.), *African Negro Art,* p. 11.
27. Sweeney (Ed.), *African Negro Art,* p. 21.
28. Von Hornbostel in *Africa,* January, 1928, p. 34.
29. *Ibid.,* p. 39.
30. *Ibid.,* p. 60.
31. Evans-Pritchard in *Africa,* October, 1928, p. 446.
32. Frobenius, *Voice of Africa,* Vol. I, pp. 14–15.
33. *Ibid.,* Vol. I, p. 272.
34. *Journal of Negro Education,* Vol. III, pp. 499 ff.
35. T. R. Garth, *Journal of Negro Education,* Vol. III, p. 322.
36. Keane, *Africa,* Vol. II, pp. 117–118.

CHAPTER VII

---◆---

The Trade in Men

The new thing in the Renaissance was not simply freedom of spirit and body, but a new freedom to destroy freedom; freedom for eager merchants to exploit labor; freedom for white men to make black slaves. The ancient world knew slaves and knew them well; but they were slaves who worked in private and personal service, or in public service like the building of pyramids and making of roads. When such slaves made goods, the goods made them free because men knew the worker and the value of his work and treated him accordingly. But when, in the later fifteenth century, there came slaves, and mainly black slaves, they performed an indirect service. That service became for the most part not personal but labor which made crops, and crops which sold widely in unknown places and in the end promised vaster personal services than previous laborers could directly give.

This then was not mere labor but capitalized labor; labor transmitted to goods and back to services; and the slaves were not laborers of the older sort but a kind of capital goods; and capital, whether in labor or in goods, in men or in crops, was impersonal, inhuman, and a dumb means to mighty ends.

Immediately black slaves became not men but things; and were valued as things are valued, by the demand and supply of their labor force as represented by their bodies. They belonged, it happened, to a race apart, unknown, unfamiliar, because the available supply of people of that race was for the moment cheaper; because religious feuds and political conquest in Africa rendered masses of men homeless and defenseless, while state-building in feudal Europe conserved and protected the peasants. Hence arose a doctrine of race based really on economic gain but frantically rationalized in every possible direction. The ancient world knew no races; only families, clans, nations; and degrees and contrasts of culture. The medieval world evolved an ideal of personal worth and freedom for wide groups of men and a dawning belief in humanity as such. Suddenly comes America; the sale of men as goods in Africa; the crops these goodsmen grew; the revolution in industry and commerce; in manufacture and transport; in trade and transformation of goods for magnificent service and power. "The Commercial Revolution of the sixteenth century through the opening of new trade routes to India and America, the development of world markets, and the increased output of silver from the German, Austrian and Mexican mines, made possible the productive use of capital which had heretofore been employed chiefly in military operations, and which resulted in its rapid increase. Great companies flourished and a new class of wealthy merchants arose to vie in luxury not only with the great landed proprietors but even with princes and kings. Many parallels are to be found between this and the Industrial Revolution three centuries later."[1]

It was not a mere case of parallelism but of cause and effect: the African slave trade of the sixteenth and seventeenth centuries gave birth to the Industrial Revolution of the eighteenth and nineteenth. The cry for the freedom of man's spirit became a shriek for freedom in trade and profit. The rise and expansion of the liberal spirit were arrested and diverted by the theory of race, so that black men became black devils or imbeciles to be consumed like cotton and sugar and tobacco, so as to make whiter and nobler men happier.

There are two reasons why the history of Africa is peculiar. Color of skin is not one that was regarded as important before the eighteenth century. "I am black but comely, O ye daughters of Jerusalem," cries the old Hebrew love song. Cultural backwardness was no reason—Africa, as compared with Europe, Asia, and America, was not backward before the seventeenth century. It was different, because its problems were different. At times Africa was in advance of the world. But *climate:* hot sun and flooding rains made Africa a land of desert, jungle, and disease, where culture could indeed start even earlier than in ice-bound Europe, but when, unaided by recent discoveries of science, its survival and advance was a hard fight. And finally, and above all, beginning with the fifteenth century and culminating in the eighteenth and nineteenth, *mankind in Africa became goods*—became merchandise, became even real estate. Men were bought and sold for private profit and on that profit Europe, by the use of every device of modern science and technique, began to dominate the world.

How did Africans become goods? Why did they submit? Why did the white world fight and scheme and steal to own them? Negroes were physically no weaker than others, if as weak; they were no more submissive. Slavery as an institution is as old as humanity; but never before the Renaissance was the wealth and well-being of so many powerful and intelligent men made squarely dependent not on labor itself but on the buying of labor power. And never before nor since have so many million workers been so helpless before the mass might and concentrated power of greed, helped on by that Industrial Revolution which black slavery began in the sixteenth century and helped to culmination in the nineteenth.

A new and masterful control of the forces of nature evoked a Frankenstein, which Christianity could not guide. But the Renaissance also gave birth to an idea of individual freedom in Europe and emphasized the Christian ideal of the worth of the common man. The new industry, therefore, which was as eager to buy and sell white labor as black, was canalized off toward the slavery of blacks, because the beginnings of the democratic ideal acted so as to protect the white workers. To dam this philanthropy and keep it from flooding into black slavery, the theory of the innate and eternal inferiority of black folk was invented and diffused. It was not until the nineteenth century that the floods of human sympathy began to burst through this artificial protection of slavery and in the abolition movement start to free the black worker.

Fortunately, as Gobineau rationalized this subjection of men, Marx saw the virus of labor exploitation, of labor regarded and treated as goods, poisoning Europe. He saw the social revolution; revolution in ideas which traffic in labor force for power and personal enjoyment, brought; and he saw this becoming the object of that very industrial revolution to which black slavery gave birth. Freedom then became freedom to enslave all working classes and soon the emancipation of the new wage slaves, arising out of the hell of the Industrial Revolution, was hindered by chattel slavery and then men began dimly to see slavery as it really was.

Then chattel slavery of black folk fell, but immediately and in its very falling it was rebuilt on African soil, in the image and pattern of European wage slavery of the eighteenth and nineteenth centuries, which at the time was yielding before a new labor movement. The abolitionists, however, did not realize where the real difference between white and black workers had entered. Initially the goods which the white workers made had made them free; because they began to get their share; but the goods which black slaves made did not make them free. It long kept them slaves with a minimum share, because these workers were isolated in far and wild America. The eaters and wearers and smokers of their crops, even the owners of their crops and bodies, did not see them working or know their misery or realize the injustice of their economic situation. They were workers isolated from the consumer and consumers bargained only with those who owned the fruit of their stolen toil, often fine, honest, educated men.

Those then who in the dying nineteenth century and dawning twentieth saw the gleam of the new freedom were too busy to realize how land monopoly and wage slavery and forced labor in present Africa were threatening Europe of the twentieth century, re-establishing the worst aspects of the factory system and dehumanizing capital in the world, at the time when the system was diligently attacked in culture lands. They did not see that here was the cause of that new blossoming of world wars which instead of being wars of personal enmity, of dynastic ambition, or of national defense, became wars for income and income on so vast a scale that its realization meant the enslavement of the majority of men. They therefore did not finish the task, and today in the twentieth century, as the white worker struggles toward a democratization of industry, there is the same damming and curtailment of human sympathy to keep the movement from touching workers of the darker races. On their exploitation is being built a new fascist capitalism. Hence the significance of that slave trade which we now study.

Greece and Rome had their chief supplies of slaves from Europe and Asia. Egypt enslaved races of all colors, and if there were more blacks than others among her slaves, there were also more blacks among her nobles and Pharaohs, and both facts are explained by her racial origin and geographical position. The fall of Rome led to a cessation of the slave trade, but after a long interval came the white slave trade of the Saracens and Moors, and finally the modern trade in Negroes.

Slavery as it exists universally among primitive people is a system whereby captives in war are put to tasks about the homes and in the fields, thus releasing the warriors for systematic fighting and the women for leisure. Such slavery has been common among all people and was widespread in Africa. The relative number of African slaves under these conditions varied according to tribe and locality, but usually the labor was not hard; and slaves were recognized members of the family and might and did often rise to high position in the tribe.

Remembering that in the fifteenth century there was no great disparity between the civilization of Negroland and that of Europe, what made the striking difference in subsequent development? European civilization, cut off by physical barriers from further incursions of barbaric races, settled more and more to systematic industry and to the domination of one religion; African culture and industry were not only threatened by powerful African barbarians from the west and central regions of the continent, but also by invading Arabs with a new religion precipitating from the eleventh to the sixteenth centuries a devastating duel of cultures and faiths.

When, therefore, a demand for workmen arose in America, European exportation was limited by unity of religious ties and economic stability. African exportation was encouraged not simply by the Christian attitude toward heathen, but also by the Moslem enmity toward the unconverted. Two great modern religions, therefore, agreed at least in the policy of enslaving heathen blacks; while the conquest of Egypt, the overthrow of the black Askias by the Moors at Tondibi, brought economic chaos among the advanced Negro peoples. Finally the duel between Islam and Fetish left West Africa naked to the slave-trader.

The modern slave trade began with the Mohammedan conquests in Africa, when heathen Negroes were seized to supply the harems, and as soldiers and servants. They were bought from the masters and seized in war, until the growing wealth and luxury of the conquerors demanded larger numbers. Then Negroes from the Egyptian Sudan, Abyssinia, and Zanzibar began to pass into Arabia, Persia, and India in increased numbers. As Negro kingdoms and tribes rose to power they found the slave trade lucrative and natural, since the raids in which slaves were captured were ordinary inter-tribal wars. It was not until the eighteenth and nineteenth centuries that the demand for slaves made slaves the object, and not the incident, of African wars.

There was, however, between the Mohammedan and American slave trade one fundamental difference which has not heretofore been stressed. The demand for slaves in Mohammedan countries was to a large extent a luxury demand. Black slaves were imported as soldiers and servants or as porters of gold and ivory rather than industrial workers. The demand, therefore, was limited by the wealth of a leisure class or the ambitions of conquest and not by the prospect of gain on the part of a commercial class. Even where the idle rich did not support slavery in Africa, other conditions favored its continuance, as Cooley points out, when he speaks of the desert as a cause of the African slave trade.

"It is impossible to deny the advancement of civilization in that zone of the African continent which has formed the field of our inquiry. Yet barbarism is there supported by natural circumstances with which it is vain to think of coping. It may be doubted whether, if mankind had inhabited the earth only in populous and adjoining communities, slavery would have ever existed. The Desert, if it be not absolutely the root of the evil, has, at least, been from the earliest times the great nursery of slave hunters. The demoralization of the towns on the southern borders of the desert has been pointed out, and if the vast extent be considered of the region in which man has no riches but slaves, no enjoyment but slaves, no article of trade but slaves, and where the hearts of wandering thousands are closed against pity by the galling misery of life, it will be difficult to resist the conviction that the solid buttress on which slavery rests in Africa, is—The Desert."[2]

In Mohammedan countries there were gleams of hope in slavery. In fiction and in truth the black slave had a chance. Once converted to Islam, he became a brother to the best, and the brotherhood of the faith was not the sort of idle lie that Christian slave masters made it. In Arabia black leaders arose like Antar; in India black slaves carved out principalities where their descendants still rule.

Some Negro slaves were brought to Europe by the Spaniards in the fourteenth century, and a small trade was continued by the Portuguese, who conquered territory from the "tawny" Moors of North Africa in the early fifteenth century. Later, after their severe repulse at Al Kasr Al Kebir, the Portuguese swept farther down the West Coast in quest of trade with Negroland, a new route to India and the realm of Prester John. As early as 1441, they reached the River of Gold, and their story is that their leader seized certain free Moors and the next year exchanged them for ten black slaves, a target of hide, ostrich eggs, and some gold dust. The trade was easily justified on the ground that the Moors were Mohammedans and refused to be converted to Christianity, while heathen Negroes would be better subjects for conversion and stronger laborers.

In the next few years a small number of Negroes continued to be imported into Spain and Portugal as servants. We find, for instance, in 1474, that Negro slaves were common in Seville. There is a letter from Ferdinand and Isabella in the year 1474 to a celebrated Negro, Juan de Valladolid, commonly called the "Negro Count" (El Conde Negro), nominating him to the office of "mayoral of the Negroes" in Seville. The slaves were apparently treated kindly, allowed to keep their own dances and festivals, and to have their own chief, who represented them in the courts, as against their own masters, and settled their private quarrels.

In Portugal, "the decline of the population, in general, and the labor supply, in particular, was especially felt in the southern provinces, which were largely stripped of population. This resulted in the establishment there of a new industrial system. The rural lands were converted into extensive estates held by absentee landlords, and worked by large armies of black bondmen recently brought from Africa. Soon the population of Algarve was almost completely Negro; and by the middle of the sixteenth century, blacks outnumbered whites in Lisbon itself. As intermarriage between the two races went on from the beginning, within a few generations Ethiopian blood was generally diffused throughout the nation, but it was notably pronounced in the south and among the lower classes."[3]

Between 1455 and 1492 little mention is made of slaves in the trade with Africa. Columbus is said to have suggested Negroes for America, but Ferdinand and Isabella refused. Nevertheless, by 1501, we have the first incidental mention of

Negroes going to America in a declaration that Negro slaves "born in the power of Christians were to be allowed to pass to the Indies, and the officers of the royal revenue were to receive the money to be paid for their permits."

About 1501 Ovando, Governor of Spanish America, was objecting to Negro slaves and "solicited that no Negro slaves should be sent to Hispaniola, for they fled amongst the Indians and taught them bad customs, and never could be captured." Nevertheless a letter from the king to Ovando, dated Segovia, in September, 1505, says, "I will send more Negro slaves as you request; I think there may be a hundred. At each time a trustworthy person will go with them who may have some share in the gold they may collect and may promise them ease if they work well."[4] There is a record of a hundred slaves being sent out this very year, and Diego Columbus was notified of fifty to be sent from Seville for the mines in 1510.

After this time frequent notices show that Negroes were common in the New World.[5] When Pizarro, for instance, had been slain in Peru, his body was dragged to the cathedral by two Negroes. After the battle of Anaquito, the head of the viceroy was cut off by a Negro; and during the great earthquake in Guatemala a most remarkable figure was a gigantic Negro seen in various parts of the city. Núñez had thirty Negroes with him on the top of the Sierras, and there was rumor of an aboriginal tribe of Negroes in South America. One of the last acts of King Ferdinand was to urge that no more Negroes be sent to the West Indies, but, under Charles V, Bishop Las Casas drew up a plan of assisted migration to America and asked in 1517 the right for immigrants to import twelve Negro slaves each, in return for which the Indians were to be freed.

Las Casas, writing in his old age, owns his error: "This advice that license should be given to bring Negro slaves to these lands, the Clerigo Casas first gave, not considering the injustice with which the Portuguese take them and make them slaves; which advice, after he had apprehended the nature of the thing, he would not have given for all he had in the world. For he always held that they had been made slaves unjustly and tyrannically; for the same reason holds good of them as of the Indians."[6]

As soon as the plan was broached, a Savoyard, Lorens de Gomenot, Governor of Bresa, obtained a monopoly of this proposed trade and shrewdly sold it to the Genoese for twenty-five thousand ducats. Other monopolies were granted in 1523, 1527, and 1528.[7] Thus the American trade became established and gradually grew, passing successively into the hands of the Portuguese, the Dutch, the French, and the English.

At first the slave trade was of the same kind and volume as that already passing northward over the desert routes. Soon, however, the American trade developed. A strong, unchecked demand for brute labor in the West Indies and on the continent of America grew, until it culminated in the eighteenth century, when Negro slaves were crossing the Atlantic at the rate of fifty to one hundred thousand a year. This called for slave raiding on a scale that drew slaves from most parts of Africa, although centering on the West Coast, from the Senegal to St. Paul de Loanda. The Mohammedan trade continued along the East Coast and the Nile Valley.

Carleton Beals says: "This vast labor army, conscripted for developing the Americas, represented a force of many millions of man power. It was taken from all parts of Africa; from Angola and from the deep Congo, from Bonny River and the central Niger and Hausaland, from Lagos, Dahomey, Old Calabar; from Madagascar and Ethiopia and Gabun. The Portuguese, Spanish, Flemish, Dutch, English, French recruiting agents with their platoons of soldiers reached far above Stanley Pool to the Mozambique, clear south of Kunene River. Portuguese Guinea and the Gold Coast poured forth their contingents. Not only the Yoruba, Egba, Jebu, Sokoto, the Mandingo, but the Hottentots and Bushmen gave up forced levies.

"Mohammedan Negro settlements are found in Brazil, the Guianas and elsewhere. Some of them still speak and use Arabic."

Herskovits believes: "From contemporary documentary evidence that the region from which the slaves brought to the New World were derived, has limits that are less vast than stereotyped belief would have them. . . . That some, perhaps in the aggregate; even impressive numbers of slaves, came from the deep interior, or from East or South Africa, does not make less valid the historical evidence that by far the major portion of the slaves brought to the New World came from a region that comprises only a fraction of the vast bulk of the African continent."[8]

There was thus begun in modern days a new slavery and slave trade. It was different from that of the past, because more and more it came in time to be founded on racial caste, and this caste was made the foundation of a new industrial system. For four hundred years, from 1450 to 1850, European civilization carried on a systematic trade in human beings of such tremendous proportions that the physical, economic, and moral effects are still plainly to be remarked throughout the world. To this must be added the large slave trade of Mussulman lands, which began with the seventh century and raged almost unchecked until the end of the nineteenth century.

These were not days of decadence, but a period that gave the world Shakespeare, Martin Luther, Raphael, Haroun-al-Raschid and Abraham Lincoln. It was the day of the greatest expansion of two of the world's most pretentious religions, and of the beginnings of modern organization of industry. In the midst of this advance and uplift, this slave trade and slavery spread more human misery, inculcated more disrespect for and neglect of humanity, a greater callousness to suffering, and more petty, cruel, human hatred than can well be calculated. We may excuse and palliate it, and write history so as to let men forget it; it remains a most inexcusable and despicable blot on modern history.

The Portuguese built the first slave-trading fort at Elmina, on the Gold Coast, in 1482, and extended their trade down the West Coast and up the East Coast. Under them the abominable traffic grew larger and larger, until it became far the most important in money value of all the commerce of the Zambesi basin. There could be no extension of agriculture, no mining, no progress of any kind where it was so extensively carried on.[9]

It was the Dutch, however, who launched the overseas slave trade as a regular institution. They began their fight for freedom from Spain in 1579; in 1595, as a war measure against Spain, which at that time was dominating Portugal, they made their fight for slaves in their first voyage to Guinea. By 1621 they had captured Portugal's various slave forts on the West Coast and they proceeded to open sixteen forts along the coast of the Gulf of Guinea. Ships sailed from Holland to Africa, got slaves in exchange for their goods, carried the slaves to the West Indies or Brazil, and returned home laden with New World produce. In 1621 the private companies trading in the west were all merged into the Dutch West India Company, which sent in four years fifteen thousand four hundred and thirty Negroes to Brazil, carried on war with Spain, supplied even the English plantations, and gradually became the great slave carrier of the day.

The commercial supremacy of the Dutch early excited the envy and emulation of the English. The Navigation Ordinance of 1651 was aimed at them, and two wars were necessary to wrest the slave trade from the Dutch and place it in the hands of the English. The final terms of peace, among other things, surrendered New Netherlands to England and opened the way for England to become henceforth the world's greatest slave trader.

The English trade began with Sir John Hawkins' voyages in 1562 and later, in which "the Jesus, our chiefe shippe," played a leading part. Desultory trade was kept up by the English until the middle of the seventeenth century, when English chartered slave-trading companies began to appear. In 1662 the "Royal Adventurers," including the king, the queen dowager, and the Duke of York, invested in the trade, and finally the Royal African Company, which became the world's chief slave trader, was formed in 1672 and carried on a growing trade for a quarter of a century. Jamaica had finally been captured and held by Oliver Cromwell in 1655 and formed the West Indian base for the trade in men.

The chief contract for trade in Negroes was the celebrated "Asiento" or agreement of the King of Spain to the importation of slaves into Spanish domains. The Pope's Bull of Demarcation, 1493, debarred Spain from African possessions, and compelled her to contract with other nations for slaves. This contract was in the hands of the Portuguese in 1600; in 1640 the Dutch received it, and in 1701, the French. The War of the Spanish Succession was motivated not so much by royal rivalries as to bring this slave trade monopoly to England.

This Asiento of 1713 was an agreement between England and Spain by which the latter granted the former a monopoly of the Spanish colonial slave trade for thirty years; and England engaged to supply the colonies within that time with at least one hundred and forty-four thousand slaves at the rate of forty-eight hundred per year. The English counted this prize as the greatest result of the Treaty of Utrecht (1713), which ended the mighty struggle against the power of Louis XIV. The English held the monopoly for thirty-five years until the Treaty of Aix-la-Chapelle, although they had to go to war over it in 1739.

It has been shown by a recent study made at Howard University that the development of England as a great capitalist power was based directly and mainly upon the slave trade.[10] English industry and commerce underwent a vast expansion in the early seventeenth century, based on the shipment of English goods to Africa, of African slaves to the West Indies, and of West Indian products back to England. About 1700 Bristol became an important center of the slave trade, followed by London and Liverpool. Liverpool soon overtook both Bristol and London. In 1709 it sent out one slaver of thirty tons burden; encouraged by Parliamentary subsidies which amounted to nearly a half million dollars between 1729 and 1750, the trade increased to fifty-three ships in 1751; eighty-six in 1765, and at the beginning of the nineteenth century, one hundred and eighty-five, which carried forty-nine thousand two hundred and thirteen slaves in one year. In 1764 a quarter of the shipping of Liverpool was in the African trade and Liverpool merchants conducted one half of England's trade with Africa. The value of all English goods sent to Africa was 464,000 pounds sterling of which three-fourths was of English manufactures.

This growth of Liverpool indicated the evolution of the capitalist economy in England. Liverpool did not grow because it was near the Lancaster manufacturing district, but, on the contrary, Lancaster manufacturers grew because they were near the Liverpool slave trade and largely invested in it. Thus Liverpool made Manchester.

Karl Marx emphasized the importance of slavery as the foundation of the capitalist order. He said, "Slavery is an economic category just as any other. Direct slavery is the pivot of bourgeois industry, just as are machinery and credit, etc. Without slavery there is no cotton; without cotton, there is no modern industry. It is slavery that has given value to universal commerce, and it is world trade which is the condition of large scale industry. Thus, slavery is an economic category of the first importance."[11]

The tremendous economic stake of Great Britain in the African and West Indian trade is shown by these figures, after Bryan Edwards: from 1701 to 1787 British ships took to Africa goods to the value of twenty-three million pounds sterling. Of these, fourteen million pounds sterling were of British manufacture. Slaves, gold and other products were purchased with these goods. The slaves were transported to the West Indies. From the West Indies in the century from 1698 to 1798 Great Britain imported goods to the value of over two hundred million pounds.

The basis of the English trade, on which capitalism was erected, was Negro labor. This labor was cheap and was treated as capital goods and not as human beings. The purchase of slaves furnished a large market for British manufacture, especially textiles. African gold became the medium of exchange which rising capitalism and the profits of African trade demanded. The large fortunes which were turned to industrial investment, and especially to the African trade, stimulated industries like ship building, which helped make England mistress of the seas. The West Indies too as a seat of slavery furnished an outlet for British manufacture and a source of raw materials. From this again large fortunes arose which were transferred to the mother country and invested.

All this spelled revolution: world-wide revolution starting in Europe; sinister and fatal revolution in West Africa. The city-state represented by Yoruban civilization had fought with the empire builders of the Sudan and retreated toward the Gulf of Guinea. Here they came in contact with the new western slave trade. It stimulated trade and industry; but the trade was not only in gold and oil and ivory, it was in men; and those nations that could furnish slaves were encouraged and prospered. The ruder culture of Ashanti and Dahomey outstripped Yoruba. Benin was changed. Blood lust was encouraged and the human culture which the slave trade helped build up for Europe, tore down and debauched West Africa.

The culture of Yoruba, Benin, Mossiland and Nupe had exhausted itself in a desperate attempt to stem the on-coming flood of Sudanese expansion. It had succeeded in maintaining its small, loosely federated city-states suited to trade, industry, and art. It had developed strong resistance toward the Sudan state builders toward the north, as in the case of the fighting Mossi; but behind this warlike resistance lay the peaceful city life which gave industrial ideas to Byzantium and shared something of Ethiopian and Mediterranean culture.

The first advent of the slave traders increased and encouraged native industry, as is evidenced by the bronze work of Benin; but soon this was pushed into the background, for it was not bronze metal but bronze flesh that Europe wanted. A new state-building tyranny, ingenious, well organized but cruel, and built on war, forced itself forward in the Niger Delta. The powerful state of Dahomey arose early in the eighteenth century. Ashanti, a similar kingdom, began its conquests in 1719 and grew with the slave trade because the profits of the trade and the insatiable demands of the Europeans disrupted and changed the older native economy.

Thus state building in West Africa began to replace the city economy; but it was a state built on war and on war supported and encouraged largely for the sake of trade in human flesh. The native industries were changed and disorganized. Family ties and government were weakened. Far into the heart of Africa this devilish disintegration, coupled with Christian rum and Mohammedan raiding, penetrated.

Few detailed studies have been made of the Mohammedan slave trade. Slave raiding was known in the Nile Valley from the time of the Egyptians and with the advent of Islam it continued, but it was incidental to conquest and proselytism. Later, however, it began to be commercialized; it was systematically organized with raiders, factories, markets, and contractors. By the nineteenth century African slaves were regularly supplied to Egypt, Turkey, Arabia, and Persia; and also to Morocco there came from the Western Sudan and Timbuktu about four thousand annually.

Egyptians in the nineteenth century tried to stop this slave trade, but they encountered vested interests making large profits. The trade continued to exist as late as 1890. The English charge that under the Madhi in the Egyptian Sudan, slavery and slave raiding were widespread; but this was the result of the very misrule and chaos which caused the Madhist movement and for which it was not responsible. Doubtless many of the Madhist followers were enslaved and robbed under cover of religious frenzy; but the Madhi could not in the midst of war curb an evil which forced recognition even from Chinese Gordon. From the East African coast and especially the lake districts a stream of slaves went to the coast cities, whence they were sent to Madagascar, Arabia and Persia. In 1862, nineteen thousand slaves a year were passing from the regions about Lake Nyasa to Zanzibar. Minor trade in slaves took place in and about Abyssinia and Somaliland. Turkey began to check the slave traffic between 1860 and 1890. In Morocco it continued longer.

The face of Africa was turned south and west toward these slave traders instead of northward toward the Mediterranean, where for two thousand years and more Europe and Africa had met in legitimate trade and mutual respect. The full significance of the battle at Tondibi, which overthrew the Askias, was now clear. Hereafter Africa for centuries was to appear before the world, not as the land of gold and ivory, of Gongo Mussa and Meroe, but as a bound and captive slave, dumb and degraded.

The natural desire to avoid a painful subject has led historians to gloss over the details of the slave trade and leave the impression that it was a local African West Coast phenomenon and confined to a few years. It was, on the contrary, continent wide and centuries long; an economic, social, and political catastrophe probably unparalleled in human history.

Usually the slave trade has been thought of from its sentimental and moral point of view; but it is its economic significance that is of greatest moment. Whenever the human element in industry is degraded, society must suffer accordingly. In the case of the African slave trade the human element reached its nadir of degradation. Great and significant as was the contribution of black labor to the seventeenth, eighteenth, and nineteenth centuries, its compensation approached zero, falling distinctly and designedly below the cost of human reproduction; and yet on this system was built the wealth and power of modern civilization. One can conceive no more dangerous foundation; because even when the worst aspects were changed and the slave trade limited and the slave given certain legal rights of freedom, nevertheless the possibilities of low wages for the sake of high profits remained an ideal in industry, which made the African slave trade the father of industrial imperialism, and of the persistence of poverty in the richest lands.

As Marx declared: "Under the influence of the colonial system, commerce and navigation ripened like hot-house fruit. Chartered companies were powerful instruments in promoting the concentration of capital. The colonies provided a market for the rising manufactures, and the monopoly of this market intensified accumulation. The treasures obtained outside Europe by direct looting, enslavement, and murder, flowed to the motherland in streams, and were there turned into capital."

The exact proportions of the slave trade can be estimated only approximately. From 1680 to 1688 we know that the English African Company alone sent two hundred forty-nine ships to Africa, shipped there sixty thousand, seven hundred eighty-three Negro slaves, and after losing fourteen thousand, three hundred eighty-seven on the middle passage, delivered forty-six thousand, three hundred ninety-six in America.

It seems probable that 25,000 Negroes a year arrived in America between 1698 and 1707. After the Asiento of 1713 this number rose to 30,000 annually, and before the Revolutionary War it had reached at least 40,000 and perhaps 100,000 slaves a year.

The total number of slaves imported is not known. Dunbar estimates that nearly 900,000 came to America in the sixteenth century, 2,750,000 in the seventeenth, 7,000,000 in the eighteenth, and over 4,000,000 in the nineteenth, perhaps

15,000,000 in all. Certainly it seems that at least 10,000,000 Negroes were expatri-
ated. The Mohammedan slave trade meant the expatriation or forcible migration
in Africa of millions more. (Many other millions were left dead in the wake of the
raiders.) It would be conservative, then, to say that the slave trade cost Negro
Africa from a fourth to a third of its population. And yet people ask today the
cause of the stagnation of culture in that land since 1600!

Such a large number of slaves could be supplied only by organized slave
raiding. The African continent gradually became revolutionized. Whole regions
were depopulated, whole tribes disappeared; the character of people developed
excesses of cruelty instead of the flourishing arts of peace. The dark, irresistible
grasp of fetish took firmer hold on men's minds. Advances toward higher civilization became more difficult. It was a rape of a continent to an extent seldom
if ever paralleled in ancient or modern times.

In the American trade, there were not only the horrors of the slave raid, which
lined the winding paths of the African jungles with bleached bones, but there
were also the horrors of what was called the "middle passage," that is the voyage across the Atlantic. As Sir William Dolben said, "The Negroes were chained
to each other hand and foot, and stowed so close that they were not allowed
above a foot and a half for each in breadth. Thus crammed together like herrings
in a barrel, they contracted putrid and fatal disorders; so that they who came to
inspect them in a morning had occasionally to pick dead slaves out of their rows,
and to unchain their carcases from the bodies of their wretched fellow-sufferers
to whom they had been fastened."[12]

It was estimated that out of every one hundred lot shipped from Africa only
about fifty lived to be effective laborers across the sea; and among the whites
more seamen died in that trade in one year than in the whole remaining trade of
England in two. The full realization of the horrors of the slave trade was slow in
reaching the ears and conscience of the modern world, just as today the treatment
of natives in European colonies is brought to publicity with the greatest difficulty.
The first move against the slave trade in England came in Parliament in 1776, but
it was not until thirty-one years later, in 1807, that the trade was banned through
the arduous labors of Clarkson, Wilberforce, Sharpe, and others.

Denmark had already abolished the trade, and the United States attempted to
do so the following year. Portugal and Spain were induced to abolish the trade
between 1815 and 1830. Notwithstanding these laws, the contraband trade went
on until the beginning of the Civil War in America. The reasons for this were the
enormous profit of the trade and the continued demand of the American slave
barons, who had no sympathy with the efforts to stop their source of cheap labor
supply.

However, philanthropy was not working alone to overthrow Negro slavery
and the slave trade. It was seen, first in England and later in other countries,
that slavery as an industrial system could not be made to work satisfactorily in
modern times. Its cost tended to become too great, as the sources of supply of
slaves dried up; on the other hand, the slave insurrections from the very beginning threatened the system, as modern labor strikes have threatened capitalism,
from the time when the slaves rose on the plantation of Diego Columbus down

to the Civil War in America. Actual and potential slave insurrections in the West Indies, in North and South America, kept the slave owners in apprehension and turmoil, or called for a police system difficult to maintain.

The red revolt of Haiti struck the knell of the slave trade. In North America revolt finally took the form of organized running away to the North. All this with the growing scarcity of suitable land led to the abolition of the slave trade, the American Civil War and the disappearance of the American slave system. Further effort stopped the Mohammedan slave raider, but slowly because its philanthropic objects were clouded and hindered by the new Colonial Imperialism of Christian lands, which sought not wholly to abolish slavery but rather to re-establish it under new names, with a restricted slave trade.

Such is the story of the Rape of Ethiopia—a sordid, pitiful, cruel tale. Raphael painted, Luther preached, Corneille wrote, and Milton sang; and through it all, for four hundred years, the dark captives wound to the sea amid the bleaching bones of the dead; for four hundred years the sharks followed the scurrying ships; for four hundred years America was strewn with the living and dying millions of a transplanted race; for four hundred years Ethiopia stretched forth her hands unto God.

NOTES

1. Lichtenberger, *Development of Social Theory*, p. 153.
2. Cooley, *The Negro Land of the Arabs*, p. 139.
3. Williams, *The People and Politics of Latin America*, p. 100.
4. *Cf.* Helps, *Spanish Conquest*, Vol. IV, p. 401.
5. Helps, *op. cit.*, Vol. I, pp. 219–220.
6. Helps, *op. cit.*, Vol. II, pp. 18–19.
7. Helps, *op. cit.*, Vol. III, pp. 211–212.
8. Herskovits, "On the Provenience of the New World Negroes," *Social Forces*, December, 1933, pp. 251, 252.
9. Theal, *History and Ethnography of South Africa before 1795*, Vol. I, p. 476.
10. Williams, "Africa and the Rise of Capitalism," in *Howard University Studies in the Social Sciences*, Vol. I, No. 1.
11. Quoted in Williams, p. 28.
12. Ingram, *History of Slavery*, p. 152.

CHAPTER VIII

◆

Western Slave Marts

The West Indies, or Antilles, consist of 90,000 square miles of land, among the most beautiful spots in the world, strewn through endless areas of tropical waters and inhabited today by ten million persons mostly of Negro descent.

Late in the fifteenth century these islands were discovered; beautiful, fertile but sparsely inhabited. In the sixteenth century the treasure hunt started. Columbus, Balboa, Cortez, and Pizarro searched and killed for gold and found it; but the real wealth of the Indies was not discovered until the seventeenth century, when sugar planting began in 1650, followed by cotton, coffee and other crops. All that was needed was labor and for that the Indians were enslaved and nearly exterminated. Then Negroes from Africa began to arrive. The main African labor supply came in the eighteenth century. England had kept Spain from falling into the lap of either Austria or Louis XIV by the war of Spanish Succession and extracted as her pay not only Gibraltar but the right to the Spanish slave trade, the Asiento. She poured slaves into the New World and thus began her mastery of the seas, her manufactures and her trades. By the middle of the eighteenth century new finance capital based on African and American gold, new wealth based on West Indian crops, established the capitalistic system in Europe. The buying of labor and selling of goods, thus encouraged throughout Europe, brought prosperity and self-assurance to capitalists and employers.

France built in Haiti the richest colony in the world and thus encouraged her merchants, trade and manufacturers to throw off the yoke of a lazy, elegant and wastrel nobility. The revolution beginning in a cry for commercial freedom, rose rapidly to a demand for a political dictatorship of the proletariat. Before this was curbed, its fire caught the tinder in the West Indies—a contingency wholly undreamed of—and under Toussaint the Savior, actually in the end abolished Negro slavery, posing a new problem for nineteenth century democracy.

We can only sketch the history of the Negro in the West Indies, here and there, for lack of complete and accessible data. But even fugitive facts are illuminating. According to some accounts Alonzo, "The Negro," piloted one of the ships of Columbus,[1] and it has been claimed that Negroes reached America from Africa in prehistoric times. Some Negroid and Australoid skulls have been found, and Leo Wiener traces direct cultural connection between Africa and America in art, food, language and religion.

Continually Negroes appear with the explorers. Nuflo de Olana, a Negro, was with Balboa when he discovered the Pacific Ocean,[2] and afterward thirty Negroes helped Balboa direct the work of over five hundred Indians in transporting the material for his ships across the mountains to the South Sea.[3]

Cortez carried Negroes and Indians with him from Cuba to Mexico and one of these Negroes was the first to sow and reap grain there. There were two Negroes with Velas in 1520, and two hundred black slaves with Alvarado on his desperate expedition to Quito. Almagro and Valdivia in 1525 were saved from death by Negroes.[4]

As early as 1528 there were about 10,000 Negroes in the New World. We hear of one sent as an agent of the Spanish to burn a native village in Honduras. In 1539 they accompanied De Soto and one of them stayed among the Indians in Alabama and became the first settler from the Old World. In 1555 in Santiago de Chile a free Negro owned land in the town. Menendez had a company of trained Negro artisans and agriculturists when he founded St. Augustine in 1565.[5]

In the seventeenth century began systematic transportation of black labor from Africa to the developed slave markets of the West Indies and America. Slaves imported under the Asiento treaties reached all parts of the Americas. Spanish America had, by the close of the eighteenth century, ten thousand Negroes in San Domingo, eighty-four thousand in Cuba, fifty thousand in Puerto Rico, sixty thousand in Louisiana and Florida, and sixty thousand in Central and South America.

The history of Negroes in the West Indies and South America falls naturally into two parts: that before and that after the emancipation of the slaves; and the history of slavery may best be considered according to the exploiting nations. Spanish American history is centered in Cuba, San Domingo, Puerto Rico, Central and South America, as well as in Jamaica and other islands which early were lost to Spain. It was the role of the Spaniards to explore and to make some beginnings of the plantation system with slave labor.

English and French pirates came to Cuba in the sixteenth century. The Indians were exterminated or mingled their blood with an increasing number of Negro slaves, and illicit trade in contravention to Spanish law was the early basis of Cuba's wealth. Havana was captured by the British in the eighteenth century but exchanged for Florida. The Spanish part of San Domingo was ceded to France and afterwards became independent. Cuba was practically independent during the latter part of the eighteenth and the first part of the nineteenth century, because of the wars in Europe and the freedom of trade.

Intensive exploitation of the Spanish slaves did not begin until the second quarter of the nineteenth century. A desire to be revenged on England and encouragement of shipping and industry under Charles III led to efforts to develop Cuba. Slaves were rushed in between 1753 and 1790; the Cuban sugar crop multiplied tenfold. After the French Revolution Cuba replaced San Domingo as a producer of sugar. This development led to increased exploitation of the slaves until after the San Domingan revolt. Then the Cuban slaves under José Aponte also attempted an uprising. Estates were burned and owners killed but the leader was finally captured and hanged. In 1774 Cuba had a population of 160,000 which increased rapidly to over a half million in 1817. As early as the sixteenth century Negroes formed over half the population.

In the nineteenth century the island was threatened with annexation by both European and American countries. It was ruled at the time by irresponsible captains-general and the increased exploitation led to a bloody persecution of Negroes in 1844 because of a slave plot. Toward 1850 the pro-slavery interests in the United States schemed to annex Cuba. The Ostend Manifesto proclaimed this and Presidents Pierce and Buchanan encouraged it. There were three filibustering expeditions.

Corrupt administration, heavy taxes and harsh driving of labor led finally to the Cuban Ten Years war in 1866, in which Negroes and white rebels joined. They demanded the abolition of slavery and equal political rights for natives and foreigners, whites and blacks. The war was cruel and bloody, but ended in 1878 with the legal abolition of slavery, while a further uprising the following year demanded civil rights for Negroes. The majority of Cuban Negroes, however, were not really freed until the eighties.

In Puerto Rico, Spanish exploitation early exterminated the Indians. They were followed by hordes of Negro slaves, and by invasion of Indians from other islands. Hurricanes, pirates and the attacks of Europeans made the island unhappy for years. Both the English and Dutch attempted its capture, but it remained in the hands of the Spanish until 1898. East of Puerto Rico are a hundred little islands long known as the Virgin Islands. They were the favorite resort of buccaneers in the seventeenth century and were subject to English and Danish rule in the early nineteenth century.

The Spaniards settled the lowlands of Central America, and Venezuela, Ecuador, Colombia and Peru in South America. They introduced there considerable numbers of slaves and encountered repeated slave insurrections. On the coast of Mexico there were in the second half of the sixteenth century nearly twenty thousand Negroes. They took part in various expeditions and before 1530 led a desperate insurrection.

It was from Mexico that the expedition started out to discover the land which is now New Mexico. It was led by Steven Dorantes or Estevanico, an intelligent black man who came to America with the Narvaez expedition in 1527. He and three Spaniards survived a succession of disasters and reached Mexico from Florida by the overland route. Because of his knowledge of Indian tongues, Estevanico guided the expedition to the "Seven Cities of Cibola," as the land of the Zuñis was supposed to be. He reached the pueblos but was killed by the Indians and the expedition following him turned back. The legend of his visit is still current among the Zuñi Indians. It was forty years before further attempts were made to penetrate New Mexico.

In Cuba and Central America bands of fugitive slaves who took refuge in the mountains were known as "maroons." They were a continual cause of trouble in Jamaica and San Domingo, and fought fiercely with the Spanish in Mexico. In the middle of the sixteenth century they were attacking the treasure trains

PRESENT DISTRIBUTION OF NEGROES IN THE NEW WORLD

107

crossing the isthmus, and under a black leader, Bayano, organized a regular government. The colony started a campaign against them in 1560 and eventually captured Bayano and sent him to Spain. His followers founded the city of San Diego de Principe.

The maroons spread, organized new revolts, and intermarried with the Indians, and finally formed the race known as the Mosquitoes. By the seventeenth century they mustered forty thousand soldiers and later, in alliance with the Indians, swept the Spaniards from the coast.

The Isthmus of Panama has seen strange vicissitudes. An order of black monks was inaugurated by the Catholic Church in Spanish America early in the sixteenth century and by the middle of the seventeenth a Negro freedman and charcoal burner saw his son, Francisco Xavier de Luna Victoria, become Bishop of Panama, the first native Catholic bishop in America.

A Negro landed with the first Spaniards in Peru and Negroes were among those who later welcomed Drake and offered him aid. They repeatedly led rebellions and furnished one saint for the Catholic Church, Brother Martin de Porres. This black priest was a Franciscan monk and suffered much racial discrimination. He gave his life to helping the poor. In the Argentine, the Indian slaves, killed off by severe labor, were replaced by Negroes, many of whom later became household servants and formed a considerable part of the population of Buenos Aires and Cordoba.

The Portuguese followed the Spaniards in America. Their empire, because of the Bull of Demarcation, centered in Brazil, which juts far enough to the eastward to fall within the western limits set by the pope. Slaves were not introduced in considerable number until the middle of the eighteenth century, after the discovery of gold and diamonds. Gradually the seaboard from Pernambuco to Rio de Janeiro and north was filled with Negroes. The slave trade was abolished by Portugal north of the equator in 1815 and south of the equator in 1830, but the illicit trade persisted long after this. Between 1800 and 1850 probably two million Negroes were poured into Brazil.

By the aid of Negroes, the Portuguese penetrated the valley of the Amazon from the Parana to Guiana. Negroes helped them conquer the land, fighting against the French in Rio de Janeiro in 1711. Nash writes in the *Conquest of Brazil*, "When gold came to dominate the economic life of Brazil, the Negro assumed the entire load. Every panful of earth from which the gold was washed, every clod of cascalho from which diamonds were gleaned, and all the millions of tons that yielded nothing at all, were moved by Negroes carrying upon their stalwart heads the loads their masters were too stupid to move on wheelbarrows. Negroes carried upon their well-muscled backs the full weight of that Portuguese Empire in the eighteenth century, as they alone carried the weight of the Brazilian Empire for the first half of the new nineteenth century."

There were repeated insurrections among the Brazilian Negroes. The Palmares in 1695, a tribe of slaves, held back an army of seven thousand and their leaders committed suicide when finally defeated. In 1719 there was a widespread slave conspiracy and between 1828 and 1837 Mohammedan Negroes revolted repeatedly.

The Dutch supplanted the Portuguese as slave traders on the African coast and brought the first slaves to the North American continent. In South America they settled Guiana in 1616 and began the cultivation of sugar cane. Later, to curb the revolting Negroes, they brought in East Indian coolies. The so-called Bush Negroes in the interior of Guiana were descendants of runaway slaves, and early established villages and an organized government. By the end of the seventeenth century they had large settlements on the Suriname River and before the middle of the eighteenth century they were making repeated raids on the plantations. From 1715 to 1763 fighting continued until at last formal treaties between the Dutch and Negroes were made. Today the Bush Negroes retain their independence and when they drink with the white man their toast is "free."[6]

Eventually the English forced the Dutch out of the slave trade and became the great slave traders of the world. Their empire in America centered in the Barbados, Jamaica and other West India islands and in the American colonies on the mainland. Large numbers of Negroes were imported, reaching a total of over 50,000 annually late in the eighteenth century. Between 1680 and 1786 it is estimated that over two million slaves were imported into the British West Indies. Even young Irish peasants were "hunted down as men hunt down game, and were forcibly put on board ship, and sold to the planters in Barbados."[7]

Barbados, seized in 1625, developed a savage slave code, and the result was slave insurrections in 1674, 1692, and 1702. These were not successful, but a rising in 1816 under the leadership of a mulatto, Washington Franklin, destroyed much property. A Negro insurrection in Dominica under Farcel greatly exercised England in 1791 and 1794 and delayed slave trade abolition; from 1844 to 1893 further uprisings took place.

The chief island domain of English slavery was Jamaica. It was Oliver Cromwell who, in his zeal for God and the slave trade, sent an expedition to seize San Domingo. His fleet, driven off there, took Jamaica from Spain in 1655. The English found the mountains already infested with fifteen hundred or more runaway slaves known as maroons, and more Negroes continually joined them. In 1663 the freedom of the maroons was acknowledged, land was given them, and their leader, Juan de Bolas, was made a colonel in the militia. He was killed, however, in the following year, and from 1664 to 1738, three thousand or more black maroons fought the British in guerilla warfare. Soldiers, Indians, and dogs were sent against them, and finally in 1738 Captain Cudjo and other chiefs made a formal treaty of peace with Governor Trelawney. They were granted twenty-five hundred acres, their freedom was recognized, and they were promised bonuses for runaway slaves returned by them.

The peace lasted until 1795, when, inspired by Haiti, they rebelled again, killed planters, and tried to incite a general slave insurrection. They gave the British a severe drubbing. Bloodhounds again were imported. The maroons offered to surrender on the express condition that none of their number should be deported from the island, as the legislature wished. General Walpole hesitated, but could get peace on no other terms and so gave his word. The maroons surrendered their arms, and immediately the whites seized six hundred of the ringleaders and transported them to the snows of Nova Scotia! The legislature then voted a sword worth twenty-five hundred dollars to General Walpole, which he indignantly refused to accept. Eventually many of these exiled maroons found their way to Sierra Leone, West Africa.

The pressing desire for peace with the maroons on the part of the white planters arose from the new sugar culture introduced in 1673. A greatly increased demand for slaves followed, and between 1700 and 1786 six hundred ten thousand slaves were imported. In 1768 there were exported from Jamaica 56,000 hogsheads of sugar; 15,500 puns of rum; 2,500 bags of cotton; 4,000 bags of coffee and, in addition to this, pimento, ginger, log-wood, mahogany, molasses, and hides. In 1774 these exports had increased and in 1787, they were worth two million pounds sterling. At the close of 1791 Jamaica had seven hundred sixty-seven sugar plantations with 140,000 Negroes; six hundred seven coffee plantations with 21,000 Negroes; 1,047 grazing and breeding farms with 31,000 Negroes; and a number of small settlements for cotton, ginger, pimento, etc., employing 58,000 Negroes.

The revolution in San Domingo cut off the French colonies from Europe. The price of sugar in London rose from thirty-two shillings a cwt. in 1793 to fifty-eight shillings, and then advanced until the end of 1798 when it touched eighty-seven shillings. Jamaica made every effort to increase its output with additional slave labor and the introduction of a different species of cane. Several sugar islands were captured and the British slave trade rose from twenty-five thousand to fifty-seven thousand a year.

At the beginning of the nineteenth century the value of Jamaica "as British property" was estimated at twelve and a half million pounds sterling in 250,000 slaves and twenty-six and a half million in land and other property; or thirty-nine million pounds in all.[8]

But already change was in the air. The American Revolution stopped the English continental slave trade and brought rivalry in the shipping trade. The French Revolution threatened all property and the Haitian revolt cut security of investment from beneath the feet of slavery. Sugar, then the chief slave crop, reeled drunkenly from twenty-two dollars a hundredweight after Toussaint had burned Haitian plantations, to a low of seven dollars, when not only Jamaica but Cuba began to pour increasing amounts on the glutted market.

In Hamburg, where British ships sold their sugar, there were eighty-three bankruptcies in four months, in 1800–01, and Parliament had to loan the West Indian merchants of Liverpool two and a half million dollars. The profit in American slavery and the slave trade was beginning to disappear. English capital turned to Africa and Asia.

When now the deadening manacles of profit, chaining English commerce to the slave trade and slavery, began to loosen, there was a chance for humanity and philanthropy to express itself in England; and this chance was broadened by the French Revolution and the Haitian Revolt. A splendid and unselfish crusade for human freedom arose, led by Sharpe, Wilberforce and Buxton and by philanthropists throughout the world. The first fruit was the suppression of the African slave trade, which was begun in 1807 but not finished until after the American Civil War. There followed the abolition of slavery, beginning in 1833 and ending legally in 1838 in the British islands, but continuing actually in some other West

India islands down to 1870. It was accompanied by wide unrest, as, for instance, the insurrection in northwest Jamaica in 1831, when Negroes destroyed nearly three and a half million dollars' worth of property and brought wide ruin on the planters.

In many of the minor islands under English control curious bits of slave history may be unearthed. In the island of St. Vincent, Indians sought to enslave fugitive Negroes, but the Negroes drove the Indian men away and took the Carib women. The black Caribs fought with the English and others for three-quarters of a century when finally the British took possession in 1763. Eventually the black Caribs received a third of the island as their property. Then they helped the French against the British and were deported to the island of Ruatan off Honduras.

The tiny island of St. Lucia is one of the most charming spots in the tropics. It was long held by the French who fortified it and held it with two thousand Negro soldiers. In 1796 England tried to seize it and stop the spread of French revolutionary ideas of equality. It took eleven thousand English soldiers a month to secure the fortifications and then the Negroes took to the woods. Abercrombie and Sir John Moore nearly lost their lives fighting against these guerillas. They finally were induced to lay down their arms on condition that they remain free. Later they were formed into an English regiment and sent to fight on the coast of Africa.

Owing to wars with England, the French never became great slave traders and their West Indian possessions were supplied mainly by the Dutch and Portuguese in the earlier days, although the French Royal Senegal Company held the coveted Asiento from 1701 to 1713. On the other hand, the French developed on the island of San Domingo a system of slavery which had great influence upon the Negro race and the economic history of the world.

French slavery centered in San Domingo, Guadeloupe, Martinique, some other small islands and French Guiana. Later the French introduced slaves into Louisiana and on the Alabama coast. Martinique and Guadeloupe were seized in 1639 and Guiana in 1674. There was much trouble with the Indians and with the British, but eventually these colonies remained French. In Martinique, the Indians were exterminated and sugar planting began there in 1650. Within a century there were sixty thousand slaves in the island and it took three revolts and a civil war to make them free.

It was in the island of San Domingo, however, that French slavery centered. Ovando arrived there in 1502. He imported 40,000 Indians from the Bahamas to replace the local Indians who were rapidly disappearing. Sugar cane was planted in 1506 and immediately became an important product. Diego, son of Columbus, was the next governor, but in six years the Indian population of 60,000 had decreased to 14,000. Africans began to be imported as early as 1510, and by 1522 the new blacks had already staged a rebellion.

Trade was carefully guarded as a Spanish monopoly, but the English and French broke into it by force. The Spaniards did not proceed with the cultivation and organization of the sugar traffic and as the buccaneers gradually invaded the island, cultivation dwindled. In 1586, Drake attacked San Domingo City and secured a ransom of thirty thousand dollars; by the beginning of the seventeenth century the commerce between San Domingo and Spain had been practically destroyed.

The French West India Company gradually began to occupy the island and their right to the western part was recognized in the Treaty of Ryswick. By 1685 there were so many slaves and mulattoes that Louis XIV issued his celebrated Code Noir, which was notable in compelling bachelor masters, fathers of mulatto children, to marry their concubines. Children followed the condition of the mother as to slavery or freedom; slaves could have no property; harsh punishments were provided for, but families could not be separated by sale, except in the case of grown children; emancipation with full civil rights was made possible for any slave twenty years of age or more. Indigo, cocoa and sugar cane were planted and by 1728 there were 50,000 Negroes, who increased to 172,000 in a quarter of a century.

From the middle of the eighteenth century to the French Revolution, French San Domingo was counted as being the richest colonial possession in the world. Intense and complete organization of the plantations became general. There were windmills, coffee plantations, sugar factories, acres of vanilla bushes, wide fields of cotton and sugar cane. Thousands of black slaves were at work and slept in huts at the edge of the cultivated land. Many of the owners lived in luxury almost barbaric, with palaces, gilded coaches, scores of horses, well-trained servants and unbounded power. Probably nowhere else in America was existence more delightful for the white man than in San Domingo in the eighteenth century. Ten thousand square miles produced more sugar, coffee, chocolate, indigo, timber, dye-woods and spices than all the rest of the West Indies put together.

The French bourgeoisie, even shackled as they were by the privileges and pretensions of the nobility, developed fast in the eighteenth century. Between 1714 and 1789 French commerce quadrupled. At the outbreak of the French Revolution there were three thousand indigo plantations and an equal number of coffee plantations in San Domingo. Eight hundred great estates produced sugar and as many others produced cotton. Cocoa was a great crop and there were distilleries, lime kilns, brick yards and potteries. In 1788 there were imported from France into the French part of San Domingo, goods to the value of $21,000,000, including flour, wine, clothing and manufactures. These importations were carried in five hundred eighty vessels, and ninety-eight other French ships plied from the coast of Africa. In 1788 there were brought to San Domingo twenty-nine thousand five hundred slaves in ninety-eight vessels, including fifteen thousand men, seven thousand women and seven thousand children. In ten years, 1782 to 1792, the number of slaves employed on its plantations probably doubled.

French San Domingo in 1791 exported one hundred seventy-seven million pounds of sugar, seventy-four million pounds of coffee, seven million pounds of cotton and nearly seven million pounds of dye-woods. The value of the exports was about fifty million dollars and the total value of the plantation and slaves was over one hundred-ninety million dollars. The taxes laid on San Domingo were a considerable source of French revenue and its commerce employed most of the French shipping.

There was great increase in the white emigration from France to San Domingo in the middle of the eighteenth century. This included a class of poor whites (petits blancs), persons with little capital, but eager to get rich, and jealous and bitter against the mulattoes and free Negroes, who were their economic rivals. There also came numbers of marriageable young French women without dowry. These, however, found themselves in little demand, the Frenchmen preferring to marry rich mulatto girls. Jealousy and envy thus arose between the petits blancs, the white women and the colored folk. After the Peace of 1763, a number of young mulattoes educated in the new philosophy of France returned to San Domingo and wanted to take part in public affairs.

Color prejudice grew in intensity and gradually mulattoes were deprived of civil and political rights and restricted in their occupations. Edicts regulated their clothing, names and social intercourse. All this was patently illegal since article fifty-nine of the Code Noir declared that freed slaves enjoyed the rights and privileges of citizens.

In 1771 the Minister of Colonies declared against granting mulattoes certificates of citizenship and said that Louis XV was determined to maintain the principle that colored people and their posterity could never be permitted the same advantages as whites. After 1777 mulattoes were refused the right to come to France.

The outbreak of revolution in France in 1787 had extraordinary repercussions in San Domingo. Here the planters (grands blancs), the poor whites (petits blancs) and the mulattoes were all aroused. The planters demanded sole recognition as citizens, excluding both the petits blancs and the mulattoes. The mulattoes were excluded because of their race and the petits blancs because they did not own at least twenty-five slaves. The grands blancs wanted membership in both the French Constituent Assembly and in the provincial assembly limited to grands blancs. They also supported the monarchy against the general trend of the revolution.

The petits blancs wanted membership in both assemblies and they supported the revolution against the king. Both groups opposed the demands of the mulattoes, while the mulattoes sought alliance with either or both groups of whites in order to achieve their rights.

As soon as the States-General was summoned, the planters of Haiti secretly elected delegates to represent the island in the Constituent Assembly. Six of these finally were admitted. But the mulattoes were also alert. Numbers of them were resident in Paris. They and others in the West Indies had been inspired by current radical thought and by the American Declaration of Independence.

Indeed in 1779, when the French undertook to help American independence, Comte d'Estaing was able to raise eight hundred volunteers among Haitian blacks and mulattoes, including Rigaud and the great Christophe, who at the siege of Savannah saved the American army from annihilation by the British. It was here that Pulaski and Sergeant Jasper were killed, and among the British leaders was Maitland, who later tried to seize San Domingo.

Colored people suffered civil and political disabilities in San Domingo, but on the other hand they held a considerable amount of land and wealth. In France they had a number of distinguished and influential friends. In the fall of 1789 they sent a delegation to Paris, including Julien Raymond and Vincent Ogé. They also sent six million francs in gold and a promise to contribute this and one-fifth of the property which the mulattoes owned in San Domingo to the public debt. These delegates were received by the National Assembly October 22, 1789, and they presented a petition asking citizenship rights in San Domingo for free Negroes. The presiding officer replied politely if vaguely that "not a single part of the nation shall ask in vain for its rights from the assembly of the representatives of the French people."

However, the Club Massiac, the Paris rendezvous of the San Domingan planters, moved swiftly and their advice was backed by petitions from the manufacturers and merchants of the great French cities. Consequently March 8, 1790, the Constituent Assembly voted by a large majority not to interfere with the interior government of the colonies, or subject them to laws "incompatible with their local establishments"; and also buttressed the slave trade by declaring that the National Assembly would not cause any innovation to be made, directly or indirectly, "in any system of commerce in which the colonies were already concerned."[9]

This was the beginning of a series of extraordinary and contradictory pronouncements on the part of the government of France. The Amis des Noirs bestirred themselves and on March 18 secured supplementary instructions to the vote of March 8, declaring that free Negroes were citizens and could vote in parish elections.

On May 15, 1791, came a strong and definite pronouncement giving the privilege of French citizenship to free Negroes in the colony and the right to vote and sit in colonial assemblies. Notwithstanding this, on September 24 the same year, just before it went out of existence, the Constituent Assembly virtually repealed this decree, leaving the fate of the free Negroes and the mulattoes in the hands of the Colonial Assembly.

This was the last effort of the bourgeoisie in the Constituent Assembly, before the meeting of the more radical Legislative Assembly. In the Legislative Assembly in April, 1892, the right of free Negroes to vote was affirmed and this decree was signed by the king. As the government got more radical under the Committee of Safety in 1793, July 22, the emancipation of slaves was announced and confirmed February 4, 1794. Notwithstanding this, in 1801 Napoleon, by decree, re-established slavery.

These contradictory decrees registered the gradual advance of French public opinion to the point of admitting the manhood rights of Negroes; and at the same time showed the contradictory and restraining effect of colonial planter opinion and economic power in France.

Let us follow this history more in detail both in France and San Domingo. The Negroes from San Domingo and other colored folk in Paris after their demands upon the Constituent Assembly, were set upon, assaulted and in some cases murdered. Others escaped to San Domingo. As we have said the Amis des Noirs succeeded in getting the decree of March 8, 1790, supplemented March 28 by "instructions recognizing the right to vote in parishes of all free persons twenty-five years of age." The authorities of Martinique, Guadeloupe and San Domingo all decreed that this applied only to white persons.

Meantime, the white planters became divided into bitter factions. The great landholders and large investors regarded the revolution as a movement to turn over the conduct of the colony into their hands; while the petits blancs proposed taking it from the hands of the great landholders and proprietors into their own; some of the officials, hoping for a restoration of royal power, were waiting to sail in with that tide. None of these factions envisaged any real division of power with the mulattoes, and against this attitude the mulattoes began to plot and even to fight.

Bitterly disappointed with the decision of the French assembly in 1790, Ogé returned to America. He went by way of the United States in order to collect arms and escape observation. Landing secretly in the north of San Domingo, he collected a force of three hundred men. They were immediately attacked by a much larger force from Cap François and compelled to take refuge in the Spanish part of the island. The governor surrendered them, and Ogé and Chavannes, the two leaders, March 12, 1791, were sentenced "whilst alive to have their arms, legs, thighs and spines broken; and afterward to be placed on a wheel, their faces toward Heaven, and there to stay as long as it would please God to preserve their lives; and when dead, their heads were to be cut off and exposed on poles."[10] This sentence was executed in the presence of the members of the Northern Provincial Assembly gathered in state.

When the news of this barbaric treatment reached France, there was a storm of indignation. A pantomime on the story of Ogé was given in the theaters and planters were afraid to appear in the streets of Paris. They and their friends threatened that if anything was done against slavery, the colonies would be destroyed. "Perish the colonies," said Robespierre, "rather than sacrifice one iota of our principles." The majority reiterated the sentiment, and the famous decree of the 15th of May, 1791, was pronounced "amidst the acclamation and applause of the multitude."[11]

The decree of May 15, 1791, gave the privilege of French citizenship to free Negroes in the colonies and the right to vote and sit in the parochial and colonial assemblies. When the news of this decree reached San Domingo, the white people went quite crazy; a caste war was predicted and the whites swore they would never yield. There was talk of secession, of confiscating French goods; and the national cockade was thrown into the gutter to be trampled upon. The representatives of the planters withdrew from the Constituent Assembly. On the eighth of June, 1791, Abbé Gregoire, protagonist of the blacks, wrote his famous letter to the citizens of color in the French West Indies: "You were men, you are now citizens."

A newly elected colonial assembly met in San Domingo August 9 and then adjourned to await three commissioners which France was sending to pacify the colony. Up to this point practically the whole public controversy had turned, first, upon the future repositories of power in the colonies, whether it was to be the former great proprietors or whether the poorer whites would share; these together formed forty thousand of the inhabitants. This controversy had resulted in the beginning of civil war between the whites and into this situation was precipitated the question of the future status of the twenty-eight thousand free Negroes and mulattoes, which threatened to add a race war.

Up to this point practically nothing definite had been said about four hundred and fifty-two thousand black slaves. Although Lameth, in his great speech before the Constituent Assembly, had mentioned the possible liberation of the blacks, this was regarded only as a vague and indefinite matter of the future.

Then suddenly at midnight, August twenty-second, the representatives of the half million black slaves of Haiti rose in a bloody revolt that shook the modern world. "In an instant twelve hundred coffee and two-hundred sugar plantations were in flames; the buildings, the machinery, the farmhouses, were reduced to ashes; and the unfortunate proprietors were hunted down, murdered, or thrown into the flames, by the infuriated Negroes. The horrors of a servile war universally appeared. The unchained African signalized his ingenuity by the discovery of new methods and unheard of modes of torture."[12]

The revolt was all the more startling because while it had been in the fears and imagination of the colonists for two hundred years, it was always undreamed of as an actual occurrence. There had been numberless revolts, which had spread terror to whites all over the West Indies, Central America and the mainland of the United States; but once they were quickly suppressed, their details and facts were minimized, the records destroyed and the memory forgotten.

In San Domingo itself the dangers of slave revolts were not unknown. For years runaway slaves had hidden in the mountains, especially in the northeastern part of the island. There were serious slave revolts in 1679, 1691 and 1718, and in the middle of the eighteenth century a Negro, Macandel, carried out systematic poisoning which created a panic.

After eight years of open warfare with the French and Spanish, these maroons had completed a treaty of peace with the French in 1780. The maroons were organized under chiefs, among whom were Père Jean in 1679; Michel in 1713; Colas in 1720; Polydor, 1730; Macandel, 1758; Canga, 1777; and Santiague, 1782. The great chief at the time of the slave revolt was Jean François, who was soon succeeded by Biassou and after Biassou came Toussaint L'Ouverture.

Pierre Dominic Toussaint, known as Toussaint L'Ouverture, joined these maroon bands, where he was called "the doctor of the armies of the king," and soon became leading aid to Jean François and Biassou. Upon their deaths Toussaint rose to the chief command. He acquired complete control over the blacks, not only in military matters, but in politics and social organization.

Toussaint was one of the great men of the world. He made an extraordinary impression upon those who knew him personally or studied his life, whether they were friends or enemies. August Comte included him with Washington, Plato, Buddha and Charlemagne as worthy to replace all the calendar saints. Morvins, biographer of Napoleon, calls him "a man of genius." Beauchamp refers to him as "one of the most extraordinary men of a period when so many extraordinary men appeared on the scene." Lamartine wrote a drama with Toussaint as his hero. Harriet Martineau wrote a novel on his life. Whittier and Wordsworth published poems about him. Sir Spenser St. John, consular agent in Haiti, called him "the one grand figure of a cruel war." Rainsford, a British officer, refers to him as "that truly great man." Chateaubriand charges that Bonaparte not only murdered, but imitated him.

There seems to be little doubt that Toussaint planned and led the revolt of 1791. He was at that time about forty-eight years of age, a small, rather ugly black man, without a drop of white blood. His plans and those of the maroons generally were hidden behind the veil of heathen rites. Much has been written about West Indian voodoo. Its ceremonies and sacrifices were matters of curiosity and ridicule among planters and travelers. They represented, at first, a survival of primitive African animism. Later, equipped with a priesthood, weird African ceremonies and the signaling of drums and tomtoms, they called slaves to worship in the dark mountains of central San Domingo; but they also concealed and protected the plotting of their leaders and directors.

Here it was that, at the time of the revolution, Toussaint laid his plans. He watched the developments in France carefully. There is even a story that he was in France with Ogé, but this is doubtful. While a man with no formal education, he read and thought, and had not only a singular and impressive dignity of bearing, but a character which for combined persistence, absolute unselfishness and deep wisdom, has seldom been duplicated. He knew that the new colonial assembly, elected in defiance of French law, since free Negro voters were excluded, was to meet in August. On August fourteenth, in a raging thunder storm, Toussaint and his black leaders made final plans. Their object was to let loose a terror which would make the world pause and give attention to the demands, not only of free Negroes, but of the slaves. Toussaint was convinced that the partial and temporizing attempts of the mulattoes to gain their rights would never be effective. He was determined to strike a tremendous and unheard-of blow.

For four days, the revolt increased. For three weeks the flames spread. Carteau, a planter, who saw it, said: "Picture to yourself, the whole horizon a wall of fire, from which continually rose thick vortices of smoke, whose huge black volumes could be likened only to those frightful storm-clouds which roll onward charged with thunder and lightnings. The rifts in these clouds disclosed flames as great in volume, which rose darting and flashing to the very sky. Such was their voracity that for nearly three weeks we could barely distinguish between day and night, for so long as the rebels found anything to feed the flames, they never ceased to burn."[13]

The governor of the colony helplessly called on the revolting Negroes to surrender. In answer Toussaint wrote: "Sir,—We have never thought of failing in the duty and respect which we owe to the representative of the person of the King, nor even to any of his servants whatever; we have proofs of the fact in our hands; but do you, who are a just man as well as a general, pay us a visit; behold this land which we have watered with our sweat or rather, with our blood,— those edifices which we have raised, and that in the hope of a just reward! Have we obtained it? The King—the whole world—has bewailed our lot, and broken our chains; while, on our part, we, humble victims, were ready for anything, not wishing to abandon our masters. What do we say? We are mistaken; those, who next to God, should have proved our fathers, have been tyrants, monsters unworthy of the fruits of our labours: and do you, brave general, desire that as sheep we should throw ourselves into the jaws of the wolf? No! it is too late. God, who fights for the innocent, is our guide; he will never abandon us. Accordingly, this is our motto—*Death or Victory!*"[14]

Thus while the slaves arranged themselves with the king as symbolic head of the state, the new colonial assembly August 24, 1791, instead of appealing to France, begged protection, especially for their property, from England: "Fire lays waste our possessions, the hands of our Negroes in arms are already dyed with the blood of our brethren. Very prompt assistance is necessary to save the wreck of our fortunes—already half-destroyed; and confined within the towns, we look for your aid."[15]

The governor of Jamaica was wily. He sent five hundred muskets but no other active aid. Meantime the commissioners authorized to pacify the colony arrived in December. They were surprised and shocked at conditions, since no word of the slave revolt had reached Paris before they sailed. Immediately Toussaint showed the statesmanship which was always his strongest card. He sent a white prisoner with a flag of truce and offered to submit. He did not ask complete and immediate abolition of slavery but what was the beginning of it. He demanded general pardon for himself and followers; for a certain comparatively small number of the revolted slaves, comprising probably his most trusted confederates, he asked complete emancipation. For the great body of slaves he demanded that hereafter they work three days a week for their owners and that the other three days they should have the right to work for themselves, presumably on land furnished them by the owners or by the state. There was a current report that France had proposed this step toward emancipation.

It was of course a revolutionary demand, but under the circumstances it should have been treated with consideration. It was not. The commissioners handed the matter over to the Colonial Assembly. The Colonial Assembly at first did not deign to answer. Patiently Toussaint sent a second message by two free Negroes. The bearers were received with contempt and told to return for a reply within ten days. This reply to "revolted slaves" simply asserted that the assembly "cannot hold communication with people armed against the law, against all laws" and then ordered the messengers pre-emptorily "to withdraw!" The French commissioners, however, at this breakdown of preliminary negotiations, tried to propose a general amnesty; but this suited no one and two of the commissioners returned to France in the spring of 1792.

Nevertheless this terrible uprising had already brought results. The rebellion had spread to the southwest and was joined by the mulattoes. Two thousand of them rose in one parish and began murder and destruction. They approached Port au Prince, but at that point the mulatto leaders refused further to co-operate with the blacks and told the white colonists that they had been fighting not for the slaves, but to support the decree of May fifteenth which gave mulattoes the right to vote. Immediately the Colonial Assembly, in order to get the support of the mulattoes and separate them from the slaves, proposed to recognize free people of color as citizens, including even those born of slaves, which the decree did not require. It looked as though the mulattoes had won their fight.

Meantime, however, the National Assembly in France on the point of dissolution passed a decree, September twenty-fourth, putting the whole question of the status of slaves and free Negroes in the power of the Colonial Assembly. Early in November news of the new decree arrived in Haiti. The whites, again sure of French support, immediately repudiated their agreement with the free Negroes, arrested colored people and burned several alive. The free Negroes reorganized their forces and renewed their fight.

In France the revolution was developing. The Constituent Assembly had not established democracy but had placed the state in the control of property holders. It now gave way in October, 1791, to the Legislative Assembly where the power of the workers and their radical leaders was definitely increased. This was shown by the decree of April 4, 1792, which said that "The persons of color, mulattoes and Negroes, free, shall be admitted, as the white colonists, to vote in all the electoral assemblies, and shall be eligible to all positions when they have also the requisite qualifications."[16]

This decree led in San Domingo to a joining of forces between the governor and the mulattoes and the capturing of Port au Prince from the white colonists. The enfranchisement of the free Negroes and the mulattoes in the south was celebrated July fourteenth, but the whites took no part; and in the north the blacks still fought on.

A new commission headed by the Jacobin, Santhonax, arrived in the island and was immediately interrogated by the Colonial Assembly as to their policies. The Assembly declared that the Constituent Assembly of France had agreed with them that there could be no agriculture in San Domingo without slavery; and certainly five hundred thousand savage slaves could not become French citizens. Santhonax replied, "We declare that never was it the intention of the National Assembly to abolish slavery"; Polverel added that if France should interfere with slavery he would give up his commission and return home.

On the other hand, the commission insisted on recognizing the citizenship of the free Negroes, and they proceeded to show this by dissolving the Colonial Assembly and appointing an Intermediary Committee of six whites and six mulattoes. This brought the commission into sharp antagonism with the white colonists and with the new French governor, which opposition finally flared into a civil war and reduced Cap François to ashes. The commission had to abandon the town and found themselves face to face with the black revolt in the north.

These slaves realized the change in their position. They were fighting not only the white planters but the mulatto planters also; and in addition to that, they were now fighting the power of the French government which was evidently recognizing slavery. Great Britain and Spain were now at war with France, and Spain approached Toussaint with an offer of freedom to the slaves; while Great Britain, again appealed to by the planters, planned to help them. In the midst of this France killed her king.

Immediately Toussaint took service under Charles IV of Spain, and joined his forces to the Spanish part of San Domingo. He was amazed and repelled by regicide. He had believed in the King's justice. He and his colleagues were made Spanish generals. He immediately issued a manifesto to all Negroes and

120 + BLACK FOLK

mulattoes. "I am Toussaint L'Ouverture; my name is perhaps known to you. I have undertaken to avenge your wrongs. It is my desire that liberty and equality shall reign in San Domingo. I am striving to this end. Come and unite with us, brothers, and fight with us for the same cause."[17]

Through the prowess of Toussaint, the Spanish pushed the French farther and farther back and in a short time secured possession of nearly the whole north of the island and part of the south. The French commission found themselves in a tight place and tried to extricate themselves in June, 1793, by offering to free all slaves who would enroll in their army. In August they went even further and proclaimed universal emancipation in San Domingo, and this action was confirmed by the French National Convention, February 4, 1794.

The first proclamation had no influence upon Toussaint. As a Spanish general, he refused to recognize the authority of the French. But when the English invaded San Domingo, the aspect of things changed. They landed in September and soon had captured the whole western coast except Port au Prince. Finally they captured that city with its heavy artillery and two million dollars' worth of shipping in its harbor. Toussaint knew the British as slave traders, and he now suspected that Spain wanted vengeance on France rather than freedom for the slaves. When, therefore, the French government affirmed universal emancipation early in 1794, he returned to French allegiance to the open delight of the commission. They said, "Remember that distinctions of color are no more!"

The blacks under Toussaint now proceeded to restore San Domingo to France. The mere magic of his name did much without fighting. In April Toussaint left the Spanish army; in May the French flag was flying at Gonaives. From now on Toussaint was known as L'Ouverture, the Savior. Gradually the whole northern part of the island was in his possession. As Santhonax wrote in his diary, "These Negroes perform miracles of bravery."[18]

In France, the desperate position of the republic in July, 1793, had been changed under the National Convention. The mountain radicals gained the upper hand; the commune ruled Paris and Robespierre ruled France. Horrible as was this Reign of Terror, it was by this means that the traitors within were driven out and France galvanized into self-defense. By the treaty of Basel in 1795, Spain surrendered her portion of San Domingo to France.

Meantime Rigaud and the mulattoes had been making desperate resistance against the British, and the French commission had recognized them by bestowing high office upon colored men. By the end of 1793 they were exercising wide political power. When, however, after the return of Toussaint to allegiance, both he and Rigaud were made brigadier-generals, the old jealousy and mistrust arose between the blacks and mulattoes. It was emphasized by the continuing success of Toussaint and the stalemate between the mulattoes and the British.

Despite Rigaud, the English had captured Port au Prince, but Toussaint attacked them from the east and even after reinforcements brought them under General Howe, he totally defeated them and was made commander-in-chief of the army of San Domingo in May, 1797. Just as Toussaint was getting ready to besiege Port au Prince, the British agreed on a truce giving up the city and retiring to Jeremie. Toussaint's entrance into Port au Prince was an ovation. Flags were flying, flowers were heaped on him and many distinctions and honors proffered. The British after five years were sick of their attempt to conquer Haiti. By September 30, 1796, out of the whole number of white troops, British and foreign, who had landed in Haiti since 1795, at least 15,000 men, only 3,000 were left alive. April 22, 1798, the British Commander Maitland evacuated all towns in Haiti except Mole St. Nicholas. He had only about a thousand troops alive.[19]

The brilliant success of Toussaint not only aroused the envy of the mulattoes, but the suspicion of France. The commission of Santhonax, who had returned, reported to the new government of the Directory in France, the facts concerning Toussaint, and they thought it best to send a governor who would curb his power. Hédouville, the new governor, arrived April 20, 1798, and proposed to take charge of the negotiations with the English; but Maitland, the English commander, was only too glad to affront France by dealing directly and exclusively with Toussaint and to attempt to gain for England by flattery and bribery what he could not take by force. After five years of fighting, the loss of thirty thousand men and the expenditure of one hundred million dollars, he offered to surrender.

On October 1, 1798, Toussaint entered Mole St. Nicholas as conqueror. The white troops saluted him. He was dined in the public square, on a silver service which was afterwards presented him in the name of the King of England. A treaty was signed by which the English gave up the island, recognized Haiti as independent, and entered into a commercial agreement. They then tried secretly to induce Toussaint to declare himself king, but he refused.

Hédouville, insulted, returned to Europe, taking with him a band of eighteen hundred equally disgruntled whites, mulattoes and blacks. As a final thrust he encouraged open strife between Toussaint and Rigaud by recognizing Rigaud as independent ruler in the south. Despite every effort on the part of Toussaint, the breach between his followers and the mulattoes flamed into open hostilities; but by the summer of 1800 Rigaud had been induced voluntarily to leave Haiti for France, where he got his revenge by later joining Le Clerc's expedition.

Toussaint next took possession of the Spanish part of the island and thus became master of the whole island. His next step was a critical one. Haiti was conquered but it had to be organized and governed, and no one was so capable of establishing this government as Toussaint. He, therefore, proceeded to draw up and promulgate a constitution of seventy-seven articles. It abolished slavery forever, and declared all men born there free citizens of the French Republic; and everyone of whatever color eligible for all kinds of employment. Agriculture was especially encouraged; and for the first time in the history of the world, a state constitution provided for free trade.

Beyond these political provisions, he turned attention toward the economic; the island was divided into districts with inspectors who were to see that the freed men returned to their work. A fifth part of the produce of each estate was to go to the workers. Commercial arrangements were made with the United States and England.

This constitution he sent to France for approval, a year after the Eighteenth Brumaire, when the bourgeoisie returned to power with Napoleon as First Consul.

The course of the French Revolution had again changed. The dictatorship of the workers with its welter of blood, gave the owners of capital a chance and excuse to seize the reins of government, hiding behind the patriotism which the attack of all Europe on France had evoked.

To Napoleon, the planter interests appealed. They wrote to Josephine, soon to be Napoleon's wife, that "a black ape, a certain Toussaint," has made himself ruler of the island with the connivance of Santhonax. "Take your kerchief, as you have always done in difficult situations, put it to your weeping eyes, and entreat Barras and the Egyptian hero who has just returned to Paris, General Bonaparte, the victor of Lodi, Arcole, Milan, and Marengo; entreat them by all the saints still surviving in France to put colonial affairs in order at the earliest possible moment, before they become unmanageable. A slave cannot be free, according to the counsel of the gospel."[20]

Napoleon, when he received the constitution from Toussaint, was thirty-two years of age, and in the full tide of his extraordinary career. He could not tolerate colored or black men. He had relieved General Dumas, son of a French Marquis, from his command for no reason but color. Dumas was the father of the author of *The Three Musketeers*, and grandfather of the author of *Camille*.

Napoleon would have ordered an army to San Domingo as soon as he seized power in France, but the English blockade hindered him, and affairs in Egypt were going badly. As soon as the peace of Amiens was signed with the English, Napoleon felt free to handle Toussaint and the blacks. He intimated that Toussaint was usurping French power and not recognizing the paramount authority of the mother country. "A constitution of a Haitian Republic, with a black consul at its head, would be a violation of France's sovereignty, just as the liberty of the Blackamoors is an insult to Europe."

Napoleon gradually elaborated his own plans for the restoration of French colonial power in America. He wanted to know to what extent the French bankers "will assist the republic which is striving to gain a strategic vantage ground on the American continent." Islands were not enough. He wanted foothold in North America.

He admitted that Toussaint, by bringing together the blacks and mulattoes, had prepared San Domingo for France. "We should be making a mistake, if France did not turn to account the prosperity which this black general has brought to our richest island. How can this be done? The Negroes must be reduced to submission. We have grounds for dissatisfaction. Toussaint has submitted to me for confirmation a Negro constitution for the Republic of Haiti. This is an insult to France, and we will make war on Haiti. We will put an announcement in the papers that there is no slavery in our colonies. I, as First Consul, will write a flattering reply to Toussaint L'Ouverture. But what we must achieve is: first, the complete restoration of the former status of the Negroes; secondly, the cautious removal, after careful preparation, of all Negro leaders."[21]

Napoleon's plans were backed not only by the large number of disaffected colonials and exiled planters living in Paris, by speculators and merchants who wanted again to handle the labor and crops of the West Indies, but also the mulatto colony in Paris let their hatred of Toussaint blind them to the real aims of Napoleon and were eager to co-operate with him.

Napoleon figured that by reconquering the queen of the Antilles he would not only keep his large and expensive army active but acquire new prestige. Also he would find a berth for his obscure brother-in-law, Charles Victor Emmanuel Le Clerc. Napoleon's preparations to conquer San Domingo were on a tremendous scale and no expense was spared. Bodies of troops were collected in France, Holland and Spain. Every dockyard was busy. Napoleon gave more personal attention to organizing this expedition than he had to his Egyptian campaign. The army included veterans who had distinguished themselves in all the Napoleonic campaigns. He summoned the young sons of Toussaint, flattered them and sent them as hostages along with the fleet. He promised a bishopric to any of Toussaint's confessors who would induce him to surrender.

Le Clerc sailed with a fleet of five squadrons, leaving Europe on December 14, 1801. He had twenty-one thousand troops on more than eighty vessels; thirteen major generals and twenty-seven brigadier-generals accompanied him and all of the expelled leaders of the mulattoes: Rigaud, Petion, Birot. The orders given to this fleet were a combination of threats, promises and dastardly lying which seem today almost incomprehensible for the head of a great state. "No mistaken notions of soldierly honor," Napoleon admonished Le Clerc. "Remember that Negroes are not human beings."

He sent an open letter to Toussaint, thanking him for restoring San Domingo to France and commending certain things in his constitution, but declaring that much of it conflicted with the dignity and supreme authority of the French nation. At the same time secret instructions were given Le Clerc. The campaign was to be divided into three periods: the first period, from fifteen to twenty days, was to be given up to occupying the forts, quieting the people and getting acquainted with the topography, and taking possession of the plains. The second period, the rebels were to be pursued to death and the confidence of their leaders gained. In the third period, the leaders to be sent to France as prisoners and their remaining followers pursued into the hills to be finished off at leisure.

Late in January, Le Clerc assembled his fleet at the eastern tip of the island. One glance at it convinced Toussaint that the object was conquest and slavery. He had about nineteen thousand men under Christophe, Dessalines and his brother, Paul L'Ouverture. When Le Clerc approached Cap François, Christophe refused to let him enter. After a parley, a battle began which lasted all day and sank one of the chief vessels. Christophe then burned the town, beginning with his own palatial headquarters and destroying more than twenty million dollars' worth of property. He then took to the hills with his troops, leaving only the ashes for Le Clerc to occupy.

This exploit was characteristic of the extraordinary campaign between Le Clerc and Toussaint. With his trained soldiers and his supplies, Le Clerc easily and quickly captured the whole San Domingan coast. The blacks fighting retreated to the hills. Le Clerc closed in upon them. They eluded him, burst through his lines, fell upon him with fierce onslaught and disappeared into thin air. With desperate valor, his veterans captured the central almost inaccessible fortress, Crête à Pierrot. But that exploit alone cost the French twenty-seven hundred men, and they had to adopt various expedients to conceal their losses. Le Clerc called for reinforcements from France. He sought to restore to the planters their former power over their slaves, and at the same time declared that slavery was not to be restored. But San Domingo remained unconquered. His lines of communication and commissary department broke down.

Then Le Clerc tried duplicity: he had already sent Toussaint's own sons to plead with him, but Toussaint merely told them that they could stay with him or go back to the French; and added, "I must warn you that to remain with me means to remain with your race and with its cause, to remain in the Land of Mountains, and to regard the Land of Mountains as the Mother of the Earth. We must remold human relations here—we must alter human society here—and from here, liberty will go out to the whole world."[22]

Now Le Clerc made subtler approach. He promised San Domingans, "before the face of the Supreme Being," to respect their liberty. He argued that he simply represented the authority of France which the leaders willingly acknowledged. Why could there not be peace? He seduced Christophe, Dessalines and other leaders until Toussaint found himself stripped of co-operation. He did not believe Le Clerc, but there was nothing for him to do but submit.

His progress to the Cap to make a treaty of peace was like a triumphant procession. He signed the treaty and sat silently at a great banquet in his honor. He said, "I accept everything which is for the advance of the people and the army. As for myself, I wish to retire."

For a month he was allowed to live in peace, and then responding courteously to an invitation to consult with General Brunet, he was seized, imprisoned and sent to France. Le Clerc wrote to Napoleon, "Toussaint must not be left at liberty. Shut him up somewhere in the republic so that he never again sees San Domingo." Napoleon sent him to Fort Joux in the cold and snow of the Jura Alps.

Meantime and in less than two weeks after the peace treaty, yellow fever struck the French army; within three weeks, three thousand French soldiers were dead, and many more thousands were being nursed by the blacks. Le Clerc fairly shrieked his complaints to the strangely silent Napoleon. Already in May, 1802, Le Clerc was wailing that "sickness is destroying the army under my command. Not another second is to be lost. Send reinforcements immediately." Then came the arrest of Toussaint. "I implore you earnestly," he wrote, "to send reinforcements. I am without supplies. I am not master in the colony. Send me money. The army is in desperate straits. Do something for us."

Not only did the scourge of fever increase but signs of distrust and rebellion multiplied among the blacks. The news of restored slavery in Martinique and Guadeloupe leaked out. "No general of an army has ever been in such an unfavorable situation. The troops which arrived last month have ceased to exist. The rebels are attacking the valley every day; they open fire, which can be heard in Le Cap. It is impossible for me to defend myself; my regiments have been crushed, and I have no means for carrying on the defence or for utilizing the advantages which they offer me."[23]

The tom-toms rolled darkly in the hills. By September the revolt was in full sway. Even the mulattoes deserted the French. Earlier in the spring of the same year Toussaint died or was murdered at Fort Joux. He had not been allowed the services of a physician because as his jailor explained, "The health of Negroes is in no way similar to the health of Europeans." After studied humiliations and deprivations he was found dead April seventh.

Thus perished the greatest of American Negroes and one of the great men of all time, at the age of fifty-six. A French planter said, "God in his terrestrial globe did not commune with a purer spirit."[24] Wendell Phillips said, "You think me a fanatic, for you read history, not with your eyes, but with your prejudices. But fifty years hence, when Truth gets a hearing, the Muse of history will put Phocion for the Greek, Brutus for the Roman, Hampden for the English, La Fayette for France; choose Washington as the bright, consummate flower of our earliest civilization; and then, dipping her pen in the sunlight, will write in the clear blue, above them all, the name of the soldier, the statesman, the martyr, Toussaint L'Ouverture."

Santhonax, a wily Jacobin, who knew him, said, "Toussaint is the real leader of the Negroes, and the white inhabitants, who have been conciliated, regard him as a friend. Sometimes I feel that this fanatic man is inflamed with an unquenchable fire of love for humanity."[25]

Wordsworth wrote:

There's not a breathing of the common wind
That will forget thee: thou hast great allies;
Thy friends are exultations, agonies,
And love, and Man's unconquerable mind.

In 1802 and 1803 nearly forty thousand French soldiers died of war and fever. Le Clerc himself died in November, 1802. Rochambeau succeeded to his command and was promised soldiers by Napoleon; but already in May, 1803, Great Britain started new war with France and communication between France and San Domingo was impossible. The black insurgents held the land; the British held the sea. In November, 1803, Rochambeau surrendered and white authority died in San Domingo forever.

The effect of all this was far-reaching. Napoleon gave up his dream of American empire and sold Louisiana for a song. "Thus, all of Indian Territory, all of Kansas and Nebraska, Iowa and Wyoming, Montana and the Dakotas, and most of Colorado and Minnesota, and all of Washington and Oregon states, came to us as the indirect work of a despised Negro. Praise, if you will, the work of a Robert Livingstone or a Jefferson, but today let us not forget our debt to Toussaint L'Ouverture, who was indirectly the means of America's expansion by the Louisiana Purchase of 1803."[26]

NOTES

1. Of course it has been explained that he was no real "Negro," but only "dark."
2. J. F. Rippy, *Journal of Negro History*, Vol. VI, p. 183.

3. Helps, *op. cit.*, Vol. I, p. 421.
4. Rippy, *loc. cit.*
5. *Cf.* Du Bois, *Gift of Black Folk*, Chap. 1.
6. Herskovits, *Rebel Destiny*, p. 7.
7. Williams, *Whence the "Black Irish" of Jamaica?* p. 5.
8. Edwards, *History of the West Indies*, edition 1805–06, Book II, p. 259.
9. Edwards, *History of the West Indies*, p. 27.
10. Leger, *Haiti*, p. 46.
11. Edwards, *History of the West Indies*, p. 66.
12. Thiers, *French Revolution*, Vol. II, p. 35.
13. Waxman, *The Black Napoleon*, p. 79.
14. Beard, *The Negro Patriot of Haiti*, p. 61.
15. *Ibid.*, p. 60.
16. Steward, *The Haitian Revolution*, p. 58.
17. Waxman, *op. cit.*, p. 101.
18. See Vinogradov, *The Black Consul*, p. 299.
19. Edwards, *History, Civil and Commercial of the British Colonies in the West Indies*, p. 236.
20. From Santhonax's diary, in Vinogradov, *The Black Consul*, p. 311.
21. Vinogradov, *The Black Consul*, p. 324.
22. Vinogradov, *The Black Consul*, p. 359.
23. Vinogradov, *The Black Consul*, p. 413.
24. Marquis d' Hermonas. *Cf.* Johnson, *Negro in the New World*, p. 158.
25. Santhonax's diary, in Vinogradov, *The Black Consul*, p. 309.
26. DeWitt Talmage in *Christian Herald*, Nov. 28, 1906.

CHAPTER IX

---◆---

Emancipation and Enfranchisement

One has but to notice significant dates in the emancipation of Negro slaves and the enfranchisement of white workers to become aware of the close connection between the two series of events. Especially since the French Revolution, the white workers of Europe were striving to better their condition through the achievement of political power. There was in the minds of their leaders no question but that with the right to vote all things economic were possible. Slowly through the reform bills and subsequent legislation in England, through the revolutions of 1830 and 1848 in France, and by analogous steps in many other countries, including the revolution in the United States under Andrew Jackson, the great mass of white workers were enfranchised. At the same time in the West Indies and South America the working class was being made legally free and in some cases also achieved the right to vote. In the rest of the world and among the darker peoples, the workers remained for the most part in semi-serfdom.

Meantime the power of capitalism expanded enormously. Capital actually gained that freedom of action and irresponsibility of power which had been dreamed into reality in the eighteenth century as an attribute of the free individual citizen. The power of capital in the state increased much faster than the participation of workers in the direction of the state. Moreover, the power of capital rested upon legal property and property was the thing that was most tenaciously withheld from the democratic power of the new workers.

England stopped the slave trade in order to defeat Napoleon. She was enabled to do this because a moral revolt was sweeping England against the methods of the slave trade; and this revolt was allowed scope because continual slave uprisings and new conditions in Africa were reducing the profits of slavery. Moreover, a new era of capitalism was approaching. It was gradually becoming possible to transfer capital to places where labor was available instead of, as formerly, being compelled to transfer labor to available land and capital.

This increased ease in the transfer of capital came through the establishment of stock exchanges. In 1773 the "Stock Exchange Coffee House" was established in London and business grew so fast that in 1801 the members raised capital and provided a building and opened it in 1802. Thus while particular recipients of profits might be ruined, and were ruined, in the stopping of the slave trade and the abolition of slavery, nevertheless the general flow of profits to the masters of capital could be and was enormously increased at the beginning of the nineteenth century by possibilities of investment in Europe, Asia, and Africa.

On the other hand, recalcitrant groups of laborers who revolted against capitalists' methods, like those in the West Indies Islands, could now be starved into submission. Instead of transporting labor from Africa to the rich lands of America, it was possible to transfer capital to the labor of Africa and Asia and thus control increasing amounts of necessary raw materials. With this new capitalistic era went new methods of controlling democracy through wealth, through investment in colonial labor. The wealth and power of capitalist classes in democratic lands became so large that directly and indirectly they controlled votes and public opinion. The forms of democracy remained but the substance began steadily to decay as colonial imperialism increased.

The main problem of the West Indies is not political, but economic, and the problem of race is only important as it affects economic status. The labor of the islands, ignorant and degraded and exploited for centuries, was freed only in the sense that the importations of Africans ceased. There was some division of lands varying in different islands from the complete peasant proprietorship of Haiti to complete land monopoly under landlords in many other islands.

The taxes direct and indirect on the poor are high; the officials, especially in the British Islands, receive large salaries and perquisites. For instance, in West Indian, Central and South American British colonies, nine governors receive as salaries and allowances $175,000 a year, not to speak of other governmental expenses. Yet the work of these nine men could easily be concentrated into the hands of two or three executives. Such federation, however, would mean increasing power and democratic control among black people, attack on investment returns, with all of the slow and painful training of those folk into self-government. This task Great Britain is not disposed to undertake. The markets in which the island produce can be sold are monopolized and directed by white capital in European centers, and the carrying trade is entirely in their hands. Capital for local enterprise can only be obtained from them and the local labor employed is paid at the lowest competitive price.

Revolt has been controlled by the rise of a small local bourgeoisie composed of whites and reinforced gradually by mulattoes and a few blacks, who are recognized as part of the dominant white community and associate and often intermarry with them. All signs of revolt and leadership are thus persistently taken away from the Negro masses and honors, appointments and recognition by the mother country are so arranged as to keep the status quo.

Here and there despite this, revolts arise. One of the most spectacular was the case of Marcus Garvey. He was a leader of the Jamaica peasants and, migrating to the United States, tried from that base to emancipate the Negroes of the world by commercial enterprise. It was of course a dream far beyond his power or ability, but it aroused the Negro world and led to precautionary measures both in the West Indies and in Africa. Recently widespread labor troubles have broken out both in the French and the British West Indies. The only systematic

attempt to meet the grievances of this peasantry has been taken in the producers' and consumers' co-operative movement, which the English government
has subsidized, chiefly to offset the monopoly of the American owned United
Fruit Company.

The West Indies still remain remote exploited provinces, cut off from union
with the world labor movement or with their racial groups, and distracted by
petty internal jealousies and provincialisms. It is the tragedy and paradox of a
land where life might be easy, healthy and happy, with a minimum of toil for
simple needs, or even luxury with adequate technique, that the investing races
of the world have for centuries lived on the toil of this proletariat, raping its land
and labor; impoverishing it with taxes and interest; monopolizing its sugar, coffee and fruit; depressing the prices of its products in the world market and sad-
dling it with eternal debt. Today the white world visits the land either to play or
to rule; to reap large profit and to throw pennies and guffaws at little, lithe, black,
begging swimmers.

The racial problem in these areas is biological, but even more cultural. The people are European in speech and outlook, but largely African in their unconscious
memories and survivals; and still so filled with a naive joy and exhilaration from
an awful experience in slave trade and slavery that there survives art and laughter and joy of living, sprung today from emancipation, and not embittered as yet
by memory of a fall from decent standards of living or lost dreams of wealth.

Human beings are apt to be naive in their plans of righting social wrongs,
particularly if it seems possible to execute these plans without loss of income to
themselves or others. If the stealing of men instituted slavery, their emancipation meant freedom and happiness. It was a commonplace among abolitionists
to prove beyond peradventure that a free laborer could do more work and better work than a slave and create more wealth. It was not, on the other hand, at
all clear that while the profit which the slave made went almost exclusively to
his master save for the pittance which kept him alive, on the other hand, the
profit of the free laborer was divided: an increased proportion went to the
laborer himself in the form of wages or of leisure; and he might easily have no
direct interest in making the total profit large.

Of course those who had invested in the West Indies knew that under slavery
or freedom, under political control or independence, they owned the land, they
would handle the crops, they would pay the labor. Unless then the land was confiscated or the crops seriously decreased in amount, or the labor inefficient or
intractable, they might still make profit. It happened after West Indian emancipation, that only in one country was the land definitely and entirely taken from
the former proprietors.

Sugar, coffee, cocoa, tobacco and rum, and later oil and tropical fruits were the
raw materials eventually turned out by the West Indies in increasing amounts.
Their value was enhanced at first by the Napoleonic wars and later by the prosperity and increased demand of the industrial development of the nineteenth
century.

Labor varied in efficiency and docility. The first impulse of the freed slave
was to rest, to realize his freedom in leisure and absence of driven toil. If he had

his own land as in Haiti, he worked only irregularly and when his wants compelled him. On the other hand, in Cuba he remained a slave long after legal emancipation, being driven to work by land monopoly and the low wages paid. In Jamaica there was at first widespread ruin among the planters. They were already in debt to English financiers and the demand of the free laborers in wage and leisure was more than they could pay and keep solvent.

On the other hand, the owner and exploiter was not without weapons against the laborer: he could refuse to furnish capital except this was accompanied by at least some political control. Foreign capital could be attracted to these regions of emancipation only by the payment of large interest and the promise of excessive profit. Even when emancipated labor began to get political power and to vote, nevertheless this power could be controlled by limiting its scope to the selection of powerless officials and carefully keeping control of property and industry out of the hands of the voters.

Unfortunately, all the interesting details of this economic development in the West Indies have not been seriously studied by sociologists and economists. Usually the explanation of everything that has taken place there is purely racial: Negroes are lazy and inefficient and consequently poor and turbulent; with a different kind of labor the West Indies would flourish, but their racial fate is upon them.

Despite this oft-repeated belief, it is quite clear that if the West Indian laborers were paid decent wages and given a modern education; if they could control capital and income through a free vote; there might arise there a center of world industry; and more than that, a center of thought and art. But so long as the labor is isolated on these islands, given but limited education, paid a starvation wage, kept largely from the use of the land, and taxed on consumption, some art may emerge and some individuals of note, but on the whole the islands and the adjacent mainland will remain a sort of world slum, illustrating and making clear the exploitation which planted it in the past and prolongs it today.

The future development of this interesting and fundamentally important part of the world may come through the economic emancipation of its preponderantly dark peasantry and the raising of them to higher standards of living. On the other hand it may come by the persistent effort which one sees today to subject them to a bourgeoisie partly risen from their own masses and partly foreign, which will build a prosperity of wealth on the continued subjection of the masses of labor. It is for the promise of this latter purpose, that these groups are held today apart, not only by general economic exploitation but by studiously encouraging provincialism in small and separate islands and groups, with every difficulty of intercourse and contact and in the face of the general neglect of the world.

To illustrate the development of the West Indies, since the emancipation of the slaves, we may take certain typical examples: the drama of the West Indies typified itself in the story of San Domingo. Here was the nadir of labor, a great amorphous mass of black commodity flesh dumped into a little island of heavenly beauty and exploited with every ecstasy of cruelty and blood, from the mass murder of Indians in the fifteenth century to the sugar-cane exploitation of the eighteenth. And then suddenly, in a night, there came the revolution. It came as Marx would have had it, not so much from the educated and rich mulattoes, as from the great black mass of slaves, led by an incredible man; those slaves drove out the imperial Spaniards and the commercial English and ruined Napoleon Bonaparte's dream of empire in the Valley of the Mississippi; they set up a free and independent state.

The result of the Haitian revolution was not so much the independence of a small island with its half million or more inhabitants, but rather the ideas which it spread among many million black laborers in America, and their exploiters; and even beyond that, the challenge to democracy which it eventually instituted.

The world alternately grew red with laughter and white with fear as this little independent state, born of slavery and revolution, started its tempestuous career. Its real problem was not political, although it had to struggle for political independence against France and the United States. The essential struggle was for economic survival; for feeding and sheltering these slaves and enabling them to barter with the world for a share in world goods. Commercial isolation was not permitted. They must trade and on such terms as white folk willed. They established under the great Christophe, whose monument is still the most marvelous building in America, a replica of the African tribal government with emperor, chieftains, clans and family life, and raised Haiti from the inertia of reaction to organized and fairly efficient beginnings of economic life.

Above all, this regime accomplished the most astonishing thing in the modern world: it divided the land among the peasantry in fee simple, sharply in contrast with the land monopoly of Europe, the current land theft of Africa, the other West Indies and America. Land-holding by foreigners was forbidden and large holdings by natives were neither politically wise nor profitable. The plantation system disappeared.

This was the result not so much of edict as of custom. Toussaint, Christophe and Petion all were compelled to drive the black laborers back to their land; but they gave them holidays to work for themselves and they gave them customary rights of tenure. Gradually it came to be Haitian law that peasants could not be evicted and this law stood until the Americans did what they could to overturn it during their occupation. But, after all, this island of communal effort and peasant proprietorship was in the midst of a sea of private profit organized during the Industrial Revolution and coming, in the early nineteenth century, to its perfect flower.

The kidnapping and death of Toussaint opened the eyes of his followers; Dessalines and Christophe and mulattoes like Petion, who had joined the French, soon saw their mistake. The result was that Rochambeau was literally driven into the sea and had to surrender to the English. After the loss of sixty thousand Frenchmen, Haiti became independent and in 1804 Dessalines tore out the white stripe from the French tricolor and threw it on the ground and put the red and the blue together as the standard of a new state, which he called Haiti, "Land of Mountains."

He and his successor, Christophe, were curious combinations of primitive African chieftains and shrewd modern men, uneducated and violent but determined and shrewd. Through the Napoleonic wars they maintained the political independence. Political subjugation could not be forced on Haiti, but economic subjugation was almost inevitable. Crops decreased; Haitians were not raising sugar for the world but food for themselves; they were not toiling for the ease of white folk, but for their own enjoyment. The Sugar Empire passed to the slaves of Cuba. The French later insisted on enormous tribute, which Boyer reduced in actual figures, but which still remained more than this poor community could pay and live.

The pressure of American investment began, culminating in demands for strategic coaling stations and finally in attempted subjugation. The result in Haiti was that the people limped forward, wavering between the attempted leadership of presidents analogous to African chieftains, and presidents who represented the French élite of capital.

The élite could establish no exploitation in modern form because they could furnish neither land nor cheap labor to investors, nor did the island have technical skill for industry. The agriculture of Haiti was at the mercy of colonial imperialism throughout the world, with a low value set on raw materials, by those world centers where profit was made and expected, not from the raising of crops, but from their transformation into manufactured goods. Such foreign capital as was offered Haiti was offered only on the severest terms with a demand for more or less political control in the background and with the additional demand, peculiar to colored countries, that white representatives be the local repositories of all expenditure and control.

During these years the fight in Haiti was between an incipient bourgeoisie with a fine tradition of French culture but small wealth, and a black peasantry fanatic in its insistence upon land ownership and freedom from compulsory labor. Civil disturbances, rapid succession of officials and social unrest in Haiti can practically all be explained in these terms.

Finally the United States conceived of Haiti as a way station to the Panama Canal, and President Wilson, at the behest of American investors and commercial freebooters, seized the country. The resistance was not mainly, and could not be, physical. The new engines of war were too terrible; but Haiti put in action a "sit-down" strike, a silent refusal to co-operate; it made use of all of the difficulties of a language which the Americans did not know, and of a law code with which they were not familiar; the inability of the conquerors legally to monopolize land; and above all a determined propaganda among the Negroes of the United States which threatened their allegiance to the Republican party, the party of finance capital, in many critical centers.

There were only two ways out: murder and subjugation, which the Republican party with its Negro supporters did not dare inaugurate; or compromise. That compromise consisted of compelling Haiti to accept a debt which was nothing less than highway robbery, and included every alleged "contract" that it could, under the most disadvantageous terms. Haiti again became "free," but her existence depended upon a dictatorship which must, on the one hand, keep the peace; and, on the other hand, pay enormous and continuous tribute to the banks of New York. An American fiscal officer sits in Port au Prince with his hands on the treasury, seeing that the profit of foreign investors, made permanent by the debt agreement, is paid before anything can be done for Haitian labor in wage, education, health or social advance.

Under such circumstances no new orientation of object could easily take place. The new voices of industrial democracy were sternly repressed and perhaps had to be if the threat of American subjugation was not to return. Nevertheless, the voices were there and the effort. The voices declared that the true ideal of Haiti is to raise its land-holding peasantry to economic independence and intelligence; and perhaps the most significant prophecy of this thought was when Bellegarde, delegate of Haiti, alone raised his voice against the South African murder of the Bondelswartz, voicing the complaint of a whole world of exploited black folk in the League of Nations.

The Spanish end of the island of San Domingo is known today as the Dominican Republic. It remained separate from Haiti until Toussaint and his revolting slaves united the island. When Haiti was established as an independent republic, the Spanish part of the island reverted to Spain, but became independent in 1821. The Haitians under President Boyer dominated the whole island from 1822 to 1844. Since then the Dominican Republic has been independent, except for the intervention of American business, 1916 to 1924. The greatest leader of the country was the mulatto, Ulisse Heureaux.

Much Negro and less Spanish blood make up the people of the republic, but the Dominicans are anxious to be regarded as white because they want to be treated like white people and preserve the social and cultural bonds which they still have with Spanish-speaking countries. They, therefore, discriminate against Negroes in their immigration laws. On the other hand, their workers form a part of the low paid exploited labor of the West Indies, working under the control of foreign capital.

Turning now to Jamaica, we find a development different in many ways. Two hundred fifty-five thousand slaves were set free in 1838 for which the planters were paid nearly thirty million dollars. There ensued a discouraging condition of industry. This was partly due to unwilling and lazy Negro labor, trained by slavery to despise common work; but it was also in part due to English commercial adjustments. The capital invested in the West Indies by Englishmen was more and more concentrated in the carrying trade and that trade even after emancipation remained large and lucrative. The Jamaica crops of sugar and coffee markedly decreased at the time of emancipation, but crops from other islands and new crops more than made up the difference.

The losses fell principally on the plantation owners who had borrowed from the financiers and already paid them handsome profit. Tariff protection on Jamaican sugar in the English market was withdrawn after emancipation and the price of sugar which had been about ten dollars a hundredweight fell to six dollars. The overvalued estates were burdened with mortgages and debts owed largely to English consignees, who had formerly bought the sugar crop. There was a severe financial and banking crisis in England. Nine-tenths of the Jamaican land and estates in Jamaica were owned by absentee landlords and administered by agents. They proceeded to cut the wages of labor from fifty cents to twenty-five cents a day and finally even to sixteen cents a day. And often at that they had no money to pay the wages due.

Thomas Carlyle came forward as the extreme protagonist of the planters with his *Discourse on Niggers* in 1849: "You are not slaves now; nor do I wish, if it can be avoided, to see you slaves again; but decidedly you have to be servants to those that are born wiser than you; . . . servants to the whites, if they are (as what mortal man can doubt they are?) born wiser than you! That, you may depend upon, my obscure black friends! Is and was always the Law of the world for you and all men."[1]

The white officials sent out in these days were arbitrary and corrupt. Little was done for the mass of people and there was outrageous over-taxation. Nevertheless the backwardness of the colony was attributed solely to the Negro. Governor Eyre complained in 1865 that the young and strong were good for nothing and were filling the jails.

The colored people were aroused and a mulatto, George William Gordon, began agitation for reform. Gordon was the son of a white planter by a Negro slave woman, who taught himself to read and write and eventually bought his own and his mother's freedom. He became a prosperous storekeeper, and when his white father became insolvent redeemed the home and maintained his father and the white family in it, although they refused to recognize him or let him enter the house. The minister of the Scotch church in Kingston characterized him as "a man of princely generosity and unbounded benevolence." He married a white woman and by allying himself as a planter with the whites, as so many of the mulattoes did, he might have escaped the difficulties of black folk. But he espoused the cause of the blacks and as a parish official tried to help them in many ways.

Meetings were held, and finally the Negro peasantry began a riot in 1861, in which twenty-two people were killed, only three of whom were white. Thirty-four persons were wounded. The result was that Governor Eyre tried and executed by court-martial three hundred and fifty-four persons, and also killed without trial eighty-five, a total of four hundred and thirty-nine. In addition to this, one hundred and forty-seven were killed after martial law ceased. One thousand Negro homes were burned to the ground and thousands of Negroes flogged or mutilated. Children had their brains dashed out, pregnant women were murdered, and Gordon himself, whose direct connection with the riot was never proved, was tried by court-martial and hanged. In fact the punishment was, as the royal commissioners admitted, "reckless and positively barbarous." Eyre was never punished, but the island was made a crown colony in 1866 and twenty years later the voters were given the right to elect a majority of the legislature.

Nevertheless this right to vote was seriously curtailed. It could not touch the returns on old investments made by the English dating back to slavery days. It had but limited control over the land, and its right of taxation was strictly curtailed by the governor and colonial office and could not impede the freedom of capital. The peasantry remains with elementary education, little land, low wages and uncertain employment.

Above the mass has arisen a considerable class of educated, well-to-do Negroes and mulattoes, who achieve on the whole political and social equality with the whites. Good education is available for them and commercial and political preferment. But their ranks could be multiplied tenfold and their horizon infinitely widened in industry, literature and art, if the barriers of slavery did not hold the great flood of ability and genius imprisoned in the black peasantry.

Emancipation wrought no sudden miracle in Cuba. Economic oppression continued after emancipation. The mass of the Negroes were still beasts of burden on the sugar and tobacco plantations and manumission gave them no settled economic status. They were continually uprooted by war, disorganized, politically unstable, and even when enfranchised the victims of demagogues and fuel for further revolution.

It was the Negroes and mulattoes who made Cuba politically independent of Spain and started her on her torturous climb to economic justice. The Ten Years War brought legal emancipation, but when oppression and injustice followed, Antonio Maceo, a handsome mulatto, took the field with numbers of Negro soldiers in 1895. The wealthy Spanish and creole capitalists denounced this war as a race struggle of Negroes against whites. From the beginning it was bitter. For fourteen days Maceo and his companions were hunted over hills and valleys and through forests. Some of his companions were killed, others captured, and he himself was wounded twenty-five times. Finally in December, 1896, he was killed "too soon to witness the final triumph of his cause," but he lived long enough "to stamp him the greatest military leader in Cuba's history." His bronze monument today dominates Havana.

Through the intervention of the United States, Cuba secured her freedom. American Negro regiments played a leading role, among other things rescuing Theodore Roosevelt and his Rough Riders from threatened annihilation. But the American intervention had its price. It was motivated by no desire to see Negroes free and politically independent in Cuba, but rather with the distinct design of dominating the Cuban sugar fields and concentrating in that island the sugar culture which formerly had centered in Haiti and Jamaica. With the rule of American capital and under such officials as Wood, Brookes and Lagoon, labor exploitation was accomplished and helped by racial discrimination which was now emphasized in Cuba to an extent never known before.

Notwithstanding this, the political leaders, whether they were puppets of the Americans or local demagogues, had to be careful of their Negro political support. Estrada Palma, who was the first independent Cuban official and a direct representative of American finance, depended upon Martin Delgado, the black leader, for political backing. He managed, however, in deference to American prejudice, to refuse recognition to Delgado's wife at social functions.

Palma subjected the government to foreign capital, closed the doors to native development and favored foreign banking. The sugar lands were increasingly monopolized. Whole towns on the sugar estates were subject to American law, with private company railways and private ports. A wave of purely racial resentment swept over Cuba for the first time. Under the leadership of Estenoz, born in the black capital, Santiago de Cuba, a new Independent Colored Party was formed and incorporated in 1907. Within a year it had a membership of over sixty thousand Negro voters. The result was race riots and clashes, in one of which at Oriente, three thousand Negroes were killed.

President Gomez depended again upon Delgado and by his aid an electoral law was introduced forbidding the formation of any political party along racial lines. But the lesson had been learned. Negro officials began to be appointed. They have occupied cabinet and other high positions. Under President Grau, the Havana chief of police was a capable mulatto. A black judge was appointed and the number of Negro Army officers increased. Indeed the present military dictator of Cuba, Fulgencio Batista, who came to power in 1933, is a mulatto with white, Negro and Indian blood.

The present Negro population of Cuba probably runs to about seventy per cent despite official statistics. The Negroes form naturally the bulk of the poor, ignorant and untrained. The American economic penetration has monopolized the resources of the island and made the Negro's opportunity worse. There are now Negro and white jobs and open discrimination in pay. As Beals says, if present tendencies persist, "Cuba will be converted into a vast sugar plantation with a population of West Indian Negroes, a cowardly native bureaucracy; a government receiving orders from Wall Street, and a flag—symbol of its independence."[2]

Puerto Rico was annexed to the United States after the Spanish American war and in 1917 the inhabitants became American citizens. Education has been provided widely but the poverty and low social status of the people as a result of long history of exploitation and misrule are notable and have led to clashes with the officials, labor controversy and other sorts of unrest.

Turning now to South America, we may center our attention upon Brazil because this country represents a rather different attempt to solve the problem, not only of the worker but of the workers of different races. The submerged peoples here were the Indians and the Negroes. The Indians were only partially enslaved and lived apart in the swamps and forests. Their exploitation as porters and laborers did not reach the concentration of effort characterized by the importation of Negro slaves. It is probable today that white folk form only one-third of the population of Brazil, the other two-thirds being Indians, Negroes, and mixtures of these races and the whites.

Emancipation of Negroes did not come in Brazil until 1888, but before that gradually large numbers had been freed; and also before and after emancipation, Negroes, whites and Indians were amalgamating into a new race. Some of the most intelligent Brazilians have possessed Negro blood. Indians and Negroes made up the lowest class in Brazil, and the white element the highest; but nevertheless race and color have played only a secondary part in social life. Discriminatory laws existed in the past, until the close of the colonial era, those having Negro blood being legally disqualified from becoming priests or holding civil office; yet individuals evidently Negro secured such positions. Even in the eighteenth century there were black clergy and bishops; indeed the Negro clergy seem to have been on a higher moral level than the whites. Negroes rose to high posts even in colonial times. A recognition of the equality of the two darker races with the white one was shown when four persons were decorated and ennobled for services in driving out the Dutch; one was an Indian chief and another a Negro captain of a black regiment. Later patents of nobility were repeatedly conferred upon persons known to have Negro blood.[3]

A Brazilian writer said at the First Races Congress: "The cooperation of the metis in the advance of Brazil is notorious and far from inconsiderable.[4] They played the chief part during many years in Brazil in the campaign for the abolition of slavery. I could quote celebrated names of more than one of these metis who put themselves at the head of the literary movement. They fought with firmness and intrepidity in the press and on the platform. They faced with courage the gravest perils to which they were exposed in their struggle against the powerful slave-owners, who had the protection of a conservative government. It was owing to their support that the republic was erected on the ruins of the empire."

At other parts of South America we can but glance. Colombia, Venezuela, Peru and Ecuador, and some parts of Mexico have considerable amounts of Negro blood. Slavery was abolished by Guatemala in 1824 and by Mexico in 1829. Argentina, Peru, Bolivia, Chile, and Paraguay ceased to recognize it about 1825. Between 1840 and 1845 it came to an end in Colombia, Venezuela, and Ecuador.

When Bolivar announced his war in Colombia and Venezuela, many Negroes flocked to the standard, and, after his first failure, it was President Petion of Haiti who twice provided him with filibuster forces of black troops to start the war anew, with the proviso that Bolivar would at once free the slaves. Paez, Sucre, and other South American leaders used Negro soldiers in their fight for freedom. In general, in South America, Negroes found the army a short cut to social improvement and were especially used as soldiers in many civil wars and rebellions.

In Colombia, Venezuela, Peru and Ecuador there are today whole towns predominantly or entirely Negro. All along the coast of Colombia, Guatemala and Honduras there are numbers of Negroes and mixed people of Negro, Spanish, and Indian blood. The Negroes of Nicaragua are mostly on the Pacific side and form a notably handsome group of people; but throughout this country the economic disintegration and social squalor are tremendous. These lands are largely without guiding ideals or encouragement and receive little help from the civilized world, which in turn has not yet reduced them to profitable wage slavery.

Negroes have always exercised an important political role in Venezuela, where most of the leaders of revolts have had Negro and Indian blood. There are perhaps thirty thousand Negroes in Ecuador, where they have led many of the recent revolts. They are interbred widely with Spaniards and Indians, "and today give a distinct flavor to the whole coast culture, ever so separatist, so resentful and mistrustful of highland Quito rule."[5]

When the French Panama Canal Company began to dig, they brought large numbers of black laborers from the British and French West Indies and Haiti, and began a trade in transferring labor from island to island and to the coast, which is still carried on by none too honest contractors. It has not very greatly improved the lot of the laborers, but it has begun to get them acquainted with each other and conscious of their common wrongs. When the United States took up the work of digging the Panama Canal they used thousands of these laborers and dumped the surplus across the borders into the new republic of Panama. Thus Panama became a distributing center for labor all along the Central American and South American coast.

In the Canal Zone the United States drew the color line strictly by law and custom, discriminating in wages and particularly in housing. The housing of black laborers in Panama and Colon has been described as horrible. "No more tragic contrast is presented between these people, dumped originally on Panama by the Zone authorities, and the great civilized symbol represented by the remarkable operation of the canal itself."[6]

In general, throughout South America, the situation differs from that in the West Indies. First of all, here the migration of Europeans has been large enough to establish a group of local capitalists in most of the countries, who proceeded to exploit the mass of Indian and Negro labor. They were encouraged to borrow large amounts of capital from Europe and the United States and for a time fell into continuous revolutionary squabbles over the division of the profits.

Gradually, however, their ranks were penetrated with Indian and Negro blood, and a new patriotism arose which looks upon these countries as places of development for the mass of their people. Endeavors to break down land monopoly in countries like Mexico and to reorganize the state on less oligarchic lines, as in Brazil, went on and still, with halting and retrogression, are proceeding. On the other hand, in Brazil, the Argentine and elsewhere European capital is playing a menacing role and increasing in power.

The ignorance and inexperience of the masses here are partly compensated for in a certain carefree life in the forest and on the plains, for a people who have developed a love of mere existence even on a low plane. There is a good chance, therefore, that in South America, despite the power of European capital, a democracy in industry and agriculture will eventually arise and that people of mixed Indian, Spanish, Portuguese and Negro blood will form a new amalgam with increasing economic equality and a rich cultural life.

The widespread mixture of races in the West Indies and South America: Indian, Spanish, Dutch, English, and Negro, has given rise to exceptional men and women. Yet systematically their relation to any of these races except the Negro is stressed; and if any West Indian insists that he or his ancestors were not of Negro descent, it is a matter of courtesy to agree with him; and of course documentary proof is nearly always impossible. On the other hand, there were few white women in the West Indies, especially in earlier days, and those few were protected by wealth, law and custom. An illegitimate child, therefore, in the West Indies in the earlier days was almost proof positive of Negro descent. Thus Alexander Hamilton, the great American statesman, and the forebears of Robert Browning were probably of Negro descent; but the facts can naturally never be proven.

Today only one country in the West Indies openly acknowledges and even boasts of its Negro blood, and that is Haiti, although as a matter of fact there are more Negroes in Cuba than in Haiti. Haiti has often been tempted to stress her mulatto element and forget her black peasantry, but the temptation to this lies primarily in the insult and discrimination which she had suffered, even at the hands of the Pan-American Union.

Beyond the physical results of this mixture, come certain cultural developments. In Brazil "at the present moment there is scarcely a lowly or a highly placed federal or provincial official at the head of or within any of the great departments of state that has not more or less Negro or American-Indian blood in his veins."[7]

Lord Bryce says, "It is hardly too much to say that along the coast from Rio to Bahia and Pernambuco, as well as in parts of the interior behind these two cities, the black population predominates. . . . The Brazilian middle class intermarries with mulattoes and quadroons. Brazil is the one country in the world, besides the Portuguese colonies on the east and west coasts of Africa, in which a fusion of the European and African races is proceeding unchecked by law or custom. The doctrines of human equality and human solidarity have here their perfect work. The result is so far satisfactory that there is little or no class friction."

Waldo Frank writes: "The dark folk alone that dwell in Brazil can create an authentic Brazilian culture. This dark folk does not make republics and has not learned yet sufficiently how to direct one. It has not studied the intricacies of international commerce. Its potency is a deeper level. It is already forming the vision, the art, the play of its world. It is the living plasm of Brazil, whence must rise its spirit."

From the French West Indies many people of mixed blood have arisen to distinction both there and in France. Olivier fought as an officer in the German wars. Chevalier de St. Georges was knighted by Louis XVI. The Dumas family furnished a general under Napoleon and two of the leading literary men of France; and finally Josephine Tascher de la Pagerie, granddaughter of a Negro, became first the mistress of a member of the Directory and later wife of Napoleon and first empress of France.

The art influence of the Negro in the West Indies and Latin America has been deep. He is responsible for much of its spiritual heritage. Ruben Dario, a Nicaraguan mulatto, is perhaps the greatest poet of Latin America. In Cuba there was the poet Placido and today there is Guillen. In Peru there are two mulatto poets, Abujar and Yerovi. José de Patroncinio was of Negro descent and not only one of Brazil's greatest writers but a leading abolitionist. Negro language customs and folklore have been preserved in Guiana, in Cuba, in Jamaica and Haiti. There are few dances in America that have not been influenced by the Negro.

The future of Latin America is with no single race but with a new amalgam which is already setting its pattern. Often the fear is expressed that parts of Central America and the West Indies will grow black and that drink, disease and sexual immorality will degrade the people. But the danger does not lie here. It lies rather in the determination to pauperize any people with black blood and thus deliver it into the arms of disease and crime. For hundreds of years the development of ability among West Indians and the opening of doors, particularly, of economic opportunity, were confined to white people or to those light mulattoes who by courtesy passed as white. The great mass of laborers became a proletariat reduced in the days of the slave trade to the very lowest labor status. There is no sufficient reason to doubt that economic opportunity and social justice will raise, out of this part of the world, people not only capable of supporting present human civilization but of creating new centers for a greater and finer culture.

NOTES

1. *Critical and Miscellaneous Essays,* Vol. IV, p. 379.
2. Beals, *The Crime of Cuba,* p. 316.
3. Williams, *The People and Politics of Latin America,* p. 270.
4. The author used "metis" as indicating the Negro-white mixture and not the Indian-white. *Cf.* Spiller's *Inter-racial Problems,* pp. 377–382.
5. Beals, *America South,* pp. 150–153.
6. Beals, *America South,* pp. 156–159.
7. Johnston, *Negro in the New World,* p. 109.

CHAPTER X

———————◆———————

The Black United States

There were half a million slaves in the confines of the United States when the Declaration of Independence declared "that all men are created equal; that they are endowed by their Creator with certain unalienable rights; that among these are life, liberty, and the pursuit of happiness." The land that thus magniloquently heralded its advent into the family of nations had supported the institution of human slavery for one hundred and fifty-seven years and was destined to cling to it desperately eighty-seven years longer. The greatest experiment in Negro slavery as the base of a modern industrial system was made on the mainland of North America and in the confines of the present United States.

There were in the United States and its dependencies, in 1930, 11,891,143 persons of acknowledged Negro descent, not including the considerable infiltration of Negro blood which is not acknowledged and often not known. Today the number of persons called Negroes is probably about thirteen millions. These persons are almost entirely descendants of African slaves, brought to America from the sixteenth to the nineteenth centuries.

The importation of Negroes to the mainland of North America was small until the British obtained the coveted privilege of the Asiento in 1713. After the Asiento treaty the Negro population in the confines of the United States increased in the eighteenth century from about 50,000 in 1710 to 220,000 in 1750 and 462,000 in 1770. When the colonies became independent, the foreign slave trade was soon made illegal; but illicit trade, annexation of territory and natural increase enlarged the Negro population from a little over a million at the beginning of the nineteenth century to four and a half millions at the outbreak of the Civil War and to about ten and a quarter millions in 1914.

The present so-called Negro population of the United States is:

1. A mixture of the various African populations: Bantu, Sudanese, Nilotic and West Coast Negroes; some dwarfs, and some traces of Semitic blood.
2. A mixture of Negro and American Indian blood.
3. A mixture of Negro with the blood of white Americans through a system of concubinage of colored women in slavery days, together with some legal intermarriage then and later.

The census figures as to mulattoes[1] have been from time to time officially acknowledged to be understatements. This blending of the races has led to interesting human types, but there has been little scientific study of the matter. In general the Negro population in the United States is brown in color, darkening to almost black and shading off in the other direction to yellow and white, and in some cases indistinguishable from the white population.

It has been estimated on admittedly partial data that less than twenty-five per cent of American Negroes are of unmixed African descent, the balance having in varying degrees Indian and white blood.[2]

The slaves, landing from 1619 onward, were usually transported from the West Indian marts, after acclimatization and training in systematic plantation work. They were received by the colonies at first as laborers, on the same plane as other laborers. For a long time there was in law no distinction between the indented white servant from England and the black servant from Africa, except in the term of their service. Even here the distinction was not always observed, some of the whites being kept beyond term of their service and Negroes now and then securing their freedom.

The opposition to slavery had from the first been largely stilled when it was stated that this was a method of converting the heathen to Christianity. The corollary was that when a slave was converted he became free. Up to 1660 or thereabouts it seemed accepted in most colonies and in the English West Indies, that baptism into a Christian Church would legally free a Negro slave. Masters, therefore, were reluctant in the seventeenth century to have their slaves receive Christian instruction. Maryland declared in 1663 that Negro slaves should serve durante vita, but it was not until 1667 that Virginia finally plucked up courage to attack the issue squarely and declared by law: "Baptism doth not alter the condition of the person as to his bondage or freedom, in order that diverse masters freed from this doubt may more carefully endeavor the propagation of Christianity."

During the seventeenth and eighteenth centuries there was a considerable forced slave trade of whites from Europe under the guise of indentured servants. It met, however, not only the monopoly of feudal labor, but the new demand for labor purchase in the expanding industries of Europe. And, on the other hand, these very industries were encouraged and enlarged by the raw material raised in America by slave labor. The profits of the slave trade and of the plantations, together with the ease of obtaining black slaves through the systematic organization of the trade, increased the importation of black slave labor, while white free labor gradually replaced indentured workers.

The African family and clan life were disrupted in this transplantation; the communal life and free use of land were impossible; the power of the chief was transferred to the master, bereft of the usual blood ties and ancient reverence. The African language survived only in occasional words and phrases. African religion, both fetish and Islam, was transformed. Fetish survived in certain rites and even here and there in blood sacrifice, carried out secretly and at night; but more often in open celebration which gradually became transmuted into Catholic and Protestant Christian rites. The slave preacher replaced to some extent the African

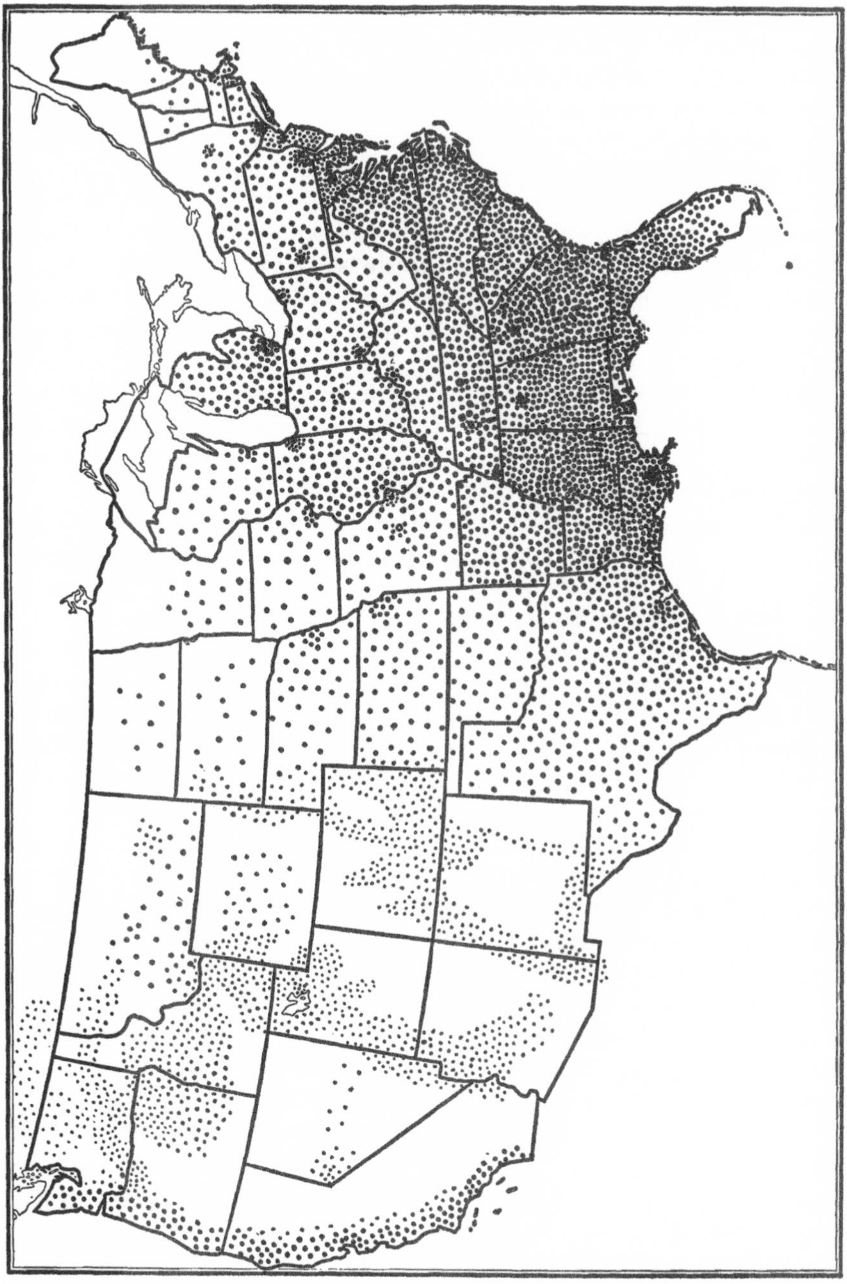

DISTRIBUTION OF THE NEGRO POPULATION IN THE UNITED STATES, 1930

medicine man and gradually, after a century or more, the Negro Church arose as the center and almost the only social expression of Negro life in America. Nevertheless, there can still be traced not only in words and phrases but in customs, literature and art, and especially in music and dance, something of the African heritage of the black folk in America. Further study will undoubtedly make this survival and connection clearer.

The war of the American colonies against England in 1776 was an effort to escape the colonial status, in which the profits of agriculture and industry went to the mother country. In this struggle for industrial freedom and independence of England, the Negroes took part in considerable numbers, while others helped the Tories, tempted by offers of freedom. It was natural that at the conclusion of the war and at a time when the profits of the slave system were low, the small number of slaves in the northern colonies should be emancipated, partly in gratitude for their help during the war, and partly because the extinction of slavery in the new nation seemed inevitable.

The series of laws emancipating slaves in the North began in Vermont in 1779, followed by judicial decision in Massachusetts in 1780, and gradual emancipation in Pennsylvania beginning the same year; emancipation was accomplished in New Hampshire in 1783, and in Connecticut and Rhode Island in 1784. The momentous exclusion of slavery in the Northwest Territory took place in 1787, and, helped by Haiti, gradual emancipation began in New York and New Jersey in 1799 and 1804.

There early began to be some internal development and growth of self-consciousness among the Negroes: for instance, in New England towns during colonial times, Negro "governors" were elected. This was partly the African chieftainship transplanted, in an endeavor to put the regulation of the slaves partly into their own hands. Free Negroes voted in those days: for instance, in North Carolina until 1835, the constitution extended the franchise to every freeman, and when Negroes were disfranchised in 1835, several hundred colored men were entitled to vote. In fact, as Albert Bushnell Hart says, "In the colonies, freed Negroes, like freed indentured white servants, acquired property, founded families, and came into the political community, if they had the energy, thrift, and fortune to get the necessary property."

In order to forward this movement, the Constitution permitted and subsequent legislation spurred by the Haitian revolt confirmed the abolition of the foreign slave trade. This meant not simply putting a stop to the further importation of slaves but also, and closely bound up with this, the firm conviction of all Americans that without an active slave trade the slave system would disappear. The Act of 1808, therefore, was conceived as a first and decisive step toward the overthrow of the old slave system and represented a triumph of abolitionism both North and South. Even then, however, there was some opposition to this legislation and open violation of it for many years because of the loss of slaves during the war and the consequent curtailment of the labor force on Southern plantations.

Two things ensued: Slavery changed in the United States from a slave-consuming to a slave-conserving system, and the Negroes, being more carefully treated, increased rapidly in number from a million to a million and three-quarters between 1800 and 1820. It was evident that the American Negro unassisted by the slave trade would not die out, and for that reason there arose the movement begun by the American Colonization Society in 1816 which resulted in the establishment of Liberia.

The forces back of colonization were fatally divided. Some wished to repatriate American Negroes in Africa and others wished to get rid of free Negroes so as to buttress the slave system. Simultaneously with this, came an increase of the cotton crop from 8,000 bales in 1790 to 650,000 bales in 1820. This phenomenal increase of a comparatively new crop was accompanied by the westward movement of the slave-cultivated area and by the birth of the Cotton Kingdom in the vivid minds of men, and the death of the colonization idea.

A new slavery began to appear, whose aim was production rather than consumption as represented by house service. It led to slave conspiracy and revolt dangerous in portent if not in actual fact. Several small insurrections are alluded to in South Carolina early in the eighteenth century, and one by Cato at Stono in 1739 caused widespread alarm. The Negro plot in New York in 1712 put the city into hysterics. There was no further plotting on any scale until the Haitian revolt, which shook the whole slave edifice to its foundation and terrified the New World. There were laws and migrations and a new series of plots. Gabriel in Virginia, in 1800, made an abortive attempt. In 1822 a free Negro, Denmark Vesey, in South Carolina, failed in a well-laid plot, and ten years after that, in 1831, Nat Turner led his insurrection in Virginia and killed fifty-one persons. The result of this insurrection was to crystallize tendencies toward harshness, which the economic revolution was making advisable.

A wave of legislation passed over the South, strengthening and enforcing the laws prohibiting the slaves from learning to read and write, forbidding Negroes to preach, and interfering with their religious meetings. Thus between 1830 and 1850 the philosophy of the South changed: it strongly repressed the slaves by a more careful patrol system; and it began to rationalize slavery with theories of race inferiority. In reaction from this there came the "Underground Railway" which systematized the regular and increasing running away of slaves toward the North, thus adding fuel and giving practical examples to the rising abolition movement.

The most effective revolt of the Negro against slavery was not fighting, but running away, usually to the North, which had been recently freed of slavery. From the beginning of the nineteenth century slaves began to escape in considerable numbers. Four geographical paths were chiefly followed: one, leading southward, was the line of swamps along the coast from Norfolk, Virginia, to the northern borders of Florida. This gave rise to the Negro element among the Indians in Florida and led to the two Seminole wars of 1817 and 1835. These wars were really slave raids to make the Indians give up the Negro and half-breed slaves domiciled among them. The wars cost the United States ten million dollars and two thousand lives. The great Appalachian range, with its abutting mountains, was the safest path northward, and this John Brown plotted to develop. Through Tennessee and Kentucky and the heart of the Cumberland

Mountains, using the limestone caverns, was the third route, and the valley of the Mississippi was the western tunnel.

These runaways and the freedmen of the North soon began to form a group of people who sought to consider the problem of slavery and the destiny of the Negro in America. Negroes passed through many psychological changes of attitude in the years from 1700 to 1850. At first, in the early part of the eighteenth century, there was but one thought: revolt and revenge, with possible return to Africa. The developments of the latter half of the century brought an attitude of hope and adjustment and emphasized the differences between the slave and the free Negro. The African background was forgotten and resented. The first part of the nineteenth century brought two movements: among the free Negroes, an effort at self-development and protection through organization; and among slaves and recent fugitives, a distinct reversion to the older idea of revolt and migration.

On the other hand, the cotton crop leaped from 650,000 bales in 1820 to 2,500,000 bales in 1850 and was destined to reach the phenomenal height of four million bales in 1860. This new and tremendous economic foundation for a new Negro slavery increased the economic rivalry between the cotton-raising South and the increasingly industrialized North.

There seemed to the South two ways of escape from the domination which northern industry exercised over them by its larger capital, close organization and concentrated aims: one was to encourage industry in the South. Already there was a considerable number of slave artisans and some faint beginnings of a factory system. But if this was to be increased, slaves must be trained and educated or white artisans imported. Either alternative was dangerous for the slave system. The South feared free Negroes, and free Negroes were showing increasing group consciousness. They began to develop writers who expressed their reaction against slavery. They organized beneficial and insurance societies. They set up independent churches and fought in the War of 1812. In cities like Cincinnati and Philadelphia they came into sharp physical conflict with the white workers and as a result began to consider the possibilities of emigration from the United States. After a series of conventions, large numbers went to Canada where they were offered asylum, and later agents were sent to Central America, Haiti and Africa. Leaders arose like Frederick Douglass, who made his first speech in 1841, and a number of educated Negroes and others of ability went to Liberia and West Africa.

The second path which the white South considered for the development of an economy based on slavery was to build up an agricultural monopoly in the South and in slave territory which might eventually be annexed, and then make terms with industry both in the northern United States and in the world. This latter plan, however, called for accumulating capital in a spending and luxury-loving group, and for discipline and practical self-control to which the South had never been used. Nevertheless, the increasing cotton crop, and an almost unlimited world demand for it, seemed to insure the prosperity of the South, unless the slave system was interfered with; and the interference which the South would not and, in defense of its system, could not brook, was limitation of its political power by which it had hitherto maintained ascendancy in the nation. This political power was increased by counting three-fifths of the slave population. Slavery was forced north of Mason and Dixon's line in 1820; a new slave empire with thousands of slaves was annexed in 1850, and a fugitive slave law was passed which decreased fugitives even if it endangered the liberty of every free Negro and nullified the Common Law; finally determined attempts were made to force slavery into the Northwest in competition with free white labor, and less concerted but powerful movements arose to annex Cuba and other slave territory to the south and to reopen the African slave trade.

It looked like a triumphant march for the slave barons, but each step cost more than the last. Missouri gave rise to the early abolitionist movement. Mexico and the fugitive slave law affronted the democratic ideal in the North, and Kansas developed a counter-attack from the free labor system, not simply of the North, but of the civilized world. The result was war; a war not to abolish but to limit slavery. It was fought to protect free white laborers against the competition of slaves, and it was thought possible to do this by segregating slavery.

At this critical point the South proposed to establish a separate and independent state where the slave system would be absolutely protected politically and from which economically fortified retreat it could make terms with the industrial world. The North, on the other hand, was determined not to surrender a part of its territory which was not only a market for its manufactures and agricultural products but the source of raw materials—tobacco, sugar, and cotton.

In the revolution which ensued, the possible reaction of the slaves was ignored by all except the small party of abolitionists, with its contingent of free Negroes. In the end, however, this great mass of four million slaves settled the physical conflict, even though the mass of them remained on the plantations. They were from the first a source of great anxiety, and a considerable percentage of them at every opportunity ran away to the area occupied by Northern armies and became servants and laborers; eventually, to the number of 200,000, they became actual soldiers bearing arms.

The first thing that vexed the Northern armies on Southern soil during the war was the question of the disposition of these fugitive slaves, who began to arrive in increasing numbers. Butler confiscated them, Frémont freed them, and Halleck caught and returned them; but their numbers swelled to such large proportions that the mere economic problem of their presence overshadowed everything else, especially after the Emancipation Proclamation. Their flight from the plantation was not merely bewildered swarming; it was the growth of an increasingly purposeful general strike against slavery, after the well-known pattern of the Underground Railway. Lincoln welcomed and encouraged it, once he realized that even the idle presence of the Negroes was so much strength withdrawn from the Confederacy.

It gradually became clear to the North that here they had tapped a positive source of strength to their cause, which would balance the indisposition of large numbers of white Northerners, especially laborers and foreign immigrants, to enter the army; and also the South saw just as quickly that here was a point of fatal weakness which they had unconsciously feared. The moment that any considerable number, not to mention the majority, of their four million slaves stopped work, much less took up arms, the cause of the South was lost.

The Emancipation Proclamation was forced not simply by the necessity of paralyzing agriculture in the South, but also by the necessity of employing Negro soldiers. During the first two years of the war no one wanted Negro soldiers. It was declared to be a "white man's war." General Hunter tried to raise a regiment in South Carolina, but the War Department disavowed the act. In Louisiana the Negroes were anxious to enlist, but were held off. But the war did not go as swiftly as the North had hoped, and on the twenty-sixth of January, 1863, the Secretary of War authorized the Governor of Massachusetts to raise two regiments of Negro troops. Frederick Douglass and others began the work of enlistment with enthusiasm, and in the end one hundred and eighty-seven thousand Negroes enlisted in the Northern armies, of whom seventy thousand were killed and wounded.

The conduct of these troops was exemplary. They were indispensable in camp duties and brave on the field, where they fought in two hundred and thirteen engagements. General Banks wrote, "Their conduct was heroic. No troops could be more determined or more daring." Abraham Lincoln said, "The slightest knowledge of arithmetic will prove to any man that the rebel armies cannot be destroyed with Democratic strategy. It would sacrifice all the white men of the North to do it. There are now in the service of the United States near two hundred thousand able-bodied colored men, most of them under arms, defending and acquiring Union territory. . . . Abandon all the posts now garrisoned by black men; take two hundred thousand men from our side and put them in the battlefield or cornfield against us, and we would be compelled to abandon the war in three weeks."

Emancipation thus came as a war measure to break the power of the Confederacy, preserve the Union, and gain the sympathy of the civilized world. It was this fact even more than the exhaustion of Southern resources and the success of Northern armies, which induced the South to surrender long before they had reached the theoretical limits of their resources. The emancipation of the slaves, promised during the war both as a moral sop to abolition sentiment and a needed addition to Northern resources, became a fact after Lee's surrender. And then for the first time the nation had to sit down and consider a situation which it had never before envisaged realistically.

The initial settlement of the problem, proposed by the South, and at first not strongly opposed in the North, was to substitute serfdom for slavery; and a series of Negro codes to this end were passed by the Southern states. These were so unnecessarily drastic that they increased the sympathy with Negroes in the North, already well-disposed because of the military service of black soldiers.

To protect Negroes therefore, a Freedmen's Bureau was proposed

1. To oversee the making and enforcement of wage contracts for freedmen.
2. To appear in the courts as the freedmen's best friend.
3. To furnish the freedmen with a minimum of land and of capital.

4. To establish schools.
5. To furnish such institutions of relief as hospitals, outdoor relief stations, etc.

Such an institution was bitterly opposed in the South as interfering with labor control, and given but half-hearted support in the North because it was too costly and a bad precedent in labor relations. The temporary makeshift which was actually enacted had neither time, sufficient funds nor proper organization for wide success.

Even under such conditions, the Freedmen's Bureau in its short hectic life accomplished a great task. Carl Schurz, in 1865, felt warranted in saying that "not half of the labor that has been done in the South this year, or will be done there next year, would have been or would be done but for the exertions of the Freedmen's Bureau. . . . No other agency except one placed there by the national government could have wielded that moral power whose interposition was so necessary to prevent Southern society from falling at once into the chaos of a general collision between its different elements." Notwithstanding this, the Bureau was made temporary, was regarded as a makeshift, and soon abandoned.

Philanthropy poured out of the North to help the freedmen and establish schools; but the mass of Northerners were chiefly interested in the restoration of production and commerce and willing to leave the Negro to the control of the South, if this could be accomplished peacefully and profitably. The South was not satisfied with this and demanded increased political power, larger in proportion to its population than it had had before secession. This arose from the fact that each American Negro now counted for representation in Congress as one citizen instead of as three-fifths of a person, in accordance with the celebrated three-fifths compromise of the Constitution. Even with their normal political power, the returning South was a threat to Northern bond-holders, to the new national bank system, to the high tariff of manufacturers and to various other privileges and concessions which Northern industry had reaped during the war.

Northern industry gradually gained the support of an increasing feeling among the former abolitionists and ordinary American citizens, that the nation was rather shamelessly deserting its Negro allies; but the South, led blindly and stubbornly by Andrew Johnson, repudiated the Fourteenth Amendment and the establishment of a real Freedmen's Bureau. As a result the North placed its reliance upon what was at once a settled American political doctrine and a new political expedient: the political doctrine of democratic control exercised by newly emancipated black slaves, which was in reality now a political expedient, by which the South with this threat of black labor dictatorship over it, would consent to the industrial policies which the dominant North wanted.

An experiment in democracy followed which instead of being a complete failure as most Americans no doubt thought it would be, was so successful that a new revolutionary bargain was needed to overthrow it. In 1867, a Dictatorship of the Proletariat was established in a large part of the South, with black and white workers in the majority. It was not a dictatorship conscious of any plan for continuing labor control of government. On the contrary, it was vitiated by the old American doctrine which assumed that any thrifty worker could become a capitalist. And yet this temporary dictatorship envisaged a chance for the poor freedman and the poor white to control enough wealth and capital to overturn the power of the former planters and slave barons. As steps toward this, they introduced democratic control in states where it had not been the rule; they began a new social legislation which gave government aid to the poor; they essayed protection from crime and furnished state capital to enterprises like railways. And above all, led especially by the blacks, they established a public elementary school system.

The chief charges against these labor and Negro governments are extravagance, theft, and incompetency of officials. There is no serious charge that these governments threatened civilization or the foundations of social order. The charge is that they threatened property and that they were inefficient. These charges are undoubtedly in part true; but they are often exaggerated. The South had been impoverished and saddled with new social burdens. In other words, states with smaller economic resources were asked not only to do a work of restoration, but a larger permanent social work. The property-holders were aghast. They not only demurred, but, predicting ruin and revolution, they appealed to "race" pride, secret societies, intimidation, force and murder. They refused to believe that these novices in government and their friends were aught but scamps and fools. Under the resulting circumstances directly after the war, the wisest statesman would have been compelled to resort to increased taxation and would have, in turn, been execrated by property-holders as extravagant, dishonest, and incompetent.

Much of the legislation which resulted in fraud was basically sound. Take, for instance, the land frauds of South Carolina. The Federal Government refused to furnish land. A wise Negro leader said, "One of the greatest slavery bulwarks was the infernal plantation system, one man owning his thousand, another his twenty, another fifty thousand acres of land. This is the only way by which we will break up that system, and I maintain that our freedom will be of no effect if we allow it to continue. What is the main cause of the prosperity of the North? It is because every man has his own farm and is free and independent. Let the lands of the South be similarly divided." From such arguments the Negroes were induced to aid a scheme to buy land and distribute it. Yet a large part of eight hundred thousand dollars appropriated found its way to the white land-holders' pockets through artificially inflated prices.

The most inexcusable cheating of the Negroes took place through the failure of the Freedmen's Bank. This bank was incorporated by Congress in 1865 and had in its list of incorporators some of the greatest names in America, including Peter Cooper, William Cullen Bryant, and John Jay. The bank did excellent work in thrift and saving for a decade and then through neglect and dishonesty was allowed to fail in 1874, owing the freedmen their first savings of over three millions of dollars. They have never been reimbursed.

Many Negroes and whites were venal, but more were ignorant and deceived. The question is: Did they show any signs of a disposition to lean to better things? The theory of democratic government is not that the will of the people is always right, but rather that normal human beings of average intelligence will, if given a chance, learn the right and best course by bitter experience. This is precisely what the Negro voters showed indubitable signs of doing. First, they strove for schools to abolish ignorance, and, second, a large and growing number of them revolted against the extravagance and stealing that marred the beginning of Reconstruction, and joined with the best elements to institute reform. The greatest stigma on the white South is not that it resented theft and incompetence, but that, when it saw the reform movements growing and even in some cases triumphing, and a larger and larger number of black voters learning to vote for honesty and ability, it still preferred a Reign of Terror to a campaign of education, and disfranchised men for being black and not for being dishonest.

In the midst of all these difficulties, the Negro governments in the South accomplished much of positive good. We may recognize three things which Negro rule gave to the South: (1) democratic government, (2) free public schools, (3) new social legislation.

There is no doubt that the thirst of the black man for knowledge, a thirst which has been too persistent and durable to be mere curiosity or whim, gave birth to the public school system of the South. It was the question upon which black voters and legislators insisted more than anything else, and while it is possible to find some vestiges of free schools in some of the Southern States before the war, yet a universal, well-established system dates from the day that the black man got political power.

Finally, in legislation covering property, the wider functions of the state, the punishment of crime and the like, it is sufficient to say that the laws on these matters established by Reconstruction legislatures were not only different from and even revolutionary to the laws in the older South, but they were so wise and so well-suited to the needs of the new South that, in spite of a retrogressive movement following the overthrow of the Negro governments, the mass of this legislation, with elaboration and development, still stands on the statute books of the South.

In the process of accomplishing this revolutionary change in Southern economy there was waste and theft due in part to ignorance and in part to the deliberate connivance of the best elements in the community, who were determined that Negro suffrage and labor control should cease. The old planter class was decimated by the war and hard experiences after the war, and their place taken by new capitalists, some trained after the Northern industrial pattern and all eager to follow it. This new leadership of the South was eager to strike a bargain with the industrial North and they did so in 1876.

The bargain consisted in allowing the Southern whites to disfranchise the Negroes by any means which they wished to employ, including force and fraud, but which somehow was to be reduced to semblance of legality in time. And then that the South hereafter would stand with the North in its main industrial policies and all the more certainly so, because Northern capital would develop an industrial oligarchy in the old South.

Forcible overthrow of democratic government in the South followed from 1872 to 1876. Negroes were kept from voting by force and intimidation, while whites were induced to vote as employers wished by emphasizing race hate and fear. The disfranchisement of 1876 and later was followed by the widespread rise of "crime" peonage. Stringent laws on vagrancy, guardianship, and labor contracts were enacted and large discretion given judge and jury in cases of petty crime. As a result Negroes were systematically arrested on the slightest pretext and the labor of convicts leased to private parties.

In more normal economic lines, the employers began with the labor contract system. Before the war they owned labor, land and subsistence. After the war they still held the land and subsistence. The laborer was hired and the subsistence "advanced" to him while the crop was growing. The fall of the Freedmen's Bureau hindered the transmutation of this system into a modern wage system, and allowed the laborers to be cheated by high interest charges on the subsistence advanced and in book accounts.

The black laborers became deeply dissatisfied under this system and began to migrate from the country to the cities, where there was a competitive demand for labor and money wages. The employing farmers complained bitterly of the scarcity of labor and of Negro "laziness," and secured the enactment of harsher vagrancy and labor contract laws, and statutes against the "enticement" of laborers. So severe were these laws that it was often impossible for a laborer to stop work without committing a felony.

Nevertheless competition compelled the landholders to offer more inducements to the farm hand. The result was the rise of the black share tenant; the laborer, securing better wages, saved a little capital and began to hire land in parcels of forty to eighty acres, furnishing his own tools and seed and practically raising his own subsistence. In this way the whole face of the labor contract in the South was, in the decade 1880–90, in process of change from a nominal wage contract to a system of tenantry. The great plantations were apparently broken up into forty and eighty acre farms with black farmers. To many it seemed that emancipation was accomplished, and the black folk were especially filled with joy and hope.

It soon was evident, however, that the change was only partial. The landlord still held the land in large parcels. He rented this in small farms to tenants, but retained indirect control. In theory the laborer was furnishing capital, but in the majority of cases he was borrowing at least a part of this capital from some merchant at usurious interest.

Nevertheless, Negroes had begun the accumulation of land and property and had eagerly accepted the democratic ideals of popular suffrage and the eventual accomplishment of social and economic salvation by means of the vote. In the two decades from 1880 to 1900 they tried desperately to put this program into accomplishment by efforts to regain their lost political power; but these were the years of tremendous expansion of industry and wealth in the United States and the world over; government was dominated by business and the possibility of any real political influence on the part of a poor and socially excluded minority was extremely small.

The illegal disfranchisement of the Negro, against which he was protesting in season and out, now began to be buttressed by law. In 1890 Mississippi disfranchised Negroes by a literacy test, securing the acquiescence of the ignorant whites by requiring on the part of the prospective voter either the ability to read or "understand" a part of the Constitution read to him by sympathetic officials. South Carolina followed in 1895 by an illiteracy or property test and the Mississippi "understanding" clauses. In 1898 Louisiana enacted an illiteracy and property test and added to that the celebrated "Grandfather Clause" which allowed persons to vote whose father or grandfather had had the right to vote before Negroes were enfranchised. Variations and elaborations of this kind of disfranchisement followed in Alabama in 1901, Virginia in 1902, in Georgia in 1909. Not only were these laws clearly unfair if not unconstitutional, but their administration was openly and designedly discriminatory. Yet in the cases rushed before the courts, they were invariably upheld; indeed it was not until 1915 that even the "Grandfather Clause" was declared unconstitutional.

To all this was added a series of labor laws making the exploitation of Negro labor more secure. All this legislation had to be accomplished in the face of the labor movement throughout the world, and particularly in the South, where it was beginning to enter among the white workers. This was accomplished easily, however, by an appeal to race prejudice. No method of inflaming the darkest passions of men was unused. Racial sex jealousy was especially emphasized. The lynching mob was given its glut of blood and egged on by purposely exaggerated and often wholly invented tales of crime on the part of perhaps the most peaceful and sweet-tempered people the world has known. Labor laws were so arranged that imprisonment for debt was possible and leaving an employer could be made a penitentiary offense. Negro schools were cut off with small appropriations or wholly neglected, and a determined effort was made with wide success to see that no Negro had any voice either in the making or the administration of local, state, or national law.

The acquiescence of the white labor vote of the South was further insured by throwing white and black laborers, so far as possible, into competing economic groups and making each feel that the one was the cause of the other's troubles. The neutrality of the white people of the North was secured through their fear for the safety of large investments in the South, and through the fatalistic attitude common both in America and Europe toward the possibility of real advance on the part of the darker peoples.

It was natural that a leader should arise at this time who should point out the necessity of economic adjustment before political defense was possible. Booker T. Washington in his celebrated speech in Atlanta in 1896 enunciated this principle and united under his leadership Southern whites who wanted nothing so much as an end to political pretentions on the part of Negroes; Northern whites who wanted to encourage the development of a dependable labor force in the South not dominated by the labor class consciousness of the North; and by Negroes who were willing to give up their right to vote and hold office if they but had a chance to earn a living.

What Mr. Washington did not see or understand was the connection of his movement with the labor movement of the world. His idea was to develop skilled labor under the benevolent leadership of white capital; and out of wages to save capital so as to develop a Negro bourgeoisie who would hire black labor and co-operate with white capital. He did not know the difficulty, indeed the practical impossibility, of this program, when capital was willing to exploit race prejudice and the rivalry of race groups in industry, and at a time when the possibility of accumulating capital on the part of laborers and in competition with the great monopolies of capital in the industrial world was rapidly coming to an end. Even more than that, he did not foresee, perhaps could not have foreseen, the disappearance of special technical skills before mass production and the impossibility of establishing a permanent system of education based on the handing on of skills which might easily become obsolete in a generation or even in a day.

The political revolt of white labor against prevalent conditions began about 1880 and American farmers joined the movement by 1890. Populism arose both in the West and in the South, but Negroes paid little attention to it. They were bound up in the Washington idea that their salvation lay in close alliance with capital. The result was that there was some alliance between black and white labor in the South, as for instance when Negro Republicans and white Populists elected a congressman in North Carolina in 1896; in Georgia on the contrary, Tom Watson, exasperated because the Populists did not get a larger Negro following, tried the experiment of joining the forces for Negro disfranchisement and anti-Semitism, and thus cut the labor foundation from under his own feet.

This failure on the one hand of Negroes to make common cause with white labor and the failure of white labor on the other hand to invite or desire their co-operation, together with the bitter agitation for disfranchisement, increased mob violence and lynching. The lynchings in one year, 1892, numbered two hundred thirty-five. In the period between 1882 and 1927 nearly five thousand persons were lynched in the United States, and three thousand five hundred of these were Negroes. Race hatred reached an apogee, and with it came the series of laws in the South and some Northern states which established persons of Negro descent as a caste with curtailed civil rights in matters of marriage, travel, residence, and social intercourse.

The twentieth century saw a determined effort on the part of Negroes to stem this tide. They had made efforts at general organization within racial lines since the first convention in 1830; and just before and during the Civil War they had held a number of very effective general congresses. In the nineties they started the Afro-American Council as a national organization, which held annual meetings and served to consolidate public opinion. But the real effective effort came in 1905 with the Niagara Movement which clarified and laid down a new clear bill of rights. In 1910 the leaders of the Niagara Movement were joined by a large number of white liberals and the resulting organization was the National Association for the Advancement of Colored People. The Association proved, between 1910 and the World War, one of the most effective organizations of the liberal spirit and the fight for social progress which the Negro race in America has known. It won case after case before the Supreme Court, establishing the validity of the Fifteenth Amendment, the unconstitutionality of the "Grandfather Clause" and the illegality of residential segregation. Above all, it began a determined nation-wide and interracial fight against lynching which eventually reduced this relic of barbarism from two hundred thirty-five victims a year to eighteen.

The World War radically altered this whole situation. First of all came the economic results. Immigration since the Civil War had poured into the North such a mass of laborers that industry had a reservoir of labor at low prices which they could discharge and rehire at will. This abundance of labor had kept the Negro largely out of industry in the North, because of exacerbated race prejudice and fear of wage under-bidding, which on the other hand largely repelled foreign immigration to the South; and in the whole land excluded Negroes, by competition and lack of opportunity, from learning skilled operations.

The War stopped this flow of immigrants as early as 1914 and with equal suddenness the Negro began to pour into the North, until by 1920 black workers and their families to a total of two million had left the South. This caused difficulties of competition for jobs with whites, which resulted in riots in East St. Louis, Chicago, Pennsylvania, Washington and elsewhere. Despite this the Negro found work and the best paid work that he had been able to do since emancipation.

The result was a great increase in his economic power, and also his political influence as a voter, especially in Northern cities and as part of a new labor movement with which he began to make tentative alliance. When the United States was drawn into the war, his power was revealed. The government had to pay him special attention. German propaganda was feared. A conference of Negro editors was held in Washington; a Negro was made adviser to the Secretary of War; and when the War Department determined not to appoint Negro officers, a nationwide Negro agitation compelled the opening of a special camp for their training. Eventually seven hundred Negro officers were commissioned. Of all the white nations that took part in the World War, the United States was the only nation that recognized its colored constituents to any such extent. England did not have a single officer of acknowledged Negro blood; France had many, but no such number as America.

After the war and with the depression, the Negro's position again became critical. Mass production gave him entrance into industry formerly largely monopolized by skilled white workers, but the general depression threw the Negro first into the ranks of the unemployed. He was saved from something like economic annihilation by his increased political power, based on the black population in cities like New York, Philadelphia, St. Louis, Pittsburgh and Chicago. After a lapse of thirty years, one Negro congressman appeared in Washington and Negroes became members of state legislatures in a dozen different states and were represented on city councils. While they lost a good many of the more spectacular political jobs that were formerly set aside for them, they gained representation for merit and training in a number of less conspicuous but important positions under the New Deal.

But above all they had to examine again the balance of importance between political and economic power. It was pointed out that the casting of a ballot must not be simply for the election of officials or to settle at infrequent times, broad contrasting matters of policy; but rather that real democracy can be attained only when the laborer can express his wishes in industry; when he has a voice in the production and distribution of wealth. And while the broad accomplishment of this great advance in human progress is not in the hands of the Negro voter today, he has the opportunity of starting toward it through the organization of his power as a consumer and by utilization of the cultural bands of his racial grouping to secure industrial emancipation.

Meantime the American Negro forms an important group. It has a population larger than Sweden, Norway and Denmark together and owned, before the depression, land equal to half the area of Ireland. He forms nine and seven-tenths per cent of the population of the land, with nine and one-third million of its population living in the South and two and one-half million in the North. Fifty-six per cent live in towns and cities of two thousand five hundred or more. The crude death rate in the registration area is 18.7 per 1,000 of population, but most Negroes live outside this area. The illiteracy of this population ten years of age and over is reported as 16.3 per cent, although probably in reality it is considerably larger than this. Two and one-half million Negro children are in school.

The Negroes are occupied as farmers, laborers and servants; 36 per cent being engaged in agriculture; 19 per cent in manufacture and mechanical industries, chiefly as laborers and porters; and 28 per cent in domestic and personal service. In addition to these there are 25,000 clergymen, 56,000 teachers, 4,000 physicians, 2,000 dentists, 1,200 lawyers, 6,000 trained nurses and 11,000 musicians. Beside these there are 34,000 barbers and hairdressers, 108,000 chauffeurs and truck drivers, 28,000 retail dealers, 6,000 mail-carriers, 11,000 masons, 21,000 mechanics, 15,000 painters.

At the Census of 1930, the number of Negro farm operators was 882,850, with 37,597,132 acres; the value of the land and buildings, $1,402,945,799. Their ownership was 20.5 per cent; the number of farms owned, 181,016, and the value of their owned land and buildings $334,451,396. Negro representation is weakest in the higher ranks of skilled labor, business and commerce. Nevertheless, Negroes are so integrated in American industry that they are for the present at least indispensable.

There are 42,500 Negro churches with five million members and property worth $200,000,000. In American poetry, prose literature, music and art, the Negro has gained notable recognition. In sports and physical prowess, representatives of this race have continually come to the fore.

It is astonishing how the African has integrated himself into American civilization. The first national holiday, the fifth of March, commemorated the death of Crispus Attucks. In the War of 1812, the Civil War, the Spanish War and the World War, Negro soldiers were prominent.

Paul Cuffee began agitation and a movement to Africa, and David Walker's Appeal anticipated the abolition movement. That movement received indispensable aid from Douglass, Remond and Sojourner Truth. After the Civil War, Lynch of Mississippi, Cardozo and Eliott of South Carolina, and Dunn and Dubuclet of Louisiana were recognized as able political leaders.

In science, Banneker issued early American almanacs and assisted in surveying the city of Washington. Later Just made a record in biology; Turner in entomology and Fuller in psychiatry; Hinton is today a leading American authority on syphilis.

In religion, Richard Allen was a national leader; Payne and Turner prominent and forceful; and Pennington received his doctor of divinity from Heidelberg in 1843. Chavis and Booker Washington were leading educators; George Leile and Lott Carey led in American foreign missionary effort. As inventors Matseliger founded our pre-eminence in shoe manufacture, Rillieux in sugar and McCoy began the lubrication of running machinery.

But it is in art that the Negro stands pre-eminent: his folk song began its wide influence with the Fisk Jubilee Singers; and was followed by the compositions of the Lamberts, Rosamond Johnson, Dett, Burleigh and Handy. There are the great voices of the "Black Patti," Roland Hayes and Marian Anderson. For years, before his recent death, Henry O. Tanner was the dean of the American painters. The stage has had no comedian to surpass Bert Williams and every year brings a new dramatic figure like Gilpin and Richard Harrison.

The Negro's work in literature was begun by Phyllis Wheatley. She was not a great writer, but she led American literature in her day. In Louisiana in 1843–45, Negroes published an anthology of their poetry which represents a higher literary standard than anything contemporary in the United States. In the early twentieth century came Chesnutt and Dunbar, Braithwaite who revived appreciation for poetry in America; James Weldon Johnson and Benjamin Brawley. The record, by no means complete, is an astonishing proof of the capacity of the Negro race.

NOTES

1. Eleven to fifteen per cent, 1850 to 1890.
2. *Cf.* Herskovits, *The American Negro*.

CHAPTER XI

◆

Black Europe

So what is Africa? Guernier repeats in 1933 the ancient lie of 1833: "Seule de tous les continents, l'Afrique n'a pas d'histoire." This preludes modestly his thesis that Africa is the future field of exploitation and expansion for Europe; that Europe is being hemmed in and forced out of the teeming and revivified East; that Europe can hope for no further foothold in the American West; but that the black South can be regarded as open, virgin, empty soil.

The drama which has played itself out in Africa has been as human and dramatic and intensely interesting as that of any other continent. That it did not finally integrate into one great and unified culture, like that of Europe or of China, was the clear and logical result of its physical characteristics and of the slave trade. The human spirit that expanded in Africa was the same humanity that all the world knows. It shows itself in family and clan, in town and city, in individual genius, and above all in art, an art that connoisseurs today recognize among the great aesthetic traditions of the world. But all this was surrounded and conditioned by a plateau that warded off easy egress to the sea; by a desert that limited contact with other worlds, and by a climate the most difficult in some respects which human life ever faced.

On this continent came early, if not the earliest, writhing of humanity in its urge toward food and shelter, protection and adventure. Starting in the Great Lakes, it swept up the Valley of the Nile and probably into the Valley of the Tigris-Euphrates. Traces of it can be found along the shores of the Mediterranean and in Crete. Limited by the jealous desert, it sailed westward down the Niger and wound around the central jungle with the Congo.

In all these centers the Negro race throve, inspiring and sharing the civilization of Egypt and developing the culture of Ethiopia. Toward the west arose its groups of villages and in the center its kingdoms and autonomous tribes. Integration into great states came in the South, inspired by contact perhaps with dark India; and again when Arab culture swept the southern shores of the Mediterranean and penetrated Negroland through the gateway of ancient Ghana. Great states arose and in the fifteenth century the outlook for African civilization south of the desert and south of the jungle was comparable to the outlook for renascent civilization north of the Mediterranean. But this culture had to fight the village states of the

West and the wild tribal agglomerations of the center, and found no natural protection like the Alps and Himalayas.

Out of the war and turmoil thus induced came a chance for aggression and
violence from abroad, despite the industry and state building of the North and
South. Then came heart disease; then came the slave trade. The world has captured and sold slaves before—slaves, white, black, yellow and brown. But before,
it was always a local or temporary movement limited in demand and supply by
humanitarian development. So too was the African trade, when it first began.
And so it remained for a century. But gradually it became the center of a new
world movement. It became the founding stone of a new world-encircling, world-
integrating movement: instigating and buttressing a new industrial and commercial method—a new Capitalism; its ordinary implications and human morality
were drowned in a tremendous development, which opened new vistas of empire
and power to men.

For half a millennium the human traffic raged, beginning with a drizzle in the
fifteenth century and rising to a flood in the eighteenth and early nineteenth, and
only dying in our day. A race was forcibly transplanted. Africa lost in actual captives, killed defenders, disease and murder, not less than fifty million souls, equal-
ing the natural increase of the land and more. The rich New World was rapidly
settled and in parts overrun with an alien labor caste of workers, bereft of the
most elementary rights of men, and raising crops on which the wealth of the
world rapidly became based. It may be doubted if the descent of barbarians on
Rome, the Mongol conquest of China, or the Moslem conquest of India had greater
if as great influence on the culture of mankind.

The economic revolution thus incited and sustained rested upon the fact that
in Indian America, also, no permanent integration of social life had been achieved
upon its double continent, so as to take complete possession. Here white men put
black slaves and most of the brown Indians to work to raise new crops for the
expanding wants of Europe: tobacco, cotton, sugar and rice. Their coming incited
the ingenuity of men. It was not a series of inventions that made the Industrial
Revolution. It was the new commerce and goods made by black men that incited
men to invention and built a new world. An extraordinary class struggle arose;
not among the peoples of one land, so much as between modern civilization and
primitive black labor transported to the free land of the West.

The whole attitude of the world was changed to fit this new economic reor-
ganization. Black Africa, which had been a revered example to ancient Greece
and the recognized contender with imperial Rome, became a thing beneath the
contempt of modern Europe and America. All history, all science was changed
to fit this new condition. Africa had no history. Wherever there was history in
Africa or civilization, it was of white origin; and the fact that it was civilization
proved that it was white. If black Pharaohs sat on the throne of Egypt they
were not really black men but dark white men. Ethiopia, land of the blacks, was
described as a land of the whites. If miracles of art appeared on the West Coast
these were imported from artless Portugal. If Zymbabwe, with mine and irrigation, appeared in the East, it was wholly Asiatic. If at any time, anywhere, there
was evidence in Africa of the human soul and the same striving of spirit and the

same build of body found elsewhere in the world, it was all due to something non-African and not to the inherent genius of the Negro race.

In the eighteenth century the slave trade was systematized, and greatly increased, chiefly under the English, who gave up the policy of monopoly and threw the trade open to the public. A mass of slaves was poured into the United States. The North American colonies at times protested the influx but the profits were too great and the crops too valuable. The American Revolution struck the first blow at the trade, first by the voluntary boycott known as the Association, and then by the Revolutionary war, which seriously interrupted it.

But it was the Haitian revolt that sounded the fatal warning. The world shuddered, and, spurred by the French Revolution, awoke to some realization of what Negro slavery really meant. But what could be done? The economic foundations lay too deep to be dislodged in a day. The Cotton Kingdom arose in the nineteenth century, and a frantic attempt to rewrite science and religion in the interest of enslaving a labor class, which succeeded to an astonishing degree, until the new Labor Movement opposing Capitalism began to spread.

Labor faced a new world, based upon the immense accumulation of capital goods and economic power based on black labor, cheap, rich land and new mastery of natural forces. But changes were imminent. The cost of procuring black labor was increasing, the methods of controlling it were growing more difficult and dangerous, and the fertility of the land under slave culture was decreasing. Slavery as the basis of industry was again passing, as it had failed under other conditions centuries before.

Attack on slavery through the slave trade began in 1807, but American smuggling kept it alive until it fell in a sudden blast of blood and fire, known as the American Civil War. The freeing of four million slaves in the United States followed at least by nominal emancipation in most slave-holding lands, threatened the whole economic organization of the world. A new industrial organization was called for.

Suddenly man-stealing was loudly condemned, especially in lands like England, which had built its vast wealth upon it. Poverty in the midst of wealth, political power checked and controlled by wealth, and national aims and ideals subject to international commercial control, brought a world-wide threat of revolution as the logical outcome of a struggle between the rich and the poor. Unless a new labor force, cheap and controlled, could be used to replace slaves and hold white labor in check, nineteenth century Capitalism was doomed.

Asia and America and the islands partially supplied the increasing demand for cheap labor and raw material, and Africa was not immediately regarded as of further commercial value.

In 1815 the slave trade was still taking a decreasing stream of Negroes from West Africa to the West Indies and South America, while the Arab trade in ivory and slaves was rife in East Africa, the Nile Valley and the Sudan. There was as yet no thought of any permanent occupation of Africa by Europe. France had Senegal on the West Coast and a few islands on the East Coast. England had practically all the land of the world available for white settlement: Canada, Australia and Cape Colony in South Africa; she had paramount influence in Egypt; she retained some

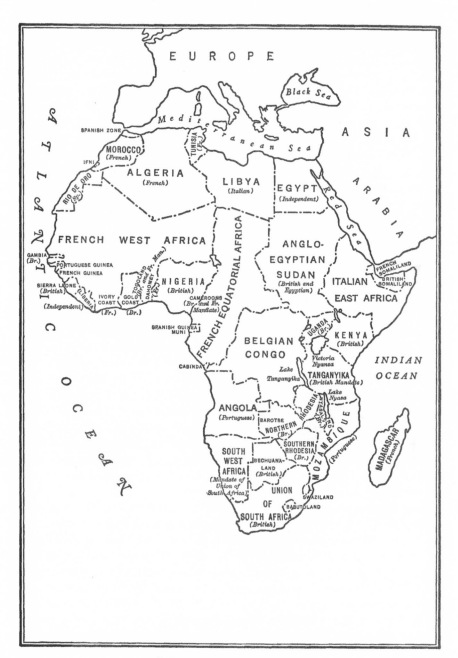

EUROPE

Black Sea

ASIA

Medi te rr anean Sea

A T L A N T I C   O C E A N

SPANISH ZONE

MOROCCO
(French)

IFNI

RIO DE ORO
(Sp.)

ALGERIA
(French)

TUNISIA
(Fr.)

LIBYA
(Italian)

EGYPT
(Independent)

ARABIA

Red Sea

FRENCH   WEST   AFRICA

GAMBIA
(Br.)

PORTUGUESE GUINEA
FRENCH GUINEA

SIERRA LEONE
(British)

LIBERIA
(Independent)

IVORY
COAST
(Fr.)

GOLD
COAST
(Br.)

TOGOLAND
(Br. and Fr. Man.)

DAHOMEY
(Fr.)

NIGERIA
(British)

CAMEROONS
*(Br. and Fr.
Mandate)*

FRENCH EQUATORIAL AFRICA

ANGLO-
EGYPTIAN
SUDAN
*(British and
Egyptian)*

ITALIAN
EAST AFRICA

FRENCH
SOMALILAND
BRITISH
SOMALILAND

SPANISH GUINEA
MUNI

CABINDA

BELGIAN
CONGO

*Lake
Tanganyika*

UGANDA
(Br.)

*Victoria
Nyanza*

KENYA
(British)

INDIAN
OCEAN

TANGANYIKA
(British Mandate)

*Lake
Nyasa*

ANGOLA
(Portuguese)

BAROTSE

NORTHERN
RHODESIA
(Br.)

RHODESIA

SOUTHERN
RHODESIA
(Br.)

MOZAMBIQUE
(Portuguese)

MADAGASCAR
(French)

SOUTH
WEST
AFRICA
*(Mandate of
Union of
South Africa)*

BECHUANA-
LAND
(British)

UNION
OF
SOUTH AFRICA
(British)

SWAZILAND

BASUTOLAND

POLITICAL AFRICA, 1939

of the West Indies Islands, and there were patches on the coast of West Africa where she was dominant. Portugal had various claims; but in all cases European claims consisted of a few factory stations and towns on the coast. The heart of Africa was unknown and its occupation unthought of.

On the other hand, beginning with the late eighteenth century and extending with increasing tempo into the nineteenth, came a stream of explorers; some urged by curiosity, some by science, some by trade. Mungo Park made his journeys in 1795 and 1805. Barth explored the Sudan in 1849 and 1851; but the great period of exploration came with Livingstone, who went to Africa in 1841 and died there in 1873. Following this came Cecil Rhodes; and capitalizing the mystery and potential wealth of Africa, came a triumph of newspaper reporting in the person of Henry M. Stanley, who went to Abyssinia in 1867. From then until 1897, he traversed the whole center of the continent, dramatizing for the world the future of Africa, in his finding of Livingstone, his rescuing of Emin Pasha, and his founding of the Congo Free State. It was Stanley who opened a new Africa to the imagination of the world as a field for European enterprise—as a Black Europe. So in the nineteenth and twentieth centuries, instead of stealing workers from Africa, the world turned gradually to enslaving workers in Africa; to the use of Africa as a reservoir of raw material, with local slave labor to supplement the industrial organization of Europe.

By curious coincidence, three distinct lines of development in the second half of the nineteenth century looked to many people as one, as simply three different views of the same forward movement; there was science moving from biology to anthropology and sociology in the race theory of Gobineau, the publication of the *Origin of the Species*, and the conclusions of La Pouge, Galton and Pearson; there was business in the triumph of the fully developed capitalist system with the transmuting of raw material into manufactures and world trade; and there was philanthropy making the Christian ideal practical in the courageous movement which had abolished the slave trade and modified slavery and was now about to undertake the material uplift and civilization of the Africans.

But in these three lines there were some fatal alliances. Science was the pensioner of business, and business and philanthropy were trying to appear as two aspects of social uplift: one of Livingstone's chief objects was to open up Africa to trade and so was Stanley's; the abolition of slavery during the Civil War in the United States was the beginning of a tremendous forward movement in industry which soon captured the imagination of the world. These movements seemed again in unity when, in 1876, Leopold of Belgium sought international effort in Africa. His plan, chameleon-like, assumed each protective coloration: first in the Brussels' meeting of 1876 it was a matter of scientific knowledge about Africa on the part of united Europe. National committees were formed in twelve different countries. But when the central committee met in Brussels a year later, already the scientific outlook had changed imperceptibly to the philanthropic and stations were to be established as "centers of civilization." Later, when diamonds were discovered in South Africa, emissaries of Leopold, who had formed a committee for studying the Upper Congo, met Stanley as he landed from his epoch-making trip across the continent in 1877 and wanted to know specifically and practically, "what protection native chiefs could give to commercial enterprises and what was the nature of the produce which could be dealt in, and how much capital a railway would need?"

The whole situation at this time in Africa was dramatized, first by the simple and unsophisticated Livingstone, who honestly saw business thrift and philanthropic effort as one, and next and especially by the more theatrical Stanley, who with all his grit and courage let nothing come between him and publicity. Philanthropy led by Livingstone concentrated on the Arabian slave trade and its abolition. Horrible pictures were painted of the murder and desolation which accompanied this surviving slavery; but it was not pointed out then nor has it been emphasized since, that this slavery differed from the West Coast American slave trade and slavery. This was, at least in the nineteenth century, apparently a trade in ivory and based upon the demand for ivory in the London market and later in Antwerp. Early in the nineteenth century London was importing three thousand hundred weight of ivory; by 1850 it had arisen to eight thousand, and by 1890 to over fourteen thousand. There must be added to this the Indian and Asiatic demand for ivory, partly supplied by Africa. Thus the Arabian slave trade of Livingstone and Stanley was a trade principally in ivory with Negroes forced to labor as porters and then sold, so that the slaves were a by-product of the world demand for ivory. These slaves were sold in the Nile Valley, the Sudan and Asia, and went into domestic service as well as labor; they were incorporated in the populations, increasing the Negro strain in North Africa and Asia, but not becoming the basis of new industry, new crops or new industrial demands.

Moreover, back of this cry for the abolition of the slave trade clothed in the shadow of great names like Wilberforce, Sharpe, Douglass, and Garrison, lurked political control. Algiers had been acquired by France in 1830, but this was a personal adventure of Charles X and his friends, for collection of a debt. After the Franco-Prussian War, however, Bismarck practically turned over Tunis to France, thus starting a vague dream of North African empire.

It began to be clear to scattered white traders of various nations in West Africa, that outside the matter of slaves, there was profit to be made. "In return for a few yards of cheap cottons, a few trinkets, obsolete guns, or the vilest and cheapest of spirits, enormous returns were obtained in oil and oil nuts, ivory, gold-dust, and other native products."[1] No sooner had the wounds of the Franco-Prussian War begun to heal than France, aroused by the developments in Egypt and South Africa, noticed again the colonial power of commercial England and started in North Africa in 1880 a series of explorations, military expeditions and business enterprises designed to secure an African empire with the idea that its produce and trade would pay. The whole world was becoming Africa-conscious.

Gradually business and philanthropy became scientific. Gobineau argued the inequality of races; the *Origin of Species* spread the doctrine of the survival of the fittest, and the "white man's burden" came later with Kipling. Conversion of the heathen in Africa did not involve living beside them as it would in America, and putting Negroes to work in Africa for the white man's profit and their own development seemed a natural and logical sequence.

Moreover, the new uplift of white labor which began with the English factory laws early in the nineteenth century and spread in the democratic movement of the Chartists and the continental revolutions of the thirties and forties, sought appeasement in the plan to supplement more highly paid European labor by the low paid labor of Africa and Asia, with the justification that even this low pay was higher than that of slavery and did away with the iniquities of the slave trade.

Thus in the shadow of the crusade for the abolition of the slave trade in the Sudan and East Africa, came increasing consciousness of the part which African labor could play in Africa and the value of indigenous crops and products like palm oil, ivory and rubber. Science, missionary enterprise, commercial exploitation and eventually political domination began to march hand in hand.

This did not necessarily involve conscious hypocrisy. This was an era when liberalism expressed itself in free individual enterprise and largely in free trade. It could be made to seem, therefore, a veritable triumph of liberalism, when instead of the slave trade, one had the local exploitation of African labor. This tendency was tremendously increased by the dramatic exposition of the wealth of the Congo Valley made by Stanley, and the discovery of gold and diamonds in South Africa.

The Belgian effort to internationalize this exploitation of Africa on a high plane of philanthropic effort at first had something of sincerity back of it; but in the cold and selfish mind of Leopold it turned into an international scramble in which he was meant to be the pawn, but turned out to be more wily than the chief actors. It became evident as the scramble for the known and dreamed-of wealth of Africa increased, that there must be some rules to this game of grab. A conference on the subject was suggested in June, 1884, and before the conference could be brought together, Germany, moving with disconcerting suddenness, outwitted England by seizing first Southwest Africa, then Togoland and the Cameroons on the West Coast; and finally, while the Berlin Conference was actually sitting in the fall of 1884, she secretly occupied parts of German East Africa and put up so bold a front that England had to yield it to her by treaty in 1885.

Portugal opposed the Congo Free State with perfectly valid claims, based on her discovery and co-operation with native governments; but Portugal was not observing color-caste and being a small and weak country she was brusquely pushed aside by England. France also had claims and ambitions and yielded only on the assurance that if the Belgian enterprise were given up, she would be heir. England also undoubtedly had the same idea, and Germany naturally would not let the Congo be divided without getting her share.

Here the business side of the whole Congo enterprise came openly to the front and the Independent Congo Free State which was eventually recognized by the world at the Berlin Conference of 1884–85, was a business organization in a day when business was regarded as philanthropy and philanthropy as business. This Stanley's proclamation of 1879 emphasized: "On the fourteenth of August, 1879, I arrived before the mouth of this river to ascend it, with the novel mission of sowing along its banks civilized settlements, to peacefully conquer and subdue it, to remold it in harmony with modern ideas into National States, within whose limits the European merchant shall go hand in hand with the dark

African trader, and justice and law and order shall prevail, and murder and lawlessness and the cruel barter of slaves shall be overcome."[2]

Thus the three chief European powers reached stalemate and balance of colonial power, where another forward step on the part of any one of them meant serious defeat for the other. Suspicions of each other therefore allowed Belgium to erect a state in central Africa, first through an international association formed at the Brussels Conference of 1876, but finally as the personal property of Leopold of Belgium—an unparalleled political development, and one designed to be temporary.

The world thereafter faced an Africa rapidly being absorbed by Europe, with 500,000 square miles under European claims and partial control in 1815; a million in 1880; six million in 1890; and eleven and one-half million in 1914. In this black Europe in Africa, there was a population of three million in 1815; ten million in 1880; seventy-five million in 1890; and one hundred and twenty-three million in 1914. At the outbreak of the World War, France had four and one half million square miles; Great Britain three and one half million; Germany and Italy a million; Belgium and Portugal each about eight hundred thousand; and Spain seventy-five thousand.

Singularly few folk have seen the inherent paradox and contradiction in the successive demands of science, business and philanthropy. In many minds slavery and religious conversion marched happily hand in hand; back of slave trade suppression lurked colonial imperialism, but when Mwanga killed Bishop Hannington, most Englishmen saw only heathen savagery and nothing of a race, back to the wall, fighting for independence. Theoretical racial inferiority becomes the firm foundation of low wages and high profits while philanthropy merits five per cent. Today as Africa becomes swiftly and increasingly an area of investment for Europe and America, of exploitation of land and labor for profit in the production of food, clothing, material for further manufacture, and luxuries, it is not easy for the world to realize the increasing contradiction between moneymakers and missionaries, between rulers and philanthropists; between education and subjection, between science and dogma. Perhaps least of all do missionaries, white officials and black students feel the fundamental stresses.

The basic difficulty of posing the present problems of Africa arises partly from the varieties of men who have represented the white world in Africa, and on whose testimony our present conceptions are based. We have sent holy men like Livingstone and Colenso; civil servants like Johnston and Guggisberg; freebooters like Lugard and Jameson; imperialists like Rhodes and Delamere, and endless commercial pirates who regarded neither God nor man. Out of these diverse strands we have sought to weave a single fabric of philanthropy and reason; but of fundamental weight in our judgments, has come lately, swiftly and increasingly, the overwhelmingly powerful influence of Africa as a source of income, as one of the foundation stones of world industrial organization.

Why are white folk in Africa today? There are two answers: economic enterprise and missionary effort, and, of these two, without any doubt economic enterprise is dominant. Just at the time, when public opinion in Europe and America is beginning with difficulty to realize that property and profit must be limited by considerations of the public weal, we are developing African colonies on the laissez faire economic philosophy, and in accord with eighteenth century racial theory and nineteenth century biology. It usually does not enter our thought that this colonial development in Africa and Asia must, in the interdependence of industry, powerfully condition all economic, political and social reform in the white world.

Ancient European and Asiatic penetration of Africa brought only cultural distinctions between Europeans, Asiatics and Negroes. In ancient Egypt there was long and bitter feud between cultural Egyptians and barbaric central African tribes, but no color line, because many Egyptians were black and most had mingled Asiatic and Negroid blood. Even when the Arabs invaded Africa and initiated a vast and organized trade in black slaves, the distinction between Asiatics and Africans was religion and culture, and never mere skin color. So too the early Portuguese explorers drew no color line.

When, however, modern Europe touched Africa, and mainly for trade, not settlement, the obvious and vivid contrasts in skin color between Europeans and Negroes were early rationalized as stigmata of a deep and eternal racial difference which justified slavery. In the century of the Renaissance, of militant Protestantism and reborn Catholicism, a new human slavery had to be justified in order to be permitted, and an incipient revolution in industry spurred men to seek such justification when by swift strides slave labor in America began to pay.

Thus the modern Color Bar arose. Europeans developed an economy in which increased profit went pari passu with color caste. This was exhibited by the steps in which various European nations became industrialized. The Portuguese, whose industrial development had not begun in the sixteenth century, treated the Negroes as prospective equals, intermarried with them and offered some of them chances for education and political development, while enslaving the mass. The Spaniards did the same, until the economic interests of their overseas empire over-bore their European interests.

On the other hand, the Dutch and the English, from the first, and, for a while, the French, had their main interest in their purchase and sale of Africans as workers, and found it safer and more profitable to treat them as an inferior creation. The growth of American slavery and the vast economic interests built upon it, led to a rationalization of this increasingly profitable form of race relations, in the modern form of the doctrine of racial inferiority.

For a century, science wasted time and stultified itself in seeking sanctions for a line of inter-racial conduct, which in reality had its only justification in the immense profits which Negro slavery brought to white Europe and America. Color, head-form, brain weight, comparative anatomy, and psychological reactions were in turn feverishly evoked, explored and distorted, to put a scientific foundation under a structure of plain, selfish profiteering, and to ward off the increasing threat of the awakening conscience of Christendom and the eventual development of a labor movement.

When the African problem changed from a matter of seizing and exporting black labor to methods of making use of labor in Africa for the raising of raw materials, the problem of the relation between whites and blacks in Africa gradually increased in complexity. During the slave trade, with some exceptions, the whites did not attempt settlement, land-ownership or dominion on the continent. Portugal tried this at first, but Portuguese enterprise did not develop into a chattel slave trade. The Dutch, English, and French established temporary "factories" on the coast, but acknowledged the independence and suzerainty of the Negro states and carried on trade with them.

When the abolition movement increased in power with the decreasing profit of the American plantation system, there came a period of hesitation when many thought that the best policy both for business and philanthropy was to leave Africa to the development of independent states both native and artificial, like Sierra Leone and Liberia, and to look forward to eventual trade with them. But the demand of world industry was too insistent and the policy of forcible partition and domination ensued. In this way the nations of Europe found themselves established more or less insecurely in Africa, with the necessity of working out a policy of relationship between whites and blacks.

One might envisage three types of race policy in Africa.[3] One policy is the individual development of whites and natives in parallel segregated areas. This answer will not suit those who wish to exploit Africa for profit, for one cannot physically segregate laborers and capitalists entirely. A second proposal might be a development of both races in a common economic structure, toward which each would make a contribution. This would call for European technique and capital and for native land and labor. But the maximum profit for whites could not be obtained unless the land was monopolized and native labor controlled; and maximum profit has usually been the goal of the imperialists. A third development would be a native economy built and controlled by the natives with the temporary guidance and advice of whites. This would be an ideal development, but it would yield a minimum of private profit and call for extraordinary and costly philanthropy.

Or to put the problem in another way, suppose white men settle and live in Africa, what will be their method and object? What shall be the relative weight of the three forces impinging on Africa today: the missionaries representing the church, the administrators representing political control, and industry aiming at profit? Concentrating our attention upon this matter of economic policy, shall we try to have two lines of economic development in Africa, one for whites and one for blacks, with a line of segregation between them; or shall we have them built into a single economic structure; or shall we think of African economic development with the European as temporary adviser and teacher? Due to varying conceptions and adaptations of these policies, and always impelled forward more or less blindly by the demand for income of European investors, there has arisen in modern Africa a series of paradoxical situations and conflicting ideals.

The study of the African Negroids and their relation to the white world might remain a matter of leisurely scientific study, but for one arresting fact; and that is, that in an age of unprecedented economic development and in a world knit together by industrial interdependence and torn even to the threat of cultural extinction by wealth rivalry, Africa is looming each year as a greater and greater reservoir of labor and materials. The tensions, jealousies and fears over the ownership and direction of this potential wealth are not only a direct world threat to

168 ◆ BLACK FOLK

peace, but an indirect hindrance to economic adjustment in culture lands. We have fared far since the day when Africa was valuable chiefly as a labor reserve for the sugar and cotton plantations of America. It cannot be too strongly emphasized that today it is the economic significance of Africa, and not the racial, that looms largest in the action of the world.

Today the possibilities of investment in Africa, investment in labor, land and materials, are not only attracting capital but the imagination of capitalists and statesmen. As Lord Olivier has pointed out, diamonds, one of the most valuable products of Africa, are peculiarly the sign of kept women and pawn brokers, with a value entirely emblematic, and for this reason "the most appropriate foundation imaginable for a policy of commercial imperialism." But beyond this, today Africa furnishes nine-tenths of the vegetable oils so widely used in manufacture; over one-half the gold; nearly one-fifth of the chrome ore; over one-fifth of the copper; fourteen per cent of the asbestos; 8.6 per cent of the tin; 14.4 per cent of the manganese; 10.9 per cent of the platinum; 7.5 per cent of the graphite, and a slowly but regularly increasing amount of cotton, wool, and hides. Thus in the basic raw materials of modern industrial life—metals, minerals, rubber, textiles and vegetable oils—Africa looms large in actual production. Of foods, sixty per cent of the cocoa, much fruit, and spice come from Africa; five million dollars worth of ivory is still exported annually.

This is but part of the story. The world is increasingly aware that the possibilities of Africa in production have only been lightly touched. Frenchmen like Guernier look upon Africa as a possible extension of Agricultural and Industrial Europe. They see wheat and corn for all Europe raised in Africa; cereals, fruits and vegetables as preponderant crops; the banana crop could surpass that of the West Indies. Vegetable oils in huge quantities might sometime replace mineral oils. The cotton crop could excel the American, not to mention other vegetable fibers. Cattle and sheep, hides and wool can be indefinitely expanded. Not only copper, but iron, manganese, chromium, cobalt, vanadium, radium and the rarer minerals are found, while possible African power production is among the greatest of all the continents.

Most significant in this respect is the argument which Germany with increasing vehemence is putting forward to prove the necessity of African colonies for any European state. Germany, it is reiterated, is obliged to import food and raw material in order to feed and clothe the population and maintain the activities of industry. Tropical and subtropical countries are of increasing importance as sources of supply. Before the World War they accounted for nearly one half of Germany's total imports. Germany's own colonies supplied only a small proportion of these imports, but that was due not to lack of capacity, but because they were only in the early stages of economic development. Fat, rubber, fibers, minerals, timber, cocoa, coffee, bananas, tea, lemons, and tobacco are instanced as necessary supplies from Africa, and it is pointed out that the German colonies were rapidly being developed to supply these needs. The recent and frantic efforts of the German four-year plan to supply "ersatz" for needed raw material is designed not simply for development of such materials in Europe; but even more clearly for the development of tropical fields in the future.

The white oligarchy in Kenya in 1923 drew this picture of the economic possibilities of Africa. "The development of British territories in Africa opens up a vista of commercial expansion so endless that calculated description is difficult. The bare facts are that the area of these territories is 4,000,000 square miles, as compared with India's 1,900,000; that India's overseas trade is about 350,000,000 pounds sterling, and British Africa's (excluding Egypt) is about 292,000,000 pounds; that the non-self-governing territories, whose total area is 2,628,498 square miles, already produce an overseas trade of 76,500,000 pounds sterling, although their development can hardly be said to have begun; that the average fertility and mineral wealth of their soil are at least equal to those of any other great land mass; that they hold an intelligent fast-breeding native population of about sixty millions, waiting for guidance to engage in the production of the raw materials of industry and food stuffs. . . ."[4]

The present economic significance of Africa is often minimized by pointing out that Africa's share in the world production is still small. It is small if we regard value alone; "The share of the whole continent (and not merely of that part which lies south of the Sahara) was in 1929, according to calculations made by the Economic and Financial Section of the League of Nations, approximately 4.5 per cent of the world's export trade and 4.8 per cent of the world's import trade. The shares of Africa south of the Sahara were no more than 2.8 and 2.6 per cent, respectively." But who sets the value of raw native produce the world over, as compared with the value of manufactured goods and the freight charges of transport? The merchants, carriers and transformers set it and at almost any minimum they will; hindered only by competition among themselves, which they cut to the lowest by combination and national monopoly. At a fair valuation, with civilized labor costs, the proportion of Africa's production would be far higher.

So Europe annexed Africa. It demanded the right to exploit and develop an unexploited land, pointing out that already Africa is furnishing vast quantities of necessary materials. And knowing too that this supply may be almost infinitely increased. When Italy and Germany call for a share of these raw materials, what they really mean is the control of the labor back of the raw material, and it is this demand of the countries of modern Europe and America to have at their disposal the cheapest human toilers, that makes the real problem of Africa, just as it makes the problem of Asia and the South Seas.

NOTES

1. Keltie, *The Partition of Africa*, p. 196.
2. Keltie, *The Partition of Africa*, p. 132.
3. *Cf.* Mair, *Native Policies in Africa*, Chap. I.
4. Cobb, *The Thermopylae of Africa*, p. 40.

CHAPTER XII

◆

The Land in Africa

The basic activity which, past and present, has conditioned all other human activities is the necessity of earning a living; of defending life and getting food, clothing and shelter. With our present phenomenal control of physical forces and our technical advance, we may forecast the time when this basic necessity of work can be subordinated in its dominating influence to the larger aspects of human life—Science, Art, Love, and Joy. But this time, perhaps already foreseen, is not yet realized.

The relation of a people to the land is the basic problem of its economic life, because the land is the source of the raw materials upon which life depends. A study of Africa and the problems of its population begins therefore with the study of the relation of these people to the land in Africa.

It has been estimated that nearly two-thirds of the world's population is engaged in agriculture. Moreover, instead of agriculture being today as it so long was, a matter of local, national or even continental interest, it is of international interest because of the sale from one country to another of the surplus of agricultural products. All the farmers of the world are in increasingly active competition; a situation, which has begun since 1850 and now covers one-half the world. In the early part of the twentieth century it looked as though the free exchange of crops was going to influence the form of agricultural effort. Then came war and depression, and free trade was clogged. Today in world agriculture confusion reigns.

Meantime in Africa the old methods of production, for the tribe and the village, have been increasingly influenced, first, by the demands for certain African products outside of Africa; and, secondly, by the strain put upon native agriculture through the partially or wholly industrialized native, who more or less permanently has left the tribe; and, thirdly, and especially, by the slavery or serfdom of the African laborer in competition with the farm laborer of the world.

The systems of land tenure in native Africa were varied and often complicated. The tenure of the soil was connected with the system of kinship and there were magical and mythological rights as well as agricultural customs connected with its use. There was abandoned land in all parts of Africa, and yet each tribal unit knew the boundaries of its territory and guarded them jealously. Individual ownership of land was seldom recognized, but Africans were hospitable in assigning strangers land for habitation, and they readily gave missionaries and guests dwelling places.

Indeed it was through the abuse and misinterpretation of this land hospitality that much of the European claim to African land today is based. The Belgian title to more than 900,000 square miles in the Congo is founded on "treaties made with four hundred fifty independent African chiefs" by Henry M. Stanley, through which they were represented as giving away tribal lands for nothing; although in accordance with the usual African custom the chief could assign land for temporary use but could never give it away. In parts of Africa, influenced by Moslem law, the head of the state had often some additional power with regard to the disposal of land, but even here his power was curtailed by ancient tribal custom.

The process by which the land of Africa has been alienated reminds one of that celebrated chapter in Karl Marx on "primary accumulation," where he shows that the peasants of Europe between 1801 and 1831 did not "ever get a farthing's worth of compensation for the 3,511,770 acres of common land stolen from them." And he adds that the expropriation of peasants from the land formed the basis of the capitalistic method of production.

A study of present day Africa will give some idea of the way in which colonists and capital entering Africa are beginning land monopolization. Unfortunately complete accuracy cannot be claimed for the following figures. Official statistics are reticent when it comes to facts unfavorable to the ruling power. Nevertheless every effort has been made to approximate the truth.

In the *Union of South Africa* today, natives forming eighty per cent of the population possess eight per cent of the land. The six and one-half million natives resident in the Union have acknowledged rights in twenty-one million acres. Recent legislation, not yet carried out, proposes to increase this to thirty-seven million acres. In the event this legislation is carried out, which is not altogether certain, the proportion of the Union left to the natives will be thirteen per cent. Or, in other words, ninety-one per cent of Cape Colony; sixty-seven per cent of Natal; eighty-one per cent of the Transvaal; and ninety-nine per cent of the Free State are now in possession of whites. Yet only five per cent of the land owned by whites is in actual use.

The history of this land alienation may be indicated, although neither South Africa nor any of its constituents have made any detailed investigation of native land rights, and the whole history is complicated by a long series of invasions and tribal dislocations due to invading Bantu tribes since the seventeenth century.

The early settlers took enormous farms and the capitalist land speculators took more. In the Transvaal, thirteen land companies hold nearly five million acres of land, most of which is unused. Even the right of natives to buy land is now limited. Indeed land sequestration went so far that it was recognized in the early twentieth century that something must be done to preserve for the natives even such rights as would give them a chance to earn a living; to furnish the labor which the whites needed; to pay taxes and especially to meet their rising discontent. As early as 1903 the Commission on Native Affairs reported that the reserves and locations were insufficient to support the population.

172 ◆ BLACK FOLK

The first comprehensive proposal came from the government of Louis Botha in the Native Lands Act of 1913, which proposed a policy of racial segregation, dividing the Union into native and European areas and restricting purchases of either race outside the area. This Act of 1913 sought to narrow the economic basis of the natives outside the reserves. Before that, natives could buy or rent land from the white farmers and, if fortunate, become peasant proprietors; but as this decreased the labor supply of landlords and mine owners, they induced Botha to enact this law, which made it illegal for a native to occupy land except as a farm laborer, and penalized heavily any white farmer who permitted native cattle to graze on his land. Thousands of native farmers were thus compelled to give up their holdings and sacrifice their stock.

This Botha policy had a certain logic, but it did not at all correspond with the realities of the situation. The white farmer and capitalist did not want the Negro laborer segregated; what they wanted was to limit the amount of land that he occupied so that it would be necessary for him to work for whites for a living. The Beaumont Commission appointed to carry out the provisions of the Act soon realized this. It proposed in 1916 to add about twenty-one million acres to the native area, giving five million natives nearly thirteen per cent of the land, and one and one-half million whites eighty-seven per cent. Cape Colony assented, but all the other provinces scaled down the proposal so that as a matter of fact nothing was accomplished.

The war intervened, and, in 1926, Hertzog at the head of the home-rule-labor coalition proposed a compromise; suggesting an area of twelve million acres where both natives and Europeans might purchase land, but making this contingent upon the disfranchisement of colored people in the Cape Provinces. This bill failed, but it was reintroduced in different form in 1935 and passed the next year as the "Native Trust and Land Act." It provided an additional area of fifteen million acres for acquisition by the natives, making a total of thirty-seven million acres for eventual native occupation, and it promised that the Union government would assist in purchasing this land. Up to November, 1937, the purchase of 824,000 acres had been approved at a cost of nearly 1,304,000 pounds sterling, and it is hoped that 10,000,000 pounds sterling will eventually be available for the acquisition of such lands as the law permits. If the trust acquires this land, six and one-half million natives will have nearly forty million acres or thirteen per cent of the area of the Union.

The situation in the various provinces of the Union varies greatly. In the Cape Province, where the whites hold the largest proportion of the land, they have been in many respects also the most liberal. In 1894 the Glen Gray Act abolished communal tenure among the natives in the Transkei, the largest native district in the Cape, and cut the land into family lots of eight acres each, for which the occupants were given titles. The government collects a quit-rent of 15s. The land can neither be sold nor mortgaged, but may be forfeited for disloyalty or failure to pay rent. The Orange Free State has made but meager allowance for the natives in three official reserves which total about 150,000 acres. The Transvaal has only two million acres, which are much congested. Natal has the Zululand district with four million acres, and two and one-fourth million acres in other reserves.

When British capital pushed north toward Central Africa, it first seized Bechuanaland, eventually annexing part of it to Cape Colony and retaining the rest as a British protectorate. The protectorate has 275,000 square miles, but much of it is desert and tsetse fly country. In this area 102,000 square miles are reserved for 260,000 natives and 7,500 square miles have been given to a thousand whites. The remainder of 165,000 square miles is held as "Crown land," that is, as land which the government claims as its own and which can be alienated or reserved for natives. The eventual disposition depends, of course, on the motive power back of the government. If British capital should find profitable mining investment or South Africans need labor supply, most of this land will go to whites. If, on the other hand, natives or their friends in South Africa or England have any decisive influence, some of it may go to the natives. The South Africa Company still owns the entire district of Tati, which has an area of 700,000 acres, and this is being exploited for minerals by a company with many distinguished Englishmen and South Africans as directors. They pay no government royalty on gold production.

Northeast of Bechuanaland lies territory now known as Southern and Northern Rhodesia, consisting of an area equal to Great Britain, France, and Prussia. Under the migrations and conquests of various tribes the control of this land has changed many times in the last few centuries and it was finally penetrated by the British South Africa Company under native permission to search for minerals.

When Dr. Jameson invaded Matabeleland in 1893 he promised each member of his force six thousand five hundred acres and from fifteen to twenty mining claims. Rhodes told them later, "You will be the first entitled to select land. It is your right for you have conquered the country."

The Colonial Office later ordered the British South Africa Company to assign land to the natives in *Southern Rhodesia*: but the first attempt in 1894 to herd the natives into two reserves resulted in a fierce insurrection in 1896. Rhodes rushed from London and found the settlers huddled in Bulawayo besieged by ten thousand Matabele. He met the chiefs on the Matopo Hills and pacified them. Finally in 1920 the company gave 834,000 natives about twenty-two million acres of land, of which three million acres or more were unsuitable for settlement; while 35,000 whites were given about fifty million acres. It is planned to divide the land so that 40,000 Europeans have forty-seven million acres and 800,000 natives have twenty-nine million acres. This leaves an unassigned area of eighteen million acres. Crown lands are not reserved and may be sold or leased to natives or whites; but wherever mineral deposits are found, native reserves will doubtless be taken away.

In *Northern Rhodesia* there has been set up by original treaty with the tribes, a native reserve, Barotseland, with thirty-seven million acres of none too good land, where 350,000 natives live. In other parts of Northern Rhodesia, 10,000 whites own about nine million acres, chiefly in mining claims, while a million natives have thirty-five million acres reserved for them. There remains a hundred million acres in the hands of the government as Crown land. Some 300,000 Africans are squatters on lands owned by whites, while many natives live in mine compounds and in towns.

The conditions in Northern Rhodesia are different from those in Southern Rhodesia, because the main interest of the whites is in mining, and so long as they can secure a sufficient number of miners, there is no reason for monopolizing agricultural land. Less than five per cent of Northern Rhodesia is at present actually owned by Europeans, but most of the Crown lands and all mining regions are for them when they wish. A policy of giving twenty acres each to white civil servants was inaugurated in 1934.

Basutoland is a protectorate by treaty where a half million natives hold twelve thousand square miles of land. The soil suffers from widespread erosion and cannot support the whole working population.

More than half the habitable land in the protectorate of *Swaziland* was secured by whites from a drunken chief who had no power under native law to dispose of it. Nevertheless, after the Boer War, British concessions of 3,767 square miles were made to the whites, while the natives held 2,261 square miles. Land distribution was eventually based on the Coalition Ordinance of 1907, which said that from every concession one-third would revert to native use and the remaining two-thirds to whites. The Swazi protested against the ordinance and sent a delegation to England, but were unable to get any satisfaction. The result of the proceedings of 1907 left the total area of 4,290,000 acres, divided roughly into a native area of 1,638,000 acres and a Crown area of 1,115,000 acres; and the rest in the hands of European concession holders who received freehold title from the Crown.

So much land had been taken from the Swazi that when the British took over the administration, they had to buy back 40,000 pounds sterling worth of land held by the concessionaires. This was paid for out of taxation levied on the Swazi. Since then the Swazi have bought about 80,000 acres by borrowing money. The present figures are 1,700,000 acres held by 100,000 natives, while less than three thousand whites own nearly two and one-half million acres. Indeed the government has alienated so much land to the whites that only 150,000 acres are left as Crown land. Of the European owners, forty per cent are absentee and most of the best grazing land is held by Transvaal farmers for winter grazing and speculation on future values.

Both Northern Rhodesia and Nyasaland occupied territory to which, of all European countries, the Portuguese had a prior claim by reason of discovery; but the control of this territory was necessary for Rhodes' "Cape to Cairo" scheme and for control of the mineral wealth which he was sure it contained.

The history of land alienation in *Nyasaland* is one of the most extraordinary on record and shows the peculiar relation between missionary proselytism and business enterprise, which sometimes develops. Livingstone went to Africa in 1840 with the idea that business development would be one of the best aids to his missionary effort. He married the daughter of the missionary Moffat. Moffat's son became a co-worker with Cecil Rhodes and helped secure the celebrated Rudd concession which eventually gave to Englishmen most of the mineral wealth of South Africa.

Missionaries and capitalists in Nyasaland formed the African Lakes Company, but native rebellions brought the company near bankruptcy. It passed into the hands of Cecil Rhodes, who acquired 2,700,000 acres for the South Africa Company in northern Nyasaland; another million acres became the private property of whites through efforts of various sorts. But the amount of cultivable land is limited by the tsetse fly and malaria. Native rights to the land have not been regarded, and the Land Commission of 1921 could only propose recognition and supervision of their tenancy. They have no legal protection against eviction, for the most part, and are not satisfied with the wage offered; so much so that in 1915 this led to widespread rebellion. Despite the amount of land which the whites own, only 66,000 acres were under cultivation in 1922.

Later the British South Africa Company sold its surface rights, amounting to 2,700,000 acres, to the government in return for more valuable mineral rights. This left a total of 1,303,000 acres alienated, and owned mostly by eleven large estates.

In *Kenya* the natives forming eighty per cent of the population occupied but twenty per cent of the land area in 1935; and this land was the least fertile, and in part desert, swamp and habitat of the tsetse fly. The history of this land theft is in part as follows: the Masai were pastoral tribes in the southern Sudan and Kenya whose wealth was entirely in cattle. The whites began to seize the land in 1902. After the first seizure the Masai agreed on the condition that no more grants be made. They were reported to be well-behaved and orderly, but the aggression went on. In 1904, the British signed a formal treaty agreeing that certain territories should be reserved to the tribe. The chiefs agreed on condition that the "settlement now arrived at shall be enduring as long as the Masai shall exist." Nevertheless, they were later moved again and they tried to sue the government for breaking the agreement. There was great unrest and the Masai were cheated out of their land and not allowed to sue or to appeal to the Privy Council because they could not pay costs. One-third of their new reserve is uninhabitable.

In 1903, three or four hundred Dutch farmers came from South Africa to Kenya, and this contingent formed over one-half the Kenya white settlement. After the World War settlement in Kenya was stimulated by offers to ex-service officers and privates. Governor Northey confiscated two million acres of land belonging to the Nandi tribe; divided it up into small estates and gave it to demobilized British army officers. The Nandi broke out in open rebellion. In all, 4,560 square miles were allotted to soldier settlement farms. The land was given in freehold or on long leases. In 1922 the governor so drew a native reserve boundary as to leave a million and a half acres open for European settlement. The highlands and the good land with water was thus taken for Europeans.

The total area of Kenya is about 225,000 square miles, of which by liberal estimate 40,000 square miles are capable of cultivation. The government has given eleven thousand square miles of this land to Europeans, mostly in large blocks and at a nominal price. Lord Delamere, long the leading Kenyan politician, acquired over 100,000 acres of the finest land at one penny per acre. The Crown Land Ordinance of 1915 granted settlers the right to obtain property up to five thousand acres for ninety-nine years at the price of one penny an acre. The East Africa Estates, Ltd., with many distinguished directors, owns 350,000 acres of land and other valuable property. British East Africa Corporation has a capital of 400,000 pounds sterling. The Dwa Plantation, Ltd., has 20,000 acres of coffee and sisal land. These companies declare large dividends annually.

The increase in land values has already been phenomenal. A farm of six hundred and forty acres sold in 1903 for eighty-five pounds; it was re-sold for six hundred and forty pounds in 1905 and in 1913 with improvements was sold for 17,500 pounds sterling. An Ordinance of 1915 empowered the governor to establish and reduce native areas while the Barth judgment of 1921 declared that the natives were tenants at will of the Crown.

The Kikuyu, after carrying on a long agitation against the confiscation of their land, ended in open revolt in 1922 under Harry Thuku. This led in 1924 to a British Commission under Ormsby-Gore. After the report of this commission, the Crown Land Ordinance of 1926 set aside twenty-seven native reserves totaling nearly thirty-one million acres; but those still were not the property of the natives, who continued to be tenants at will.

The area which these operations withdrew from the tribes for the purpose of European settlement was made 16,000 square miles; while the area of the reserves assigned to the natives in the neighborhood of the highlands amounted to about 43,500 square miles. Unfortunately, the area withdrawn from European settlement was thickly populated with natives, the density running as high as two hundred and eighty-three persons per square mile; while other areas untouched had less than one person per square mile. The commission on closer union in East Africa in 1929 emphasized the necessity of some security for the natives in their land tenure. The settlers at the time were considering a Land Trust Board to take charge of reserves, but they were going to give it considerable discretion, even to the extent of allowing land for whites within the native reserves, when this was deemed "beneficial" for the natives.

The commission secured a revised ordinance in 1930, declaring that the reserves were set "aside for the benefit of native tribes forever" and placing them under a board composed of the governor, colonial secretary and attorney-general of the colony. In case land in a reserve should be taken for any reason, it must be with the approval of the native council; and in such case land equal in quality and quantity and value must be substituted. In 1932 gold was discovered on the native reserve occupied by the Kavirondo. The 1930 ordinance was promptly amended, nullifying the principal clauses, allowing the annexation of gold-bearing land without native consent and payment therefore by money and not by land.

At the time the Commission reported, the area already definitely alienated to whites was 10,345 square miles; 11.8 per cent of this was cultivated, 40.7 per cent used for stock, twenty per cent occupied by native squatters, and 27.5 per cent unused. The native areas were increased fifteen per cent and the European area sixty per cent; in addition to this there were 99,000 square miles of Crown lands opened theoretically to both races, but much of this is desert. Thereupon Parliament, in dealing with the report of the Commission, instituted an inquiry into this ordinance of 1930 and into the present and prospective land needs of the natives.

The Carter Land Commission report in 1934 proposed an addition of 2,629 square miles. This would bring the total area reserved for 2,750,000 natives to about 50,000 square miles, while 16,700 square miles were to be reserved for 16,500 whites. The commission recommended more convenient boundaries and amalgamation of reserves; and appropriated 50,000 pounds to finance the cost; but this 50,000 pounds sterling represents part of the unclaimed balances of pay overdue 40,000 natives employed as soldiers and carriers during the war, who died or disappeared. All these recommendations have not yet been carried out.

In 1931, there were in Kenya 16,500 white men, women and children of whom 2,100, including a large number of absentees, owned 11,000 square miles of land. There are 30,000 Indians and three million Africans. The land reserved for the natives is still inadequate. Many have as little as two acres a head, and where they have fifteen acres, much of the land cannot be cultivated. The average native farm has only eight acres and there are probably 40,000 landless African families in Kenya.

The assumption of Leopold was that the land of the *Congo Free State* belonged to him to dispose of as he thought best. There were always various general statements as to the rights of the natives in the land they actually occupied, but in practice these rights never interfered with the profit-making objects of Leopold. The disposal of land under his regime, on paper at least, reached fantastic proportions. The grants were of three kinds: nine million hectares were given to railway companies in proportion to the mileage constructed. Then there were two types of concessions: the Katanga concession really set up a commercial company as an administrative government with freehold property in one-third of the territory used. The old company was finally put under a special committee, two-thirds of whose members represented the government and one-third the company. This concession had forty-five million hectares. Another type of concession was monopoly of forest areas. They included immense tracts of territory but did not confer freehold rights.

When Belgium annexed the Congo Free State it was calculated that twenty-seven million hectares had been granted to whites in freehold. Later, as a result of negotiations with certain companies, nine million hectares reverted to the state. Thereafter concessions of another type were made, by which the right to land in freehold depended on the development. In 1911, for instance, the Huilieries du Congo Belge received grants which, on the fulfillment of conditions, would entitle them to 750,000 hectares in separated areas. These conditions must be fulfilled by 1945. In a similar way the company Sucrière Congolaise is promised 30,000 hectares.

In 1929 it was decreed that no further mining concessions would be given, and that two-thirds of the territory was to be open to small scale and large scale agricultural concessions. In the Kivu region, where European colonization is possible, a railway company has an option of over 400,000 hectares, and a committee which the government controls is charged with the development of colonization on eight million hectares. In this region native lands will be subject to government control. So far 23,000 hectares have been alienated.

In recent years the Congo State has alienated 84,000 hectares in 1932; 69,000 in 1933; 32,000 in 1934; and 14,000 in 1935. The total area alienated is about 5,275,000 hectares as compared with the resident white population of 18,000, and out of a total area of 235 million hectares. Nevertheless it would seem that according to present plans the eight million natives will eventually have indeterminate title to less than seventy-five million hectares.

The Belgian system with modifications extended for a time into *French Equatorial Africa*, chiefly with Belgian and English capital. For a long time the French government exercised no effective control; having overthrown dominant native states, the component units were let to drift into administrative anarchy and the whole area became a sort of no-man's land for marauding corporations. In these stretches of desert and jungle, the population is sparse; and while native lands for the cultivation of food were reserved, vacant lands were declared the property of the state and in this way vast areas were opened to concessionaires. The raid began under Delcasse, French under-Secretary of State, who in 1893 secretly granted concessions of land in the Congo and Ivory Coast. There was one concession alone of twenty-six and a half million acres.

Popular outcry caused a revision of these concessions, but the French courts in many cases upheld and indemnified the companies. In 1899, the need of revenue caused the appointment of a commission and forty concessions in the French Congo were granted, about four-fifths of the capital being furnished by Belgians, and the territory granted covering nearly one-third of the French Congo. A low annual rental was required and fifteen per cent of the profits was to go to the state. On fulfillment of certain indications of development, the land was to be granted in freehold. Most of the companies failed and those who began to make profit did so through forced labor which led to open revolt.

Again revulsion of feeling in France forced a revision of the system in 1910–1912. Some thirty-one million hectares out of the eighty-seven million alienated were eventually returned to the state; the fate of land in other concessions is apparently still pending.

In occupying French Africa the government both in French West Africa and in the Congo made numbers of treaties guaranteeing native rights to the land and the power of the chiefs over the land. Indeed the so-called conquest of France over French Africa was much more a matter of treaty arrangement than actual conquest.

In 1904, in *French West Africa*, public domain and private, were recognized and public domain as collective property could only be alienated by the lieutenant governors in council. At present about 93,000 hectares is held on provisional tenure and 57,000 as permanent concessions. Many concessions granted were later abandoned. On the whole, the land of French West Africa has been left to native use and largely in native ownership. The right to land can be proven under native law, and both individual and group ownership are legalized.

In *British West Africa* the land pattern differs markedly from the Union of South Africa and Kenya, and more nearly resembles French West Africa. But the reasons for the land development here are quite different from those in the

French domain. They arise from the peculiar economic and political history of British West Africa. West Africa was not conquered like most of South Africa; nor was it annexed by pretense of treaty like the Belgian Congo; nor by actual treaty as in French West Africa. It was, from the beginning of the American slave trade, held by powerful native states and communities, which grew more powerful by monopoly and which made treaties and arrangements with the slave-trading powers, allowing whites usually no ownership of land at all or at most the right to erect coast stations for the storage of slaves and goods.

When the slave trade dwindled, various Negro states set up more or less independent existence, but through long connection with the Europeans extended their trade with them and allowed more settlements. Disputes arose and military clashes. They were long drawn out, resulting usually in stalemate; but gradually the power of the Europeans and especially of the British, backed by the persistent strong demand for industrial profit, increased the rule and influence of the whites.

Moreover, no considerable number of Europeans attempted to settle in West Africa. The whites were there as representatives of business concerns and administrators, so that the ideal of a Negro economy, guided and assisted by white experts and technicians and by white capital, approached realization. The difficulty was, however, that two ideals were here inextricably mixed: the ideal of using this set-up for the largest possible income to English investors; and the opposite ideal of using it for the best interests and highest development of the Negro peoples. Attempt has been made and is being made to prove that there is nothing incompatible in these two ideals. But such a conclusion in the light of facts does not make sense.

The fundamental Nigerian principle, for instance, is that all the land of the country belongs to some stool, i.e., Throne or State; and so too, in the Gold Coast, the natives opposed the Crown land idea. Apart from stool lands there are family lands and private lands. In the cocoa-growing provinces, individual freehold or private land has come into use. The land question has, however, been complicated by land grants from chiefs and mortgages to moneylenders on the cocoa crops.

In Lagos, Southern Nigeria, the land originally belonged to the tribes and could not be sold. After the colony was ceded in 1861, the British declared the territory Crown land and issued individual freehold deeds. The result is much confusion. There are now 4,000 peasant proprietors side by side with the old communal system. In 1901 the chiefs of Lagos challenged the government ownership of land and received some support from the English Privy Council.

In Yorubaland, Northern Nigeria, there is native land and Crown land. Under the Lands Acquisition Ordinance of 1917, no one except a native can buy land without obtaining the sanction of the governor; nor can a native buy land outside the territory of his tribe without the consent of the paramount chief. Rent for the land, in case it is thus alienated, goes to the communal chest. Some Europeans, Assyrians and companies have secured leases. Thus land-ownership is vested in the chiefs and councils as trustees for the people.

In Hausaland, Northern Nigeria, the land in the north is vested in the governor as trustee for the natives, according to the Ordinance of 1916. The governor alone can dispose of land to natives and non-natives, and the blacks are tenants at will. In return for the use of the land, the government taxes the natives according to the amount of use or the value of the crops. This was easier in Hausaland, because the British in fact took over the land rights of the emirs, while on the other hand the emirs had never really interfered with the tribal land rights. The overwhelming majority of the natives of Nigeria are independent peasant producers. The total concessions permitted by the High Court covered, in 1935, some 8,805 square miles out of 23,937 in the colony, and 2,986 square miles in Ashanti out of 24,379 square miles.

The net result on the whole in West Africa is that on the Gold Coast and in Southern Nigeria the state itself makes no claims over the land. In Northern Nigeria, on the other hand, the state claims right over all the land, but exercises great care in alienating land to whites, so that in practice the land remains largely in the hands of the blacks. The dominant idea in West Africa is that of perpetuating and defending native land-ownership. Vigorous assaults upon this policy have been made from time to time by those who would establish plantations for palm oil, for cocoa and for rubber. For instance, after the World War, the Empire Resources Development Committee of England, advocated a monopoly of palm products in West Africa to pay the cost of the war and declared that "the natives were an undeveloped national asset." The association of West African merchants of Liverpool demanded drastic laws to facilitate diverting the lands from natives' bands.

Profits from products under a regime of native land-ownership have been large enough to defeat schemes of land alienation, especially when the cost of such a policy in the face of stubborn native resistance and strong tribal organization would have been large, if not quite prohibitive.

Next to Kenya lies *Uganda*, and it presents a contrast to Kenya in its land policy. Uganda was seized by the British in order to checkmate the advance of the Germans; but Uganda was held at the time by a strong feudal organization in contrast to the loosely organized and wandering herdsmen who occupied Kenya. The land in Buganda, the most advanced part of Uganda, was of three kinds: state lands owned by the Kabaka as trustee, clan lands, and private lands. When Sir Harry Johnston came as English commissioner, he found that, on account of war, there was anarchy and financial difficulties. He tried to consolidate the country by dividing up the clan land among the chiefs as freehold property. This was embodied in the agreement of 1900.

The Kabaka received five hundred square miles for himself and 3,700 of his feudal retainers received private holdings amounting to over 9,000 square miles. All remaining Buganda lands, forests, etc., were vested in the state. Thus between 10,000 and 20,000 new landlords arose and began to rent out their holdings to 200,000 farm tenants, whose original rights to this land as members of clans had been ignored. Europeans and Asiatics began to get hold of some of this land and as the cotton industry increased, the peasants protested, declaring that the clan lands which had been divided up really belonged to them.

Largely by the aid of the profits of cotton cultivation, the peasant succeeded in partially re-establishing his position by the purchase of clan lands; these transactions have amounted probably to 20,000 in number, and many of the larger estates have now been broken up. In 1925 the Agrarian Law was enacted by which renting peasants were given certain rights. This was strengthened by a new law in 1927 which fixed the rent and charges on crops and prevented eviction.

In the other three states, the native land system was left theoretically intact by claiming all lands not actually occupied as Crown land. Ruling families were given private estates of two hundred square miles each.

Out of a total area of 80,371 square miles in Uganda, not including lakes, 9,627 square miles represent the areas given to chiefs and others under the agreements of 1900 and 1901; of the rest, less than five hundred square miles are in non-native hands, and of this area only 115 square miles of freehold and sixty-one of leasehold represent alienations by the Crown. The rest has been acquired from natives after the 1900 Agreement.

Nevertheless there remain 71,000 square miles under white government control, on which the natives are tenants at will. Already 250,000 acres of this are in the hands of whites and Indians, and there is a movement to encourage white planters in the west plateau along the Ruwenzori Range. There is danger that pressure from white Kenya may lead to land monopoly and cotton plantations in this part of Uganda. Since 1913 a land commission has been trying to work out a settlement and there is a plan by which four-fifths of the land will be allocated to the natives and one-fifth to the Crown. But this remains a plan only.

"Indirect rule" is a phrase that should be applied to the economic control of the Egyptian Sudan, ancient Ethiopia and medieval Nubia, through English investment; and the similar French control of Algeria, Tunis and Morocco. In these cases, the ancient tribal land-ownership has long since disappeared under war and conquest, and in place has come the ownership of land by landlords, with a large number of tenants and farm laborers. In the *Egyptian Sudan*, however, there was a peculiar opportunity to dominate the whole area by large investment in irrigation schemes. In fact the recapture of the Sudan from the black Madhists was made imperative by the necessity of controlling the flow of the Nile in order really to dominate Egypt. English economic control began with investments in railways and then turned to the extraordinary feat of so regulating the waters of the Nile as to bring larger annual crops and stabilize the labor force.

Since the twelfth century Egypt had been threatened by the possible diverting of Nile waters and silt. The Aswan Dam above the First Cataract was recommended in 1867, before the opening of the Suez Canal. It was financed by a Jew and built under great difficulties between 1898 and 1902 and later twice rebuilt. It irrigates seven million acres; and was followed by the Sennar Dam on the Blue Nile and the Gebel Aulia on the White Nile.

Further plans for dams in the great swamps to the south will bring eventually not only almost perfect control of the Nile waters, but a command over Egyptian agriculture and the whole Egyptian economic and political structure, which will make Egypt an investment of higher European finance.

The Egyptian peasant farmer is keen to own his farm. Between 1902 and 1913 the number of native landholders increased from one million to one and a half million; and in 1920, 1,859,000 Egyptians owned five million acres. The cultivable area in 1926 was over eight million acres but nearly three million acres of this was used for public utility purposes or was unreclaimed. Of the five and one-half million acres cultivated over two million were held in farms of fifty or more acres, or thirty-nine per cent. There are a large number of landless laborers working for landlords under ancient and customary labor conditions.

The land policy in the various *mandates* of German colonies may be illustrated by the case of Tanganyika. The policy of the German government favored European settlement in the highlands and the development of the plantation system. The government took land from the natives and gave it to whites for cultivating coffee, cotton, rubber and sisal. After the war 860 German plantations totaling two million acres were confiscated by the British and sold. Other property and buildings were sold chiefly to East Indians and Greeks who were largely agents of former German owners. Since 1925 Germans have returned and many have re-acquired their former plantations.

A dual farming system characterizes the British administration, with plantations in the highlands and native peasant farms on reserved areas in the rest of the country. The Land Ordinance of 1923 divided up a number of German plantations among the natives. This law and amendments in 1928 gave to the governor the right to alienate the land. Pressure is being brought to bear to alienate more land to the whites.

The Planters Association supported by the Kenya Association asked the Tanganyika government to prohibit natives from raising coffee. Governor Cameron would not yield; but he did give the whites more land for plantations in the southwest. About 800,000 acres have been alienated in Tanganyika by the mandate government. In 1930, 4,232 square miles out of a total of 340,500 square miles are in the hands of 4,500 whites and 15,000 Arabs and Indians. This leaves 336,000 square miles as the possible territory of four million natives.

In Southwest Africa the discontent of various tribes under German administration caused the Herero and Namaqwa rebellions, which were punished by confiscation of their land. The decree of 1905 permitted reserves for the natives to be made, and in this way about a million hectares were given to native communities. When the Union of South Africa took over Southwest Africa as a mandate, it tried to extend the segregation policy. Between 1923 and 1932 eleven native reserves with an area of nearly three million hectares were proclaimed and about six and one-half million hectares in addition were earmarked for acquisition by the natives in the future. In 1935, the Hereroes and the Ovambos and a few other small tribes lived in twenty-three reserves. The detribalized natives are in town locations. The total land held by natives was forty million acres in 1936, much of it suitable at best only for grazing. It was occupied by 200,000 native Negroes and colored folk. The remainder of the territory equal to 275,000 square miles is reserved for 24,000 whites.

It is not possible to estimate accurately the total amount of the land already alienated in Africa to white control. From the data in hand we may roughly calculate a half million square miles of the best and most accessible land in Africa is now owned by whites and in addition to that there are at least a million square miles held as Crown lands or under state control, which would seem without much question to be ear-marked for white ownership, making a territory in all half the size of the United States.

The crucial question with regard to this land is, In whose interests is it going to be divided and administered and how far are other lands in Africa eventually to come under similar administration? If the African land were controlled by the state in the interest of African people, we might see here a most interesting economic development. Indeed at one time the single tax advocates of England sought to introduce this system in West Africa, but the proposal raised a fury of protest among the natives who did not consider that the English government was likely to administer the land for the benefit of the natives. They knew well that, in the past, administration of West Africa to some extent, and much more so of other parts of Africa, had been carried on in the interests of those who were investing or working in Africa for profit. Here they touched the kernel of the African land question.

A fundamental difficulty in the proper development of Africa, and through Africa of the world, is illustrated by the land question which has been discussed. The real power in control of the distribution of land in Africa is European industry. This European control is carried on by local representatives. They exercise persistent pressure and have been given wide political recognition by their inclusion as members of the governors' councils. Business and capital is controlled by colonial administration at home but here it has always had strong representation. Administration however has been made to feel and respect philanthropy and is subject to such political changes as represented by the English, Belgian and French labor administrations.

Administration has thus been driven to call in the aid of science. Modern anthropology and social science have done excellent work, but it is on the whole to the discredit of these sciences that they have so easily loaned themselves to manipulation as servants of administration. Anthropology in recent years has been called upon, not so much to state the truth and lay down reasonable ideals of development, as to tell the administration what scientific paths it may follow so as to keep peace with the natives and appease public opinion at home. And especially has it joined the administration in discrediting the educated African and belittling his co-operation in science and in social development.

Thus the indispensable democratic control which should gradually be built up in Africa to direct administration and science in the interest of the real development for the sake of the Africans is ignored and even ridiculed; and so deep and fundamental a question as the distribution of land and control of the natural resources is reduced to a question of successful administration from the point of view of the business man.

CHAPTER XIII

◆

The African Laborer

The buying and selling of labor for the purpose of property in its ultimate products began its modern phase with the African slave trade. Labor purchase has since dominated the modern economic world, and as that world now turns renewed attention towards Africa, the central theme must naturally again be the investment which white Europe and America are making in the black labor force of Africa.

The European demand for land in Africa was in effect a demand for labor; first a demand for slave labor; then for forced labor with a nominal wage; later it became a demand for wage labor with indirect compulsion by sequestration of land to such an extent that the laborer could not support himself on his own acres; with this went poll, hut and other taxation which could be met only by a cash wage system.

There followed indirect inducements to work: flattering deception on the part of recruiting agents, pressure brought to bear by chiefs, and finally the lure of new imported goods: first for ornament, then for convenience, and then for new necessities. One can trace here in miniature the exact steps by which the European laborer has been reduced to regular work through total separation from his ancient source of livelihood on the land.

The demand for labor in Africa brought out certain fundamental differences between the native and European attitudes toward work. Before the arrival of European enterprise, paid labor was practically unknown in Africa. The chief could demand certain labor as a service to the community; like contributing to his support or keeping pathways open. It was a sort of labor tax and not a burden; it lasted but a short time and the community was interested in it. It did not resemble in the least the kind of forced labor which the Europeans imported.

European legislation concerning labor is based upon the fact that the worker is practically divorced from land and capital; he must work for a living; and he wants desperately to retain his job, since the labor supply exceeds the demand. In Africa this is not yet true. The demand for labor still exceeds the supply, except in certain overdeveloped areas during the late depression. The mass of workers are still connected with tribal lands and villages, and use money wages for taxes and for luxuries rather than necessities. African laborers are directly dependent upon wages only in the Union of South Africa and in the vicinity of the mines of Northern Rhodesia and Katanga. It is not possible yet, therefore, to exploit the African laborer as thoroughly as the European laborer; yet the standard of tribal living is so low that the African is on the whole much worse off than the European and it is possible not only fatally to curtail the possibilities of tribal life, but also to monopolize natural resources so as to mortgage the economic future of millions of blacks.

Work for the primitive African was largely a source of pleasure. When it demanded effort and unpleasant effort, this was turned into a sport rather than a task. Among those advanced tribes where the organization of work demanded regularity and concentration, and the use of tools, as among the weavers of cloth and makers of hats and weapons, even then there was a much larger degree of voluntary varied and pleasurable effort for artistic satisfaction and much less of compulsion and irksomeness than among modern factory workers. The artisan could be to considerable extent an artist.

Then again the object of work in the African tribe was not individual income. The native stressed the importance of work for the welfare of the family and clan. Each person considered himself as a member of a group rather than as an individual, and in turn he relied upon the aid and guidance of that group in all his daily life. Imagine then the results of the impact of the European type of forced labor upon the African tribesman, even when it was mainly agricultural; but especially when it became labor in mines and industry.

Africa is a vast reservoir of cheap labor, which can compete with and replace to a considerable degree white labor the world over, and yield at the same time a much larger profit to capital. Common labor in Africa costs on an average twenty-five cents a day. Moreover, this labor is capable of more than ordinary toil. There has been a remarkable acquiring of skill for producing goods for export among African laborers. In British West Africa and elsewhere, cocoa-growing has developed in native hands from insignificant beginnings to one of the important industries of the world. The palm tree belt covers central Africa from Lake Tanganyika to the Atlantic Ocean and is worked by blacks; the oil is shipped to Europe and America, where it is used for soap, tin plating and in other ways. The United States imports annually over 30,000 tons of oil from Nigeria alone, and some 275,000 tons of palm kernels. Cotton is being raised in Africa in the Nile Valley, Uganda and Nigeria. Sixty-nine per cent of the coffee raised in Tanganyika is grown by the natives. All over Africa, natives are being used for skilled work in mining, on the railways and in other industries. The total number of skilled workers is still small but it is rapidly increasing.

Today this labor is not leaving Africa either by means of a slave trade or by migration; on the other hand, capital is entering Africa from Europe and America in commodities representing larger and larger sums, and this capital is being used to monopolize land and natural resources. This process can be traced in a general way, although exact figures and careful studies are not always available.

The present extraordinary situation in the *Union of South Africa* is woven of a dozen twisted threads, including colonization of South African land by actual white farmers, long-continued war with the native tribes, sudden and colossal industrialization through the mines, and widespread investment in mining and commerce on the part of the middle class and well-to-do English public. English wealth and comfort, therefore, has a stake in South Africa which cannot be easily disturbed. On the other hand, not only do African farmers want cheap labor, but African industry is based upon it. Along with this goes the rivalry of the poor whites and the bitter fear of the skilled white workers. The problem of building a just native policy under such circumstances is indeed baffling.

In 1824 there were 60,000 slaves and serfs in South Africa and when slavery was abolished by Great Britain in 1838 it affected nearly 40,000 Negroes and Malays. Forced labor for farming and for porterage followed, and later for building of railways.

As the South African native lost his legal right to the land, he stayed on the land of the whites as squatter or contract laborer, or retired to native reserves. Settlement on the native reserves not only compelled him usually to leave his ancestral tribal home, but also afforded him too little land for support.

The squatter, on the other hand, stuck doggedly with a certain moral justification. He was usually an African whose tribal lands had been seized and were in the legal possession of whites, but who clung to his native soil. Such natives were not in reality trespassers as recent laws have described them, but historically, or in their own belief, precisely the reverse. The white man was the trespasser, but he had the law back of him and could compel the native to work on his land or pay rent. Today in the Transvaal alone there are 300,000 squatters. They are increasingly under the power of the owner. Their share of the produce is small, often a third.

The native farm laborers may enter into contract and become regular tenants, but the labor laws reduce them practically to the position of serfs. The older contracts were traps for the workers. The newer contracts give the laborer better protection but nothing like modern freedom of contract. The cash wages paid for contract labor are small, amounting to two dollars, or two dollars and fifty cents a month, with a small food ration; less than this is paid in the Transvaal and the Free State. The working hours are from sunrise to sunset, six days in the week. The laborer usually builds his own house and has only Sunday and one or two days at Christmas as holidays. The average income of a family of three adults and five children is reported at something over fifty dollars a year. As a result of these conditions five or six thousand native contract workers desert each year.

The Native Service Contract Act of 1932 makes laborers liable to criminal prosecution if they leave. Up to eighteen years of age they can be punished by flogging. The *Cape Argus* called the Act a "barbaric" piece of legislation. It allows no farmer to hire a native unless he produces a document signed by a previous employer, permitting him to leave for finding work. The native rural population of the Union of South Africa is estimated at about five and one-half million. The pass laws to control the movement of labor are especially harsh. The majority of natives must have at least four passes, consisting of a labor contract, a special pass for moving from one district to another, a night pass, and a receipt for payment of poll tax. In the Transvaal, a native may have to produce twelve different passes. Pass laws are sometimes used by the police to harass the natives and to breed criminals. Of the court convictions of Union natives, eleven per cent are under the pass laws, while forging of passes is a profitable business. Over 40,000 natives were imprisoned for violating the pass laws in 1934.

In 1867, on land owned by a Hottentot mulatto, the first diamond was discovered in South Africa near the Orange River, and later the main mines were found near Kimberley. Through this discovery, the annual world output of diamonds rose from four million dollars a year to twenty million dollars in the nineties, and ninety million dollars in the 1930s.

The whole history of capital investment in South Africa has yet to be written. Cecil Rhodes began digging diamonds in 1870 and was rich within a year. Within a decade he had consolidated the mines at Kimberley and become a member of the Cape Colony assembly. In 1884 he encouraged Warren to seize Bechuanaland and make it a British protectorate. He sensed there must be gold and other minerals further north. His agents, helped by the missionary Moffat, brother-in-law of Livingstone, secured the Rudd concession in 1888, through which Lobengula gave the right to search for minerals in Matabele-Mashonaland, in return for a thousand rifles with ammunition and 1,200 pounds sterling.

In 1889 Rhodes organized the British South Africa Company with a capital of a million shares of one pound each, three-fourths of which were privately issued to directors and supporters and the remainder held for contingencies. It was not until 1886, two years after the London convention which acknowledged the independence of the South African Dutch states, that the greatest gold field of the world was discovered in the Transvaal. The magic city of Johannesburg arose on this field, which has furnished nearly a quarter of the gold produced in the world since the fifteenth century, and still yields over half of the annual output.

There was an enormous influx of Englishmen and others into Johannesburg until the strangers outnumbered the Boers five to one. Rhodes became Prime Minister of Cape Colony in 1890. On the one hand he was seeking British monopoly of the new mines, and on the other pushing toward Central Africa, where he knew there were further mineral deposits and where he wished to consolidate British industrial dominion in South Africa with her grip on the Nile Valley.

Rhodes was now the executive director of stock companies which controlled both the diamond and the gold fields. The Matabele war was a turning point and Southern Rhodesia became the keystone of Rhodes' Empire. In September, 1895, the price of one pound shares of the chartered company was nine pounds. In order to control the investment which England and America were making in South Africa, Rhodes took a fatal step, and through his agent, Jameson, having overthrown the Matabele in 1893, tried to seize political power in the Transvaal. In December, 1895, came the Jameson raid on Johannesburg. Momentarily the raid was a failure, but gold production in the South African mines rose from thirty-four million dollars in 1894 to eighty million in 1899. There ensued from 1899 to 1902 a bitter war between Britons and Boers for the mastery of the mineral wealth of South Africa; a war that cost 10,000 lives in the field and at least forty thousand wounded.

The world has not realized how fateful a step this was. The Rhodes imperial plan changed the face of Africa, modified the trend of civilization, and began a movement that ended in the World War. The gold and diamonds of South Africa fired the imagination of the investing world. The discovery was sudden and dynamic. Men talked of Ophir and King Solomon's mines; of the Manifest Destiny of the white race and especially of Britain. In America the industrial and technical triumph following the Civil War and Reconstruction was at its height, breeding millionaires. In England, the middle class had a new dream of power and dominion. Leopold of Belgium was fired to begin the seizure of Central Africa. Germany suddenly realized the meaning of Africa. England and France renewed their rush for North and West Africa.

The development of South Africa and the fate of the natives there changed. Hitherto a farming community desired land and labor to help them farm; but, after all, there was land enough for white and black. Now farmers began to change into speculators and investors. They wanted land monopoly and slaves. They ruthlessly pushed the natives back and out, while the industrialists began to tap the reservoir of primitive native labor in the interior. White labor from Europe was attracted by high wages and preferred status, and the sons of white South African farmers began to join the ranks of prospectors for mineral wealth and skilled workers. To the riches of African vegetable oils and ivory were added diamonds and gold and then copper and tin, but above all power and empire. Europe prepared to divide up Asia after the Boxer troubles. Japan impatiently shook off the threat of China and toppled Russia over, as Russia was already collapsing from interior dry rot. The Madhi and Menelik started to drive Europe out of Northeast Africa, while France and England in jealous rivalry at Fashoda nearly precipitated a world war.

But a balance of power was effected because of the prospective profits of capital, under peace and compromise. The world expanded enormously in imperial industry, until in 1914 came the collapse. It was almost exactly one hundred years after England by the Treaty of Utrecht received the monopoly of the African slave trade and pushed it into enormous expansion. A century later came the decline of the West; the end of that Purple Era which so long seemed to spell the apogee of human civilization, but can only be regarded today as an uneasy incident in the ups and downs of civilization.

In South Africa, as mining and industry expanded, an increased demand for workers arose and the natives began pouring in to work the mines. The land legislation of 1913 increased the migration. The wages paid were low; the conditions were irksome, but both wages and conditions in mine work were much better than on the Boer farms.

A native urban population also arose, of servants and laborers, helpers of all sorts, auxiliary to the main mining industry. Thus began the so-called native locations. These locations were long allowed to develop haphazard. Wherever a European settlement appeared, at its door sprung up a motley native slum filled with black men and women who worked for the white men. They were bleak, treeless wastes, with discontent, sickness and crime. Usually they were separated by at least three miles from the main European town and this allowed curfew regulations and taxation upon the workers for transportation. Sixteen per cent of the total native population of South Africa, or over a million persons live in the city. Johannesburg, for instance, has 500,000 natives and 227,000 Europeans.

The bulk of native mine labor is recruited from the reserves and protectorates. The South African government has an agreement with Portuguese Mozambique for an annual supply of labor which amounted to 90,000 natives in 1932 and 80,000 in 1933. Native miners live in huge concentration camps called compounds, guarded night and day, and are seldom allowed to leave until the year's contract is up. There are no beds and the food is poor. Flogging is not unusual. They work from 2:30 o'clock in the morning until 4:30 o'clock in the afternoon, with a cold breakfast and a warm dinner. The mines are hot and often flooded. Miners sometimes work lying on their backs or standing up to their waist in water. As the Minister of Mines said in 1926, "We cannot deny that the natives of the Witwatersrand, nearly 190,000, are really in a semi-servile condition."

The South African Labor Party in 1911 had carried a Mines and Work Act which shut out non-Europeans from many employments on the excuse of safety and health. Bantus were thus excluded from certain skilled occupations, although the Transvaal courts later held such discrimination to be unconstitutional. In general, labor unions in South Africa excluded colored workers, although a few have been admitted in the Cape Province. Refusal was regularly made by the authorities to grant natives the right to act as traders and merchants in certain town locations, and the bargaining power of black labor was hampered by laws under which a breach of contract was a criminal offense and strikes were illegal except in the case of day laborers and weekly employees.

White workers were still dissatisfied with the conditions of work and continued to blame native competition. There was in 1913 a strike in the gold mines and a threat of a native uprising, and in 1914 a more serious general strike of whites which had to be put down by armed force. The upheaval and readjustment of the World War and the depression had profound effect in South Africa and tended to fester around the color problems, as is usual in such cases. The whole fabric of capitalism was shaken. During the War, not only were 93,000 natives used in various war capacities, including 8,000 as soldiers, but many mines, in order to reduce the cost of production, expanded the field of work for cheap black labor and gave it such skilled work as the natives were able to do. A report of 1925 attests to "the native's almost phenomenal advance in efficiency during recent years," and says that if the development was unhampered, the European worker would be eliminated "from the entire range of mine operation."

The result was labor unrest: among the whites, fear of losing their jobs to cheap black labor; among the blacks, fear of always being held down to starvation wage. In 1918 the white employees at the Johannesburg Power Station struck and the city council capitulated. The native sanitary workers tried to do the same, but were punished under the criminal law. There was passive resistance in 1920 by natives in the Rand; a student strike at Lovedale College and a serious native strike at Port Elisabeth. The nearly one hundred-sixty native religious sects became centers of agitation. In 1921 the police shot down scores of one sect called Israelites.

Attempts to reduce wages in 1922 led to a strike of the white skilled workers which threw 20,000 whites and 180,000 natives out of work on the Rand. Finally, in March, the Federation of Labor was induced to call the strike off and disown "Communism." Smuts, then Prime Minister, in return appointed a commission to investigate, and Hertzog announced that in the next election the Nationalists would work with Labor. A new frank and determined policy actively to suppress the economic and political development of the native thus appeared.

By an act of 1922 further trades were barred to natives by the Apprenticeship Act. This required that a native should have an education up to standard six, which very few natives could reach, because of their limited public schools. Since 1922, the Chamber of Mines and the white trades unions have had an agreement by which the ratio of employment is put at one white man to 10.5 natives.

This whole movement culminated in the Color Bar Act of 1926, an amendment of the Mines and Work Act. It empowered the ministry to make regulations which would exclude natives from occupations requiring special skill and thus make legal the established practice of reserving the best work for Europeans. This was one of the most extraordinary acts of a white civilized government and was in effect a public admission of the inability of white labor to compete with Negroes on equal terms. It was a surrender of the dogma of inborn Negro inferiority in learning industrial technique.

In another aspect of the question, this legislation cuts curiously athwart the Marxian dogma, for instead of class conscious labor solidarity, land monopolists and skilled industrial workers here joined with capital to exploit black labor. Thus white skilled labor in South Africa gets a larger share of the product of industry, but to compensate the owners, native labor is wretchedly under-paid; so that in a sense the higher wage of the white worker is taken from the wage of the black worker and not from the profits of capital. The democracy of the Union of South Africa became an oligarchy in which highly paid white skilled labor had no real control of wealth and income but was induced to sacrifice even unskilled white labor to the competition of the artificially depressed wage of the native—a fact which explains the poor white problem of South Africa.

In 1931, there were thirty thousand European workers and miners on the Rand; and 350,000 native miners who constituted ninety per cent of the total labor force. This number fell to 240,000 in 1933 and 270,000 in 1934. Perhaps 200,000 black miners and 15,000 white skilled laborers is the norm. Also, in addition to the miners, there were 120,000 natives in manufacturing and production, or sixty per cent of the labor force, and 40,000 natives in transport, or thirty-five per cent of the total. Thousands were in secondary industries such as clothing, food, laundry, furniture and handicraft. Practically all servants were native men.

Despite the fact that fluctuations in the general price levels in South Africa have amounted to nearly fifty per cent, native pay has stayed at practically the same rate since the war. While the white worker averages nearly $4.50 a day the colored mine worker gets a little over fifty cents, in addition to simple rations and a place in the compound. The white miner on the Rand is less skilled and does poorer work than the California miner but receives nearly twice the pay. Since the war his wages have risen about twenty per cent, not including funds for pensions and an increased number of holidays.

It has been variously estimated that since 1927 white wages have amounted to something between seven and ten times the native wage. Padmore reports that the income of the South African mining industry was 46,206,000 pounds in 1931, out of which 16,600,000 pounds were paid in wages. This was about equally divided between 23,000 white miners and 240,000 blacks. In 1934, 30,000 white miners received 11,000,000 pounds while 270,000 Africans got less than 9,000,000 pounds. In secondary industries white workers get at least twenty-five dollars a week while natives receive from five to seven dollars and fifty cents. The 20,000 natives employed on the railways get an average monthly wage of fifteen dollars and seventy-five cents.[1]

Black labor has not submitted to this wage slavery without a struggle. The Industrial and Commercial Workers Union, known as the ICU, was the first organized effort on the part of native workers and it had for a while phenomenal success. It was organized in 1919 by a young native of Nyasaland, Clemens Kadalie, one of the results of missionary educational effort and an illustration of the reason that industry opposes native education. Kadalie's organization began its efforts with a docker's strike at Cape Town. Within a few years it had enrolled 100,000 members in the chief industrial and agricultural centers of the Cape Province. From 1924–1926 it spread into the Transvaal and the Orange Free State.

From the nature of the situation it had to become a political as well as an industrial organization, and Hertzog himself appealed to the ICU to rally the voters of the Cape behind him in his fight against Smuts in 1924. On the other hand, the farmers were alarmed at the organization, and the laws against native organization which could be evoked meant its eventual doom. Strikes on the part of natives were for the most part illegal; and agitation of almost any kind could be interpreted as sedition. The only thing that could save the ICU was white labor alliance.

This Kadalie attempted when he secured recognition by the Trades Union International at Amsterdam. He appealed then to the white Cape Federation of Laborers and the Trade Union Congress. They refused to recognize colored trades unionists, but did propose that there should be periodic consultation between the ICU and the federation. This meager concession Kadalie ought to have accepted, or better the whites should have insisted on; but Kadalie stood firmly on the principle of full recognition and the negotiations fell through.

The ICU thereupon was attacked in the courts. During one year, 1927, it is said to have paid out twenty thousand dollars for litigation. Inner troubles ensued, natural among untrained workers, not used to this kind of co-operation. The result was that the ICU was disrupted; there now exist three native industrial organizations: the ICU (now led by an English trade unionist), a separate but similar organization in Natal, and a communist organization.

There is some social uplift work among native workers. The mortality of native miners has been greatly reduced and accident compensation has been increased. Up until 1919 the native victim of an accident received only about one-tenth as much as the white worker. Today he receives about one-half. In 1931, out of 243,000 workers, 2,250 died of disease and six hundred from injuries received at work. Native workers, when they are no longer able to work, are sent back to the reserves. The law provides compensation for white miners and for the dependents of those killed. Up to 1929, eleven million pounds compensation had been paid Europeans. Blacks are not taken care of in the two tuberculosis sanitaria where white miners may go.

Sanitary conditions in the locations became so bad that effort is now being made to correct them. The church and white women have undertaken social work in the locations, including hospitals, clinics and social settlements. Up to the end of 1932 Johannesburg had expended 1,100,000 pounds sterling, Cape Town 300,000 pounds sterling and Durban 170,000 pounds sterling, to improve native housing. Bad conditions are still reported in many cities.

Black labor in the union may be divided into a higher group of forty thousand professional men, teachers and clerks; 360,000 miners, 475,000 farm laborers, and 165,000 common laborers and artisans. These blacks and colored people are to a large degree integrated into the economic system of the whites. About one-third of the total native labor belongs to this system. Of these, ninety per cent are unskilled laborers but they are fast acquiring skill. Despite opposition, natives have learned how to build houses, make implements, spin and weave cloth, work metals, form social and political institutions and teach school.

Thus labor, assisted by the bounty of nature and capital goods raised and made by other laborers, produced minerals as follows in South Africa up until 1935: gold to the value of 2,817 million pounds sterling; diamonds to the value of six hundred thirty-seven million pounds sterling and a total of mineral production including gold, diamonds, coal, copper and tin to a value of 3,733 million pounds sterling. The South African mines and allied industries employed in 1935, 360,000 natives and colored persons, forty-three thousand Europeans and eight thousand Asiatics.

In the four *South African protectorates*, it is not easy at first sight to sense the economic situation. Politically these protectorates are under direct British control, but economically they are bound hand and foot to the economy of the Union of South Africa. They control most of their own land, but the land is poor and eroded by bad methods of agriculture and cattle raising. This makes it impossible for the tribes to raise enough food to support themselves and pay their taxes. South Africa, through customs duties and other regulations, dominates their import and export trade; she exploits their labor in the mines and leaves them no method by which they can get adequate revenue or modern industrial guidance. They are being starved into union with South Africa on the one hand, while the imperial government is being threatened to make it hasten their surrender. It has been openly stated by South Africans that one reason for annexing the protectorates is that this will assist in the solution of the poor white problem.

Bechuanaland is engaged in cattle raising and dairying on the part of the natives and some gold and silver mining by the whites. It has an area of 275,000 square miles and a native population of 260,000 in four chief tribes. There are about a thousand European inhabitants. Wheat, corn, beans and live stock are exported to the amount of 150,000 pounds sterling a year. At least seven thousand natives seek work outside the protectorate annually.

Swaziland, with 7,000 square miles and 150,000 natives, raises tobacco, corn, cotton, vegetables and live stock. Over 10,000 young men each year work in the Rand mines and on the Natal farms. Basutoland has 10,000 square miles and over 550,000 natives. It produces barley, oats, vegetables, corn, sorghum and wheat. There is sheep breeding and seven million pounds of wool were exported in 1935. Basutoland has not nearly enough land for the workers, and in 1932 about 58,000 Basutos, or fifty-five per cent of the adult males, worked away from home; 26,000 in the mines; 12,000 on farms; 19,000 in domestic service. Barotseland, the native reserve in Northern Rhodesia, has 350,000 people on 60,000 square miles and sends annually from 40,000 to 80,000 laborers out of the reserve to find work.

South Africa has also two other race and cultural problems in addition to the native problem; one has to do with 800,000 so-called "colored" people. They are descendants of the Boers and the Hottentots in the earlier days, and of intermixtures between these and the Malays. They form a class of people with considerable education and culture. They sent two corps to East Africa to help the Allies during the World War, and have made good citizens and skilled workers. They are however subject to caste restrictions almost as severe as those visited upon the natives. They vote under property and literary restrictions in Cape Colony but can at present elect only a restricted number of white members to the provincial and Union legislatures, no matter what the number of their voters may be.

There are also in South Africa, East Indians who began to be imported from India to South Africa about 1860 as indentured laborers to work on the sugar and tea plantations of Natal. Some 150,000 were originally imported. They were actively recruited and assured that no disability or limitation of legal rights would ever be imposed on them by reason of race, color, or religion. Importation was stopped in 1866, started again in 1874 and was abolished in 1911. There are now 170,000 resident Indians, and thousands have been repatriated. There are capitalists among them, especially in Natal, but the majority of them are poor artisans and laborers with a middle class of retail traders and professional men.

Eventually the Indians were subjected to all sorts of discrimination. There was open conflict in 1910 on the legality of Indian marriages and then economic strife over the question of buying land and trading. They had proved more successful than the whites in exploiting the natives. An act prohibiting them from owning land in Natal, the Transvaal and other places and restricting their right to trade was enacted.

Gandhi organized the Indians for agitation, initiating in South Africa his technique of "satyagraha." He brought forward a five point program, demanding a repeal of the racial stigma on Asiatics; the right of Indians born in the Cape to return there; the abolition of special taxes, etc. He was really claiming the rights of British citizens for Indians. He carried out his passive resistance and marched his protesting Indians into the Transvaal. His arrest was followed by strikes. He gained some of his demands in 1914, and in 1926 a settlement was arranged between South Africa and India. The Indians were to be encouraged to return home, the South African government paying their passage and giving each of them a bonus of one hundred dollars. Indians born in South Africa do not usually leave and are victimized under the Color Bar Act and other laws.

The white labor group in South Africa fears the competition of the Negro worker and tries to ward it off by trade union organization and government action. This has not only forced down the wage and social condition of the native, but also of an increasing proportion of whites. The gulf between the rich and the poor in the white group is becoming deeper. The older theory was that the white people were to represent an upper caste, rich, experienced, trained and powerful. They were to dominate black labor by their ability as well as by their capital and political power. But, in fact, where they appeared in any numbers, some of them fell from their high estate or never reached it.

The problem came insistently to the attention of the Union of South Africa as early as 1888, and in 1927 the Carnegie Report estimated that 300,000 of the white population were "very poor." Thus when a population of two million white people tried to a large extent to live on the land and exploit the labor of seven million Negroes, one of the results was that at least fifteen per cent of the exploiting group fell into the exploited class.

There is a tendency in South Africa to look upon the poor whites as a burden to society, since they cannot be so effectively exploited as a source of income as can the natives. As one white South African said, "The poor whites are like children in a large family who are looked upon as a burden, while the natives are like the cattle who are regarded as assets." The poor whites form a dangerous slum population, with indolence, dishonesty and prostitution; yet practically all of them have the vote and in many constituencies hold the balance of power. These poor whites look to the state for help and say that they must not be allowed to sink to the level of "the Hottentot." Economic competition between them and the native increases. In the northwest Transvaal there are sections where Dutch whites are wage laborers for native employers; while, on the other hand, the white farm laborer is no longer a social equal with the white landholder.

For several reasons the British government has been less disposed to yield to the exploitation of black labor in *Kenya* than in South Africa. First of all, there were until lately no such large investments in Kenya on the part of the English public as in the South African mines, and consequently less propaganda to make Great Britain think that exploitation in Kenya was absolutely necessary to English well-being. Then too, experience in the development of the West African native as a peasant proprietor, and the ensuing profitableness of his commercial exploitation made South African methods seem less necessary. Finally the first English labor government came to power just as the Kenya dispute was hottest.

There has gone on between England and Kenya an acrimonious debate over the native laborer, which at one time threatened armed rebellion. From the beginning the white settlers were determined to have forced labor and when the Colonial Office tried to lay down restrictive rules, the settlers forced their withdrawal. They sought the resignation of one governor and declared that it was unfair to invite settlers to the country, give them land and then not supply them with cheap labor.

By alienation of land, restriction of their crops, inaccessability to the markets, increased taxation and the direct pressure of the government, the natives have been forced into European employ rather than attracted to it. In 1912, 12,000 were employed and natives testified that through pressure on the chiefs they were compelled to hire out to the white farmers and were further forced by native taxation.

As Norman Leys reminds us, one of the great boons promised the natives was Pax Britannica—cessation from the losses of inter-tribal war. Yet during the World War, from Kenya alone, fourteen thousand natives were enrolled as fighters and one hundred and fifty thousand as porters and stevedores. Of these black men, 1,743 were killed and 44,875 died of disease—a total loss of 46,618, which is greater than any loss through tribal wars for generations. The relatives of most of these dead men have never been traced and there was in 1924 a balance of pay and wages due them unclaimed, amounting to $775,000.

In 1919 the work of recovery from the war began in Kenya and there was naturally a shortage of labor. The governor declared that the natives must be compelled to work and by exercising compulsion through chiefs ninety thousand were in white employment by 1920. The resident white bishops, representing the missionaries, were alarmed at this attitude and issued in 1919 an astonishing but characteristic memorandum. They said, "We do not believe that there is the least intention on either side [government and the settlers] of exploiting natives for private ends . . . we believe that ideally all labor should be voluntary. We recognize that *at present this is impossible and that some form of pressure must be exerted* [our italics] if adequate supply of labor necessary for the development of the country is to be secured."

Low wages and high taxes increased the black labor force to one hundred eighty-five thousand in 1927, but under the depression it fell to one hundred thirty-two thousand in 1929 and rose to one hundred fifty thousand in 1935. In 1934 native laborers in Kenya were paid from two to two and a half dollars a month. In 1929 the average peasant family living in a native reserve had an income between seventeen dollars and fifty cents and twenty-two dollars and fifty cents a year; while the wage earner received about twenty-two dollars and fifty cents, except in the case of skilled laborers and miners. Labor tenancy under contract is the chief form of labor. Contracts may be made for a period up to three years and must involve not less than one hundred and eighty days' work for wages each year. In 1933 over three thousand natives were punished for breach of contract under the Masters and Servants Ordinance. The Kavirondo Native Association pointed out that ten thousand natives had been turned off their land and forced to make labor contracts for periods of six months at two dollars and fifty cents a month.

The produce on native farms is restricted. Natives formerly were not allowed to grow either tea or coffee and until recently there was no effort to help them in marketing their produce, as in Uganda and Tanganyika. "A new marketing scheme was recently introduced which gave the native producer protection, ensures fairer prices, and by a system of inspection bettered the quality of native produce."[2] The produce raised by the native goes through many hands before he gets his share, so that of the five hundred thousand pounds sterling which his produce is worth annually, only about two hundred thousand pounds actually reach him, because of four to six European and Indian middlemen. The produce of native farms was valued at $2,730,000 in 1924, but that same year $4,380,000 was collected in native taxes. Of this $1,250,000 came from customs and the rest from the hut and poll taxes.

The squatters law is more drastic than in South Africa. In Kenya squatters must do six months' contract labor and this is often increased. A labor registration ordinance has been enacted which makes the laborer carry a wallet with his fingerprints and labor record. Failure to have the certificate is a criminal offense. Trade union organization and collective bargaining are strictly prohibited by law. There is no social legislation such as unemployment benefits or old age pensions; no workmen's compensation act nor minimum standards in housing.

Lately big business is invading Kenya. The largest mining claims are held by the Tanganyika Concessions, Ltd., the Kenya Developments, Ltd., and French and American capitalists. The Imperial Chemical Industry, Ltd., a British trust with a capital of over four million pounds sterling, has a concession to exploit soda at Lake Magadi, where there is a deposit of two hundred million tons.

There are also in Kenya thirty thousand Indians. They came to build the Uganda railway and as soldiers during the war. They work as clerks, artisans and traders; and in the native reserves the trade is nearly all in their hands. Effort has been made to exclude them entirely from the Colony and has been successful in excluding them by administrative policy from the land reserved for the whites, in restricting their commercial rights, in segregating them in residence and partially disfranchising them by putting them on a separate election roll. They have fought continuously for full rights as English subjects.

Southern Rhodesia forms a variation of the South Africa-Kenya labor pattern. The aim of Southern Rhodesia, as expressed by Prime Minister Huggins, is to make Southern Rhodesia a "white man's country," despite the fact that today fifty-five thousand whites face 1,300,000 blacks. The whites are engaged in agriculture, stock culture and mining and are depending on African labor. Labor is supplied from Nyasaland, Northern Rhodesia and Mozambique, as well as from Southern Rhodesia. Today there is enough land for whites and blacks and the available labor force from Southern Rhodesia itself and neighboring territory gives an ample supply of low-priced labor. High taxation and limited land have not yet been necessary in Southern Rhodesia to secure labor. When the natives grow in education and compete in farm produce, as mining and industry increase and more white workers appear, the South African pattern will be reproduced.

In 1932, sixty-five per cent of the native population lived on the reserves and from one hundred and fifty to two hundred natives annually were purchasing land in the undetermined areas. Village settlements are planned near the urban centers for natives in employment and three have been provided for. A large

number of natives have remained upon the land of white landlords as squatters. The number of such tenants was limited in 1908 to forty on a single farm.
The customary rent charge is five dollars a year. The Native Affairs Commission
of 1910 advocated the substitution of labor for cash rent and prohibition of
natives living outside the reserves, unless they were employed by Europeans
for a definite period.

Native agricultural laborers receive three dollars and seventy-five cents per
month of thirty working days, but during the depression this fell to two dollars
and fifty cents. In 1935, 127,000 natives were in the employ of white farmers and
77,000 in the mines. Over 120,000 of these workers were from outside Southern
Rhodesia. The average monthly wage in the mines is about three dollars to
seven dollars and fifty cents a month for unskilled and semi-skilled labor.
Skilled workers such as machinists in the mines get from eleven to fifteen dollars per month.

The investment of capital on which the Rhodesias rest is illustrated by the fact
that in 1923, when the British South Africa Company withdrew from the administration of Rhodesia, it received 3,750,000 pounds sterling from the Imperial
Government and at the same time retained ownership in lands amounting to
10,195,000 acres, and mining rights yielding an annual income of over 100,000
pounds sterling. The assets of the Company were 7,065,000 pounds at that time.
In 1933 the Company sold its mining rights to Southern Rhodesia for 2,000,000
pounds. Its total profits in 1934 were 328,797 pounds.[3]

Some natives employed in government service are messengers, interpreters,
railway guards, jailers, police, agricultural and industrial demonstrators. They
average twenty-five dollars per month. All supervisory positions and skilled
jobs are reserved for whites. After a strike, the government and the Chamber of
Mines have promised white miners a minimum of five dollars a day for an eight-
hour day. White organized labor is hostile to black labor and allows no African
to receive the pay of a skilled worker even if he does the work.

Unionization among colored workers is forbidden. Labor legislation such as
workmen's compensation and hours does not apply to Africans. The Masters and
Servants Act and the pass system regulate native labor. All natives must obtain a
pass before they can enter Southern Rhodesia and are allowed thirty days to find
work. After that they are liable to arrest as vagrants. If a native quits a job without
consent he is liable to a fine of fifty dollars or two years' imprisonment or both.

It will be seen that Southern Rhodesia proposes to arrange for a class of governing capitalists and planters and a Negro proletariat. It is trying to avoid the
rise of a poor white problem and does not expect the black worker to gain any
considerable voice in government.

The copper region of Africa lies in the southern part of the Belgian Congo
and in *Northern Rhodesia*. The fields are said to contain over a third of the world's
known resources. For a thousand years natives have mined small quantities of
copper in what is now Northern Rhodesia and the present mines were first
pointed out to Europeans by native chiefs. Gold mines were worked with black
labor in 1906 but use of Negro miners on a large scale began in the Belgian Congo
in 1911.

Northern Rhodesia is one of the lowest cost copper-producing areas in the world and is able to deliver in Europe copper at a cost forty or fifty per cent lower than is possible for mines in the United States. It is said that the mines of Northern Rhodesia could produce a quarter million tons a year for a hundred years.

The effect of South African diamonds and gold upon the world is fairly well-known. But in the case of copper we have an astonishing illustration of the economic interdependence of the world, including Africa, and of the curious linking of social and racial problems. From a world production of a quarter of a million tons in 1880, the age of electricity brought, in 1929, nearly two million tons of copper. This increase has been accompanied by manipulation of price in the world market, by war and depression, by tariff restrictions and cartels. For the first part of the nineteenth century, the British Empire produced a large percentage of the world's copper. Just before the World War, the United States was producing fifty-six per cent. The production fell during the war, but afterward consumption increased rapidly and speculation sent the price to five hundred dollars a ton in 1929. Then came the depression and mines began to close.

Next to the abundance of the metal itself, the great commercial advantage of the African copper region lies in the presence of an inexhaustible cheap labor force. When the Rhodesian mines first became active, the process of recruiting labor reached to centers three hundred to six hundred miles distant. There was the usual bribery of chiefs and misrepresentation; and mission work, agriculture and education were interfered with over wide stretches of African village life. In some districts sixty per cent of the able-bodied men were away from home during the construction boom in the copper belt. The wages offered, though low, were so much higher than the workers had ever been given, that very soon recruiting was unnecessary and a stream of volunteers presented themselves at the mines. When the demand fell, they were sent back to their villages; so that the mining companies had all the advantages of a vast labor reserve which they could discharge at will without responsibility.

There were in Northern Rhodesia in 1930–31, one and one-fourth million natives and about fourteen thousand whites. The wage-earning natives formed then something over 100,000, and of these thirty-eight thousand found work outside of the territory on farms and in mines. Perhaps in no other area of the world has there been so sudden an economic transformation or such an intensive application of scientific knowledge to a region so large and so primitive as in the territories on the watershed between the Congo and Zambesi Rivers. The richest products of European knowledge and American enterprise are harnessed together for exploiting the vast resources of Africa so as to enhance the wealth of the world for the benefit of the white investor, with scant reference to native welfare.

Thus in Northern Rhodesia during the last twenty-five years an essentially urban economic organization has been imposed upon a native rural economy and has brought with it all the vicissitudes of modern industrial systems. For instance, during the boom, Northern Rhodesia was producing copper, zinc, lead and vanadium. In January, 1927, there were about 8,500 natives employed, not counting servants and town employees. By December, 1927, the number rose to nearly 11,000; it reached 16,000 by 1929 and by September, 1931, it reached a peak of nearly 32,000. Labor was in constant demand. Then came the catastrophic fall in the price of copper. Six of the mines were closed and the demand for labor dropped. Throughout 1931 there came a gradual decrease to 21,000 in May; 16,000 in October; and 13,000 in December. The decrease went on until 1933, when in July, only 7,500 Negro miners were at work.[4]

There was among the natives great astonishment, disappointment and suffering. Northern Rhodesia was following the fate of countries which depend on a single product and suffer with all the fluctuations of a world market. Under favorable trade conditions, perhaps 12,000 natives will eventually be required to operate the mines, with some eight thousand additional servants, shop men and laborers near the mines, making twenty thousand in all.

The work of the native Rhodesian miners follows the tendency of so much modern labor. Only a few highly skilled workers are needed. The actual production of copper is very largely an automatic machine process. The ore is dug by manual labor, but for raising of the ore and taking it to the smelter, the only labor needed is to oil the machinery and stop blockage. In smelting, converting and casting only a few workers are needed.

Unskilled native labor in the Rhodesian mines formerly received from three dollars and sixty cents to seven dollars a month. The average cash wage for adult employees in the mines is about twenty-five cents a day, rising to forty-two cents for a skilled carpenter. Bonuses up to eight cents a day are sometimes paid for satisfactory work. In addition to this the laborers get food, rent and medical care which can be estimated at perhaps twenty-two cents a day, a total wage of forty-seven to fifty cents. Since the depression the average level of wages has been lowered. On the other hand, in the last seven years price levels have risen in Northern Rhodesia as much as two hundred per cent; living standards among the natives also have risen. Missions have to pay more for salaries and food and to charge the pupils more.

It was estimated, in 1931, that the 110,000 natives at work inside and outside the colony earned $4,500,000; of this the native was paid $900,000 in cash; $1,250,000 in goods which they bought; and $250,000 in taxes which they paid. Of $500,000 earned by natives at one mine, $280,000 was spent on trade goods; $60,000 spent at the beer halls run by the proprietors of the mine; $14,000 for taxes and licenses; $95,000 was sent or taken home, and the rest spent for food and miscellaneous items. At one time, between ten and fifteen per cent of the natives had savings accounts of about thirty dollars when they left employment. A few had accounts of over two hundred and fifty dollars.

The capital used in the mining sections is almost wholly imported: of the thirty-six and one-half million dollars which Northern Rhodesia annually pays out, eighty-two per cent are payments for borrowings. Of the goods imported, thirteen million is in consumption goods for Europeans; two million dollars consumption goods for natives, and one hundred and fifty million dollars, goods for industry and construction.

A most significant fact is, that this work which the natives do has objectives which have no direct relation to their life. They use little copper. There is no local brass industry; and there is no connection of the mines with other work carried on by local craftsmen. There is almost no internal cycle for the satisfaction of wants. Manufactured articles which are brought in for native consumption amount to nearly a million dollars' worth annually. Native spinning has disappeared. Picks, hoes, pots, and pans might be manufactured but native blacksmiths have been hampered and discouraged by the government.

The system is having a disintegrating effect upon the native village economy. The new industrial individualism comes into contrast with the communalism of the tribe. The village, the huts, the native agriculture change little. There are some new goods: cotton is worn, candles are used, blankets, knives, axes, mirrors are desired, and in addition gramophones, sewing machines and bicycles. Sugar, tea, rice, cigarettes and canned goods are in demand; but the money to buy these things must come almost entirely from work in industry and not from anything that the village can furnish. Even the possibility of subsistence agriculture is reduced, because of the absence of men from their homes and farms.

In 1931, for instance, it is estimated that one-tenth of the total population, or one hundred and fifty thousand men, were absent from the native villages over long periods, leaving the old men, the children and the women in the isolated village. Such a long absence is a strain upon the fidelity of husband and wife, leading especially in the mines to temporary unions, prostitution and disease.

Since there is no competition from Indian traders, the natives have ventured into trade to some extent. In 1931 there were seventy-two native stores and six hundred and seventeen peddlers; but these traders are discriminated against at many of the mine centers. Their credit is limited and the banks furnish only a six-cent piece as the smallest unit of currency.

A black labor movement is evident in Northern Rhodesia. All the native miners in the copper industry of Northern Rhodesia went out on general strike in May, 1935, because of a proposed increase in taxes without wage increase. Armed clashes occurred between the blacks and troops at the Roan Antelope mines, where the soldiers opened fire and killed over ten and wounded several others. For days the entire mining district of Ndola, Luanshya and Nkana were disturbed and there was a sympathetic strike by native domestic servants.

All the white towns have segregated areas for Negroes, usually across a railway or a stream. The natives usually outnumber the whites and all live in the native location, except some of the servants. About thirty per cent of the residents in the locations are married and live in quarters separate from the single men.

The problem of competition between white and colored labor has already risen, since Northern Rhodesia had to import skilled labor for work in the mines and especially for work on the railways. On the railways the English trade union rules prevail and these prevent natives from being employed. Also government policy requires that on all government building, fifty per cent of all skilled labor shall be white. Already many of the whites in Northern Rhodesia are demanding complete political control of the black population.

Nyasaland was one of the main areas of David Livingstone's activities between 1866 and his death in 1873. It early became, therefore, a mecca for missionaries and had a larger proportion of mission schools and missionary effort than most African colonies. The result is that today more Negroes with sufficient training to act as teachers and clerks are found in Nyasaland than in neighboring territories. The natives of Nyasaland are not in large reserves but have areas scattered throughout the territory. On these there were fifty-three thousand native tobacco growers and thirteen thousand, two hundred and sixty cotton growers in 1932. They raised sixty per cent of the cotton crop; but in disposing of their produce they were largely at the mercy of European and Asiatic traders. On the other hand, there are thousands of landless natives who are on the plantations of the whites. They are liable for a cash rent of one to two dollars, but usually this is demanded in labor; otherwise the tenants are evicted. The coffee plantations use this sort of forced labor largely.

The Nyasaland Planters Association is opposed to black peasant proprietors. In 1931 an English commission advocated the setting aside of six million acres for native occupation but this recommendation was not followed. In 1933 a new lands' bill was introduced investing native territory in the governor as trustee. This proposal so far has not been followed. An ordinance of 1928 put some safeguards around the tenants, requiring cash wages and short labor contracts. Maximum rents were fixed and evictions limited. Notwithstanding this, the sixty thousand wage earners working as farm hands, servants and mechanics have insufficient security.

Lately the English government has called attention to the fact that the hut and poll tax is forcing the native out of the colony to find work, and keeping him from agriculture. The continued migration of able-bodied natives, since the depression, has become a considerable problem. The Nyasaland Committee on Emigrant Labor (1935) put the total of Nyasaland natives employed out of the territory as one hundred twenty thousand. Forced labor is used for transport, road and railway building, public buildings, sanitary work, telephone lines. The crisis was severe in 1932.

The wages paid are low. Common labor receives from one dollar and a half to a dollar seventy-five a month; skilled laborers between five and ten dollars a month. Clerical and government employees, of whom there are a considerable number, receive from twelve-fifty to twenty-five dollars a month.

Possibly Leopold of Belgium in his earlier years had some philanthropic plans for the *Belgian Congo.* Certainly he encouraged scientific study of the tribes, which resulted in the beginning of an encyclopedia of Belgian Negro culture; he collected a marvelous museum at Tervueren, although even here the private profit motive was emphasized. Certainly, after 1891, Leopold let loose in the Congo "the most ruthless system of exploitation which even Africa has known—

"One, Leopold claimed to exercise his absolute powers of Sovereign to tax his subjects. Since he could not collect taxes in money, he argued that he would tax them either in kind or labor.

"Two, he also claimed the right to demand from his native subjects the obligation of military service.

"Three, he claimed that the land was the property of the State and therefore of himself, the Sovereign of the State.

"Four, it was by exercising these 'rights' and claims through decrees, that he established his water-tight system of monopoly and exploitation."[5]

By decrees in 1891 and 1892 a state monopoly of all ivory and rubber was created. The natives were forbidden to either collect or sell these products. They were on the other hand taxed in kind and in labor, so that the produce could be collected and brought to the coast for transport and sale in Europe. Under the decree of December 5, 1892, the officers of administration were ordered to take any steps necessary for assuring the exploitation of the Crown land thus sequestered. This meant that the natives were forced to collect ivory and rubber and the collecting officers were paid a percentage upon the amount gathered. Forced labor and slavery were thus established. This forced labor was used not only in the interests of the king himself, but was delegated to private corporations. In addition to this, every year the governor-general was ordered to raise a stated number of troops and this military tax was distributed by the governor among his subordinates. Such native troops were subjected to military service for twelve years.

Thus humanity and commerce did not replace the Arab slave traders. Rather, European greed and serfdom were substituted. The land was confiscated by the state and farmed out to private corporations. The wilder cannibal tribes were formed into a militia to prey on the industrious, who were taxed with specific amounts of ivory and rubber, and scourged and mutilated if they failed to pay. Harris declares that King Leopold's regime meant the death of twelve million natives.

"Europe was staggered at the Leopoldian atrocities, and they were terrible indeed; but what we, who were behind the scenes, felt most keenly was the fact that the real catastrophe in the Congo was desolation and murder in the larger sense. The invasion of family life, the ruthless destruction of every social barrier, the shattering of every tribal law, the introduction of criminal practices which struck the chiefs of the people dumb with horror—in a word, a veritable avalanche of filth and immorality overwhelmed the Congo tribes."[6]

So notorious did the exploitation and misrule become that Leopold was forced to take measures toward reform, and finally in 1908 the Free State became a Belgian colony. The state took over the colony in 1909, reluctantly and in the face of widespread world criticism. To some extent Belgium has faced the realities of the situation. She has realized that the demands of European enterprise are apt to clash not only with the well-being but even the survival of the natives and that at least to that extent it must be curtailed. This is the clear explanation of the status of the Congo. Belgium has bettered the condition of the native and made the situation more hopeful than in the Union of South Africa, the Rhodesias or Kenya. Some attempt has been made to develop native life. The average wage at the mines is low, but higher than in Rhodesia or South Africa. It amounts to about seventy-five cents a day—thirty-three cents in cash and forty-five cents in health, housing, and rations.

The mines have faced the problem which we have seen in Northern Rhodesia and South Africa, of demoralized village life by large withdrawals of adult workers. Belgium has therefore set about a systematic curbing of labor recruiting with gradual and partial detribalization. Natives are transplanted in limited numbers to new government and corporation villages, where the plan is to make them spend their lives under different conditions, but with guidance and welfare work. The mines have undertaken to some extent to educate their children, safeguard the families and care for them in old age.

The depression was severe. There was the same great drop in working forces at Katanga as in Rhodesia: the 17,000 workers of 1929 shrinking to less than four thousand in 1932; but there was greater effort in Katanga to maintain a dependable resident labor force. There were in the Congo in 1935, 377,531 laborers, divided as follows: natives employed at a long distance from home 119,442; at a short distance 126,177; and near home 131,932. In the mandate of Ruanda-Urundi there were 7,470 permanent and 26,344 non-permanent employees.

Moreover, the Congo has no problem of competition between white and colored laborers, because the white persons who come in are mainly officials, merchants and agents. There are less than twenty-thousand whites in the country. Some of these are technicians and skilled laborers, but the proportion of these is small. Orde Browne says, "The train from the south reaches the Belgian border, with a staff that is European in all the important posts; there the traveler changes to a train which is managed almost entirely by Africans." The natives are locomotive-engineers in charge of machines and tools; they repair the railway coaches and they do all the skilled work in the mines. This has a double result. Not only does the Belgian investor get skilled work cheap and thus make up in profit for what he may lose by social uplift work, but he also is avoiding the menace and demands of white labor with European affiliations. On the other hand, he inspires the natives of other parts of Africa with ambition to be allowed the same work and with the knowledge that it is only their color which keeps them from the opportunity; and this threatens the preferred status of resident white artisans.

Uganda, while near Kenya, departs from the South Africa-Kenya labor pattern and approaches the West African labor situation. There were in Uganda, in 1931, three and one-half million Africans, fourteen thousand Asiatics and two thousand Europeans. Whites are chiefly government officials, with merchants and bankers in the towns, and about three hundred planters. The East Indians are artisans, government clerks and small traders. There are thirty large Indian landlords holding fourteen thousand acres and an Indian has the largest sugar factory.

The Africans are engaged in farming and stock raising. Only forty-seven thousand are in the service of whites as farm laborers, porters, and dockers; at cotton-picking time there are large numbers of temporary workers; and there are a few in the civil service, in British and native administration. In general the labor laws in Uganda are as follows: 1. the pass law; 2. reduced taxes for those who work for the whites; 3. heavy taxes to drive native traders out of business; 4. forced labor for single men, two months every year.

The Chambers of Commerce, Planters Association, Cotton Spinners Association and Indian Commercial Association have united to bring pressure upon the government for recruiting native wage labor. The result is a Masters and Servants Ordinance which makes leaving an employer a criminal offense with arrest without warrant. In 1934 the average wage in Uganda for unskilled labor was two dollars and fifty cents to three dollars and seventy-five cents a month, without food. The average native peasant farmer has an income between one hundred and one hundred twenty-five dollars a year. Mining has begun and the Tanganyika Concessions, Ltd., one of the largest mining syndicates in East Africa, has penetrated Uganda. During 1934 there were a hundred mining claims granted to whites. Natives exported 316,000 bales of cotton.

In studying the condition of the laborers in *French Africa* one must differentiate between French West Africa and French Equatorial Africa. In French West Africa there is an organized territory with some cities like Dakar and Saint Louis, where modern conditions of work and some self-government are manifest; throughout the colony there is recognition of land ownership by natives and individual farming. Labor legislation was introduced in 1926 and contracts provided for, with limited hours of work, minimum wage, compensation for accident and death. There is medical attendance, and saving is encouraged. Arbitration councils are provided to settle labor disputes. There are no regular labor inspectors but on the whole the labor conditions are not bad. On the other hand, military service is required and sometimes the soldiers are used for public work. There is general conscription for public work to build roads and railways, and the government still furnishes labor for transport and on some large farms. The amount of forced labor, however, is not large and seems to be decreasing.

On the other hand, in French Equatorial Africa one has a vast territory thinly populated, not well organized, where exploitation has in cases run wild and been as bad as anything in the Belgian Congo or elsewhere. There is no military conscription in Equatorial Africa, but railway construction and the attempt to collect wild produce have caused the use of forced labor on a large scale. The construction of the Congo Ocean Railway involved a mass of laborers, among whom there was one contingent which had a mortality of six hundred per thousand. A head tax to be paid in products of the soil was used as a means of forcing labor in 1900. It was charged that the tax was five or ten times as high as it ought to have been, because of the prices arbitrarily put on products. In 1904, armed guards were forcing the natives to gather rubber; some were shot; one thousand and five hundred were massacred in one area, which resulted in a successful revolt. Other workers revolted in 1928 and Chinese coolies were introduced but were not retained. Between 1922 and 1932, ninety-three thousand men were used in forced labor with the result that some eighty thousand natives migrated to the English Gold Coast searching for better conditions. In 1930, compulsory labor for private enterprise was legally forbidden and in 1933 further restrictions on forced labor were issued.

In all French Africa the profit motive, while curbed by certain general restrictions and especially by the beginnings of popular education, is nevertheless present and dominant. French Africa is in the main organized for profit. Great corporations, great banks, great shipping agencies, great railroads, all unite in well-known and stereotyped ways to overthrow native industry, to make economic development in French West Africa mechanical and methodical, and, above all, profitable. The great excesses of the past in land-grabbing and serfdom

are guarded against; but the retail profiteer and the wholesale price-manipula-
tor are here in their glory. They are underbidding and displacing the native
merchants by methods which the natives cannot meet. The native, to live, must
raise what the world makes him raise and raise it at the world's price; and white
world business too determines the native's share of the profit.

We now turn to *British West Africa*, where instead of the tenant farmer, we
have predominantly the peasant proprietor; the industrial worker and trader,
while a considerable and growing factor, is a small and not dominant one in the
economic situation.

Nigeria is as large as the British Isles and has some nineteen million inhabitants. This colony perpetuates the old town culture of certain parts of Africa,
with perhaps a hundred towns having from ten thousand to four hundred
thousand inhabitants. The northern provinces carry on the village and rural life.
In the whole of Nigeria, in 1935, there were only 200,000 of the natives in European
employ, or about two per cent. The mass of the people are peasant proprietors.
The total export trade of Nigeria has varied from seventeen million pounds sterling in 1928 to nine and one-half million pounds sterling in 1932; the imports
from sixteen and one-half to seven and one-fourth million during the same time.
The chief products are palm oil, palm kernels, cotton, cocoa, mahogany, tin, gold,
groundnuts and skins.

British economic penetration and control consist in practical monopoly of
transportation of all goods by ship to Europe; of various monopolies such as the
British Cotton Growers' Association, which does all the ginning; and returns on
invested capital for mining and transport facilities. Great trading companies
have divided the entire country into commercial zones. The agents of various
companies have organized Chambers of Commerce and other methods of fixing
profits and regulating trade. Local Chambers of Commerce are connected with
the Liverpool Chamber, through a special West African section. The Liverpool
Chamber is controlled by British bankers, merchants, and manufacturers. These
chambers have long been represented directly in the governing councils of the
various colonies.

The depression and manipulation of the market by British merchants have
caused a good deal of dissatisfaction and misunderstanding. The spread between
prices in Liverpool and in Nigeria is sometimes very large. It is charged that in
1932, for instance, palm oil fetched ten pounds a ton in Nigeria and eighteen to
twenty pounds in London.

Although the plantation system has not been introduced into West Africa,
exploitation by monopoly and invested capital is universal: first of all the state
gives every facility to these companies. The state has built railways in Nigeria
at a cost of about twenty-two million pounds. This has involved the use of forced
labor. Harbors have been built at an expense of eight million pounds sterling
and the money loaned to colonial governments must be spent in British-made
machinery and material.

The gold fields are owned by the government. In 1934, seventy thousand mine
workers were employed in Nigeria with some protective labor legislation. The
average wage is twenty-five cents a day for underground work and eighteen

cents a day for work on the surface. The workers furnish their own food. All skilled and supervisory work is done by whites.

In Southern Nigeria and Lagos there are sixty thousand wage earners employed on railways, public works and forests. There are a large number of clerks and civil servants. Skilled mechanics are trained in government shops as engineers, carpenters, masons, and painters. These employees receive from two hundred fifty dollars to one thousand dollars a year. In Benin and the Cameroons there are lumber workers under six months' contract cutting mahogany, with low wages and hard work.

The *Gold Coast* is the most advanced of the West Coast colonies and the richest. There are three and one-half million natives in the colony and its associated territories, and only five per cent of the adult males are in European employ. In 1934 these employees included twenty-four thousand miners and ten thousand general employees.

The Gold Coast is the largest producer of cocoa in the world. With Nigeria it raises sixty per cent of the world's total production. The story of this development is of interest. A native Gold Coast laborer, William Tetteh Quarshie, was working in Spanish Fernando Po, where cocoa had been introduced from Mexico. When he returned to the Gold Coast in 1876 he brought some beans and planted them. He sold seeds to other farmers and by and by the whole population around began planting cocoa. The first shipments abroad amounted to eighty pounds in 1891, five hundred and thirty-six tons in 1900 and in 1911 to forty thousand tons. The expansion of the cocoa industry was rapid from 1906 to 1915, but was curtailed during the war and then accelerated by high prices from 1919 to 1920. Then came low prices and fluctuation. Prices went as high as eighty-pounds per ton in 1920 but in 1934 it was fifteen pounds per ton.

The export rose from fifty-three thousand tons in 1914 to sixty-six thousand tons in 1918. In 1926, two hundred thirty thousand tons valued at eight million pounds sterling were exported to Europe and America. Prices since have fallen so that the 1931 crop of two hundred forty-four thousand tons was valued at only five and one-half million pounds; in 1935, two hundred eighty-five thousand tons were raised. There are a few white plantations, but the bulk of the cocoa is raised by over fifty thousand black peasants on 950,000 acres.

The cocoa crop is handled by European commercial houses who maintain local stores. Naturally the crop is subject to world markets and to combinations on the part of buyers. A local buying pool fixes the price and this pool is linked with the local banks and shipping companies and the Liverpool Chamber of Commerce. While the price paid is thus kept low in order to make the maximum profit for the exporters, on the other hand the natives pay high prices for manufactures in stores owned by trading companies. Cheap Japanese goods are kept out by high tariff and English goods must be bought. An export duty on cocoa which, of course, favors the English importers, furnishes about sixty per cent of the colonial income.

Back of all this has gone an interesting play of forces. It is charged, for instance, in Portugal that the boycott of Portuguese cocoa at Principe and São Thomé some years ago was deliberately designed by some interests to transfer the cocoa industry to British territory and start a large plantation system. Negro peasant enterprise frustrated this. These black West African growers have tried to get better banking facilities on the West Coast and lately with government aid are beginning to protect themselves through co-operative organization.

The government has done much excellent work in helping the natives improve the quality of the cocoa and maintain proper standards; there are experiment stations and a system of inspection. But there are seven hundred million cocoa trees on the West Coast and a tree may bear a hundred years. It is therefore very difficult to adjust the production of cocoa to fluctuations in demands. In 1925 the natives of the Gold Coast sold twenty-seven and one-half million dollars worth of cocoa and imported twenty-five million dollars worth of English goods. Before the depression, the Gold Coast Negroes were prosperous, with ten thousand bank accounts in 1922. Today the Colony is gradually recovering.

The Gold Coast is rich in minerals, including gold, diamonds and manganese. Gold has been produced since the fifteenth century, and in 1934 there were seven mines producing, twenty-four under development, and fifteen prospecting. The Ashanti Company, a British organization, was started in 1896, and holds a concession over one hundred square miles on a ninety-nine year lease. They declared a dividend of one hundred per cent in 1930 and one hundred thirty per cent in 1933, besides distributing free shares. Mining companies in some cases have to obtain their concessions from the native stools and the money paid belongs to the councils of the native states.

The chief employers of wage labor are the government departments, including railways and public works; and the mining, shipping and trading industries. The Negroes not only do the labor of the mines but occupy many skilled positions there as well as on the railways and in public works. Between twenty and thirty thousand are employed in the mines and about five hundred whites. Laborers get from eighteen to twenty-eight cents a day and skilled laborers from fifty to seventy-five cents. At present these wages are decreasing.

The Gold Coast has two thousand five hundred carpenters and builders, one thousand tailors, one thousand five hundred bricklayers and masons, eight hundred chauffeurs and mechanics, three hundred painters, one thousand goldsmiths and five thousand boatmen and fishermen. There are a number of cocoa brokers and also about six thousand traders and peddlers, mostly women, and eight thousand porters and carriers. There are twelve thousand Africans employed as clerks, teachers and clergymen; fifty practice law and eleven practice medicine.

In the northern territories there is forced labor for road building, in accordance with the new ordinance enacted in 1935. It requires six days' labor per quarter. The Gold Coast is the only African colony where the natives pay neither poll nor hut tax, but taxation in other forms has reached such a height that two delegations about 1934 went to London to protest, but without success. The colonial government discriminates openly between its white and colored employees: it pays black government physicians, with education identical with that of the whites, salaries and pensions sixteen and two-thirds per cent less.

On the Gold Coast and elsewhere in British West Africa, Syrians are prominent in commerce and money-lending and present a new problem.

Sierra Leone has twenty-six thousand square miles and one and one-half million natives. The chief work is agriculture, rice being raised for food, and more palm kernels being exported than from any other British territory except Nigeria. In 1922 the imperial government enacted the palm oil ordinance which gives the governor the right to grant concessions to the extent of five thousand acres for developing palm oil plantations. Lever Brothers have obtained such concessions. In 1934 the export of kernels rose to 68,000 tons valued at 112,000 pounds. The government derives most of its revenue by an export tax on palm oil and kernels.

The mines employ ten thousand native workers; three thousand are employed on railways and public construction. There are about six thousand unskilled workers in Freetown. Unskilled labor gets eighteen to twenty-five cents a day and skilled labor from fifty to seventy-five cents. The Krus are employed as stevedores, sailors and firemen on West Coast ships and are noted for efficient labor. They are paid from eighteen to twenty-five cents a day.

Gambia is the most unfortunately situated of the West African colonies for industry. Groundnuts are raised, but little food. There is a very small labor market, except for a few artisans. It is said that a Gambia peasant may make thirty-seven dollars a year but this does not near pay his expenses. Recently a debt of thirty thousand pounds sterling owed by the farmers to the state was canceled after agitation by the natives.

The labor movement in West Africa began in Sierra Leone. Usually trade unions were not allowed, and there was forced labor in the protectorate and household slavery was legal as late as 1927. In the colony of Sierra Leone, the Railway Men's Union was at one time the largest union on the African continent. It conducted a strike in 1917 and another in 1926. After six weeks' struggle, the latter strike was stopped by the armed force of the state. Thirty-seven employees, some of whom had worked for twenty years, were thrown out of employment and many others taken back at reduced pay.

There was a general strike of workers in Gambia in 1929, started by sailors whose wages had been reduced. It lasted sixty-two days but was finally settled by government pressure. Labor in Nigeria has comparatively little chance for organization. Public meetings are not permitted, except with special permission of the commissioner of peace. In 1929, thirty thousand women in one palm oil district struck on account of prices offered. Eighty of them are said to have been killed by machine guns and a large number wounded. Natives were taxed to reimburse the company.

Liberia, the only independent Negro state in Africa, has between one million and one and one-half million inhabitants, of whom sixty thousand live in modern fashion and the rest under the tribal regime. Recently the labor problems of Liberia have attracted world attention. United States capital turned to Liberia to off-set British monopoly of rubber, of which the United States was using nearly two-thirds of all produced. The Firestone Rubber Company obtained a concession from Liberia for the production of rubber with the right to select a million acres of land at the nominal rental of six cents an acre; and the right to labor supplied by the Liberian government through the native chiefs. Competition, however, for Liberian labor, between the Firestone Company and the Spanish interests at Fernando Po, led to a considerable amount of forced labor in which various Liberian officials were implicated.

The exposing of this system finally led to an appeal of Liberia to the League of Nations for assistance in reorganizing her government and labor economy. This, on the insistence of the Firestone Company, was offered only on terms that meant the virtual surrender of Liberian autonomy, and the offer was refused by Liberia. The United States withdrew recognition and for a time matters were critical. Finally, Liberia made terms with Firestone and the United States and still retained her sovereignty. The difficulty still remains that the Firestone contract is unfair, but is backed by the American government. Without this financial interest of America in Liberia the pressure of Great Britain and France would doubtless overwhelm her.

Today Liberia has an area of forty-three thousand square miles, and about three hundred and fifty miles of coastline. The revenue amounted in 1913 to $530,000 and in 1936 to $780,000. The imports in 1912 were $1,667,857 and the exports $1,199,152 and in 1936 $1,670,000 and $1,300,000. The exports consisted chiefly of rubber, palm oil and kernels, coffee, piassava fiber, ivory and arnotto.

For a long time the *Portuguese colonies* were used for the private enterprise of commercial organizations. Angola has forty thousand Europeans and mulattoes and three million natives on about a half million square miles. Mozambique on 300,000 square miles has four million natives and 35,000 mulattoes and Europeans. In Mozambique two chartered companies have the right to tax natives and dispose of their labor. For a long time labor conditions in these colonies were among the worst on the continent, involving slavery and a slave trade. The reason was that the administration of the government in the colonies has been really in the hands of English and other foreign investors or of Portuguese investors who were working solely for profit. The Mozambique Company, for instance, has a charter granting it sovereign rights for fifty years from 1891. The government has granted great estates and been foremost in providing forced labor for them.

In the case of the *Mandates* a study of labor conditions leads back to German Africa. The Germans in their colonies introduced modern and efficient sanitation, being the first to combat sleeping-sickness. They trained the natives in industrial skills and provided food and shelter. On the other hand, they were harsh in discipline, ruthless in sweeping away tribal culture, and low in sex morals.

In 1884 two German warships seized Togoland and the Cameroons. It was agreed that the natives should retain their lands, but the Germans repudiated the treaty and gave all the highlands to white settlers and joint stock companies and instituted forced labor. They used flogging and torture. The Cameroons fell to the allied forces in 1916. In Togoland, on account of the absence of highlands, the Germans did not settle as in the Cameroons, and peasant production was carried on; but there was much flogging and torture and sexual outrages. The members of the Bremen senate charged that while the white population of Togoland was only 254, there were 240 mulatto children. Togoland fell to the allies in 1914 and was divided between France and England.

Dittman, social democratic leader in the Reichstag, declared that in German Southwest Africa flogging and judicial execution of natives were widespread. In the small colonies of the Cameroons and Togoland, there were in a single year, 1910, over ten thousand convictions of natives to death, flogging, imprisonment, and fines. In Tanganyika there were 2,783 floggings in one year, not counting those of an unofficial character. The instrument used—a rhinocerous hide whip—often caused severe illness, and in many cases, death. In 1914, nearly seven thousand natives were executed, flogged, and imprisoned in a year. Dittman quoted Professor Schillings, a German expert on African affairs, as asserting that "200,000 natives in all had been done to death in German colonies,"[7]

When Tanganyika became an English mandate, the English had an opportunity to show a contrasting administration. They brought Cameron, a governor trained in West Africa, to the task, and the interests of native labor received especial attention. The labor policy in Tanganyika under Cameron was to develop native labor on its own land so that natives could choose between village production and wage labor. The cultivation of coffee, rice, cotton, corn, and other grains, tobacco and groundnuts has been encouraged, as well as trade in live stock. With regard to wage labor the rule has been laid down that there must be no compulsion and that employers must attract labor by wages and condition of work.

The direct taxation was only half of the rate in Kenya and the money was spent with some regard to the wishes of the natives. Cameron refused to adopt a policy which would force the natives to work either by increasing the tax or by other methods of coercion. Beyond that he established a labor department in 1926 which not only supervised labor laws but tried to plan and direct a labor development. Labor camps were established for migratory workers and the moving of labor long distances was discouraged. Diet and sanitation were looked into. The whole matter of recruiting of labor and contracts was given exhaustive study. Desertion by contract laborers since 1928 has no longer been an offense which the police can deal with without a specific charge by the employer. There is no pass law, but a system of registration.

Unfortunately the new governor succeeding Cameron in 1930 abolished the labor department for reasons of economy. In 1935 over 218,000 natives were employed by the government and private employers, including 110,000 farm laborers, fifty thousand porters, carriers and common laborers, eighteen thousand servants, ten thousand on railways and public works and five thousand in mining. Over twenty thousand migrated to Southern Rhodesia and the Congo to work in the copper mines during 1932.

The average wage in 1932 for natives was four to five dollars a month for thirty working days. Skilled workers got twelve and one-half to nineteen dollars per month. Whites are employed in all administrative and supervisory positions. Skilled and semi-skilled labor is done by East Indians and natives. There is much child labor, especially on the coffee plantations. Natives living far away have to walk hundreds of miles in search of jobs. In 1932, more than ten thousand natives were used as porters in military and public works.

Mining has begun but is still in its infancy in Tanganyika. Gold, tin and salt are increasing in output and employ about five thousand natives. They received three dollars seventy-five cents a month in 1933–34. In Tanganyika and East African colonies there is much usury. It is carried on by East Indians who advance loans to natives to pay taxes. In 1932 the natives contributed 150,129 pounds sterling in taxes but expenditures amounted to 162,000 pounds sterling. Loans are made by usurers to meet current expenses and planting. The crop then is taken over in the settlement of debt and the native borrows again for planting. A Native Credit Ordinance has been passed to regulate these transactions.

In the Cameroons, divided as mandates between the British and French, the German government had granted some 300,000 acres to whites for plantations and furnished them with forced labor. This has been in part stopped and the British plantations employ sixteen thousand natives while the French have fifty-three thousand workers. German property has been bought back by Germans since the war and Germans are in control of it. The British in Tanganyika and the French in Togoland and the French Cameroons did not at first allow the Germans to buy back their property. The ten thousand agricultural laborers in the British Cameroons receive twelve cents a day. Women and children get four to six cents a day.

In German Southwest Africa, natives were formerly distributed in labor battalions among the farmers and were sold with the farms; women were frequently misused. Stock raising was the principal occupation of the natives, but the best grazing lands were seized by the whites. When the colony became a mandate of the Union of South Africa, the 328,000 natives were treated by the 21,000 whites in the main like the natives of the Union, home legislation being applied without any attempt at modification. Diamond mining has declined sharply since 1931, but coffee, tin, and vanadium are produced. Native miners decreased from 7,750 in 1930 to 2,000 in 1932.

Skilled occupations are reserved for whites. Labor is recruited in the reserves. Native miners get five to twelve and one-half dollars a month; farm hands two and one-half dollars a month; servants two and one-half to five dollars a month. White miners get five dollars a day.

Some general considerations may conclude this survey of African labor. The development of African labor from hunting to cattle raising and to agriculture can still be traced in vague outline. The Hottentots emerged recently from the hunting stage. Along the whole of East Africa from the Nile region through the Congo Basin to the lower Zambezi and South Africa there is still cattle breeding. The cattle are not held for their meat and milk value, but as an evidence of wealth. They are seldom slaughtered if healthy. In the Union of South Africa, the native population owns forty-nine per cent of the cattle; but because they have so little land, the pastures are overstocked, cattle badly nourished and the soil eroded. The protectorate of Bechuanaland, with a native population of 155,000, has 426,000 head of cattle; while Kenya, with a native population of three million, has five million goats and three million sheep.

The beginning of manufacturing in Africa is shown by such work as reducing ore to ingots, preparing cotton and sisal for the market, and crushing sugar cane; and also in the processing of certain native materials like coffee, the vegetable oils and cocoa. This will increase in amount and value as the demand becomes larger for export material of more carefully selected character and in better condition for use. Indeed there is no reason why a considerable amount of primary preparation of goods for ultimate manufacture should not soon be done in Africa.

In addition to this there is some factory labor in South Africa. In these establishments 10,000 whites, 6,000 colored and natives and 500 Asiatics are working.

The main economic activity of Africa is today agriculture, including the collection of natural produce and mining. Both these bring the natives into economic contact with Europeans and cause inevitable changes in African communities. Sometimes the contact leads to chaos by the breaking down of old institutions, either with nothing to replace them, or with European institutions, that cannot function well under the circumstances. Economic individualism under this impact increases in a land where the economic unit was formerly the communalism of the village and the tribes. The older co-operative economic unit decreases in size; the families tend to become independent groups instead of units of a clan; and the members of the family, individuals instead of parts of a communal unit. Social prestige begins to depend upon a man's wealth rather than upon his generosity.

In partial compensation for this there is rising in Africa some new attempt at co-operative enterprise. The co-operative principle has special significance to African life, in making the adjustment between the inroads of individualism and industry, and the communalism of the tribe. One writer says: "The Co-operative Movement is perhaps the most potentially fruitful single development for real cultural expansion that has been started among the Native people of South Africa up to the present time. The moral sanctions implicit in the co-operative principles are natural to the Native mind, which has hitherto known no essential cleavage between the spiritual and the material world. Every major action of the Native had its spiritual significance. Co-operation is a discipline but one like in kind, if developing in application and in degree, to that of the Native's tribal past."[8]

Co-operative societies have been established in French West Africa beginning in 1910. Arrangements have been made for them to be organized in each colony. They deal with sickness and insurance, and also provide loans. There are at present 8,500,000 members and the dues are collected as tax by the government. These societies have built wells and grain magazines and have loaned seed, plows, and trucks. The societies have been successful in Senegal where there were fifteen such societies in 1926 with over a million members and a net capital of ten million francs. There is a savings bank at Dakar with branches in the postal service throughout the colony. This bank has forty branches with four thousand depositors and total deposits of two million francs. There are numerous co-operative units in schools.

On the British Gold Coast, co-operative societies have also been successful. A co-operative ordinance was passed in 1921. There was at first suspicion, indifference, and opposition, but the expansion was rapid. In five years, four hundred societies were formed with nine thousand members and a capital of forty thousand dollars. Four thousand tons of cocoa are marketed by these societies annually. The producers of other crops are also trying co-operation and have five joint marketing associations. The movement of the coast has spread more rapidly in five years than it did in India in ten years. The Gold Coast societies encourage savings, loans and marketing. Both Europeans and African experts in co-operation are being trained and hired and the co-operative societies are marketing high purity cocoa which sells at a higher price. Nevertheless, they control at present only two percent of the total exports. There are thirty-seven Negro co-operative organizations in South Africa and more being organized. Tanganyika has the Native Co-operative Union with 24,000 members. Nigeria has one hundred co-operative cocoa marketing associations. In the British mandate of the Cameroons are ninety-three co-operative cocoa societies, and there are others in French Togoland and the Cameroons.

Contact with Europe has tended to increase the capacity of Africa to consume European goods. The African laborer is drawn into this new competition, but is hindered because of his small buying power based on low wages. On the other hand, even this buying demand is replacing home-made African utensils and clothing with European trade-made goods. Indigenous arts and crafts are disappearing. The native no longer works in iron or weaves clothing. Artistic talent is smothered by cheap and often ugly goods and even by cast-off clothes. New dances are driving out the dramatic native dances. New foods are replacing the old. There is much undernourishment, due in part to the two scourges of Africa: malaria and the tsetse fly. The fly makes milk, meat and animal fats scarce, so that the native food consists of vegetable products with some fish, insects and vermin. Fruit, eggs and chicken are little eaten.

The labor legislation was designed first of all to control labor and was drawn up almost solely in the interest of the employer. The mining development led to the annoying pass laws and the labor codes tended to push the native into the criminal court, especially through the contract laws. This legislation is being gradually improved. The duration of contracts is being decreased and the breaking of a contract is not so often regarded in law as a crime. The International Labor Organization has been working to secure some general agreement with regard to contracts and wages and has made some progress.

There is a good deal of migration of labor between colonies. Uganda gets cotton pickers from the Congo. The Belgian railways in the Congo have been built by Portuguese native labor. British West Africa gets laborers from French territory. Italian Somaliland draws from the Sudan and there is thus constant movement of large numbers over international borders. The African is traveling and observing and learning about conditions all over Africa, and commenting upon them. There is little legislation covering this inter-colonial supply of labor. The Union of South Africa has made arrangement with Portuguese Africa at various times and the Belgian Congo has had understandings with Angola. These understandings, however, nearly all relate to the number of laborers and not to their status.

Buell estimates in 1926 that ten per cent of the African workers outside the Union of South Africa and British West Africa were in white employ and a part of the international proletariat. The proportion varied from two per cent in Uganda to fifty per cent in East Africa. The proportion employed during the last decade decreased during the depression and then increased. There are today in black Africa about four million native laborers in white employ. The capital investment which Europe and America have made in African land and labor is not readily ascertainable. Two statements concerning mining may be made: the total mining investment south of the Sahara has been estimated at $1,300,000,000. In the diamond mines of South Africa $100,000,000 was invested between 1886 and 1934 and paid dividends amounting to $400,000,000.

The central economic fact however is that in Africa today hundreds of thousands of laborers are working for wages as low as five dollars a month or twenty-five cents a day up to an average of ten dollars a month and seventy-five cents a day and at tasks for which civilized countries are paying five or ten times as much. Yet white labor does not recognize black labor as part of the labor problem.

NOTES

1. Padmore, *op. cit.*, Chap. VI; and Olivier, *Anatomy of African Misery*, Chap. IV.
2. Wallbank, "British Colonial Policy and Native Education in Kenya," *Journal of Negro Education*, October, 1938.
3. Padmore, *How Britain Rules Africa*, pp. 30, 31.
4. Consult Davis, *Modern Industry and the African*.
5. Woolf, *Empire and Commerce in Africa*, pp. 310–312.
6. Harris, *Dawn in Africa*.
7. Padmore, *How Britain Rules Africa*, pp. 58, 59.
8. D. R. O. Thomas, *Journal of Adult Education*, April, 1933, Vol. VI, No. 2. *Cf.* Herskovits, *Dahomey*, Vol. I, Chap. IV.

CHAPTER XIV

The Political Control of Africa

The control of land and its raw material and the purchase and sale of labor in Africa pose a problem of political domination; and this political control of Africa compels Europe to examine again the relation which this control has to the theory of democratic government. The political control of Africa, therefore, is directly connected with the fate of democracy in the world.

The political control in Africa in modern times has been almost entirely subservient to economic penetration. It has, therefore, followed no clear pattern, laid down no rules and been inspired by no clear ideals. Sometimes it has seemed as though the dominating power had in mind only the white settlers and was regarding the great mass of Negroes merely as capital goods. For instance, in the British South Africa Act of 1909, by which the British government granted autonomy to the white people of South Africa, the overwhelming native majority was scarcely mentioned.

In other cases the plight of the natives was put forward as the chief reason for political interference and then afterwards quite forgotten in the demands of the white settlers. For instance, the blue book of the British government on German colonies during the World War bewailed forced labor and asked Englishmen to fight in Kenya and release Africa from "the Hun." Yet soon after the war, a handful of white landowners were demanding the virtual control of the best land and the labor of three million natives. In still other cases, plans for the government, education and control of the natives were laid down, but difficulties of cost, extent of territory and other matters hindered any definite following up of this program over long periods. This was true in French Equatorial Africa and in Portuguese Africa.

On the other hand, with materials and labor in increasing demand, regular and profitable trade and industry could only be established when peace and order among the natives were assured. Complete control, however, was difficult. If the natives were armed with modern weapons, as was true for a long time in Abyssinia and to some extent in West Africa, the cost of subjugation more than balanced any possible profit. If, however, it became a matter of self-protection against threat of aggression, as was true often in South Africa, the subjugation of the native became a main object regardless of cost; and in this way the natives within the Union of South Africa were gradually reduced to submission. Where the development of the country was a matter of investment, what was sought was a balance of peace and labor control which would enable the dominating power to rule the natives at least expense. Usually this meant that no attempt was made completely to subjugate the Negroes or, if the attempt was made, it was eventually given up and by treaty, custom and understanding a definite relationship between the dominant power and native autonomy established.

· This was the case in West Africa, both British and French, and we may begin our study of political control in Africa here. *British West Africa* was not conquered. Such attempts as were made to this end were long drawn out and costly. With better weapons and trained soldiery, the British repeatedly inflicted severe defeats upon the natives, but to hold them afterwards in subjection called for diplomacy rather than force. Moreover, the West African investor and trader had to face in England a difficult public opinion, with large powers of democratic control.

English public opinion after the triumph of the anti-slavery crusade would not consent to open and violent conquest; but on the other hand it could be cajoled into armed action against slave traders and aroused by native customs repugnant to modern ideas. Side by side, therefore, with a distinct plan among English philanthropists of free black nations in West Africa with self-determination and democratic government, arose a system of commercial pressure by means of trade, military intervention, "punitive" expeditions, etc., which gradually brought West Africa under political control. Thus anti-slavery was linked with increasing effort to extend English trade in Africa, with wider investment in African labor and material, and with growing conviction that control of land and labor was necessary not only for large income but for the spread of civilization.

Instead, therefore, of complete conquest and direct control of West Africa there arose a system which has been called "indirect rule," but which is in reality not so much a deliberate method of controlling African colonies as a line of least resistance. Indirect rule was stooping to conquer and yielding to local and tribal autonomy in sufficient degree to insure peace, profitable trade and investment.

Local and tribal autonomy in British West Africa has come to be a method of guiding native tribes in practically any direction that the colonial power wishes. In practice everything depends on the kind of administrator who is in control, and on the pressure both from home and among the white traders in the colony which can be brought to bear upon him.

If, for instance, the administrator is the mouthpiece or tool of the investors at home or of the representatives of organized commerce and industry in the colony, then the object of his policy is the maximum of profit. If this can be attained by encouraging among the Negroes stagnation and reaction through old and conservative chiefs, and the encouragement of harmless ancient customs and ceremonies, the administration may be regarded as successful from the point of view of business. It may be the role of such administration to repress the young and educated critics of the tribe; to limit education and modern enlightenment, and to repress urges to wider self-rule. A period of such rule may leave the tribe after a generation less able to cope with modern conditions than before the experiment, and can render it putty in the hands of the industrial exploiter.

On the other hand, a far-sighted administrator, fairly independent of the influence of merchants and investors, could make tribal autonomy a method of slowly guiding the footsteps of a people to economic and social independence and of gradually training modern men capable of self-rule. In either case the prevailing institutions and the vernacular tongue would be used, but for widely different reasons; for in the latter case, the European tongue would be made from the earliest beginnings of education, a vehicle of communication with the civilized world and modern thought. And tribal institutions would be changed and modernized by scientific study and expert social control. Local autonomy, therefore, or as it is often called "indirect rule," may be a line of least resistance for the peaceful and profitable control of African colonies, or it may be a method of social education for backward races.

On the African West Coast, and especially in *Nigeria,* local tribal autonomy was encouraged by Lord Lugard, governor of Nigeria, with the avowed object of encouraging "the economic development of the colony through the native working in his own time and in his own way and for his own profit." It did not involve native democratic control or political independence, but it was a challenge to uncurbed commercial exploitation and it was easier to attempt this on the West Coast than elsewhere.

The cost of efforts at conquests and complete domination here had already been enormous. It had taken many wars partially to subdue these people and certain colonies like Lagos proudly claim to this day that they have never been conquered and exist as independent states in treaty relations with Great Britain.

Secondly, by good chance the natives of Nigeria and the Gold Coast appeased industry by proving their ability to develop, under black peasant proprietors, agricultural enterprise to such an extent that the plantation system has not been able to displace them. In this and other ways, the profit of industry has come to depend in West Africa not upon land monopoly and forced labor, so much as upon the buying and selling of produce and its transport to market. We have seen how the English by trade, war and treaty gained substantial domination on the Gold Coast and in Southern Nigeria. After the Berlin Conference of 1884, England hastened to consolidate this territory and annex the hinterland. The Beni resisted, but a large force of English was landed in 1897 and the city occupied after hard fighting. The king was deported. A second expedition was necessary in 1899. Finally, the country was included in Southern Nigeria with a British resident as adviser, but with considerable local autonomy. The ancient line of kings still rules.

In Northern Nigeria lay Hausaland. The rulers were the Fulani, who had invaded the country in the twelfth and fourteenth centuries. The country was ruled by emirs, of which the principal ones had their capitals at Sokoto, Kano, Katsina and Zaria. In 1886 the Royal Niger Company obtained a charter. This company, already mentioned, was one of the early British chartered enterprises which became a sub-government. It annexed territory, made laws, maintained an army, laid and collected taxes and signed treaties. By 1894, because of the continued resistance of the organized native states in the interior and the fear of French rivalry, the British negotiated a treaty with the king of Borgu and in 1899 took over the Royal Niger Company.

By 1903 the British held control by treaty and force over the whole of Nigeria, and Lugard became high commissioner and began to plan his policy of peaceful penetration and indirect rule. In 1906, Lagos and Southern Nigeria were united into the Colony and Protectorate of Southern Nigeria, and in 1914 all of Nigeria was united into the Colony and Protectorate of Nigeria, with Lagos as the seat of government. The protectorate is now divided into two groups of provinces, the northern and southern, and the mandate of the Cameroons is attached for administrative purposes. Lugard, who had consolidated the territory, served as commissioner from 1900 to 1906, then retired, but became governor-general from 1912 to 1919.

The method of English control in Nigeria centers on the use and development of the tribal chieftainship or of the corresponding Mohammedan emirate. Such chiefs have been recognized and make an integral part of the machinery of government. There are two hundred and fifty such native authorities representing roughly the tribal units as they existed in 1900. Native law is recognized in native courts, but a parallel system of British courts ranging from the supreme court of the whole protectorate down to the court which the British resident holds. The bulk of native litigation is handled by native judges under native law. Certain cases can be transferred from the native to British courts but this does not often take place. In the Mohammedan section native judges are well-trained and under the paramount chief or a subordinate chief, sitting with persons representing the community.

The native chiefs and rulers have regular salaries and much power both financial and judicial. The king of Benin for instance rules with a council of nine and receives a salary of $7,500 a year. The Alake who rules the Egbas has complete financial control. Three of the emirs receive thirty thousand dollars a year. The power of these rulers is limited and directed by British administrators who give advice and are enabled to enforce this advice through the power of the courts, through partial financial control, through their large power of deposing chiefs and influencing the choice of successors, and through some actual military force.

There are many evidences of progress and prosperity. The city of Kano, for instance, has public works, a system of schools and sanitation. It is building a library and putting in a system of town planning. It has an annual revenue of $630,000 a year. The government of the Egbas operates water works and electric lights. Education is carried on to an increasing extent in all these territories.

Taxes are assessed by Europeans and collected by natives. One-half to seventy per cent of the taxes goes to the native treasury and the rest to the British. The native treasury funds are used to pay salaries, keep wells in order, run the schools and public works. The native administrators in these matters are advised by European officials. There are sixty-three native treasuries in Northern Nigeria and one hundred fourteen in Southern Nigeria. There are charges, probably true, that without careful inspection the native treasuries would be subject to graft and corruption; and on the other hand native money collected from poor peasants is used to pay high salaries to British advisers or to furnish them with fine houses and automobiles.

Many examples could be pointed out to show a large degree of success in local autonomy; and yet there are certain manifest difficulties: the white administrators by careful manipulation are not always instructing the natives and leading them toward efficient home rule; and particularly they are, for instance, steadily opposing the political recognition of younger educated men and the extension of autonomy from local tribes and local chiefs to wider and wider units of general autonomy and to modern democratic methods. There are, however, some fine exceptions, and some English administrators who have had the courage and unselfishness really to lead black Africa.

In Lagos there is a considerable number of educated Negroes working as clerks and professional men and a town council with a majority of officials, but with three elected African members. The white town clerk has most of the real power. The people of Lagos have had a great deal of agitation and even riots concerning the status of the Eleko or king of Lagos. He was de-stooled but recently restored. He appoints chiefs and headmen with the approval of the British.

Before the World War, legislation in Southern Nigeria was through proclamation by the governor. On the other hand, local democratic government had long been established in the city of Lagos, although later curtailed; and pressure from the educated natives began to be applied to initiate democratic control over the whole of the southern provinces, if not further. The effective leadership of the protectorate, however, has been put largely in the hands of white men, by wealth, social prestige and law, thus emphasizing the idea that, even in Africa, progress is a matter of race and color rather than of training.

Gambia was settled by trading companies and controlled originally from Sierra Leone, but became a Crown colony in 1843. *Sierra Leone* is the pioneer British West African colony and at various periods all the other colonies have been placed under its jurisdiction for longer or shorter periods. The British by implication, if not by categorical promise, proposed eventual independence to the colony first established in Freetown; but as the new commercial policy for West Africa grew, the little democracy at Freetown was limited and held in leash, while the territory to the north was established as the protectorate of Sierra Leone and governed by proclamation.

The Freetown municipality, organized in 1893, had at that time more power than any other African community. It was ruled by two thousand black voters, who elected a council and had power of taxation. After the war, there was a deficit and a great deal of propaganda to convince the people of Freetown that British officials could give them better government than Negroes. This was true, for the British official was a better-educated, better-paid man with wider experience, while the political power of the Negroes in taxation and administration was fatally limited. Finally the mayor and other officials were convicted of conspiracy and misappropriation of funds, but the conviction was secured only by the overruling of the court assessors by the white presiding judge. The real question of actual guilt has never been settled, but a town council with a majority of official appointees replaced the former municipal government.

There is no doubt that the development of democratic government in small sections like Lagos and Freetown, with citizens of limited education and experience, presents difficulties. Nevertheless if Africa is to be developed as a Negro country, it is an experiment necessary and quite worth while. Instead of this, the attempt has been made to develop the mass of Negroes still living in tribal relations, without the intervention of educated leaders of their own race. A breach was thus developed between the white British administrator and the black educated leader, which has made the growth of self-rule difficult and was undoubtedly designed for this very purpose.

In some cases, especially in the Gold Coast, the Negroes have met this policy by stressing their tribal affinities and seeking to get in close touch with the chiefs. Some curious results have come from this. When, for instance, the Eleko of Lagos sent an educated African to England to represent his interests, the colonial whites accused both the representative and the Eleko of misrepresentation and displaced the ruler. Controversy over this episode still persists and there seems no doubt but that the real facts were deliberately misrepresented by the whites. One can easily sense here a growing struggle between the British administrative adviser, standing behind the power of the chiefs, and the rising democracy of educated black folk.

The *Gold Coast* is the colony which has led the forward movement toward increased autonomy and greater control through the educated black classes. The Ashanti and Fanti peoples, who are the chief tribes of the Gold Coast, are highly intelligent and belonged formerly to one tribe or state, moving down to the coast either because of pressure from the growing states of the interior, or because of the profit of the coast trade.

The colony of the Gold Coast is a little smaller than the state of Oregon. It was here that the Portuguese in 1482 built Elmina Castle and started the regular African slave trade. The English appeared in 1653, followed by the Dutch as soon as they gained their independence from Catholic Spain. The Swedes and the Danes followed. London merchants entered the slave trade in 1662 and in 1672 the Royal African Company was incorporated. Finally the English gained the monopoly of the slave trade from 1713 until long after its legal abolition in 1807.

The Gold Coast is made up of three areas: the coast region or colony proper; Ashanti north of the Pra River; and the region north of Ashanti called the northern territories. The colony is administered by the governor aided by a legislative council, while the protectorate is under resident commissioners. There is native administration, but the chiefs and councils are responsible to European political officers who administer the states through them. Each chief has a certain amount of autonomy in local affairs according to native law. Native law is recognized and in the regular courts conducted by the British, juries consisting largely of Africans serve—an unusual situation in Africa. Appeals from native courts to the white district commissioners may be taken in civil cases and this happens more often than in Nigeria. There is a British West African Court of Appeal.

The Gold Coast government declared its policy in 1921 to employ qualified Africans in any department of the government except in the political service and as judges. From 1919 to 1927, thirty-eight Africans have been appointed to positions formerly occupied by Europeans, including two police magistrates, a Crown councilor, an assistant Secretary of Native Affairs, four medical officials, etc. During the next twenty years the European staff will be decreased by one hundred and sixty-two and the African staff increased by two hundred and two. Lately, however, in appointments of junior officials no Negroes have been included, which has raised much criticism. Thus in the Gold Coast it has been impossible completely to drive the wedge between the educated and the primitive African and to make the white man the invariable political arbiter and leader; and indeed out of the Gold Coast with its educated leadership has come perhaps the most significant recent democratic movement in black Africa.

This movement was in three phases: first, the Fanti Confederation of 1867; then the Gold Coast Aborigines Rights Protection Society formed in 1898; and finally the National Congress of British West Africa in 1920. The Mfantsi Amanbuhu Fekuw or Fanti Confederation was agitated in 1865, organized in 1867 and adopted its constitution in 1871. When the scheme was presented to the British governor he arrested the leaders and imprisoned them on a charge of high treason; yet they were simply asserting their ancient rights, including the judicial authority of the chiefs and their financial and administrative powers. They planned schools and other institutions. Their movement finally resulted in the introduction of Crown colony government in 1874.

Meantime the trade of the Gold Coast increased and in 1895 a Crown Lands Ordinance was introduced designed to place the land of the colony in the hands of the government. The natives were aroused and the Gold Coast Aborigines Rights Protection Society was organized on the lines of the Aborigines Protection Society in England. A deputation was sent to England and engaged the services of Herbert Asquith. Nearly all the principal chiefs of the country were back of the organization and it was recognized by the government in 1898. The governor met the Society in session and commended the founding of it. Subsequent governors up until 1905 recognized the Society and discussed important matters with its executive committee. The organization still exists.

After the World War, the educated Negroes of the four West African British colonies planned for union and eventual dominion status. The movement was instigated by the reactionary demands of the English Empire Development Society and the determination of certain English commercial interests to recoup the losses of war by more systematic effort to monopolize land and control West African labor. In 1920, a conference representing the four West African colonies was held at Accra, called the National Congress of British West Africa. It demanded the right to vote and control the revenue; it opposed the impudent program of the Empire Development Society; it defended democratic government as an ancient Negro right: ". . . In the demand for the franchise by the people of British West Africa, it is not to be supposed that they are asking to be allowed to copy a foreign institution. On the contrary, it is important to notice that the principle of electing representatives to local councils and bodies is inherent in all the systems of British West Africa."[1]

The governors of both the Gold Coast and Nigeria, liberal men and defenders of local tribal autonomy, vehemently opposed these demands and tried to drive a wedge between the members of this conference and the chiefs, alleging that the Congress did not represent the native community. The Congress denied this, and to present their attitude sent a delegation direct to England. Finally the Colonial Office was forced to act, although action was taken slowly and with apparent effort, made to avoid any appearance that the government was yielding to organized pressure from black folk. Reforms came between 1922 and 1925 in Gambia, Sierra Leone, in Nigeria and at last in the Gold Coast.

In all cases, a native elective element was introduced into the legislative council, although the official majority was retained to out-vote it; as usual in Africa, white business and commerce have long had open and direct voice in the council. For instance, in Nigeria, there is an official majority of thirty members on the legislative council; then there are four elected African members; and four nominated members to represent Chambers of Commerce. These latter are always the white agents of trading companies. Also there is one member to represent the Chamber of Mines; one, banking; and one, shipping. Thus foreign capital has a larger membership on the Council than the Africans themselves. The Governor may also select seven members in those parts of the colonies and southern provinces which do not return elected representatives. In this category the missionaries come, making, at least in many cases, "triple alliance between the State Bureaucracy, finance-capital and the Church."[2] This council legislates for the colony and the southern provinces; the laws for the northern provinces are still promulgated by the governor.

On the Gold Coast in 1925, a legislative council of fifteen official and fourteen unofficial members was authorized by the Colonial Office. Of the latter, five represented shipping, banking and commerce; one is selected by the Chamber of Commerce, and one by the Chamber of Mines. Of the nine remaining members, six are chiefs and three are elected by the towns. This gave undue representation to the chiefs and to the English advisers of the chiefs. The educated Africans are protesting still against it, claiming that the chiefs are hand-picked and invariably vote with the government.

The towns in the Gold Coast since 1894 have had town councils, one-half elected and one-half nominated by the governor, who has the casting vote. In 1924, a Municipal Corporation Ordinance authorized councils with majorities of elected members. Ashanti is administered apart from the colony by a commissioner responsible to the governor. Native authority under the Asantehene was restored in 1935.

The colony and protectorate of Sierra Leone have a legislative council with eleven official and ten unofficial members. Of the unofficial members three are elected and seven are appointed by the governors. Among the seven are three paramount chiefs, two representatives of commercial interests, and two Africans from the colony. Voters must be males and there is a literary test, which is true in none of the other colonies. Elected members hold their seats for five years.

Thus black West Africa, through united action, gained some beginnings of representative government. The English, however, have worked to stem further progress in that direction. Decorations and awards have been judiciously distributed and the conservative native power encouraged by the knighting of several paramount chiefs. Formerly educated black colonials like Sir Conrad Reeves in Barbadoes and Sir Samuel Lewis in Sierra Leone were thus honored. The latter type of educated African naturally demands and receives more recognition and is able to make the problems of Africans more widely known.

Further than that, the depression has acted to discourage political agitation. The Congress of West Africa has held no meetings for the last five or six years and political representation given to commercial interests is not only a frank recognition of the power of capital, not made so openly in any other legislatures of the world, but also it tends to draw away Negro capitalists to common ground between them and the whites. This leaves the black peasants and workers without leadership. Nevertheless the determined drift toward nationhood in British West Africa is only halted and not killed; spurred by the example of India and the rise of Japan, it is bound from time to time to reassert itself.

There are still some curious discrepancies and inequalities in West African British colonies. For instance, while natives inhabiting the colonies are considered as British subjects, those living in the protectorate are only "British protected persons." In the British courts of some of the protectorates neither lawyers nor juries are allowed and appeals depend upon the decision of the judge.

There are many laws against sedition. In the Gold Coast, against the protest of all the natives among the unofficial councilors, a dangerous sedition law was enacted in 1934; and in general the right of assembly and free speech in West Africa is seriously curtailed. On the other hand, there are certain unofficial advantages given to the whites, especially in the matter of living quarters which really involve a vital lessening of their health hazards. By unwritten law in Bathurst, Accra and Lagos the whites occupy the most sanitary parts of the town along the sea front with modern bungalows built out of public funds; in Freetown they live in the highlands on the hills. These beautiful living quarters are in high and segregated localities with well-planned houses, golf and tennis facilities and schools. The white officials who occupy them are given large salaries even by English standards, with liberal leaves of absence, and have an abundance of cheap menial service. In this way a high and efficient type of Englishman can be attracted to colonial service; the contrast between such persons and the poor uneducated native tends to emphasize color caste.

In *French West Africa* there was a development which grew out of the four French settlements on the coast dating back to the seventeenth century. French penetration took place among the remains of former African imperialism in the Sudan, overthrown by invasion, rivalry and conquest. From the coast colonies all around Senegal, the French during the early nineteenth century began to press toward the Niger River and Timbuktu. Gradually they overcame the resistance of a number of independent states by treaty and proffered protection. French Africa even more than British Africa made the conquest of the blacks a matter of treaty and negotiation combined with force, which left the Negroes with their own local autonomy.

In addition to this, the French never became slave traders on the scale that the Dutch and British did, and were soon supplanted by the British, losing their vested interests. The lag, therefore, between the decline of the French slave trade and the rise of commercial imperialism in Africa was longer; the profit due to caste, less; and stimulated by the extraordinary history of Haiti, this gave a chance for the growth of an African colonial idea in France in which the Africans were considered as prospective French citizens and the African colonies as destined to be more or less integrated with France.

In theory the French guiding principle in Africa came thus to be the unity of France and her colonies. All subjects were to be children of France and have the same duties. The first duty was defense of the mother country. The second, economic organization for self-support; and the third, furnishing raw materials for French industry and a market for French productions.

French colonial effort split African imperialism into two streams. On the one hand the English, Belgians and Germans clung to the idea of colonies primarily for investment, and carried over the mercantile theory which caused the American Revolution. They could do this the more easily, because racial caste born of slavery and the slave trade hindered those countries from regarding African colonies as integral parts of the home country. The investment value of colonies stopped efforts for political independence and became the hidden cause of further race hate.

The French through ownership of the sugar crop in Haiti had tended in the same direction until the French Revolution. They then vacillated, and under Napoleon tried to restore the colonial idea, but were frustrated by Toussaint L'Ouverture. The ensuing French republic took a strong stand for the essential equality of the inhabitants of the colonies with the people of France, carrying the matter far in Algiers, and making distinct beginnings in Africa and Asia, until all colonies had some representation in the French Parliament. French administrators in Africa were not set up and encouraged as a segregated caste, and while they were more in number they received less pay than administrators in British West Africa, and had fewer special privileges.

On the other hand, the refusal of France to draw the color line in her colonies, the admission of blacks to her civil service and willingness to share with them in part political control, does not mean the complete subordination of the profit idea in colonial France to the idea of mass welfare. It merely means that admission to the ranks of the exploiting bourgeoisie is not confined by color caste to the whites as is so largely true in British Africa. Nevertheless the educated, enfranchised black West African may become as eager and successful a bourgeois exploiter as any white man. There still remains the task of securing among such potential leaders of black Africa, conversion to the idea of the paramount importance of the prosperity of the mass of natives rather than the enrichment of the few black or white at their expense.

French Africa is divided into two parts: French West Africa with one and one-half million square miles and fifteen million inhabitants, among whom are twenty-four thousand whites; and French Equatorial Africa with nearly three million square miles but only one million inhabitants. French West Africa is ruled by a governor-general and is divided into seven colonies, each colony presided over by a governor. There is an advisory body of forty-four members, of which ten are natives; and machinery for consultation between administrators and the natives has been extended throughout West Africa. The chief colony is Senegal, which has a colonial council and is divided into four communes which have municipal self-government and municipal councils under strict control from the general government.

Government in French Africa began in the four communes of Senegal, where any black man born there was early recognized as a French citizen. This led to a crowding in of uneducated natives to claim citizenship, and a good deal of difficulty with an electorate of little education and less experience. Attempts have been made to change the law, but the courts have upheld the citizenship of the blacks. Finally a citizenship law which fixes the status was passed in 1916.

Senegal is represented by a black deputy in the French Parliament and these deputies have held under-secretaryships in the cabinet at various times; one, Blaise Diagne, during the World War was made High Commissioner to West Africa, being given equal rank with governor-general. In 1920 a colonial council was established for the colony of Senegal with twenty members elected by the citizens and twenty native chiefs selected by the chiefs. In 1925 the citizens were increased to twenty-four and the chiefs reduced to sixteen. Among the citizens there are eight whites and thirty-two blacks. The council gives advice, has limited power over legislation, and approves the budget. The chiefs are hand picked and usually vote with the government. The council has more power than any other consultative assembly in Africa. It is controlled by the local population, while the executive is controlled from Paris.

The other colonies have advisory councils of native members elected by native electoral colleges. Outside Senegal there are city councils in three classes: the lowest with nominated members; the next with members elected under a restricted suffrage, and the highest with members elected by universal suffrage. Nineteen communes are in the lowest class and three in the second. None have yet been placed in the third.

There were in 1936 nearly eighty-one thousand black citizens in French West Africa. Of these, 78,376 were in Senegal. Outside of Senegal, few black men have been naturalized. The requirements are ability to read and write French, means of existence and good character, together with devotion to French interests. Only a thousand natives were naturalized between 1914 and 1936. A citizen is not subject to native taxes or liable for three years military service. He serves but eighteen months, and only in Senegal. He is not liable to forced labor and is tried before French courts. He can secure land titles and hold office.

The governor-general of West Africa declared in 1921 that "apprenticeship in public life and in the duties which it imposes, seems to me to constitute the most rational and sensible political machinery for our African population, which it is our duty to associate in an ever increasing measure in the management of all our affairs."

The comparatively slow growth of effective democracy in French West Africa is being modified and accelerated in two respects: first, the use of advisory councils and consultation among the natives by the administrators; and secondly, by the extraordinary growth of the plan of education which is spoken of elsewhere.

In their effort at social reconstruction in Africa, the French at first tried the characteristic and most logical short cut of ignoring native customs, languages and hereditary rule. Most of the native chiefs were displaced, the French language was made the main basis of education, and scant attention was paid to native custom. On the other hand, and simultaneously with this, the attempt was made to substitute changes which would not leave the cultural organization aimless and helpless. The hereditary chiefs, for instance, were replaced by black appointed chiefs and stress put upon the intelligence of such appointees and their knowledge of French and familiarity with French administration. They are paid by the colony.

French Equatorial Africa has had a long history. Its northern section formed a part of the Hausa states and of the kingdoms of Bornu and Kanem. Toward the south it includes the kingdom of the Bagirmi, which lasted up to the nineteenth century. Then came the Wadai and the Bateke.

War and the slave trade, invasion and conquest, have broken up tribes and cultures here for many centuries, and, last but not least, has been the spread of the desert into former fertile regions and the devastation of malaria and other tropical diseases in the jungles. The result is that this vast territory of over 900,000 square miles, or four and a third times the size of France, has less than three inhabitants to the square mile.

Its conquest and occupation have been very slow. The occupation began in the Congo region and extended slowly north by treaty and a policy of great caution in interfering with tribal and national autonomy. As late as 1908 only about a quarter of the territory was really under French administration. The result was that in the interstices between tribal autonomy and French administration, industrial exploitation, especially in times of stress, entered, patterned after the Belgian Congo regime.

The French theory that all children of France are to be equal, was modified in 1890 to include efforts to conserve native institutions. In 1937 the French Popular Front government showed some reaction toward the older policy and toward representative institutions for colonies. There is a separate colonial ministry in Paris for African colonies assisted by an expert advisory body including delegates from the colonies. Also the French have a colonial inspectorate and each colony is visited by inspectors every two or three years.

The scandals eventually became so marked that French administration was increased and the number of troops. Just before the World War a part of Equatorial Africa was ceded to Germany, but this was returned after the war. Also, after the war, the number of administrative officials was reduced. The French government between 1918 and 1924 paid about forty million francs to balance the budget of this territory. Between 1924 and 1926 the financial situation was improved and contributions from France ceased. In order to balance the budget, taxation on the natives has been considerably increased and welfare expenditures decreased. In 1910 the colony was federated, but in 1934 it became one colony with four regions. The local authority is empowered to establish communes and determine their composition and competence. Four such communes have been created. They have an official chairman and four nominated members, one a native, and have power to levy taxes.

South from French Equatorial Africa lies the vast bulk of the *Belgian Congo*, nearly equal in size. In 1936 it had a native population of nearly ten million and a white population of eighteen thousand. Stanley promised peace and tribal autonomy. "I am charged," he said, "to open and keep open, if possible, all such districts and countries as I may explore for the benefit of the commercial world. The mission is supported by a philanthropic society, which numbers noble-minded men of several nations. It is not a religious society, but my instructions are entirely of that spirit. No violence must be used, and wherever rejected, the mission must withdraw to seek another field."[3]

The Bula-Matadi, or Stone-Breaker, as the natives called Stanley, threw himself energetically into the work and had by 1881 built a road past the falls of the Congo to the plateau, where thousands of miles of river navigation were thus opened. Stations were established, and by 1884 Stanley returned armed with four hundred and fifty "treaties" with the native chiefs, and the new "state" appealed to the world for recognition.

The United States was first to recognize the "Congo Free State," which was at last made a sovereign power under international guarantees by the Congress of Berlin, in the year 1885; and Leopold II was recognized as king.

One of the first tasks before the new state was to check the Arab slave traders. The Arabs had hitherto acted as traders and middlemen along the upper Congo, and when the English and Congo state overthrew Mzidi, the reigning king in the Katanga country, a general revolt of the Arabs and mulattoes took place. For a time, 1892–93, the whites were driven back, but in a year or two the Arabs and their allies were subdued.

We have seen how Leopold carried out his promises to the world. Christian commerce proved far worse than the Mohammedan slave trade. The political autonomy of the land and even the marvelous indigenous culture came near destruction here under the Leopoldian regime. By encouraging and increasing tribal animosities, a police force of black soldiers led by white officers destroyed tribal organizations and murdered and maimed large numbers of people.

The Belgian state, which succeeded to control, was impeded in its plans by no large amount of tribal and local autonomy. The resident agents of the Belgian government and the representatives of European industry ruled the country, but because of its vast extent, the smaller administrative force and the large number of natives, they have been compelled in some degree to recognize and even reconstitute tribal government. In 1906 native chiefs were given some recognition. In 1910 the native people were to be grouped under traditional authorities. Over 2,500 such authorities are now recognized. These are of two types: one has the customary native powers and the other administrative duties put upon him by the government. The chiefs receive small salaries and a few native treasuries are allowed. Recent attempts have been made to create new centers out of native industrial cities, dividing them according to tribes and employment. Such a center may raise taxes, keep law and order, and transmit native wishes to the white governors of the province.

In the Katanga mining district, native and European quarters are separated by a "neutral zone" occupied either by parks or by hospitals, schools and prisons; elsewhere it is usual to find the native location at a short distance from the town, and non-natives are not allowed in the "native city" without permission. Trading by natives is allowed. As yet the Congo native, while increasing in industrial efficiency and paying increasing dividends to European investors, has practically no voice in his general government and only restricted tribal autonomy.

It must be remembered that the contrast between the objects of Leopold and the objects of the state in the Belgian Congo was one of method and not of basic principle. Leopold sought immediate profit for himself on short term investment and by almost any means. Belgium seeks eventual and continuous profit for white folk on long term investment, for which a proper labor force must be provided. Into this latter plan some social betterment plans for the Negro himself must necessarily enter, but this would be incidental to the main object of profit for white Belgium.

The role of Belgium in the Congo is not mainly the uplift and civilization of Negroes—it is private profit on large and growing investment. Nothing must interfere with this. Belgians look upon the Congo as their chief source of wealth and prosperity. The great profit from Congo enterprises is necessary for the present Belgian standard of living and international position. They are proud to be masters of a colony eighty-five times the surface of the Mother Country. Nor does the Belgian working-class conceive of the black Congolese as fellow workers, whose status should in sheer self-defense be safeguarded and raised by political action in Belgium; rather they are means of raising Belgian wages and lowering taxes.

While Leopold, working swiftly, was ruthless in his treatment of the natives and invited revolt, the consequences of which were only avoided by playing up inter-tribal jealousies, Belgium, on the other hand, realizes that peace and a fair degree of contentment in the Congo must be maintained by a country of eight million people in an area of twelve thousand square miles, who are exploiting ten million people occupying 900,000 square miles. Nothing but the united forces of Europe could save Belgium from any determined revolt of the Black Congo, with even a minimum supply of modern arms.

We turn now to the East Coast. The British seizure of East Africa began with the desire to guard the Suez Canal; the domination of Egypt made this possible and the seizure of the Sudan maintained the water supply of Egypt. Egypt is today partially independent, but England is still her predominant partner in the *Anglo-Egyptian Sudan*. The Sudan has nearly a million square miles and a population of nearly six million, including seventy thousand non-natives. It is divided into nine provinces under governors and the administration is carried out through British district commissioners. Under these are native Sudanese officials. There is a nominated advisory council but little democratic control. The civil service, however, is being filled increasingly with black native officials.

The excuse which English merchants and imperialists could best use for their interference with Zanzibar and East Africa was the suppression of the slave trade, which had a strong emotional hold upon the English middle class and the descendants of the abolitionists. The slave trade here was large, until it was finally suppressed about 1870. However, the aim of the English went beyond the slave trade and Zanzibar, and was extended to the mainland of East Africa, which was dominated by the sultans of Zanzibar.

In order to frustrate the expansion of Germany in East Africa, British commercial interests seized Zanzibar and Pemba and they are still under British control, but have maintained partially their local autonomy. A sultan reigns in Zanzibar with an Englishman as permanent prime minister. The legislative council has eight official and six unofficial members, the latter representing the various races. These races are a few hundred Europeans, fourteen hundred Indians, thirty-three thousand Arabs and the rest Negroes. The sultan receives sixteen thousand pounds sterling annually as his share of the revenue.

Thus commercial English and German joint stock companies seized what is now Kenya and Tanganyika, the division between the two taking place by treaty in 1890. This division, however, did not preclude the Germans from working north toward the headwaters of the Nile and to circumvent this, the British pressed through Kenya to Uganda.

Uganda was then the most prosperous and advanced of the African states. The history of the rulers of Buganda, one of the provinces, goes back by tradition thousands of years, covering a line of six hundred Kabakas. They developed an "extraordinary social and political and even legal system." From 1890 on Uganda passed through extraordinary experiences. The British East Africa Company received a charter in 1888 and paved the way for the annexation of Uganda and Kenya. Uganda came completely under British protection in 1900 through agreements signed with the rulers of the native kingdoms of Buganda, Toro and Ankole. According to the terms of these agreements, the native rulers retained jurisdiction over their kingdoms in internal affairs affecting native administration. The king of Buganda, the most developed state of the protectorate, is called the Kabaka, and by treaty rights with the British Government is officially accorded the title of "His Highness" and flies his own flag.

The British are represented by the governor and legislative and executive councils. The native rulers are responsible to the governor and their administration must conform to his policy under the Uganda agreement. Buganda has an oligarchic parliament called the Lukiko of eighty-nine members and a cabinet. For a long time the late Sir Apolo Kagwa, a very able man, was prime minister, serving under three kings. He died in 1927. The present king is paid one thousand five hundred pounds sterling a year beside revenues from his private estates. The kings of the other kingdoms also get salaries. The whole of Uganda is about the size of Sweden and has about three and one-half million people. Taxation and court processes under native law are in the hands of the natives but with little democratic control and with supervision on the part of the British.

The demand for "self-government" on the part of the white settlers in *Kenya* is in effect a demand on the part of twenty thousand white settlers to have virtual control over three million natives and partial control over fifty thousand Asiatics. This demand has been so insistent that it became a test of English democracy

especially during the two administrations of the Labor Party. The right of Great
Britain to have some voice could not be denied, after the large appropriations
amounting to at least sixty million dollars which British taxpayers gave for the
development of the colony, and the military protection afforded it.

Immigrant speculators and agents of corporations began to come to Kenya in
1902. In 1911 there were three thousand whites; in 1921 ten thousand five hundred; in 1926 twelve thousand five hundred, and in 1936 twenty thousand.
Some local autonomy was left the tribes from the beginning, since the whites were
segregating themselves on the fertile highlands and the natives were partly
nomad herdsmen. In 1902 the custom of appointing headmen began, charged
with the duty of keeping order and maintaining roads. Native tribunals were
recognized in 1907, but the chief was displaced by a white district official,
although there was from 1913 substantial recognition of native law.

On the other hand, the handful of white settlers early began to take general
control of the government. Beginning with 1910 there were regular meetings of
associations representing the white settlers, which made proposals to the government, and censored English officials. They began to function as an unofficial
parliament. Financial control of the colony passed largely into their hands, and
even bodies and committees established to safeguard native rights invariably
had white settlers as members. All local commissions on native affairs have a
majority of white settlers. The white settlers resorted many times to terroristic
methods. In 1905 they compelled a governor to leave the colony by staging a
violent demonstration. They have used insulting language against both officials
and natives.

Kenya became a crown colony in 1920 with the coast lands still held as a protectorate. The legislative council at that time had an official majority, and in
addition to that the Europeans elected eleven members, while two members
were nominated to represent the Indians. Because of complaint and unrest,
there began in 1921 a succession of English parliamentary commissions, who
investigated conditions in Kenya either by actual visit or by report, and made a
series of recommendations.

The Wood-Winterton Commission of 1921 recommended that educated
Indians and natives be admitted to the franchise, but at the same time it confirmed the whites in their monopoly control of the best land. This proposal
raised an extraordinary storm in Kenya. Actual rebellion was threatened and a
delegation was sent to South Africa to ask aid. Kenya proclaimed itself the
"Thermopylae of Africa," the gateway that was to push back Asia and establish
white supremacy with black serfs!

The English government replied with the Duke of Devonshire White Paper
of 1923 which declared that the "interests of the African native must be paramount." And that "if and when these interests and the interests of the immigrant races should conflict, the former should prevail." It sought to appease the
settlers, however, by establishing separate electoral roles for Indians and Arabs,
and it confirmed the whites in their land monopoly. The whites in 1923 organized a vigilance committee and threatened to take over the government and
arrest the governor, Sir Robert Coryndon. Finally they sulkily refrained from

pushing their extreme demands, but with fierce denunciation of this attempt to "West-Africanize" Kenya.

Before the English general election of 1924, which put the Labor Party first in power, the party conference declared that a labor government would "transfer to the inhabitants of the countries [the colonies] without distinction of race or color, such measure of political responsibility as they were capable of exercising; while imperial responsibility will be maintained during the period preceding the establishment of democratic institutions." They declared that they would by education or otherwise prepare the whole body of inhabitants for self-government.

The Indians for a time refused to pay poll tax or elect members to the council, but decided to co-operate in 1924 through the influence of the Governor, Sir Robert Coryndon. Under him medical, educational and other services were begun for the natives, and stock breeding and agriculture encouraged in the reserves. An ordinance of 1924 provided for the creation of district native councils, and during the next twelve years twenty such councils were established. The district commissioner is ex-officio president with executive functions. The native members are appointed by the government, although members may be suggested by the natives. These councils receive no share of the general revenue, but get certain rents and licenses in the reserve and share in a small native trust fund. They may levy special additional taxes. The councils have done a good deal in forestry, fly clearance, and establishing schools.

The Labor Government appointed a parliamentary commission under the chairmanship of Ormsby-Gore in 1924. This commission, one of the best ever appointed, was for some unknown reason dismissed in 1925. That same year the liberal Governor Coryndon died and was succeeded by the reactionary Sir Edward Grigg, who came under the complete domination of Lord Delamere.

Delamere owned 200,000 acres in Kenya and was one of the worst types of white African imperialist. Grigg set up committees composed of whites, in connection with each of the departments of government dealing with education, roads, etc. They gave advice and their advice was usually decisive. Local affairs were entrusted to similar bodies and they dictated the expenditures of public funds. He encouraged indirect subsidies for the whites, like the building of branch railway lines to serve the European areas, which could only be operated at a loss of a million dollars a year or more. The railways carried corn at two cents, which cost them five cents to transport.

In 1926 the white population of Kenya declared through Lord Cranworth that the interests of the white settlers must never be swamped by native interests. They called an unofficial conference of the white settlers in Kenya, Uganda, Tanganyika, Northern Rhodesia, and Nyasaland and planned a Dominion of East Africa where the whites would rule blacks without imperial interference. This question of an East African Dominion continued to be agitated until 1932. In 1929, the Hilton Young parliamentary commission partially approved it, by commending a union of Kenya and Uganda for the purpose of a uniform native policy. This was nothing less than an attack upon black landownership and native government in Uganda. The Commission, however, further recommended a policy which would make land available for every native, sufficient to support him and his family and provide money for taxes; and they said that the available labor supply "must not be estimated solely with a view to the requirements of non-native enterprise."

The official statement of the British Labor Party to the Labor Congress held in Brussels in 1929, said that the object should be to prepare as rapidly as possible the African people for self-government. This should be done by preventing the political power from falling into the hands of immigrant minorities who would use it for their own political and economic interests; and that general and political education should aim at making them as rapidly as possible capable of dealing with the political, economic and social conditions of the modern world.

At the beginning of the second Labor Government in 1929, the British sent Sir Samuel Wilson, permanent Under-Secretary of State, to gather further information. In June, 1930, the labor government published the Passfield White Paper on native policy in East Africa. It said that the Africans were to be allowed to grow coffee; that they might own land on individual tenure; that taxation should be graded according to wealth; and that every race and religion should have a right to equal treatment. This was followed by loud and emphatic protest, in which the settlers of Northern Rhodesia joined.

Sir Joseph Byrnes went to Kenya as Governor in 1931 while the Labor Party was still in power. The settlers of Kenya wanted the imperial government to abolish the official majority in the Kenya legislature which gave the governor power to override the settlers, and they again demanded a federation of all the colonies in British West Africa so as to extend the Kenya policy.

Another joint committee of parliament was appointed in 1931. Lord Passfield, better known as Sidney Webb, presided over the hearings in England and received the white official delegates with such great courtesy and sympathy that they departed believing that their demands were going to be granted. On the other hand, the natives of Kenya at great cost and sacrifice chose delegates and sent them to London. The Select Committee refused to hear them.

The Commission reported in 1931 and decided that the time was not ripe for taking any steps toward a formal union of the three East African territories. The British government followed this Commission's opinion and decided in September, 1932, to abandon the idea of this political union; but it ordered the governors of the three territories to meet regularly in conference and to discuss co-operation, especially in customs duties and communications. Finally, in June, 1933, the Mandates Commission of the League of Nations decided that mandated territory like Tanganyika could not take part in such union as long as the mandate was in force.

Lord Moyne was appointed commissioner to Kenya in 1932 to look into the financial position. He recommended that a proportion of that taxation paid by natives be put into a native permanent fund for native interests and that the administration of this should not be reviewed by the Select Committee on Estimates dominated by white settlers. The settlers protested against this in meetings. No action has been taken yet.

Kenya colony and protectorate according to the law of 1934 was governed by an executive council of twelve members and a legislative council which had eleven ex-officio members and nine nominated official members; and, in addition to this, eleven elected European members, five elected Indian members, one elected Arab member and two nominated unofficial members to represent the Africans, and one nominated unofficial member to represent the Arabs. There are separate electoral rolls for Europeans, Indians, and Arabs. Legislation is made by ordinance with the advice and consent of the legislative council.

The natives of Kenya have several times rebelled against the assumptions of settlers and the seizing of their land. They have tried bringing action in local and English courts. The young educated natives are critical of English methods and insist in many cases on native customs. The Kikuyu native councils have made good their right to control schools maintained by their own funds, and the tribes of the Kavirondo are demanding territorial union for their separate parts. Today local whites still largely dictate the policy of Kenya, but they have been halted in their more ambitious policies, and there is growing recognition of increased autonomy for the natives and some steps toward a better economic policy.

Nyasaland is inhabited mainly by two Mohammedan tribes. The Scotch Presbyterians set up a mission in 1872. Together with English capitalists they formed the African Lakes Company. They came to open conflict with the Mohammedans and were threatened by the Portuguese. The British government intervened and Nyasaland became a British possession.

Nyasaland is about the size of Indiana, with one and one-half million natives, two thousand Europeans and one thousand five hundred Asiatics. Despite the activities of land-grabbing commercial companies moving north from South Africa, native autonomy has been retained to a considerable extent. The village headmen have recognized executive duties under the white district commissioners representing the government, and receive a small proportion of certain taxes which they collect, and fines and fees which go toward their salaries and toward a central equalization fund.

Nyasaland in a curious way represents the contradiction of earlier colonial methods. With the land grabbing and commercial exploitation in which the missionaries shared widely there was an unusual number of mission schools in which the natives received excellent training. Nyasaland, therefore, today has a considerably larger number of natives educated in the three R's and their presence brings characteristic difficulties under a colonial regime which often seeks to keep the natives as illiterate as possible.

If they are recognized in the appointment of native officials, the experience and ability of black men to rule along modern lines will increase. If they are not recognized and are made subordinate to the ignorant native chiefs, their natural criticism and dissatisfaction will make the manipulation of these chiefs by white men more possible. The government professes to find it difficult to find any place for the educated black man in local government. White settlers held a conference in June, 1935, demanding of the Colonial Office a freer hand in exploiting the natives. They organized a committee to negotiate with Northern and Southern Rhodesia for a new dominion, independent of the Colonial Office in England.

The Letters Patent of 1923 which gave responsible government to *Southern Rhodesia* retained the provision of the Order in Council of 1898 with regard to native affairs. The governor of Southern Rhodesia is obliged to give the High Commissioner for Native Affairs of South Africa any information he may demand, and the high commissioner must approve the establishment and regulation of native councils and any collective fines. Racial discrimination is forbidden and thus in theory the right to vote is open to natives. In 1933 there were fifty-eight qualified native voters.

Chiefs and headmen to the number of about four hundred are employees of the government, with power to settle minor disputes under native law, to see that taxes are paid and that laborers are furnished. Such officials operate only on the reserves and not in the locations. On the other hand, the government of Southern Rhodesia has for a long time assumed that tribal society is crumbling and has given the organization little encouragement or support. Lately this policy shows signs of change. The Native Affairs Act of 1927 gave the native chiefs some police power and in 1930 a system of native local boards with elected members was started.

Much depends upon the future development of Southern Rhodesia. If agriculture or mining so develop that there is an increasing demand for alienation of native land or a shortage of labor, the economic and political power which the state now has over its labor force will lead to the same sort of trouble that one finds in Kenya and South Africa and the same demand to control the native. Indeed the difference today between Southern Rhodesia and the Union of South Africa in the treatment of natives is only a difference of degree.

In *Northern Rhodesia* the tendency is to control and govern the native in the towns and settlements near the mines and to leave him considerable autonomy in the villages and country districts. There were in Northern Rhodesia in 1934, 1,300,000 natives and ten thousand whites living on 290,000 square miles of land, including a native reserve, Barotseland, with sixty thousand square miles of poor land and 350,000 natives. The whole economy of Northern Rhodesia is subservient to the mining industry and the natives are regarded as a labor reserve, little interfered with when living in the reserves and at the same time receiving little help; but subject to strict control in the mining areas.

A native authority has been set up which deals with liquors, fire arms, gambling, water and trees, disease, crime, labor on public works, migration, food for travelers, roads between villages, prostitution and collecting taxes. Native courts deal with marriage and inheritance. Appeals may be taken from the native courts to the white district commissioner at his decision.

Among most tribes, there are regular meetings of the chiefs under supervision of Europeans. In appointing chiefs the government tries to appoint the rightful heir and the elders are consulted. The chiefs usually appoint their own headmen for the village. They are, however, greatly curtailed in power for lack of funds. They are paid from five dollars to three hundred dollars a year by the government, the average being about fifty dollars. The authority of the chiefs has been strengthened by this procedure, but the present generation of chiefs is old and conservative and shows little initiative or originality.

Usually the government or the white city conducts a large beer hall in each one of the locations, which is open three or four hours a day. They make a monthly profit of between four hundred dollars and one thousand dollars, which is supposed to go for native clinics, recreation, churches and the rebuilding of huts. Health and recreation are given some limited attention by the mine owners, but the death rate is still high. There is compensation for accident but no insurance for unemployment, and desertion of work is a penal offense.

Thus in all these Central and South African colonies, notwithstanding attempts at absolute rule, suppression and segregation, many things have made some recognition of native autonomy imperative. First of all came the question of native law. It was impossible to subject native tribes immediately to a foreign code. If the alleged aggression involved Europeans, European law might be applied, despite the fact that this was often grossly unfair. But if the question was between natives, native law must be applied to give any satisfaction. Throughout the African colonies the Europeans have thus been compelled to give some recognition to native law.

The chieftainship is a strong African institution which foreign control has seldom been able to obliterate; even where the chiefs have been overthrown, it has been necessary in many cases to revert at least to a semblance of his former power. Primarily the African chief is father of a family; from this he may rise to be head of a clan or paramount chief over a tribe or king of a nation. He is almost invariably assisted by a council and comes to no important decision without the consent of his council. New chiefs are appointed by the council and as the chief rises in power, his authority as a rule is decentralized through subordinate chiefs and headmen.

The history of political domination in South Africa is in complete contrast to both French and British West Africa, and a logical culmination of the tendency which we have followed in Uganda, the Belgian Congo, Kenya and the Rhodesias. The *Union of South Africa* is twice the size of France, Belgium and Holland together, and has a population of two million whites, six and one-half million Bantu, 800,000 colored people and 200,000 Asiatics.

The Union is governed by a governor-general, a senate of forty members and a house of assembly with one hundred and fifty members. Of the members of the Senate, thirty-two are elected and eight are nominated by the governor; four of the nominated members are selected for their "Acquaintance with the reasonable wants and wishes of the non-European races." Some additional representation of the natives by white persons whom they select has been provided by the law of 1936. The members of both the House and Senate must be British subjects of European descent; they are elected by white voters, men and women, twenty-one years of age and over; and at present, from Cape Colony, three white men are chosen by male natives and colored people with property and literary tests.

In the constitution of South Africa of 1906 and 1907, there was an express provision against any legislation which discriminated against British subjects on account of color; but in the act of Union of 1909, this provision was omitted. A native delegation went all the way to England to protest, but it met not philanthropic England but investing England, with South Africa as a source of its long-threatened, but increasing income. The protest was, therefore, in vain. The only reference to the natives in the new constitution was the above provision in regard to four senators. The Union has in the government a Minister and Department of Native Affairs.

Parliament was finally allowed to prescribe voting qualifications, but could not disfranchise voters in the Cape Province for race and color, unless the bill was passed by a two-thirds majority at a joint session of parliament. Outside the Cape, the new Union made little effort to recognize the native in any way except as an exploitable laborer. Smuts in 1920 set up a permanent Native Affairs Commission to advise the prime minister and to extend the Cape Transkei system of local government and taxation and to summon conferences of the chiefs.

The upheaval of World War brought, however, bitter exacerbation of race hate and a determination to crystallize customary and legal discrimination into a definite body of law. After the war an alliance was made between the Dutch Nationalist Party and the Labor Party. The Nationalist Party, composed largely of Dutch farmers, had been working for the independence of South Africa; but their program was rendered superfluous in 1926 by the Statute of Westminster, which established the British Commonwealth of Nations and made the Union of South Africa politically independent, although economically and socially it is still a colony of England. The Labor Party was working for preferential treatment from capital against colored laborers. Thus a farmer-labor coalition came into control of South Africa.

The Hertzog government in 1926 introduced a bill to take away native franchise in the Cape. A second bill provided for electing a small number of white members to the Union Assembly by natives throughout the Union. A third bill proposed a Union native council with thirty-five elected members and fifteen appointed members, presided over by the white Secretary of Native Affairs.

Another bill on the program was a Color Bar law, which, after having been twice rejected by the Senate, was finally passed by a joint session of Parliament. This law not only excluded Negroes from practically all skilled occupations, but from many positions in the public service which they had formerly filled. It was strongly opposed and bitterly defended. Hertzog promised that, if it was passed, he would advocate further land reserves for the natives and make a beginning of native political institutions. The Color Bar Bill passed, but the native representation failed until 1936.

To understand this legislation we must glance at the constituent parts of the Union of South Africa. There are four provinces: the Cape Province, larger than Texas, has 800,000 whites, 700,000 colored people, ten thousand Asiatics and two million natives. Next in size comes the Transvaal, the size of Nevada, with 800,000 whites and two and one-half million natives and colored folk. The Orange Free State is the size of Louisiana, with two hundred thousand whites and six hundred thousand natives and colored. Natal, the size of Indiana, has two hundred thousand whites and one and three-quarter million native and colored folk.

Cape Colony is the most advanced community. Here there is an educated colored group, and after the emancipation of slaves was finally accomplished in

1838, public opinion ranged itself behind the dictum, later enunciated by Cecil Rhodes, "Equal rights for all civilized men south of the Zambezi." Votes were given colored people and natives, with educational and property restrictions. In 1935 some twenty-three thousand colored people and natives were registered voters, being able to read and write, or having property valued at $375, or an income of $250 a year. The increase among these voters in thirty years has been about fifteen thousand, and in half of the constituencies of the Cape the colored vote represented a proportion large enough to defeat anti-Negro candidates; thus they might influence the balance of power in the Union Legislature.

This political power of the natives of the Cape was part of Cecil Rhodes' policy and was followed by the Glen Grey Act of 1884 which encouraged the natives to take up land upon individual tenure instead of communal tribal tenure. The act was first applied in the Ciskei district and later widely extended in the Transkei.

The Transkei is a sort of black belt between the Kei River and Natal and covers sixteen thousand square miles. The natives are fairly Europeanized. No whites except officials are allowed to live in the Transkei. There are nearly two thousand paid chiefs and headmen throughout the various native districts and reserves of South Africa, who are paid from ten to thirty pounds a year. In the Transkei there are about twenty-six local and district councils. They make reports to white officials and receive instruction from them. Each council is composed of an European official who presides and six native members: two nominated by the government and the others by the chiefs. These councils are responsible for collecting taxes, making roads, and maintaining law and order. From among the councils, two are chosen from each district to serve on the general council which meets once a year.

The largest Negro general conference in South Africa is the Bunga of the Transkei. It is composed of fifty-seven elected and nominated native members, representing the district councils of the Transkei and Tembuland and Pemba. There are also nineteen whites on the council. The annual meeting is held in the capital of the Transkei and lasts about three weeks. They review the work of the district councils; receive reports and budgets from the local councils. All decisions of the general council must be approved by the white members and they are responsible to the Native Affairs department, the head of which is the Minister of Native Affairs, a member of the Union cabinet.

In 1925 there were district councils in nearly all of the Transkeian districts and by 1927, two general councils had been established, which were federated in 1931 as the United Transkeian Territories' General Council. This Council or Bunga offers advice to the chief magistrate and appoints a standing committee of four magistrates and four natives to appoint and dismiss the staff, establish agricultural institutions, control public work and institute legal proceedings. If, however, the white chairman of the Committee disagrees with any of its acts he has a suspensory veto by which the matter may be referred to the High Commissioner. The General Council since 1903 has expended nearly four million pounds. It has established three agricultural schools, four experiment farms; it employs ninety-seven agricultural demonstrators and maintains 4,500 miles of roads. There is also a Ciskeian General Council federated of eight councils.

The question of the native vote in the Cape province was, from the beginning, a matter of disagreement among the provinces and nearly prevented the efforts at union in 1909. Later anti-Negro prejudice in the other provinces was partially appeased in the Cape by making the native franchise requirements more difficult. The income of $250 a year, for instance, after 1930, was not recognized, unless the person had worked the whole previous year at that rate. Lands given the natives by legislative enactment were not to be counted in the appraisal of their property ownership. Some six thousand natives and colored persons were thus removed from the Cape register.

In the Transvaal, after the passing of the Natives Affairs Act in 1920, five native councils were set up with restricted powers. In the Orange Free State the native chiefs were denied all judicial powers under native law; but two or three now have been given jurisdiction and four native councils have been set up. These two provinces are noted for their reactionary attitude toward Negroes on the part of the predominately Dutch farming population. Natal is more liberal than the Orange Free State and the Transvaal, but less advanced in race matters than the Cape colony. It was the former seat of Bishop Colenso, who refused to obey the decision of the South African bishops in native matters and was sustained by the Church of England. Registration difficulties prevent natives from voting.

The long-continued efforts of the Zulus in Natal to strengthen their power and resist the encroachment of the whites led to several serious rebellions and to efforts to establish a more liberal native policy. This was complicated by the question of the Indians and their rights to trade and participate in government. There is one native council, and eighty chiefs have civil and criminal jurisdiction.

In 1934 the political aspect of South Africa changed again. Hertzog and Smuts united in a coalition government which represented the union of land monopoly and mining capital—of landlords and industry. They were opposed by the small farmers and the poor whites, and between these parties there was some revival of racial feeling between the British and Dutch. As a diverting issue, race feeling against Bantus and Jews was encouraged and fascist organizations formed. The military budget was increased. Oswald Pirow, the Minister of Defense in the Coalition Government, in a speech before the South Africa Defense League, said that "the white people of South Africa had the great task of determining for the next few centuries, or perhaps as long as our white civilization lasts, whether Africa, or the greatest part of Africa, shall be governed by Whites or Blacks. It was a life-and-death struggle, between Black and White, with South Africa as its rallying point."[4] Sir Abe Bailey, South African millionaire, added to this a warning against the "yellow menace!"

In 1934 the property and educational qualifications in the Cape province were abolished by the Union, so far as white voters were concerned, and the franchise extended to white women; but in the case of blacks and colored people, women were denied the right to vote and the former property and educational qualifications retained. The following year, the native representation bill was introduced into the Union Parliament in new form, and was passed in 1936. It provided that the approximately twenty-three thousand natives and colored people who were legal voters in Cape Colony were to be transferred to a special electoral roll called the Cape Native Voters Roll. On this roll will also be placed the names of Cape natives who may subsequently obtain the same qualifications. These Cape natives will elect three whites to represent them in the House of Assembly and two to represent them in the Provincial Council. Members representing these native constituencies hold their seats for five years irrespective of the dissolution of Parliament. They have the same rights and privileges as the ordinary members of Parliament elected by the whites; but their number is fixed no matter how the number of native Cape voters increases.

In the other three provinces of the Union, all natives and colored folk were to continue to be disfranchised both in the Union legislature and in the provincial councils. But in the Union as a whole, natives were to share in the government through four white senators elected by natives through electoral colleges; and through representation in the Natives Representative Council.

This Council will consist of six official members, four native members appointed by the governor-general and twelve elected native members, three to each province. The Council is to consider and report on proposed legislation which affects the native population and any matters referred to it by the minister and any matter affecting the natives in general. It has, however, only advisory power. In this way the danger of the colored voters in the Cape exercising the balance of power has been averted. On the other hand, the representation of the natives in the senate by white senators is not as important as similar representation would be in the assembly, since the senate has curtailed financial and other powers.

Nor is there much hope that the Natives Representative Council will have real influence. There was a provision in a former Native Affairs Act for summoning representative natives to consult with the government on legislation affecting them, but such representatives were summoned only once in eight years, 1926–34, and then they were expressly warned not to mention native grievances. The Natives Representative Council met for the first time in December, 1937. It included five chiefs, a high school principal, three editors, two farmers, a builder and a lawyer's clerk. The white Native Commissioner presided.

Turning to the *protectorates:* Bechuanaland is divided into eleven districts. Each district is presided over by a white magistrate responsible to a resident commissioner who represents the High Commissioner for South Africa.[5] The High Commissioner is under the Secretary of State for the Dominions in London. The country is also divided into a number of native areas or reserves, which are all within the jurisdiction of the administrative districts. The chiefs rule and administer justice according to native law except in cases involving the death penalty or when one of the parties is an European.

Basutoland has been since 1931 under the British High Commissioner, who is represented by a resident commissioner. This commissioner has legislative and executive powers and is helped by white assistant commissioners and magistrates. The native districts are divided into fifty wards, each ward governed by a hereditary chief who swears allegiance to a paramount chief. The paramount chief is a descendant of Moshesh. There is a national assembly called the Pitso. It has ninety-five members nominated by the chiefs and five appointed by the government. The resident commissioner presides over the assembly. He must approve all matters before presentation.

Some native opposition has been crystallizing in Basutoland. The Young Basuto Association demands elected representatives instead of nominated ones and opposes the conservatism and reaction of chiefs.

Swaziland was unified under Sobhuza, who died in 1839. Europeans entered first in 1878. In 1888 they demanded that the government intervene and take over the administration of Swaziland. Although the independence of Swaziland was guaranteed by British and Boers in the Pretoria Convention of 1881 and the London Convention of 1884, the British occupied the territory in 1889 and set up a government composed of fifteen British and Boers and five Swazis. The five Swazis were soon excluded by the British. The Boers demurred, but were appeased by the right to collect duty on exports and imports and levy taxes, which left the territory in partial independence. The British set up courts and paid the paramount chief one thousand pounds annually. He was made drunk and signed away most of the property of the tribe. After the Boer War the government of the country was put first under the Transvaal and then under the British High Commissioner. The Swazi have a general assembly which has no constitutional position and there are district meetings of the chiefs. Educated natives and colored persons form committees and meet twice a year.

Barotseland with 350,000 people is a protectorate (or as local whites prefer to say, a Native Reserve) in Northern Rhodesia. It came under British control by treaty with Portugal in 1891 and was declared a protectorate in 1924. It is now controlled by a paramount chief, who administers native law under a British Commissioner. There is a parliament called the Kgotla, which has legislative, judicial and executive powers subject to the approval of the white commissioners. There is a national fund paid by the natives, but controlled by white officials and missionaries. Part of this fund goes for education.

These protectorates are the remains of the unconquered or partially conquered native areas, left with something of their own local and tribal autonomy, but circumscribed not only by white political rulers but also choked by the surrounding economy of South Africa. If or when their complete government will be transferred to the Union of South Africa is a grave political question. The transfer has been categorically promised by England; but England has so often broken her word given to the natives, it would be a fine variation for her to break a promise to the whites.

Portuguese Africa is difficult to study and understand, because of the wide discrepancies between the letter of the law and actual administration. Portugal has a body of colonial legislation which in many respects is the best in Africa. Every native in a Portuguese colony is legally a citizen of Portugal with all citizenship rights. Moreover, the large amount of race mixture in Portuguese colonies makes the line between whites and natives difficult to draw. Native autonomous rule has never been legally abolished in Portuguese Africa. On the contrary, in the earlier days it was encouraged to a large extent, and the Portuguese set up an African empire recognizing a paramount chief and sending natives to Portugal for education. Legal recognition is given to native political institutions;

the chiefs should be chosen by native custom and paid by the government; a fixed amount of revenue must be paid for native welfare. The Portuguese constitution of 1933 provides for the eventual transfer of the power of commercial companies to the state. Thus in 1926, 1929 and 1933 Portugal tried to establish in her colonies freedom of labor and contract, education, and a fixed expenditure on native interests. But all this legal autonomy has had but limited recognition in practice.

One momentous factor in the political relations of Europe and Africa came with the mandate legislation of the League of Nations. The annexation of German colonies and the mandate system was in theory a tremendous step. It was a proposal for the united civilized world to take charge of certain areas of Africa formerly belonging to the Germans and administer them primarily for the benefit of the natives, allowing, and strictly limiting, the profit motive. It was thought by the promoters of the mandate system that gradually Europe would be influenced by the methods of the mandates and that much if not all colonial Africa might eventually be handed over to the League of Nations for direction and control. The Mandates Commission at Geneva bade fair to become the great agent for the development of the African native.

It is hardly necessary to say that very little of this program has been realized. Indeed the selfishness of the Allies with regard to the African colonies was the first and fatal mistake that foreshadowed the present disintegration and impotence of the League. The stone which the builders rejected—justice to black folk—has been precisely the one whose absence has brought disaster to Europe in the Ethiopian conquest and the German menace. The *mandates* almost without exception have been practically incorporated with the colonies of Great Britain, France, Belgium, Union of South Africa, and Japan, and dealt with as their own colonies. "So strong indeed was the demand of the Dominions that they should acquire complete possession of the conquered territories contiguous to their own in Southwest Africa and the Pacific, that, in the event, it was with difficulty that a form of Mandate was devised, which General Smuts described as *'annexation in all but the name!'*—and American and Japanese writers have used the same terms."

In the original fourteen points which were to form the basis of peace after the World War, President Wilson had said January 8, 1918: "The only possible program is: A free, open-minded, and absolutely impartial adjustment of all colonial claims, based upon a strict observance of the principle, that in determining all such questions of sovereignty, the interests of the populations concerned must have equal weight with the equitable claims of the government whose title is to be determined."

In a memorandum by Colonel House October 29, 1918, it was said: "What are the 'interests of the populations'? That they should not be militarized, that exploitation should be conducted on the principle of the open door; and under the strictest regulation as to labor conditions, profits and taxes; that a sanitary regime be maintained; that permanent improvements in the way of roads, etc., be made; that native organization and custom be respected; that the protecting authority be stable and experienced enough to thwart intrigue and corruption;

that the protecting power have adequate resources in money and competent administrators to act successfully."

This did not propose the high philanthropic ground of development of colonies for the best interests of their peoples; it very frankly admitted the profit of industrial enterprise of Europeans as the leading motive; but it sought at least to curb it by labor laws, sanitation, public work and tribal autonomy. The principle involved was that a colonial power act not as owner of its mandate, but "as trustee for the natives and for the interests of the society of nations; that the terms on which the colonial administration is conducted are a matter of international concern and may legitimately be the subject of international inquiry, and that the peace conference may, therefore, write a code of colonial conduct binding upon all colonial powers."

The colonies were divided into three classes: the A class, including colonies in Arabia and Palestine, with six million inhabitants and 200,000 square miles, were looked upon as nearly ready for nationhood. In the B Mandates were all of the African colonies, except Southwest Africa. A permanent Mandates Commission under the League of Nations, with eleven members selected by the council, are in control of these mandated territories. The majority of the members of the Commission are from non-mandatory states; but the Commission has very limited power. It may not deal with petitions directly from inhabitants of the mandated territories, but only with such petitions as are presented through the mandatory power. The Commission cannot visit the areas or grant oral audiences to petitioners, but must depend upon publicity and discussion in the assembly of the League, with such information as the League Secretariat provides.

The extent of the power of the League over the mandated country has not been defined. The commission and the council have declared that the mandatory power is not sovereign in the mandated territory, but on the other hand it is not clear just where the sovereignty resides. The importance of the mandate system lies in the fact that it purports to provide methods for adjusting the relations between industrialized countries and backward communities; but its success in this line has not been notable.

The Germans claim infringement upon the mandate principle: "The United Kingdom . . . has combined the Tanganyika Territory with Kenya and Uganda in a Postal Union. In respect of this measure also, the Mandates Commission expressed its misgivings; but it would not decide to place itself in open opposition. We find similar aspirations in German Southwest Africa, where those striving for a Greater South Africa, have for years demanded the incorporation of the mandated territory as a fifth province.

"The so-called 'administrative reforms,' with which France, in order to 'round off' her great colonial empire, is endeavoring to unite Togoland with the neighboring colony of Dahomey, and the Cameroons with French Equatorial Africa, may also be mentioned in this connection. According to these examples, Belgium is also trying to amalgamate her mandated territories of Ruanda and Urundi with the Congo Colony."

On the other hand, lately the British have suggested an extension of the mandate system as a cure for colonial rivalry; but it is interesting that the argument repeatedly turned solely upon economic advantage to the colonial powers while the interests of the natives received little or no mention.

The data as to conditions in the mandated territories are meager. Southwest Africa was chiefly occupied by the Dutch in the eighteenth century. In 1882 Bremen sent Germans under Lüderlitz. In 1884 Bismarck proclaimed a protectorate. War with the natives ensued between 1904 and 1908: eighty thousand Hereros, five thousand Hottentots and twelve thousand Bergdamas were slaughtered or starved to death. The war lasted four years, the Germans lost two thousand officers and men and spent thirty thousand pounds sterling. Native lands were confiscated and tribal life largely disrupted. However, Ovamboland under German rule was left to its own tribal organization. It is an area in Southwest Africa which can still be used by the mandate as an organ of government.

Botha captured the colony in 1915. Southwest Africa is now a mandate of the Union of South Africa. During the World War the sixteen thousand German inhabitants were reduced to eight thousand, and some ten thousand South Africans emigrated to the new mandate. A civil administrator replaced the military authority in 1921 with a council of advisers consisting of Germans and South Africans. The area of the country is 317,000 square miles; there are twenty-one thousand whites (1924) and 328,000 natives.

In May, 1922, the Bondelswartz, an Hottentot tribe, who had served the Union of South Africa during the war, rebelled on account of heavy taxes, especially a tax of two pounds sterling a head on their herding dogs. The administrators sent a force into their reserve and with the help of airplanes killed over a hundred men, women and children. The Mandates Commission of the League of Nations, aroused by a Haitian delegate, called for a full report and condemned the administrators' methods. The Ovambos rebelled in 1932; but the air force of South Africa came over and threatened to bomb them.

Tanganyika is larger than France and Italy, with five million natives, thirty thousand Asiatics and nine thousand Europeans. Under German rule, local administration was organized through Arab officials who represented German authority. When the British took the mandate they restored native autonomy so that, until Sir Donald Cameron came from Nigeria to be governor in 1925, about half of the territory was under tribal rule. With the arrival of Sir Donald Cameron, five native authorities were set up and a wide and thoroughgoing recognition of local rule was inaugurated. There were difficulties in certain mixed groups on the coast, but these were overcome in various ways.

Sir Donald Cameron interpreted his duty to the mandate as the training of the people to stand by themselves as part of the whole community so that "when the time comes, a full place in the political structure shall be found for the native population." He distinctly refused to envisage a political organization in which there was no place for the natives until the whites were ready to yield it. He foresaw a future constitution with a central native and central non-native council and with delegates sitting jointly for most of the legislative business. To this end he proposed to entrust native authority with increased responsibility.

In five years Cameron built up a system of local native government; he restored the original democratic constitution, which made tribal opinion rather than the power of chiefs supreme. Tribal councils were set up to collect the poll tax; have charge of roads and bridges; build and manage schools and dispensaries. Between one-tenth and one-third of the poll tax was returned to the tribes to be spent by the tribal treasuries. The accounts of these treasuries are audited by British officials. Out of 3,500,000 pounds sterling which these tribal authorities have collected, less than 1,500 pounds have been lost by defalcation. There were 148 of these tribal authorities in Tanganyika about 1925, but the number is growing less through union into larger units.

Gradually larger and larger native administrative units were built up under paramount chiefs or with chiefs presiding in rotation. Annual conferences were held in certain districts among the chiefs to discuss the marketing of produce, taxation and tribal law. These native authorities are showing initiative and intelligence. There are certain voluntary groups like the Killimanjaro Native Planters Association for co-operative marketing and buying. Native courts have been recognized and are of two grades, while tribal councils can be constituted as appeal courts. Many cases are settled by family councils and village elders.

Naturally the success of this experiment depends almost entirely upon the governor and his district commissioners. Cameron represented the most liberal aspects of the English Labor Government. He was unfortunately replaced, when the last Labor Government fell, by a new governor whose plans and objects are not yet clear. The depression has brought a good many retrenchments. Whether these mean many fundamental changes in policy is not certain.

One subject calls for special consideration and that is taxation as it is used in Africa as a power of government. Logically the taxation of a people is laid for the public benefit. But, of course, in Europe taxation has been made a method by which the money of the taxpayer has been used for the benefit of privileged classes. In the same way but much more obviously in Africa, taxation has first of all been laid, not because of the needs of the native taxpayer, but primarily as a method of compulsion to make them work for landholders and industrial monopolists. This might have been justified if the proceeds from the taxes had been spent for the uplift of black communities; but in most cases singularly enough this has not been true. The extraordinary situation has arisen in colonies like Kenya, the Rhodesias and South Africa, where the black community, poor as it is, has actually been taxed for the benefit of educating white children and paying the expenses of a government carried on primarily for the benefit of the whites.

In the Union of South Africa, natives are taxed through licenses and passes, together with a poll tax of five dollars and a hut tax of two dollars and fifty cents. Often the total tax is ten dollars a year. The native pays over $15,000,000 in taxes and receives $5,000,000 in direct government services.

The direct taxation in Kenya falls on the poorest and the indirect taxes are not simply on luxuries but on necessities like flour and cloth. Until lately the whites have refused to pay any tax on incomes, paying only a $7.50 poll tax and a special tax for the education of European children. Natives pay twenty-five per cent of the direct taxes and probably a larger proportion of the indirect.

The natives pay three direct taxes: hut tax which is nominally three dollars but averages six dollars and a half per family. This tax in 1931 brought in over $3,000,000. The second direct tax is the tax levied by the tribal council for roads and education. It amounted to $200,000 in 1930. The third tax is forced labor on public projects which amounts to six days or more every three months. Beside these, fines and forfeitures average $150,000 a year. The indirect taxes paid by the natives amount to one dollar and a half a head and make an annual total of $1,815,000. In 1929 natives paid $2,500,000 in hut and poll tax and, in 1930, nearly $3,000,000. The total native taxation yields $4,000,000. The direct expenditure on natives is $1,500,000.

The government of Northern Rhodesia taxes the natives for its support more heavily in proportion than the Europeans. There is an income tax for Europeans; a poll tax for natives; a large revenue from customs, and a personal tax for non-natives. The native poll tax is from one dollar and eighty cents to three dollars a year, according to the earning capacity of different regions. It is imposed on male natives over nineteen. Generally speaking "a month's work enables the taxpayer to discharge his obligations." No part of this tax is earmarked for native development. The tax, of course, is a method of inducing the native to work as the only way in which he can get ready money.

Of the total revenue of Northern Rhodesia, amounting to $4,280,000 a year, it is estimated that the natives pay $900,000 directly and indirectly; and, on the other hand, only about $310,000 is spent on native education and agricultural and other uplift services.

In the principal provinces of Uganda, natives pay four dollars and seventy-five cents poll tax, while in the small districts the tax is from one dollar and twenty-five cents to two dollars and fifty cents. Beside this there are a number of local taxes which go into the Uganda treasuries. In Buganda, natives pay a land tax of five dollars and must work thirty days without pay on the roads under the native rulers. Chiefs and headmen in Nyasaland, who are responsible for collecting the head tax, have at times arrested the wives and female relatives of defaulters and detained them until the tax was paid. The salaries of chiefs depend upon the tax collected. The hut tax is now the largest item in the revenue of the colony. The general revenue of the protectorate amounted to $2,500,000 in 1932 and of this the natives pay thirty-eight per cent.

In the Protectorates, salaries eat up a large part of the income. The revenue of Bechuanaland in 1936–37 was $1,235,000 and the expenditure $1,270,000. Very little was done in medicine, education or agriculture. Bechuanaland pays five dollars hut and poll tax to the British government, and from seventy-five cents to one dollar and twenty-five cents to the native administration. The hut and poll tax amounted to $165,000 in 1932 while the Europeans paid $13,500 income tax. The rest of the revenue was derived from custom duties on articles used by the natives, such as blankets, which pay twenty-five per cent.

In Basutoland the native pays an average of six dollars poll tax, collected by white officials aided by the chiefs. The total revenue in 1936–37 was $1,750,000, of which $610,000 was in direct taxes. There was a special educational fund of $70,000. An export tax is imposed by the government on all products exported.

The Swazi pay about $200,000 in poll taxes out of the total revenue of $420,000. The rest comes from customs, sale of Crown lands and dog taxes, dogs being kept to guard the native cattle.

There have been widespread tax disputes in West Africa, with the result that direct taxation on natives is spent today largely for their welfare. With indirect taxation it is different. Loans for public works, for instance, have been widely used. Nigeria has received five loans, varying from $15,000,000 to $30,000,000, and has spent them for building bridges and railways, homes for the Europeans, electric and waterworks and sewer construction. The colonial governments float loans in England, and interest and principal are repaid by taxing natives. In earlier days, grants without interest were made directly by the British Treasury, some $35,000,000 of such grants being made in West Africa. But since the war, banks and financiers furnish capital and charge interest. Payment on such debts makes money for education and welfare work difficult to obtain.

Kenya borrowed from England, 1922 to 1930, $85,000,000 at from four and a half to six per cent from London financiers. Tanganyika borrowed $15,000,000 at six and a half per cent in London from 1920 to 1926 and further loans amounting from twenty-five to thirty million dollars between 1926 and 1932. The railway from Mombasa to Lake Victoria was constructed out of a loan of $25,000,000 guaranteed by the imperial government. The South African Protectorates have similarly received loans of $750,000 to $1,000,000 from England to be repaid in taxation. In French West Africa the natives pay twenty-nine per cent of the colonial income and in the Belgian Congo twenty-five per cent. In the Congo expenditure, forty-three per cent of the budget goes for interest on debt, i.e., on European invested capital.

In general it may be said that Africa retains a modicum of self-government and some recognition of native law. The object of the European governments in general is to maintain peace and order for the purpose of profitable commercial enterprise. The welfare of the native occupies a considerable but a subordinate place. The expenses of European over-lordship are borne almost exclusively by taxation upon the natives, which in many cases becomes a severe burden amounting often to ten per cent or more of the natives' annual income. Moreover, in the majority of colonies, this taxation is for the purpose of forcing the natives to work, while its proceeds are spent primarily on matters which are for the interest of the Europeans. The tendencies toward autonomy and self-rule are vigorously opposed by the European demand for dividends and profits.

To this end Europe taxes native Africa today a total of over $30,000,000 a year in direct taxes taken from the lowest paid workers on earth; and perhaps ten millions more in indirect taxes.

It may be easily shown that this contribution of the natives is less than their share of the expense of the colonies calculated on a numerical basis. But the natives do not share in colonial objectives on a numerical basis. The colony is conducted for the defense and aggrandizement of home countries and for the profit of owners and investors, and to mulct the victims of this process for the cost of their oppression is indefensible in morals and short-sighted in politics.

NOTES

1. "Memorandum of the case of the National Congress of British West Africa," etc., p. 2.
2. Padmore, *How Britain Rules Africa*, p. 312.
3. *The Congo*, Vol. I. Chap. III.
4. Johannesburg *Star*, December 28, 1933.
5. His exact title since the Statute of Westminster is "High Commissioner for Basutoland, the Bechuanaland Protectorate and Swaziland." His former powers over natives in the Rhodesias are now exercised by the Colonial Office in London.

CHAPTER XV

✦

Education in Africa

Education in Africa did not begin with the whites. The tribal education of the native was especially addressed to teaching him to endure pain and provocation without showing it. The training of young children was intelligent; spoiled children were exceptional and punishment unusual. At the time of initiation of children into manhood and womanhood there was a systematic and intense course of training. This initiation is the most important event in the life of the young man, teaching him the past of the tribe, the magical power of his ancestors and his present duties. He becomes a new person and begins a life separate from the women and children so as to be initiated into the spiritual inheritance of his forefathers. A similar ceremony for girls instructs them in the mysteries of womanhood.

The co-operation between the African and European is not simply a matter of "Black brawn and white brains"; even today the African is doing brain work in Africa and is lessening the distance between him and the European, although the European is often inclined to keep as great a distance as possible and to use education in order to maintain the status quo.

There come, however, a number of pressing problems in the European direction of African education: first, shall the African be systematically trained at all; secondly, if trained, shall he not be trained chiefly to work; third, if he is trained to work, shall he be trained for work according to his own needs and tribal organization, or for work which is valuable and desired by the white employer; fourth, whether he is trained for his own work or the work of the employer, how far shall he be trained in intelligence, the use of the three R's and the opening up of avenues toward modern training; fifth, if he is to be trained in intelligence, shall the medium of his training be his own vernacular language or a world language like the English or the French; sixth, how far in his training shall physical science and the new sciences of anthropology, ethnology, sociology and linguistics be systematically and carefully used?

All these problems face African education; but in reality the basic problem is, no matter what the training of the African is, what is the object of the training? Is it to make him valuable to the European investor? No evading of this fundamental question can hide the necessity for its answer; and two different answers are given by the British and the French.

By the British, more especially in South Africa, but to some extent even in West Africa, there is no settled determination to deny to the African an education;

but so few facilities are provided and there is such slow development of schools that the net result is to retard the African in his education and to turn him into a laborer and producer, of more or less intelligence, of crops and material for the profit of the investor.

Conversely, the French have carried to Africa the French idea of the pre-eminence of education in any social plan; they have assumed without argument that education is best for the African and should be pursued mainly along the same lines that education is pursued in France. They propose theoretically to educate an élite class and to let this intelligentsia eventually lead and govern black Africa. This involves political rights and social equality. Practically, of course, the French have fallen far below this ideal.

Between these two extremes comes the pressing present problem: the invasion of a primitive people by organized and developed industry bent on profit and accompanied by missionary effort and religious propaganda. The missionary attitude is a hang-over and throw-back; an illogical urge toward philanthropic effort, under the pattern of a religion, which has largely lost its sanction in Europe and America; and yet out of it has sprung the one effective gift of the white man to the black man, modern education.

Education in modern Africa, outside the French possessions, is the result of missionary effort. Of this there can be no question; and at the same time it is true that missionary effort has been accompanied in all cases by industrial exploitation and in some cases has itself been the instrument for spreading such exploitation and bringing political subjugation to the African tribes.

This can only be explained by remembering what a modern missionary is. He is not usually a man trained in sociology or anthropology. He is apt to be an economic illiterate, naive in the data of the social sciences; assuming that people with customs different from his own are inferior and must be "raised," and that modern capitalism and European family customs are a part of the divine order. Beyond that, he may be a sectarian fanatic or a man of intelligence and sacrifice, pouring out energy and life itself for what he conceives to be the best interests of an alien people.

Christian missions have from the beginning developed systematic educational work in Africa. For the most part, save in French Africa, they still are in charge of the majority of the schools. The colonial governments tardily but increasingly have come to take up the burden of education. Of course the missions have not confined themselves to education. They have pushed religious propaganda, sometimes to a hurtful degree; they have interfered in native family life and tradition, sometimes beneficially, but often ignorantly and dogmatically; they have often considered religious conversion of more importance than intelligence and understanding; they have sent out numbers of enthusiastic but ignorant fanatics who have played havoc with native life and European industry.

Ludwig calls attention to the fact that missionary work has been hampered and made hypocritical by the triumph of the machine, which made so many human hands idle and reduced the price of men, and nevertheless, in the use of human labor, white capital never ventured into the open "without a moral rain coat."

In the educational program, the Protestants and Catholics have differed markedly. The Catholics in the Belgian Congo, Uganda and elsewhere have arranged their pattern of education strictly according to the political and economic limits of the state; inculcating peace, submission and contentment; with primary training and training in industry. In French Africa, the Catholics have followed the pattern of the state schools. The Protestants everywhere have usually aimed at an ideal of general intelligence, seeking to advance pupils toward high school and even college and professional training, and encouraging ability and often self-assertion.

The pioneer work of the missions in education and the fact that the government was tardy in helping, gave them a certain independence. The Protestants developed a few colleges like Lovedale in South Africa and Fourah Bay in West Africa; and by insisting on training bright pupils, brought upon themselves the suspicion and enmity of a good many government officials, which persist today in colonies like the Rhodesias, Kenya and parts of West Africa.

We may attempt here a rapid survey of present educational conditions in Africa, realizing that exact statistics are not available, due both to difficulties of distance and reporting, and also to the reticence of colonial governments.

Beginning with the *Union of South Africa,* in 1936 less than thirty per cent of the total native child population of school age was in school; the majority go to school for two or three years and even then not regularly. The inspected schools are reported as hopelessly over-crowded and understaffed and the other schools are of course much worse. The cost of native education of all kinds amounts to $10.25 per student per annum on the average enrollment. The government contribution for white pupils is ten times as large as for natives; or, comparing the white and native population, it is forty times as large. White teachers are paid sixty-three per cent higher wages than natives with the same professional qualifications.

For white children primary education is compulsory and free, including textbooks. The native child has to pay school fees and buy his own books. There is but one native college, Fort Hare, in Cape Colony, which is affiliated with the University of South Africa. This college was started by the native chiefs, who gave fifty thousand dollars in 1907 from the funds of the Transkei Native General Council. The missionaries gave the land. The college opened in 1916, with twenty students. Between 1916 and 1934, it enrolled five hundred and seventy students, and graduated fifty by 1936. It prepares students for degrees in the University of South Africa. It will hereafter train medical assistants from an endowment furnished by the mining companies.

The leading institution, of the Hampton type, is the Lovedale Missionary Institution. It was founded in 1841 by the United Free Church of Scotland and has a teaching staff of about sixty, one-third of whom are Negroes. The attendance is about a thousand, and of these about a hundred are in the high school grades. Its chief work is preparing teachers. Healdtown is also noted for its teacher training. All these are in Cape Province. In Natal is Mariannhill Institute, a Catholic school training in industries and for teachers. It is noted for training artisans and for issuing most of the printed Zulu literature.

The Union of South Africa had, in 1935, 4,419 schools for natives and colored people, with 482,000 pupils. Of these, twenty-six were government schools and the rest mission schools aided by the government.

The Union government formerly gave a grant of three hundred forty thousand pounds sterling plus one-fifth of the annual revenue from direct native taxation, which amounted to two hundred fifty thousand pounds. This has proved insufficient because the native tax has dwindled during the depression. The government has promised in the future two-fifths of the annual income from native taxation, and there is hope that the total budget for the coming year will amount to a million pounds. The annual expenditure per head of native pupils may thus be increased fifty per cent next year; but there is no proposal for making primary education free. There is, of course, a deep difference of opinion as to whether the education of natives should fit them for a caste system or should be designed for acculturation.

If we turn to the separate provinces, we find in the Cape Province, up until the nineties, children of all colors in the country districts attending the same schools. Today color discrimination is the invariable rule. There were, in 1935–37, two thousand five hundred public schools and aided private schools for natives and colored people, employing six thousand five hundred teachers with 280,000 pupils. Among these schools were seventeen industrial schools and twenty-one teacher training schools. These schools cost $4,750,000 while the white schools with 154,000 pupils cost $14,750,000. In Natal in 1936 there were seven hundred native schools and one hundred thirty colored schools conducted or aided by the government. In these schools there were ninety-two thousand pupils whose education cost $1,290,000; thirty thousand European pupils cost $3,150,000.

In the Transvaal in 1936 there were 780 colored schools with ninety-six thousand pupils. There were seven teacher training institutions. These schools cost possibly $1,000,000. The total expense for education, white and native, was $15,000,000. In the Orange Free State in 1935 there were three hundred forty colored schools with thirty-one thousand pupils and nine hundred teachers. There were two teacher training institutions. These schools cost $295,000. White schools with forty-four thousand pupils cost $4,560,000. Native teachers during the depression had their salaries cut substantially, but new appointments of teachers with certificates are now paid at the regular rate.

The protectorates with their limited income and uncertain economic condition have limited school funds. In Swaziland fifty thousand dollars are expended annually for two hundred schools with five thousand pupils. There is a national education fund into which each Swazi pays fifty cents annually. A national school is being constructed out of this fund.

In Basutoland seventy-five per cent of the black children are in 575 schools with a total of seventy-six thousand pupils, of which sixty-nine thousand are in schools aided by the government. The expenditure for these schools was $265,000 in 1935–36. In Bechuanaland there were ninety-one native and two colored schools costing about fifty thousand dollars.

In Northern Rhodesia the schools are predominantly missionary schools with some government aid. Eighty per cent of the children of school age are not in school. There are nineteen missionary societies at work. There were 127,000 native children in school in 1936 at a cost of $250,000. The schools for a thousand whites cost over twice this sum. Education is confined to the primary grades. Little is done for education at the mines. At one mine, a day school had two hundred registered and fifty in attendance. There is no compulsion, of course. The government schools in the towns are not well attended. In one location out of a school population of 960 only fifty-six were in school. There are a few night schools.

There is the usual demand that the education of the natives be practical and industrial, while the natives want education for their children on broader lines. The government does not teach the native much in agriculture, for fear it will keep him away from the mines; the agricultural school at Mazabuda had in 1931 only eight students. The mission schools carry on agricultural work and instruction in the building trades and furniture making; but there is little demand for such crafts, and some of the schools have followed the bright idea of having the people use only native tools in making things for the schools and the huts. There is no mechanical training for work in the mines. The finance commission, on the other hand, has said that one of the greatest handicaps to better industrial education was lack of knowledge of the three R's.

Southern Rhodesia had, in 1935, 100,000 native pupils enrolled and 60,000 in attendance at mission schools aided by the government, costing $285,000. There were also two government schools with four hundred pupils. In these schools were 275 white teachers and 1,800 colored teachers. The ten thousand white children cost the government $1,200,000.

Southern Rhodesia has had some difficulty in facing the problem of native education. In 1919 a system of schools was proposed to apply European knowledge to improving conditions in the native villages. Natives were to be taught how to handle skins, raise food, make furniture and to build. Two such schools were opened in 1920, but money to support them was not appropriated, and there was, of course, at this stage of development, no effective demand for skilled craftsmen. The schools taught agriculture and some building, but in 1924 there was a protest against the training of natives to compete with Europeans. In 1929, it was decided to teach in the schools things that could be used in native villages but which did not call for European implements. Jeanes Fund methods were introduced but the experiment finally broke down. Even the government training school for agricultural demonstrators was about to fail, when a mission school intervened and is now training a few excellent teachers of farming.

In Nyasaland, eighty per cent of the children of school age are receiving no education. There were in 1936 four thousand native schools with 130,000 pupils in attendance. The government appropriation is very small, amounting in 1936 to only $55,000. The missions here have long borne the burden of native education. There are twelve normal schools for training native teachers.

Education in the West African colonies has been dominated by missionary zeal, on the one hand, and on the other by fear on the part of the whites lest partially educated Negroes should increase in number and demand political and economic power. The native demand for thorough higher training has, of course, entailed increased educational expenditure, increased social contact, and inevitable political readjustments with indirectly decreased commercial profit.

It has been difficult, with the counter influence of some of the English, for the educated natives to keep the respect of the mass of natives. The "Divide and Rule" method has been subtly and effectively applied. In the case of the black Bishop Crowther, the whites charged that he did not enforce discipline over the African clergy, and after his death a white bishop with an African suffragan was appointed; Henry Carr, a colored man, has been inspector of schools and assistant Secretary of Native Affairs. He was of unquestionable character and intelligence, but had a good deal of native opposition, encouraged by many of the whites. Among the Yoruba and the Egbas, natives educated in Europe helped to remodel the government and form organizations; African engineers and surveyors were used. The British interfered in many ways and suppressed the Egba leaders, but considerable influence has been retained by educated men in the tribe.

In West Africa there are two outstanding colleges: Fourah Bay College in Sierra Leone, a missionary institution supported by the Church Missionary Society and the Wesleyan Missionary Society; and the government institution in Nigeria, Achimota College, which has but recently gone beyond high school work. Other higher institutions are the Wesleyan boys' high school, and the Church Missionary Society grammar school in Sierra Leone.

There are five missionary schools in Gambia and a special school for children; and the missionaries have furnished secondary schools. The government spent $25,000 for education in 1936 as compared with $45,000 in 1930.

Freetown in Sierra Leone is dominated by the descendants of freed slaves and early became the intellectual center of West Africa, because of Fourah Bay College, established in 1827. This has long been the only institution in West Africa where an African could obtain an education which corresponded with that of an English university. It has been affiliated with Durham University of England since 1876.

In the colony there are fifty primary schools assisted with public funds and one government primary school. There were eight assisted secondary schools. In the protectorate, education lags: there are eight government primary schools and one technical institution. In 1936 there were one hundred eighty missionary primary schools of which eighty received government assistance; five thousand two hundred pupils attended the assisted schools to which the government granted twenty thousand dollars. There is a government school for the sons and nominees of chiefs at Bo. The total expenditure for education by the government was, in 1936, seventy thousand dollars. Many of the educated Negroes from this colony seek clerical employment in other parts of West Africa and in the Belgian Congo.

Nigeria is making much effort to encourage education, but is handicapped by the comparatively small amount of her budget which is available. Medicine and health were stressed, primarily at first for the health of the white officials; but this protection against tropical diseases is gradually being extended to the blacks. Soldiers and crime call for a disproportionately large expenditure. In the northern provinces there is an unfortunate religious division in the schools; thirty-five thousand Mohammedan schools with two hundred thousand pupils are mainly of the usual type: centers of propaganda and rote learning of the Koran. The element of instruction is, however, being increased. There are two teacher-training centers, one secondary government school, and at Katsina a college with fifty-five pupils.

In the southern provinces education is carried on mainly by mission schools aided by government grants. There are 3,250 elementary and middle schools and two teacher-training institutions. There are four government secondary schools and twenty missionary high schools. At Lagos there is a secondary school, King's College, which prepares for the English universities and civil service.

In the whole of Nigeria the government schools are under the direct control of the department of education, aided by the native councils. The budget for 1932 was $30,000,000, out of which $1,240,000 was spent on education; $1,940,000 on medicine and health, and $2,500,000 on police, military and prisons.

The Gold Coast has the best educational system in Africa. A college has been established at Achimota to head the educational system of African teachers. Fifty white English university graduates have been brought in as instructors. The education in the early grades is in the vernacular and in later years English is to be used. Achimota consists of a kindergarten, primary school, secondary school, and eventually it will have a college. The government plans to spend three million dollars in equipment and $250,000 a year in operation expenses. The expense of operation will in time be doubled. It is controlled by a council of sixteen members of whom six are Negroes. In 1935 there were seventeen students taking university courses.

The Gold Coast has done a good deal to train natives in technique. The Public Works Department has courses for engineers and road foremen; postmasters have been trained and women telephone operators. There are black superintendents of police, locomotive engineers and station masters.

There were three hundred eighty assisted schools with fifty thousand pupils and four hundred forty teachers in 1936, and two hundred fifty non-assisted schools. The Basil Mission trained most of the first artisans in the country. Secondary education is in the hands of missionaries. There are two good grammar schools in Cape Coast. Excluding Achimota, the government spent $900,000 on education in 1936.

There is distinct effort being made to discourage West African students from going to England for college and postgraduate work. The desire to go is partially in answer to the criticism that Negroes are not thoroughly trained. On the other hand, their presence in England causes certain social problems in hotels and elsewhere, and especially gives these students a chance to imbibe modern radical thought. This is looked upon as a danger in West Africa and effort is being made to give some local higher education as a substitute.

For instance, Yaba College, established in 1934 in Nigeria, is going to teach medicine; but, as the natives protest, it will not give a full medical course but will train "assistants" who will be allowed to practice on natives. There have been many suspicions as to the grade of work planned at Achimota. The English attribute this attitude of young West Africa to impatience. The Africans reply: "Give us scholarships and let us go to England. We will be as patient and thorough as the whites." In a number of cases this ability has been proven.

Turning to East Africa, we find Kenya fearing the educational and industrial advance of natives in West Africa, and deprecating even what East Africa has grudgingly yielded. The native school population of Kenya is about six hundred thousand, and of these ninety-three thousand are in mission schools and four thousand in government-controlled schools. Less than sixteen per cent of the African school population is receiving any form of education, and only one-half of one per cent reach the upper grades of the primary school. Girls are receiving almost no education. In 1935, Kenya had eighty-two government schools of which twelve were European.

In Kenya fifteen hundred native schools are conducted by missions, of which nine hundred are bush schools. Bush schools do little more than give religious training. The other mission schools include five hundred elementary schools, forty-five primary and two secondary. In 1923, one hundred thousand dollars was spent for African and Arab education in Kenya. In 1937, $392,500 was spent for African education. In 1932 the state spent $415,000 for education of Africans, Indians and Arabs and $245,000 for a few hundred European children. The average annual amount spent on the white child was fourteen dollars and fifty-six cents and on an African, sixteen cents.

Uganda is struggling toward the West African model. There were two hundred seventy thousand children in school in 1936. In 1932 there were 5,353 African schools with 244,227 students, and twenty-one Asiatic schools with nine hundred forty-six pupils. The total cost of education in all schools in 1932 amounted to $357,500. There are three types of native schools: elementary schools with vernacular instruction; secondary schools with instruction in Swahili and English, and Makerere College. Two missionary schools offer finishing courses for the daughters of the upper class Baganda.

Makerere College, a future black university for East Africa, has ten years' work in primary, secondary schools and professional work. There is an attendance of three hundred forty students. It trains natives as medical assistants, agricultural instructors, veterinary demonstrators, land surveyors, etc. There is a government training school at Bukalusa, and, in 1933, there were two secondary schools preparing students for entrance into Makerere. Students of Makerere College obtain entrance certificates for English schools. Parliament may be asked to make this college and affiliated institutions a higher university for East Africa including Kenya, Uganda and Tanganyika.

In the Belgian Congo, we meet a curious case of the co-operation of modern industry and the Catholic Church. Belgian industry aims at peace, cheap labor of all grades, and profit for investors. The Catholic Church, bowing to the will of the state, proposes to proselyte among the natives and give them such training as will best carry out the object of the state and no more. The standard of education in the Belgian Congo is lower than in British West Africa. Congolese are not allowed to leave the country for studying abroad. Those who leave the Congo as seamen or servants and stay abroad more than six months are not allowed to return.

The Catholic missions lay less stress on literary subjects and concentrate on the craft demand. The aim of the large Belgian corporation is to build up a cheap labor force and train it in skill. In Elizabethville, for instance, there is a school which trains tailors, dressmakers, carpenters, printers, leather workers, blacksmiths, and bricklayers. In Katanga there is a school for locomotive engineers, railway repairing and mechanics.

The government declares that it is its policy to assist the native to rise as high as he can and as rapidly, but as a matter of fact he is not allowed higher training and does not get far beyond the semi-skilled occupations. Usually Congo education goes only to the third grade. The system has been put almost entirely under the domination of prevailing capitalism so that education is not primarily for intelligence but for practical work. Certain employers have established hygienic villages and schools. Congo natives, however, are not encouraged in too great aspiration and assumption. There is not a single native black leader in the Congo educated in modern ways.

The Protestant missions have tried to do more and higher work and are consequently pretty severely restricted. Health needs, however, have brought an attempt to train medical assistants which may force the imparting of some higher training, and perhaps the eventual training of full-fledged physicians.

In the Belgian Congo, in 1937, there were two thousand five hundred Catholic missionaries and seven hundred twenty-five Protestants. They co-operate with the government and carry on ten state schools with five thousand three hundred pupils and 4,156 subsidized schools with two hundred thousand pupils. There are state schools for boys at eight centers and one for girls. Eight schools are training native dispensers and one school medical assistants, three schools are for sanitary inspectors and there are several schools for midwives. In 1937 the government grant to mission schools amounted to eleven million francs and the total expenditure was nineteen million francs.

"When the Portuguese colonized, they built churches; when the British colonized, they built trading stations; when the French colonized, they built schools."[1] In 1903 there were seventy schools and two thousand five hundred students in French West Africa; in 1925 there were three hundred seventy schools and thirty thousand students; in 1935–36, there were four hundred and seventy schools and sixty-seven thousand pupils.

In 1935–36 there were two hundred ninety preparatory and elementary schools with 26,606 pupils; seventy-five country schools with 21,805 pupils; twenty urban schools with 5,987 pupils; seven higher primary schools with six hundred four pupils; nine technical schools with four hundred thirty-seven pupils; two lyceums with seven hundred thirty pupils; sixty-nine private schools with 11,429 pupils. These figures do not include the five thousand and more Koranic schools.

Private schools in French West Africa are conducted according to special decrees, by French Catholic and Protestant organizations. In 1934, there were fifty-seven schools for boys with 6,416 pupils; seventeen schools for girls with 3,051 pupils; a total of seventy-four schools and 9,467 pupils.

The number of children of school age in French West Africa is about 1,360,000. There is, therefore, approximately one child in school for every twenty children of school age, or nearly five per cent. Outside of new buildings, there were appropriated for education in French West Africa twenty-four million francs in 1934.

The avowed object of the French is diametrically opposed to the objects, expressed or implied, of the English, Dutch, Belgians, Germans or even Portuguese in Africa. It is to train a black élite by means of a thorough French system of education and eventually to bind these people to the French state by giving them every political, civil and social privilege. This is looked upon by the French as the only way to raise the status of the native population. It has produced much ill feeling in European colonial circles against the French and the Negroes of French Africa are the envy of other colonial Negroes.

Despite this program clearly laid down and to an increasing extent followed, the actual number of educated French Africans is still small, and therefore France has not yet to any extent faced the innumerable and baffling problems of the rise of a backward people to equality with a dominant culture group; however, her West Indian experience is of value.

There are today two systems of education in French West Africa, representing two educational problems: first a European system for European and African children who are already French in culture. The European system came first and is best exemplified in Senegal. It consists of infant schools, primary schools, secondary schools and lycée schools. These schools are identical with corresponding schools in France.

European schools provide an education specially designed for the training of Europeans and Africans to play their part later on in the French economy. Secondly, for Africans who do not know French culture, there is an African system. African schools provide an education specially designed for participation in African life, but envisage eventual integration of native life in French culture. There is no color bar in either set of schools.

The system of African schools includes: first, popular schools; second, technical schools including schools for the special needs of particular areas; third, higher schools. Each of these three groups may be divided into rural and urban schools. These three groups of schools are loosely connected into an educational ladder by means of which pupils pass from one group to a higher group; but such promotion is incidental and not the aim of a given school. Each school gives complete training for pupils who will receive no further education. Only selected children of promise may take the competitive promotion examinations.

In the African popular schools there are three stages: an initiation stage; an elementary stage; and a lower primary stage. The initiation schools are held in thatched buildings and even tents, with one teacher in charge; they initiate the children into learning spoken French and raising their standards of living. The course is approximately two years. In the main country stations, and always in the cities, there is a fully developed elementary school, including initiation and substandard classes and two year standard classes. In the earlier classes of the initiation elementary schools, local vernacular is used for instruction in certain subjects, but this is limited. The efficiency and equipment of these initiation and elementary schools were formerly low and are in many cases still, but they are steadily being rebuilt and reorganized. They teach animal husbandry and stock farming and run a school co-operative with sale of produce. The co-operative is the property of the pupils.

In gold-mining areas, blacksmithing and jewelry-making are taught instead of farming; in the fishing areas, fish nets and canoes are built. In each case the needs of the local community are studied and the instruction planned accordingly. In 1934, there were two hundred sixty-five government village schools and thirteen government urban schools of the initiation and elementary type, providing for 22,289 pupils. In addition to these there were a large number of mission bush schools.

There are seventy-five regional schools at important government stations that carry African education on two years farther. The studies include history, geography, hygiene and arithmetic. In the larger commercial centers are city primary schools with an academic curriculum.

There are special craft institutions for teaching European crafts, planned to articulate African and European technique. There were adult courses with ten thousand students in 1934 and the training of teachers is provided for in practice schools. There is effort to develop vigorous local economic units by groups of technical schools; some preparing pupils for the needs of village life; others training artisans for industrial areas, and a third group training skilled workers for government departments and factories. In Moslem areas there are four special Mohammedan schools to train leaders and chiefs, with an attendance of about four hundred.

The most nearly complete system of French schools centers in Senegal and was begun in 1816. Primary education begins in the village schools. The best students of the preparatory school below the age of thirteen are sent to the elementary schools of which there are a large number in each colony. The third school is the regional school at the capital of the colony with three grades. If the student passes after four years' work he is given a certificate to enter the higher primary school at the capital.

At the capital of each of the colonies there are higher primary schools. Entrance to these schools is by scholarships awarded by competition to the best boys from the regional schools. Board and lodging are free and sometimes pocket money is given. The staff is composed of university men of high standing.

In these schools there are special technical departments which provide for artisan training in the postal and telegraphic service, the survey department, the public work department, the railways and other government or commercial service. Then there is an academic division which provides a local education for those who purpose to be government clerks or enter commercial firms or compete for scholarships which will fit them for careers in the learned professions.

Each year, the best pupils from the academic departments of higher primary schools compete in a federal examination for the selection of candidates for the State African Secondary School, which is the William Ponty and Faidherbe School at Dakar. Fifty to eighty boys are selected each year. About one-half of these are trained as teachers and the other half for medicine, veterinary work and engineering. The course is four years and the pupils are on graduation from twenty to twenty-two years of age. Work in this school is similar to the kind of work covered in secondary schools in Europe, but the students are taught with special reference to Africa. "The graduate of the William Ponty School is so fine a product that the education there given seems a complete vindication of French educational theory and practice in Africa."[2]

"In 1935 the William Ponty School admitted seventy-two new pupils; its three departments turned out forty teachers, thirty-five pupils gained the certificate in administration, and twenty-nine passed to the Medical and Veterinary schools. The two Secondary schools at Dakar and St. Louis number six hundred twenty-two pupils."[3]

The government reported recently: "We are about to embark on the transfer of the William Ponty School to Sébikotane, where it will be not only the leading school in French West Africa, but a kind of model city, a centre of French higher education. Lastly, I have decided on the establishment of a French Institute for Africa which, in association with the French West Africa Museum and the Historical Archives Department, shall be at once the centre of those higher studies that must be given a place in a great country such as our Federation and the foundation of all African research and all understanding of African life and institution."[4]

Parallel to the Ponty school are schools of marine engineering to train for the naval service, veterinary schools for government service and a medical school at Dakar, where sixty pupils selected in open competition from the Ponty School are given a five year course as medical assistants. "Walking round these wards as we did with the students, and listening to each student in turn discussing his various cases, it was difficult to realize that we were in Africa at all. In every way the students were like their brethren in Europe, keen, enthusiastic, and interested in each new problem as it was dicussed."[5]

In Portuguese Guinea there are nine elementary and two professional schools. In Angola there are seventy primary schools, three secondary schools, including a central college at Loanda, and a national college at Lubango. There are also some professional schools. In Mozambique there were, in 1932, five hundred schools with six hundred seventy teachers and six thousand five hundred pupils. Of the latter, two thousand five hundred were mulattoes and whites. The schools include a central high school; fifty elementary schools; one hundred forty intermediate schools; two hundred ninety missionary schools, and forty professional schools; also there are seventy schools administered by the Mozambique company.

Portuguese colonial law tries to compel the employer to provide teachers for any children on his estate and some private employers maintain schools. At one mission of Angola, American Negro missionaries have been carrying on agriculture and education for ten years. The life of the district has been improved, the crop yield raised and live stock increased in number; the native farmers have become economically independent.

In the Anglo-Egyptian Sudan the education of the blacks has been pushed by the English to offset Egyptian influence and rule. Taking advantage of the long memory which the Sudanese have of Egyptian misrule, the English have proceeded to train the blacks as civil servants, judges and soldiers. If Egyptians instead of Sudanese should occupy these positions, the Sudan would easily and naturally revert to Egyptian rule.

In the northern Sudan, the government controls education. There is Gordon Memorial College, a secondary school, with three hundred pupils; and several training schools for the civil service. There are eleven intermediate schools and ninety-eight elementary schools for boys and twenty-eight for girls. Also there are thirty-four non-government schools with five thousand five hundred pupils and six hundred Koranic schools. In the southern part there are only mission schools with government subsidies; there is no higher or secondary education.

Turning to the mandated areas: In German East Africa, now Tanganyika, eighty per cent of the African children of school age are receiving no education. There were in 1936 two schools for whites with seven hundred sixty-two pupils; fifty-three Indian schools with 4,038 pupils; eighty-one government native schools with 8,105 pupils; also one hundred ninety-one aided mission schools with 19,785 pupils. Beside this are 4,643 mission schools with 197,951 pupils which do not receive government aid. The total estimated expenditure for education (1936) was four hundred thirty-five thousand dollars.

In Southwest Africa there were, in 1935, sixty government white schools with four thousand seven hundred pupils and sixty private white schools with eight hundred seventy-six pupils. The education of natives is carried on in the mission schools. There were seventy-eight government-aided mission schools with 4,608 pupils. White pupils cost $98 a head; Negro pupils $2.81.

The latest figures on schools in black Africa give the enrollment as 3,375,000; of these 1,240,000 are in schools maintained by the government or aided. In the number of pupils in school the colonies rank as follows: Belgian Congo 460,000; Nigeria 416,000, if we include 200,000 in the Koran schools; in the Belgian mandate, Ruanda-Urundi, 220,000; in Uganda 273,000; in Tanganyika 225,000; in Nyasaland 194,000; in the Cape Colony 176,000; in the Transvaal 115,000; in Northern Rhodesia 110,000; in Southern Rhodesia 104,000; in Kenya 100,000; in the French Cameroons 97,000; in Natal 87,000; in Basutoland 73,000; in the Gold Coast 63,000.

The Government expenditure per head for all African children in schools varies as follows: Gold Coast $15.20; Cape Colony $11; French Equatorial Africa $10.28; Nigeria $5.29; Kenya $4; Southern Rhodesia $3.43; Basutoland $2.79; Tanganyika $1.39; Uganda $1.31; Northern Rhodesia $1.12; Nyasaland $0.45. There are no separate figures for French West Africa although the per capita expenditure is high there; and also none for the Belgian Congo where the expenditure is low.

Allied with education as indices of social service for the natives of Africa come public health, the preservation of animal life, the regulation of liquor and similar matters. The factual data covering these matters are not at present full enough to call for extended treatment, but a word may be added concerning health.

The Union of South Africa has four hundred and two hospitals and nursing homes for the two million whites and one hundred and forty-two for the seven and a half million colored and black. Most of these are maintained by mines and factories. In the protectorates there are fifteen government hospitals. In the sixteen hospitals of Southern Rhodesia both races are provided for separately. Northern Rhodesia has seven hospitals for ten thousand whites and thirty hospitals and dispensaries for 1,300,000 natives. In Nyasaland two thousand Europeans have two hospitals while the million and a half natives have fifteen hospitals and ninety-three dispensaries. In Tanganyika the four million natives have fifty hospitals and three hundred dispensaries. In Kenya the three million natives have thirty-five hospitals. Uganda furnishes thirty-four hospital beds for its two thousand whites, fifty-six beds for fifteen thousand Asiatics and 1,273 for three and a half million natives. In Nigeria there are twelve hospitals for the few thousand whites and fifty-seven for twenty million natives. Fourteen of the medical staff are Negro physicians trained in Europe. French West Africa has eleven government hospitals with beds for 788 whites and 5,484 Africans. The white population is twenty-five thousand and the native population fifteen million, but the color line is not strictly drawn in the white hospitals. French Equatorial Africa has five hospitals and ninety-eight dispensaries and health centers. The Belgian Congo has twenty-five hospitals for twenty thousand Europeans and seventy for ten million natives.

In defense of present conditions it may, of course, be argued that the need to protect the health of whites was more immediate and the native more immune to disease. Nevertheless, here still lurks the idea that the primary goal of African administration is the European; and this is confirmed when one realizes the extraordinary fact that the offer of the Rockefeller Foundation of New York of fifty-six thousand pounds sterling to the Union of South Africa to build a medical college for the Bantu was refused by Prime Minister Hertzog. There are only eight black doctors in all South Africa. Subsequently industry came to the rescue and the Transvaal Chamber of Mines in 1935 made a grant of $375,000 for educating native medical aids. This course will be given at Fort Hare native college and it is expected that the first graduates will be available in 1940. There is no provision yet for a full medical course.

In the Belgian Congo, health teaching and hospitalization have made a good record, but perhaps the most advanced medical service in Africa is in Uganda, with twenty-three government hospitals for the natives, ten for the Asiatics and four for Europeans, beside seven hospitals under missionary control. To a very great extent the problem of Africa is a problem of health in the midst of malaria, sleeping sickness and a multitude of other tropical diseases. As Marshall Lyautey has said: "La seule excuse pour la colonisation, c'est le médecin."

NOTES

1. Mumford and Orde-Browne, *Africans Learn to be French*, p. 50.
2. *Africans Learn to be French*, p. 47.
3. *Ibid.*, p. 95.
4. *Ibid.*, p. 96.
5. *Ibid.*, p. 48.

CHAPTER XVI

♦

The Future of World Democracy

What is to be the future relation of the Negro peoples to the rest of the world? The visitor from Altruria might see here no peculiar problem. He would expect black folk to develop along the lines of other human races, with perhaps new and interesting differences and variations. In Africa its economic and political development would eventually equal or outrun the ancient glories of Egypt, Ethiopia, and Yoruba; overseas the West Indies would become a new-world Africa, built in the very pathway of the new highways of commerce between East and West—the real sea route to India; in South America a new people mingled of all the chief stocks of men would give the world a new art and social science; while in the United States, a large part of its citizenship (showing for perhaps centuries their dark descent, but nevertheless equal sharers in and contributors to the civilization of the West) would be the descendants of the wretched victims of the seventeenth, eighteenth, and nineteenth century slave trade.

This natural assumption of a stranger finds lodging, however, in the minds of few present-day thinkers. On the contrary, such an outcome is usually dismissed summarily. Most persons have accepted that tacit but clear modern philosophy which has assigned to the white race alone the hegemony of the world and assumed that other races, and particularly the Negro race, will either be content to serve the interests of the whites or die out before their all-conquering march. This philosophy is the child of the African slave trade and of the industrial expansion of Europe during the nineteenth century.

Not only the vast majority of white folk, but Chinese, Indians and Negroes themselves have been so excited, oppressed, and suppressed by current white civilization that they think and judge everything by its terms. They have no norms that are not set in the nineteenth and twentieth centuries. They can conceive of no future world which is not dominated by present white nations and thoroughly shot through with their ideals, their method of government, their economic organization, their literature and their art. To broach before such persons any suggestion of radical change, any idea of intrusion, physical or spiritual, on the part of alien races into this white heaven, is to bring down upon one's devoted head the most tremendous abuse and contempt.

In this way the preservation of the color bar has been erected into a cardinal principle of modern civilization. Its preservation is threatened today principally by Japan; then by India; then by the Negroes of the United States and West Africa. Japan has attacked the legend of invincible Europe and of a white race of unapproachable ability. Nothing that Europe and Europeans have done, but Japan is doing nearly as well and sometimes better.

On a less striking scale and with less organization, India is beginning to pose similar problems, and despite century-long disunity through caste, religion and domination by foreign powers, there is arising so fixed a determination to build an autonomous Indian state which will affect a vast change in the relation of white and colored people in Asia, that it seems not only possible but probable within the next century.

Leaving aside similar but less obvious movements in black Africa and America, let us turn for a moment to a consideration of the way in which this extraordinary problem of the color line has arisen in an age which has seen the development of liberalism and democracy in the world. Liberalism, freedom of thought and action, revolt against dogma, effort to raise standards of living, came to Europe in the sixteenth and seventeenth centuries. Ideals of perfect states arose, and coincident with all this, and tremendous in its distorting influence, came the African slave trade.

For four hundred years, labor in Europe had been a matter of serfs and souls; souls to be saved and serfs as an integral part of the farming estate, or as city artisans. This now has changed and the two aspects of labor have been torn apart. Labor became a commodity in a new world; commerce added to the exchange of inanimate goods, the bodies of men whose value lay in their labor. The black African slave trade became an immensely profitable institution because the labor could be applied on an almost endless mass of fertile land. Nor was that all. This land could and did produce a mass of goods, and new goods in the sense that they were not simply luxuries demanded by the rich but necessities wanted in increasing amounts by the poor. Thus there arose and made itself manifest, by the middle of the eighteenth century, the new method of increasing income based on the buying and selling of labor as a commodity. The profit which arose therefrom furnished the first great accumulations of capital goods and was the incentive back of the new invention and technique which startled the world between 1738 and 1830. There were the cotton gin, the steam engine, the flying shuttle, the power loom, and the beginnings of our knowledge of electricity. These things were not the cause of the Industrial Revolution; they were the result of the African slave trade and of the new crops of cotton, tobacco, rice, sugar, potatoes, indigo, and what not. A new attitude toward labor was being evolved at the same time that the new democracy was growing.

The slave trade from the fifteenth through the seventeenth century flowed westward as a small, quiet but deepening stream of black labor. It rose to a flood in the eighteenth century, eventually overflowing the market with slaves, decreasing the profits of slavery, increasing the revolt of slaves, revealing the cruelty of this new slavery and giving philanthropy a chance to check it.

For fifty years, beginning with the abolition of the English slave trade and ending with the abolition of slavery in the United States, democracy developed in Europe and the United States in the conscious effort of the laboring classes to equalize income and share in the freedom and power that had come to the new capitalists from the slave trade. But the continuing slavery in America had done something to the world. It had quickened the demand of labor for a voice not only in government but in industry, and at the same time it had made the world regard labor as a saleable commodity. It divided humanity into owners and goods, it made men callous to the sufferings of white men as well as black; to the poverty of white labor, because it was looked upon not as unfortunate and oppressed but inferior and incapable; and with this class of the incapable and inferior were bracketed all members of the darker races.

Henceforth the white labor movement, beginning as mass emancipation, became subtly transformed so as to enable certain individuals and groups of laborers to escape from their poverty and become either better paid laborers or preferably employers and owners. Even in their ranks, the attitude toward the lowest class of labor and toward colored labor was an attitude of indifference and contempt. The dream of new America came to be not the uplift of labor, but the transmutation of poor white laborers into rich employers, with the inevitable residue of the poor white and black eternally at the bottom. In time men became used to the idea that this submerged mass should form not a tenth, but nine-tenths of all men.

It was in vain that the socialists and communists of the latter part of the nineteenth century sought to stress the plight of labor as such. They were appealing to people who had learned for centuries to despise human beings and the utmost that they could accomplish in solidarity of labor action was a more or less faint vision of a higher destiny for some white laborers. Even to this day, the feeling among the masses of white laborers in Europe and America is that the industrial democracy toward which they are striving holds no goal or destiny for the laborers of Asia and Africa.

On the other hand, these dark laborers have become more and more bound up in the same industrial process with white labor. They are employed by the same capital. They come more or less into competition for the kinds of work which they do; their wages can be kept at vastly different levels, but the enhanced profit from this low black wage goes only in part to white labor, even in South Africa, where fear and race hate make an unusual and temporary situation; for the most part, cheap colored labor enhances the power of owners and employers over white labor.

The examination, therefore, of the problems of democracy includes not simply Europe but black Europe, that is, Europe in Africa; European commerce and industry in so far as it involves African materials; and African labor in so far as these materials are produced and consumed in a common world economy by laborers who are increasingly in competition.

In the midst of a critical era following World War and world-wide industrial dislocation, an examination of the future of the hard-won fruits of democratic government must involve the relation of white democracy to the colored peoples of the world. It will not be amiss then to examine the basic thought of democracy in two leading countries which are today not only leaders in democratic development but also, and in curious contradiction, in colonial expansion.

Democracy in England is limited in the matters to which it may be applied. In many of the most important matters of modern life, there is little democratic control; for instance, in the determination of the kind of work which men do; in decisions as to the sort and quantity of goods produced and the way in which goods and services are distributed among consumers; in the ownership of property and division of power based on income.

Yet these matters have to do with the primary interests of life. To be sure the English voter may approach these subjects; in matters of minimum limits to wages; in certain conditions of labor; and in relief for unemployment and extreme poverty. He may, through the income tax, redistribute income to some extent. But in the main concerns of industry and income, he has no voice. Moreover, England rules more or less completely over vast numbers of colored laborers; but the English voter has but little opportunity to determine or even to know the methods and objects of this rule.

In most of these matters, outside the present purview of English democracy, it is still said that they are in the realm of private judgment and initiative; yet they touch the most important and vital interests of all Englishmen and are matters today especially of the greatest public concern. That they may come under the control of the voters eventually, no Englishman could deny. But the power to decide what and when democracy in England shall rule lies today outside democracy entirely, and in the hands of a powerful oligarchy. This oligarchy was long an aristocracy of birth, whose power rested on land and privilege. By slow and momentous change, this basis of power became invested capital, with its opportunity for education and social training.

The present British oligarchy is perhaps the most remarkable in the world. It is rich and educated, and it is saved from degeneracy and inbreeding by constant recruiting of ability from all ranks of life in England, its colonies and dependencies, and even from foreign lands. This oligarchy controls democracy and limits its scope.

A largely unexpressed but central thesis of English rule is the conviction that ability, while inherent in the English ruling class, is, outside that class, largely accidental and a sport of nature. This deep-seated belief assumes that present methods of education and opportunity are securing for England a fair maximum of ability, while, in all probability, it is securing a dangerous minimum and thus curtailing and killing the growth of democracy at its very source. Even in England and the white British dominions, the ability and capability of mankind have not begun to be exploited. Today it is largely accident that a Ramsay MacDonald or a Keir Hardie escape jail, asylum or dumb obscurity. A system of broad education for children and adults, an increasing attempt to give wider and wider masses of men the same opportunity to develop strength and ability as is now reserved for the darlings of the gods and a few sports of fate, would in time widen the basis of democracy in England, or rather make it feasible so to broaden the limits of democratic control as to bring under its purview the whole realm of work and wage, wealth and income, production and distribution as well as the welfare of the five hundred million persons whom Great Britain rules today chiefly for the private profit of the English ruling class. Lack of faith in the possibilities of its people—English and white, as well as yellow, brown and black, is the danger of British Democracy.

But it is not mere negative lack of faith in men that limits British democracy—it is the positive demand for income and large income on the part of the English ruling class. Their high scale of expenditure is well-known and world famous. The so-called necessary expense for "comfort" on their part requires for an English family as much in a week as would support a Chinese peasant a year. The ordinary ideal of a well-to-do Englishman is to have an assured income which relieves him of all necessity for work and lets him follow Art or Politics or the life of leisure with assurance; with no temptation of petty graft or bribery, and with liberty to cultivate the amenities of human intercourse.

Thus the British "gentleman" is a type and ideal of what real existence may mean. On his shoulders rest the maintenance of certain standards of conduct and customs of living, and that elusive, but real thing called "sportsmanship." But all this requires income and regular and certain income in large sums. This has led in the past to slavery and the slave trade, and the Industrial Revolution; and still leads to a ruthless exploiting of large masses of English labor for profit.

When and as the factory legislation and the increasing political power of labor, together with the diminishing returns of investment in England, brought down this rate of profit or threatened to, England turned to forced labor in Africa and coolie labor in Asia and the South Seas. Cheap colored labor thus gradually displaced white English labor, and the British Empire becomes mainly a matter of profitable investment. English labor was long the skilled manipulator of raw material raised by blacks and yellows, until gradually, in China and Japan, colored labor began to enter skilled manufacture and to throw white labor out of employment or reduce their wage.

Brown India and black Africa will eventually follow the same path, under the pressure of the English oligarchy itself and of other peoples, for income based on present industrial control. This prospect arouses labor unrest in England, and the oligarchy must allay it at any cost. It is accepting today a staggering burden of taxation, probably heavier than in any other civilized land, and using the income for doles and other temporary expedients, so as to avoid admitting a further encroachment of democratic control over industry and income.

It is all the easier for England to accomplish this, because the English middle class and the English laborers agree with the ruling class in the fear of allowing primitive and half-civilized peoples and peoples with non-European types of culture, to act and think for themselves and share in their own government. Missionary Christianity and liberalism sought to envisage such a program, but their aims were turned away and their acts made tools of exploitation and despotism by imperial industry. This was made easy not only by the power of ownership, but also by the doubts of liberals and philanthropists themselves. They continued to regard the heathen as a human liability for whom they were sorry. They could not dream of the mass of humanity as a source of power, ability, genius, and enlightening experience. English science in the hands of Galton and Pearson and their ilk made English aristocracy rulers by divine right. The vast possibility of a pool of human knowledge as wide as the living world never

arrested their attention. They could not imagine that the freedom and development of all men would make in time a world Renaissance, beside which the little
European Renaissance would seem small and petty; that art and science could
look forward to greater and more wonderful conquests, if they contemplated
using the ability of all the world and not simply a narrow section.

Even the possibility of any such world vision had to be smashed in its very
beginning by those satisfied by present conditions. Only for a moment, in the
United States of America in 1867, when four million black slaves had enfranchisement and the possibility of economic power added to their legal freedom,
did the world trend set toward universal democratic development regardless of
race and color. Organized industry girded its loins. It swiftly nullified the Negro
vote. It quickly warned Europe with terrible fiction concerning American
Reconstruction. And in the meantime in both America and Europe capital set its
house in order for a new conquest of the world.

Much that is true of England in the working of democracy is also true of
France, but there are certain striking differences. Intellectual freedom of the
French is unparalleled in the modern world, and draws the criticism and envy
of those groups and nations which do not dare to let men think. There is consequently in French intellectual life an anarchy and enthusiasm, a variety and
inventiveness which would spell continual renaissance and undying renewal of
life, were it not for one thing which is the tragedy of France—and that is war.
For a thousand years France has been baptized in blood. Hardly an effort at culture, upbuilding, government by dictator, aristocracy or democracy has been
attempted but it has been frustrated, spoiled, or misdirected by mass murder;
by wars, civil and foreign, wars of aggression and defense.

These two things: intelligence and intellectual freedom on the one hand, and
war on the other, explain France more than anything else; explain a spiritual
expansion toward a universal soul, handicapped by a defense mechanism which
makes the individual Frenchman not only thrifty, greedy, and suspicious, but
the perfect victim of an organization of wealth and industry unsurpassed in the
modern world for power, cunning, and ruthless will to rule. French industry
knows no national boundaries and no national patriotism. It is aligned with
German industry, Russian, and Italian; and its exploitation of Africa has at times
and in certain areas been unsurpassed in English Kenya or the Belgian Congo.
All of the latest paraphernalia of organized industry for securing its power originated or was perfected in France: the Trust and the Cartel; arranged and purchased Publicity; graft and widespread bribery; ownership of the public press
and ownership of government officials; not to speak of corporations for every
human activity encircling the world.

The French laboring classes have led labor thought in the world and still do.
It was by no accident that Karl Marx sought sanctuary in France and incubated
there his "Communist Manifesto." It is natural that all socialist thought and
movement should have been started and developed in France. French labor has
never completely envisaged the color bar to which English labor is so willingly
nailed. The labor vote in France has been the backbone of French democracy; and
yet in the endeavor of the mass of Frenchmen to exercise democratic control

upon French policies and to attack the very centers and main depositories of human power today, that is, the direction of industry, the production of wealth and its distribution—these efforts have come repeatedly to naught.

This weakness of French democracy has come from two facts: first, the Revolution made the French peasant a small, jealous reactionary landholder instead of forcing him into a group with interests bound up in a national land patrimony; secondly, the French industrial worker, despite his trade unions, his socialistic and even communistic idealogy, has not been able to cope with organized industrial control. He has forced the political leaders further to the left than in any modern country save Russia, but whenever, by political force, labor has time and time again threatened political revolution, it has been held back by the threat of war, which was not simply possible but actual.

The French laborer has had to fight organized industry in England, Germany and Austria, leading against France the very laborers to whom France had given ideals of European solidarity; and, against this onslaught, French labor in modern times has had to accept the leadership of organized ability furnished by French industry and has had to pay its price, which was lip service to socialism, and industry organized for war, and exploitation for the sake of private profit.

Moreover, the paradox of French democracy is to produce not only the strife and difference of opinion which arise from intelligence and are seen in the parliamentary blocs which rightly displace artificial attempts to align thought in two or even three parties, but also by its very efforts at enlightenment and education, to evoke out of the educated masses, a leadership which misleads them. Thus French labor has educated its children to furnish the most efficient leaders for French capital, and correspondingly to weaken the labor masses and strengthen industrial forces.

What now is going to happen, not only to Africans but to Europeans when such democratic organization is made the master of African industry and development? We need not stop here to evaluate the influence of democracy in Belgium, Holland and Portugal; in Scandinavia, Russia and the United States. The imagination of Belgium is so overwhelmed with its immense colonial wealth that no inner democracy can soon change it. The black Congo supports and enriches Belgium. Holland has allowed her democracy to yield in her colonial empire to an increased division of wealth with colored labor and to a vision of still larger future increase; but she is still fattening on her colonies and her future course depends on world democracy. Scandinavia is prosperous through her alliance with colonial powers and fascist governments. She buys of them and sells to them at a profit and divides that profit more equitably among her laboring classes than most democracies; but she does not investigate the ultimate sources of that profit or greatly care. Russia has made gestures toward colored labor, but the unfortunate reaction of Chinese leadership toward European capitalism and the still more unfortunate triumph of state capitalism in Japan, with stern repression of mass control, has left Russia helpless and almost complacent in the face of the problem of the darker workers of the world.

In America we have a democracy which has almost surrendered not simply to the rule of wealth, but to the domination of race prejudice. There are democratic forces at work here, but they are largely in such opposition as to be self-destroying. You cannot have a growing labor movement and increased democratic control of industry in New England and the Middle West coincident with farm serfdom and pauperized labor in the South. And it is the South today that through its rotten boroughs dominates not only the nation but even the liberal element of the nation. The burden of democracy rests, therefore, on Europe and on Europe in Africa.

Colonial imperialism in Europe includes not simply democratic England and France but also fascist Italy and, in prospect, Hitler's Germany. These states make no bones nor excuse for their colonial objects. Germany bases her whole state philosophy on the domination, not only of white people over colored people, but of certain strains of white blood over all others; and her demand for restoration of her colonies is a demand for cheap forced labor and political and economic domination. There are indications that this demand will be granted at least in part by England and France, in return for a restoration of peaceful world conditions which will allow industry to organize for further profit in Africa and Asia.

This is proved by the case of Italy and Ethiopia. The Negus of Abyssinia chose to put his energy into modernizing and organizing his state, rather than into war and defense, and he followed in this matter the advice and criticism of the best thought of Europe and America. Despite this and at the demand of Italy for increased material resources and cheap black labor, both France and England yielded or gave half-hearted opposition. Abyssinia fell before an onslaught carefully prepared and known to the world long before actual hostilities, and we are now facing the veiled and hidden process by which two thousand years of independence of a primitive people is by force and European capital going to be subjected to a systematic exploitation for the profit of Italy. This adds to the burden of European democracy in Africa.

How far can white Europe continue to dominate black Africa for its own selfish ends? When one thinks of any possible trial of strength in Africa, it is natural for white Europe to place its present faith on the strength of its technical superiority in war as shown so strikingly by Italy in Ethiopia. On the other hand, there are certain things to remember: so far as Africa has been conquered by white Europe, this has been mainly by means of black soldiers, and Africa is held in subordination today by black troops. This could be partially ignored before the World War, but even then Great Britain had the King's African Rifles in British East Africa, the West African Frontier Force in British West Africa; and she conquered the Sudan and East Africa with black troops. The Germans in East Africa and the Cameroons had about eight thousand native military and police. In French Africa there were thirty thousand native troops and police. The Portuguese, Italians and Spanish depended on Negro guards and police, and Leopold organized and dominated the Congo by putting despotic power in the hands of the wilder tribes with a twelve year military service.

During the World War the need of Negro troops was evident; not only were Sudanese troops used in Asia and Asia Minor, but the German colonies of Tanganyika, Cameroons and Togoland were conquered by black troops fighting against black troops. Hundreds of thousands of American Negroes and West

Indian Negroes took part in the war, and ten thousand soldiers and ten thousand porters were sent from British West Africa to the East African campaign. In Kenya the King's African Rifles was expanded to over twenty thousand men and over one hundred thousand natives in Nyasaland were employed as soldiers and porters. The Germans in East Africa recruited eleven thousand six hundred natives and during the first year of the war seventy thousand black troops were raised in French West Africa. By 1918 black Africa had furnished France six hundred and eighty thousand soldiers and two hundred thirty-eight thousand laborers or nine hundred and eighteen thousand men in all. General Smuts made his celebrated pronouncement in 1917:

"We have seen, what we have never known before, what enormously valuable military material lay in the Black Continent. You are aware of the great German scheme which existed before the war, and which no doubt is still in the background of many minds in Germany, of creating a great Central African Empire which would embrace not only the Cameroons and East Africa, but also the Portuguese Colonies and the Congo—an extensive area which would have a very large population and would not only be one of the most valuable tropical parts of the world, but in which it would be possible to train one of the most powerful black armies of the world. We were not aware of the great military value of the natives until this war. This war has been an eye-opener in many new directions. It will be a serious question for the statesmen of the Empire and Europe, whether they are going to allow a state of affairs like that to be possible, and to become a menace, not only to Africa, but perhaps to Europe itself."[1]

After the war, the French frankly announced their policy of incorporating black men in their army. That is the physical force which today buttresses and protects the French nation. French West African troops are divided into twenty regiments of two thousand each and these are stationed in French Algiers and Morocco and in Syria as well as in Europe. "Through the aid of Senegalese troops, France built up and today holds an empire which probably never would have been won by European soldiers."

With the modern emphasis on history, it is easy to forget that Africa, without mention of her own civil strife, has been literally bathed in blood at the behest of Europe. Not only was there the decimation due to the African slave trade, but there were eleven Zulu wars in South Africa from 1659 to 1893; there were seven wars of the English against Ashanti; there were the wars around Benin and the French war in Dahomey and other parts of West Africa; there was the English attack on Ethiopia and in the Sudan and the rise of the Madhi; there were repeated rebellions as the English and Germans entered East Africa, to say nothing of the fights in Egypt, Tunis, Algiers and Morocco, and the sporadic rebellions in French Equatorial Africa, the Belgian Congo and German Southwest Africa. There was the Italian slaughter in Tripoli, Eritrea and Abyssinia.

There is nothing in economic history that quite parallels the mass suicide of the Ama Xosa. Between the Charge of the Light Brigade and the Relief of Lucknow, a prophet rose in South Africa and appealed with every cadence of tongue and billowing of emotion to the faith and religion and hope of fighting black thousands. He told them God would drive these white oppressors into the sea and bring back the great heroes of the Kafir nations, if only they would sacrifice to heaven the blood of their cattle, their most dearly prized and venerated possession. The Xosa rose en masse and slaughtered their cattle by the thousand. The cry of their hurt and the stench of their flesh swept over the veldt; and famine fell—a hundred thousand black men starved.

In our day, the nineteenth and twentieth centuries, there have been small revolts all over Africa. The revolt in the Belgian Congo in 1904 and 1906; the riot in Dahomey in 1923; the mutiny on the Ivory Coast in 1923 and 1924; the revolt of the Senussi in 1916; the turmoil in the French Congo in 1928; that other earlier revolt in 1904, when after the massacre of one thousand five hundred natives, a tribe arose killing and eating twenty-seven traders; the revolt of Harry Thuku in Kenya in 1922; the mutiny of black Sudanese troops under English officers and the riots by former Gordon College boys; the riot of Port Alice, South Africa, in 1920; at Bloemfontein in 1925, and Durban in 1929; the revolt of the Wahee against the Germans in 1891; the Magi-Magi in East Africa in 1905; the wiping out of the Herero; in Southwest Africa, the disgraceful massacre in Uganda by Catholics, Protestants, Mohammedans and natives; the hut-tax rebellion in Sierra Leone in 1894, which lasted three months and in which a thousand British subjects lost their lives; the Zulu rebellion in 1906. One might extend this record indefinitely. In some cases few were killed and in some cases thousands; but the total loss of life was immense.

To this have been added strikes; the strike of the railway workers in Sierra Leone in 1896; the native strike in South Africa in 1913, the strike of workers on the docks and in the mines in 1919 and 1920, and especially the organization of the ICU, a desperate attempt in the face of the law to bring together unskilled workers in one big union and finance a general strike of the black workers of South Africa.

Today the number of armed black troops in Africa, designed to hold the continent in the control of white Europe, is at least two hundred fifty thousand, in addition to a large number of police. There are less than ten thousand white officers and troops regularly in Africa, aside from the recent Italian invasion. Suppose that led by these trained soldiers and armed by the revolt of white labor in Europe and America, the black mass of Africa once rose in rebellion!

Meantime, Africa has become for the most part a land of bitter color discrimination, fading out toward the French North and intensifying toward South Africa. All through Africa the discrimination between white and black, based mainly on color, is manifest. The Bantu proverb has it: "The white man's envy forbids us the red clay, although he does not paint himself." While the Union was refusing to give the natives adequate land, it set aside nearly five million acres as a reserve for wild animals. And finally one may notice the bitter comments made on the hypocrisy of Europeans who claim to be Christian. The Union Parliament which passed the Color Bar Act inserted in the constitution the clause: "The people of South Africa acknowledge the sovereignty and guidance of Almighty God."

This racial bitterness in the southern third of the continent is less manifest in Portuguese Africa but intensified in Kenya; it smolders in the Belgian Congo and in French Equatorial Africa, but reaches perhaps its most critical stage in

British West Africa, where a class of Negroes has arisen who will not always sub-mit to caste. As one author has said, "On the coast, in the forests, and along the rivers of Africa, State meets State, and the effect of the clash of those meetings falls both socially and economically on the populations of those States far off in Europe. These populations, through their policy, their desires and beliefs, are sowing in African forests, but they reap sometimes in European cities and some-times even upon European battlefields. We cannot therefore ignore the possibil-ity that by sowing dragons' teeth in Africa we may reap a most bloody crop of armed men in Europe as well as a most lucrative rubber crop in Africa."

It is, of course, too much to expect that a program of utter altruism toward African natives can be immediately substituted for the extreme individual self-ishness of profit-making investment; but that gradually such a substitution must be made is as clear as day. "For two or three generations," said Lord Lugard, "we can show the Negro what we are: then we shall be asked to go away. Then we shall have to leave the land to those it belongs to."

Finally, one cannot forget the reciprocal influence of labor and its treatment in Africa on labor in Europe and America, and one must ask how far democratic government is going to be possible in a world supported to a larger and larger degree by products from a continent like Africa, and governed by the industrial caste which owns Africa. There is here a paradox and a danger that must not be overlooked.

It seems clear today that the masses of men within and without civilization are depressed, ignorant and poor chiefly because they have never had a chance; because they have lacked inspiring contacts; because the results of their labor have been taken from them; because the opportunity to know the facts of human life has never been presented to them, and because disease and crime have been made easier than health and reason.

For centuries the world has sought to rationalize this condition and pretend that civilized nations and cultured classes are the result of inherent and heredi-tary gifts rather than climate, geography and happy accident. This explanation, which for years was supported by the phenomenal onrush of European culture, is today, because of the decline and fall of this hegemony, less widely believed; and whatever mankind has accomplished through the ages and in many mod-ern regions of the world, is beginning to be looked upon as forecast and prom-ise of what the great majority of human beings can do, with wider and deeper success, if mere political democracy is allowed to widen into industrial democ-racy and the democracy of culture and art.

The possibility of this has long been foreseen and emphasized by the social-ists, culminating in the magnificent and apostolic fervor of Karl Marx and the communists; but it is hindered and it may be fatally hindered today by the rela-tions of white Europe to darker Asia and darkest Africa; by the persistent deter-mination in spite of the logic of facts and the teaching of science, to keep the majority of people in slavish subjection to the white race; not simply to feed and clothe them and administer to their comfort, but to submerge them with such useless and harmful luxury that the effort of their rich to get richer is making civilization desperately poor.

Poverty is unnecessary and the clear result of greed and muddle. It spawns physical weakness, ignorance, and dishonesty. There was a time when poverty was due mainly to scarcity, but today it is due to monopoly founded on our industrial organization. This strangle hold must be broken. It can be broken not so much by violence and revolution, which is only the outward distortion of an inner fact, but by the ancient cardinal virtues: individual prudence, courage, temperance, and justice, and the more modern faith, hope and love. Already the working of these virtues has increased health, intelligence, and honesty, despite poverty; and further increase is only thwarted by the blind and insane will to mass murder which is the dying spasm of that decadent exploitation of human labor as a commodity, born of the Negro slave trade; and this attitude is today strengthened and justified by persistent disbelief in the ability and desert of the vast majority of men. The proletariat of the world consists not simply of white European and American workers but overwhelmingly of the dark workers of Asia, Africa, the islands of the sea, and South and Central America. These are the ones who are supporting a superstructure of wealth, luxury, and extravagance. It is the rise of these people that is the rise of the world. The problem of the twentieth century is the problem of the color line.

NOTE

1. Beer, *African Questions at the Paris Peace Conference*, p. 275.

Further Reading

It would be superfluous to set down here the work of all the classical writers on Africa. I am only, mentioning, under certain topics, a few of the standard works and the newer and more significant works on the Negro.

Chapter I

NEGROES AND NEGROIDS

Hertz, *Race and Civilization* (translated by Levetus and Entz), New York, 1928.
Huxley and Haddon, *We Europeans*, New York, 1936.
Bunche, *A World View of Race*, Washington, 1936.
Von Eickstedt, *Rassenkunde und Rassengeschichte der Menschheit*, Stuttgart, 1937–39.
El Bekri, *Description de l'Afrique*, Paris, 1913 (de Slane translation, new edition).
al-Idrisi, *Description de l'Afrique et de l'Espagne*, Leyden, 1866 (Rozy and de Goeje translation).
Kati, *Tarikh el-fettach*, Paris, 1913 (Houdas et Delafosse translation).
al-Sa'di, *Tarik es Sudan* (translation by Houdas), Paris, 1900.
Ibn Batuta, *Voyage dans le Soudan* (de Slane translation), Paris, 1843.
Seligman, *Les Races de l' Afrique*, Paris, 1935.
—— *Races of Africa*, London, 1930.
Hooton, *Apes, Men and Morons*, New York, 1937.
—— *Up from the Ape*, New York, 1931.
Van Oberbergh, *Les Negres d'Afrique*, Brussels, 1913.
Frazer, *Native Races of Africa and Madagascar*, London, 1938.
Linton, *The Study of Man*, New York, 1936.
Barzun, *Race*, New York, 1937.
Haddon, A. C., *The Races of Man and Their Distribution*, London, 1924.
Fitzgerald, W., *Africa: A Social, Economic and Political Geography of Its Major Regions*, London, 1934.

Chapter II

THE VALLEY OF THE NILE

Budge, *The Egyptian Sudan*, London, 1907.
—— *A History of Ethiopia, Nubia and Abyssinia*, London, 1928.
Hansberry, "Sources for the Study of Ethiopia History," *Howard University Studies in History,* November, 1930.
Chamberlain, "The Contribution of the Negro to Human Civilization," *Journal of Race Development,* April, 1911.
Thompson and Randall-MacIver, *Ancient Races in Thebaid*, London, 1905.
Garstang, Sayce and Griffin, *Meroe*, Oxford, 1911.
Bent, The *Sacred City of the Ethiopians*, London, 1893.

Chapter III

THE NIGER AND THE DESERT

Frobenius, *Voice of Africa* (translated by Blind), London, 1913.
Mai Idris of Bornu, Lagos, 1926.
Cooley, *The Negro Land of the Arabs,* London, 1841.
Delafosse, *Les Noirs de l'Afrique,* Paris, 1921.
—— *Civilizations Negro-Africaines,* Paris, 1925.
—— *Negroes of Africa* (translated by Fligelmen), Washington, 1931.
Dubois, *Timbuctoo the Mysterious,* London, 1897.
Lugard, *A Tropical Dependency,* London, 1911.

Chapter IV

CONGO AND GUINEA

Torday, *On the Trail of the Bushongo,* London, 1925.
Johnston, *Liberia,* New York, 1906.
Hayford, *Gold Coast Native Institutions,* London, 1903.
Morel, *Red Rubber,* London, 1906.
Harris, *Dawn in Darkest Africa.*
Ellis, *Tshi Speaking Peoples,* London, 1887.
—— *Ewe Speaking Peoples,* London, 1887.
—— *Yoruba Speaking Peoples,* London, 1887.
Blyden, *Christianity, Islam and the Negro Race,* London, 1887.
Stanley, *Congo and the Founding of the Free State,* London, 1885.
Herskovits, *Dahomey,* New York, 1938.
Maes and Boone, *Les Peuplades du Congo Belge,* Brussels, 1935.
Perham, M., *Native Administration in Nigeria,* London, 1937.
Rattray, R. S., *Religion and Art in Ashanti,* London, 1927.
Penha-Garcia, Comte de (Editor): *Les colonies portugaises,* 1931.
Meek, C. K., *Law and Authority in a Nigerian Tribe,* London, 1937.
—— The *Northern Tribes of Nigeria,* London, 1925.
Talbot, P. A., *The Peoples of Southern Nigeria,* London, 1926.

Chapter V

FROM THE GREAT LAKES TO THE CAPE

Schweinfurth, *Heart of Africa* (translated by Frewer), London, 1873.
Hunter, *Reaction to Conquest,* London, 1936.
Huxley, *Africa View,* London, 1931.
Christian Students and Modern South Africa, Fort Hare, 1930.
Barnes, *Caliban in Africa,* Philadelphia, 1931.
Leys, *Kenya,* London, 1924.
—— *Last Chance in Kenya,* London, 1931.
Junod, H. A., *The Life of a South African Tribe,* London, 1927.
Schapera, I., *The Bantu-speaking Tribes of South Africa,* London, 1937.
—— *The Khoisan Peoples of South Africa: Bushmen and Hottentots,* London, 1930.
Cobb, *The Thermopylae of Africa,* Nairobi, 1923.
Bryce, *Impressions of South Africa,* 1897.
Stow, *Native Races of South Africa,* London, 1910.

Theal, *History and Ethnography of Africa South of the Zambesi*, London, 1910.
Walker, *History of South Africa*, London, 1928.
Johnston, *Uganda Protectorate*, London, 1904.

Chapter VI

THE CULTURE OF AFRICA

Westermann, *The African To-day*, London, 1934.
Schneider, *Die Kulturfaehigkeit des Negers*, Frankfurt, 1885.
African Negro Art, edited by J. J. Sweeney, New York, 1935.
Johnston, *Comparative Study of the Bantu and Semi-Bantu Languages*, Oxford, 1922.
Ellis, *Negro Culture in West Africa*, New York, 1914.
Cendrars, *The African Saga*, New York, 1927.
Schweinfurth, *Artes Africanae*, Leipzig, 1875.
Werner, *The Language Families of Africa*, London, 1925.
—— *Structure and Relationship of African Languages*, London, 1930.
Guillaume and Munro, *Primitive Negro Sculpture*, New York, 1925.
Hayford, *Gold Coast Native Institutions*, London, 1903.
Randall-MacIver, *Mediaeval Rhodesia*, New York, 1906.
Haardt and Andouin-Dubreuil, *La Croisère Noire*, Paris, 1927.
Africa, The Journal of the International Institute of Languages and Cultures, Volumes I-XI, Oxford University Press.
Frobenius, *Atlantis*, Munich 1921–1928.
Junod, *The Life of a South Africa Tribe*, London, 1927.
Ward, *Voice from the Congo*, New York, 1910.
Spratlin, *Juan Latino*, New York, 1938.
Thurnwald, *Economics in Primitive Communities*, London, 1932.
Smuts, General J. C., *Africa and Some World Problems*, London, 1930.
Mair, L. P., *An African People in the Twentieth Century*, London, 1933.

Chapter VII

THE TRADE IN MEN

Du Bois, *Suppression of the African Slave Trade*, Cambridge, 1896.
Wyndham, *The Atlantic and Slavery*, London, 1935.
Clarkson, *History of the Abolition of the African Slave Trade*, London, 1808.
Williams, *Whence the "Black Irish" of Jamaica?* New York, 1932.
Drake, *Revelations of a Slave Smuggler*, New York, 1860.
Foote, *Africa and the American Flag*, New York, 1854.
Williams, "Africa and the Rise of Capitalism," *Howard University Studies in History*, Volume I, No. 1.

Chapter VIII

WESTERN SLAVE MARTS

Edwards, *History of the West Indies*, London, 1793–1819.
Johnston, *The Negro in the New World*, New York, 1910.
Steward, *Haitian Revolution*, New York, 1914.
Bryce, *South America*, New York, 1912.
Vinogradov, *The Black Consul* (translated by Burns), New York, 1935.
Bolivar, *Memoirs of Simon Bolivar*, Boston, 1829.

Martineau, *The Hour and the Man*, New York, 1873.
Morand, *Black Magic*, New York, 1929.
Seabrook, *The Magic Island*, New York, 1929.
Beard, *The Life of Toussaint L'Ouverture*, London, 1853.
Welles, *Naboth's Vineyard*, New York, 1928.
Wiener, *Africa and the Discovery of America*, Philadelphia, 1920.
Leger, *Haiti*, New York, 1907.
Waxman, *Black Napoleon*, New York, 1931.

Chapter IX

EMANCIPATION AND ENFRANCHISEMENT

Balch, *Occupied Haiti*, 1927.
United States Senate: "Inquiry into Occupation and Administration of Haiti and Santo Domingo," Washington, 1922.
Bellegarde, *Pour Une Haiti Heureuse*, Port au Prince, 1927, 1929.
Mathieson, *Sugar Colonies and Governor Eyre*, London, 1936.
Olivier, *Myth of Governor Eyre*, London, 1933.
Beals, *Crime of Cuba*, London, 1934.
—— *America South*, Philadelphia, 1937.
Williams, *The People and Politics of Latin America*, Boston, 1930.
Logan, *Diplomatic Relations Between the United States and Haiti* (unpublished Thesis for Harvard Ph.D.) 1936.

Chapter X

THE BLACK UNITED STATES

Herskovits, *The American Negro*, New York, 1928.
Du Bois, *Black Reconstruction in America*, New York, 1935.
Williams, *History of the Negro Race in America*, New York, 1882.
Washington, *Up from Slavery*, New York, 1901.
Giddings, *Exiles of Florida*, Columbus, 1858.
Life of Frederick Douglass, Boston, 1845.
Johnson, *Negro College Graduate*, Chapel Hill, 1938.
—— *The Negro in American Civilization*, New York, 1930.
Wesley, *Negro Labor in the United States*, 1927.
Spero and Harris, *The Black Worker*, New York, 1931.
Consult also: "The United States Census," *The Atlanta University Studies*, 1896–1914; writings of Charles W. Chesnutt, Paul Laurence Dunbar, Countée Cullen, Jessie Fauset, and James Weldon Johnson.

Chapter XI

BLACK EUROPE

Raw Materials and Colonies, Royal Institute of International Affairs, London, 1936.
Barnes, *Caliban in Africa*, Philadelphia, 1931.
Middleton, *The Rape of Africa*, New York, 1936.
Guernier, *L'Afrique*, Paris, 1933.
Simon, *Slavery*, London, 1929.
Woolf, *Empire and Commerce in Africa*.
Statesman's Yearbook, London, 1938.
Mair, *Native Policies in Africa*, London, 1936.

Hunter, *Reaction to Conquest*, London, 1936.
Worthington, E. B., *Science in Africa*, London, 1938.

Chapter XII

THE LAND IN AFRICA

Leys, *Kenya*, London, 1924
—— *Last Chance in Kenya*, London, 1931.
Hayford, *The Truth About the West African Land Question*, London, 1913.
Olivier, *Anatomy of African Misery*, London, 1927.

Chapter XIII

THE AFRICAN LABORER

Orde-Browne, *The African Labourer*, London, 1933.
Shephard, *Economics of Peasant Agriculture and the Gold Coast*, 1936.
Olivier, *White Capital and Coloured Labour*, 2nd Ed., London, 1929.
Padmore, *How Britain Rules Africa*, London, 1936.
Maran, *Batouala*, Paris, 1921.
Davis, *Modern History and the African*, London, 1933.
"The Recruiting of Labour in Colonies," etc., International Labour Conference, Geneva, 1935.
Knowles, *Economic Development of the British Overseas Empire,* Volume II, Union of South Africa, London, 1936.
Report of the Financial and Economic Commission of Northern Rhodesia, London, 1938.
Frankel, S. H., *Capital Investment in Africa*, London, 1938.
Report of the Native Economic Commission, Union of South Africa, 1932.

Chapter XIV

THE POLITICAL CONTROL OF AFRICA

Johnson, *Toward Nationhood in West Africa*, London, 1928.
Davis, *Modern History and the African*, London, 1933.
Buell, *The Native Problem in Africa*, Volumes I and II, MacMillan, 1928.
Hailey, *An African Survey*, London, 1938.
Lugard, *The Dual Mandate in British Tropical Africa*, London, 1929.
Fox-Bourne, *Civilization in Congoland, London*, 1903.
Twain, *King Leopold's Soliloquy, London*, 1907.
De Bono, *Anno XIII*, London, 1937.
Macmillan, W. H., *Complex South Africa*, London, 1932.
Schapera, I. (Editor), *Western Civilization and the Natives of South Africa*, London, 1934.
Thurnwald, R., *Black and White in East Africa*, London, 1936.
Rogers, H., *Native Administration in the Union of South Africa*, London, 1933.
Brookes, E. H., *The Colour Problems of South Africa*, London, 1934.
—— *History of Native Policy in South Africa*, Cape Town, 1927.

Chapter XV

EDUCATION IN AFRICA

Christian Students and Modern South Africa, Fort Hare, 1930.
Jones, *Education in East Africa*, London, 1925.

—— *Education in Africa* (West, South and Equatorial), New York, 1922.
Mumford and Orde-Browne, *Africans Learn to be French*, [1936].
Oldham, *Christianity and the Race Problem*, New York, 1924.
Sharp, *The African Child*, London, 1931.
Congo Missionary Conference, 1921, Bolobo, 1921.
Loram, *Education of the South African Native*, London, 1917.
Westermann, D., *Africa and Christianity*, London, 1937.
Oldham, J. H., and Gibson, B. D., *The Remaking of Man in Africa*, London, 1931.

Chapter XVI

THE FUTURE OF WORLD DEMOCRACY

"Poor White Problem in South Africa," Report of the Carnegie Commission, Stellenbosch, 1932.
Hayford, *Ethiopia Unbound*, London, 1911.
Oldham, *White and Black in Africa*, London, 1930.
Smuts, *Africa and Some World Problems*, Oxford, 1930.
Thwaite, *The Seething African Pot*, London, 1936.

Index

United States, fugitive slaves, 145–146,
147, 148
United States, migration of Negroes, 152–153,
154–155
United States and Haiti, 132, 133

Venezuela, 106, 136–137, 138
Virgin Islands, 106
Voters, Cape Colony, 236, 237, 238, 39

Wadai, 38
Wages, native, 184–185, 186, 189–190, 191,
192, 195, 196–197, 197–198, 199, 201,
202–203, 204, 206, 207–208, 211, 212,
213–214
Waklimi dynasty, 55

Washington, Booker T., 88, 152–153, 154, 157
West Africa, 219, 220, 221–222, 223
West Africa, British, 179, 219
West African students, 254, 255
West Indies, 99–100, 104, 109, 110–111, 120–121,
127–128, 129
World War, Negro soldiers, 154–155, 264–265,
269–270
World War, South Africa, 172, 189

Yellow fever, 124

Zambesi, 8, 10, 49, 50, 54, 55
Zanzibar, 56, 228–229
Zaria, 7, 38
Zymbabwe, 54, 57, 59, 82

William Edward Burghardt Du Bois: A Chronology

Compiled by Henry Louis Gates, Jr. and Terri Hume Oliver

1868	Born William Edward Burghardt Du Bois, 23 February, in Great Barrington, Massachusetts—the only child of Alfred Du Bois and Mary Silvina Burghardt. Mother and child move to family farm owned by Othello Burghardt, Mary Silvina's father, in South Egremont Plain.
1872	Othello Burghardt dies 19 September and family moves back to Great Barrington, where Mary Sylvina finds work as a domestic servant.
1879	Moves with mother to rooms on Railroad Street. Mother suffers stroke, which partially paralyzes her; she continues to work despite her disability.
1883–1885	Writes occasionally for *Springfield Republican*, the most influential newspaper in the region. Reports on local events for the *New York Globe*, a black weekly, and its successor, the *Freeman*.
1884	Graduates from Great Barrington High School. Works as time-keeper on a construction site.
1885	Mother dies 23 March at age 54. A scholarship is arranged by local Congregational churches so Du Bois can attend Fisk University in Nashville. Enters Fisk with sophomore standing. Contracts typhoid and is seriously ill in October; after recovering, resumes studies and becomes editor of the school newspaper, the *Fisk Herald*.
1886–1887	Teaches at a black school near Alexandria, Tennessee, for two summers. Begins singing with the Mozart Society at Fisk.
1888	Receives BA from Fisk. Enters Harvard College as a junior after receiving a Price-Greenleaf grant.
1890	Awarded second prize in Boylston oratorical competition. Receives BA *cum laude* in philosophy on 25 June. Delivers commencement oration on Jefferson Davis, which receives national press attention. Enters Harvard Graduate School in social science.

1891	Awarded MA in history from Harvard. Begins work on doctorate. Presents paper on the suppression of the African slave trade at meeting of American Historical Association in Washington, D.C.
1892	Awarded a Slater Fund grant to study in Germany at Friedrich Wilhelm University in Berlin.
1893	Grant is extended for an additional year.
1894	Denied doctoral degree at Friedrich Wilhelm University due to residency requirements. Denied further aid from Slater Fund; returns to Great Barrington. Receives teaching chair in classics at Wilberforce University in Xenia, Ohio.
1895	Awarded a PhD in history; he is the first black to receive a PhD from Harvard.
1896	Marries Nina Gomer, a student at Wilberforce. His doctoral thesis, *The Suppression of the African Slave-Trade to United States of America, 1638–1870*, is published as the first volume of Harvard's Historical Monograph Series. Hired by the University of Pennsylvania to conduct a sociological study on the black population of Philadelphia's Seventh Ward.
1897	Joins Alexander Crummell and other black intellectuals to found the American Negro Academy, an association dedicated to black scholarly achievement. Appointed professor of history and economics at Atlanta University. Begins editing a series of sociological studies on black life, the *Atlanta University Studies* (1898–1914). First child, Burghardt Comer Du Bois, is born in Great Barrington on 2 October.
1899	*The Philadelphia Negro* is published by the University of Pennsylvania. Burghardt Gomer Du Bois dies on 24 May in Atlanta and is buried in Great Barrington. Publishes articles in *Atlantic Monthly* and *The Independent*.
1900	In July attends first Pan-African Congress in London and is elected secretary. In an address to the congress, he declares that "the problem of the twentieth century is the problem of the color line." Enters an exhibit at Paris Exposition and wins grand prize for his display on black economic development. Daughter Nina Yolande born 21 October in Great Barrington.
1901	Publishes "The Freedman's Bureau" in *Atlantic Monthly*.
1902	Booker T. Washington offers Du Bois a teaching position at Tuskegee Institute, but Du Bois declines.
1903	*The Souls of Black Folk* is published in April. Publishes the essay "The Talented Tenth" in *The Negro Problem*.
1904	Resigns from Washington's Committee of Twelve for the Advancement of the Negro Race due to ideological differences. Publishes "Credo" in *The Independent*.
1905	Holds the first conference of the Niagara Movement and is named general secretary. Founds and edits *The Moon Illustrated Weekly*.

1906	Second meeting of the Niagara Movement. *The Moon* ceases publication. The Atlanta riots, in which white mobs target blacks, occur in September; Du Bois responds by writing his most famous poem, *A Litany of Atlanta*. After the riots Du Bois's wife and daughter move to Great Barrington.
1907	Niagara Movement in disarray due to debt and dissension. Founds and edits *Horizon*, a monthly paper that folds in 1910.
1908	Fourth conference of Niagara Movement; few attend.
1909	The National Negro Committee, an organization dominated by white liberals, is formed (it will later be renamed the National Association for the Advancement of Colored People [NAACP]); Du Bois joins. The fifth and last Niagara Conference is held. *John Brown*, a biography, is published.
1910	Appointed director of publications and research for the NAACP; becomes the only black member of the board of directors. Moves to New York City to found and edit *The Crisis*, the official publication of the NAACP.
1911	Attends Universal Races Conference in London. Publishes his first novel, *The Quest of the Silver Fleece*. Joins the Socialist Party.
1912	Endorses Woodrow Wilson in *The Crisis*. Resigns from Socialist Party.
1913	Writes and presents *The Star of Ethiopia*, a pageant staged to commemorate the fiftieth anniversary of emancipation.
1914	Supports women's suffrage in *The Crisis*. Supports the Allied effort in World War I despite declaring that imperialist rivalries are a cause of the war.
1915	Booker T. Washington dies on 14 November. *The Negro* is published. Protests D. W. Griffith's racist film *The Birth of a Nation*.
1917	Undergoes kidney operations early in the year. Supports the establishment of separate training camps for black officers as the only way to insure black participation in combat.
1918	In his July editorial for *The Crisis*, he publishes "Close Ranks," urging cooperation with white citizens. The War Department offers Du Bois a commission as a captain in the army in an effort to address racial issues, but the offer is withdrawn after controversy. Goes to Europe in December to evaluate the conditions of black troops for the NAACP.
1919	Organizes the first Pan-African Conference in Paris, and is elected executive secretary. Returns to the U.S. in April and writes the editorial "Returning Soldiers," which the U.S. postmaster Albert Burleson tries to suppress; the issue sells 106,000 copies, the most ever for *The Crisis*.
1920	Founds and edits *The Brownies' Book*, a monthly magazine for children. Publishes *Darkwater: Voices from within the Veil*, a collection of essays.

1921	The second Pan-African Conference is held in London, Brussels, and Paris. Du Bois signs group protest against Henry Ford's support of the anti-Semitic forgery, *Protocols of the Elders of Zion*.
1922	Works for passage of the Dyer Anti-Lynching Bill, which is blocked by Senate.
1923	Writes "Back to Africa," an article attacking Garvey for encouraging racial division. Organizes the third Pan-African Conference in London, Paris, and Lisbon; declines to attend Paris session due to disproval of French assimilationists. Receives the Spingarn Medal from the NAACP. Travels to Liberia to represent the United States at the Liberian presidential inauguration.
1924	Publishes *The Gift of Black Folk: The Negroes in the Making of America*.
1925	Contributes "The Negro Mind Reaches Out" to Alain Locke's *The New Negro: An Interpretation*, one of the most influential works of the Harlem Renaissance.
1926	Founds the Krigwa Players, a Harlem theater group. Travels to the Soviet Union to examine life after the Bolshevik Revolution. Praises Soviet achievements in *The Crisis*.
1927	The fourth and last Pan-African Conference is held in New York City.
1928	Daughter Yolande weds the poet Countee Cullen in Harlem; the marriage ends within a year. Du Bois's novel, *Dark Princess, A Romance*, is published.
1929	*The Crisis* faces financial collapse.
1930	Awarded honorary Doctor of Laws degree from Howard University.
1932	Du Bois's daughter Yolande and her second husband, Arnett Williams, have a daughter, Du Bois Williams.
1933	Losing faith in the possibilities of integration, Du Bois begins to publicly examine his position on segregation. Accepts a one-year visiting professorship at Atlanta University. Relinquishes the editorship of *The Crisis* but retains general control of the magazine.
1934	Writes editorials encouraging voluntary segregation and criticizing the integrationist policies of the NAACP. Resigns as editor of *The Crisis* and from the NAACP. Accepts the chairmanship in sociology at Atlanta University. Named the editor in chief of the *Encyclopedia of the Negro*, which is never completed or published.
1935	Publishes the revolutionary historical study, *Black Reconstruction*.
1936	Spends five months in Germany on a grant to study industrial education. Travels through Poland, the Soviet Union, Manchuria, China, and Japan.
1938	Receives honorary Doctor of Laws degree from Atlanta University and honorary Doctor of Letters degree from Fisk.
1939	*Black Folk, Then and Now*, a revised edition of *The Negro* is published.

1940	Publishes his first autobiography, *Dusk of Dawn*. Founds and edits *Phylon*, a quarterly magazine examining black issues. Awarded honorary Doctorate of Humane Letters at Wilberforce.
1941–1942	Proposes and then coordinates the study of southern blacks for black land-grant colleges.
1943	Organizes the First Conference of Negro Land-Grant Colleges at Atlanta University. Informed by Atlanta University that he must retire by 1944, he attempts to have the policy reversed.
1944	Named first black member of the National Institute of Arts and Letters. Despite his protests, he is retired by Atlanta University. Although hesitant to work with Walter White, he rejoins the NAACP as director of special research and moves back to New York. Publishes the essay "My Evolving Program for Negro Freedom" in Rayford Logan's collection *What the Negro Wants*.
1945	Writes a weekly column for the *Chicago Defender*. Serves as consultant, with Mary McLeod Bethune and Walter White, at the San Francisco conference that drafts the United Nations charter; criticizes the charter for failing to oppose colonialism. In October he presides at the Fifth Pan-African Conference in Manchester, England. Nina Du Bois suffers a stroke, which paralyzes her left side. Publishes the first volume of *Encyclopedia of the Negro: Preparatory Volume* with coauthor Guy B. Johnson. Publishes an anti-imperialist analysis of the postwar era, *Color and Democracy: Colonies and Peace*. Resigns from the American Association of University Professors in protest of conferences held in segregated hotels.
1946	Invites leaders of twenty organizations to New York to draft a petition to the United Nations on behalf of African Americans; the appeal becomes an NAACP project.
1947	Edits and writes the introduction to *An Appeal to the World*, a collection of essays sponsored by the NAACP to enlist international support for the fight against racial discrimination in America. At the United Nations, the appeal is supported by the Soviet Union but opposed by the United States. Publishes *The World and Africa*.
1948	Fired from the NAACP after his memorandum critical of Walter White and the NAACP board of directors appears in the *New York Times*. Supports Henry Wallace, the Progressive Party candidate for president. Takes unpaid position as vice chairman (with Paul Robeson) of the Council of African Affairs, an organization listed as "subversive" by the U.S. attorney general. Begins writing for the *National Guardian*.
1949	Helps sponsor and addresses the Cultural and Scientific Conference for World Peace in New York City. Attends the First World Congress of the Defenders of Peace in Paris. Travels to the All-Union Conference of Peace Proponents in Moscow.
1950	Nina Gomer Du Bois dies in Baltimore in July; she is buried in Great Barrington. Elected chairman of the Peace Information

Center, an organization dedicated to the international peace movement and the banning of nuclear weapons. Organization disbands under pressure from the Department of Justice. Du Bois is nominated by the American Labor Party for U.S. senator from New York. Receives 4 percent of the vote statewide, 15 percent in Harlem.

1951 Secretly marries Shirley Graham, aged 45, a writer, teacher, and civil rights activist, on Valentine's Day. Indicted earlier that month as an "unregistered foreign agent" under the McCormick Act: Du Bois, along with four other officers of the Peace Information Center, is alleged to be agents of foreign interests. He suffers the indignity of being handcuffed, searched, and fingerprinted before being released on bail in Washington, D.C. National lecture tours and a fundraising campaign for his defense expenses raise over $35,000. The five-day trial in Washington ends in acquittal.

1952 Publishes *In Battle for Peace*, an account of the trial. The State Department refuses Du Bois a passport on grounds that his foreign travel is not in the national interest. Later, the State Department demands a statement declaring that he is not a Communist Party member; Du Bois refuses. Advocacy of leftwing political positions widens the distance between Du Bois and the black mainstream.

1953 Prints a eulogy for Stalin in *National Guardian*. Reads 23rd Psalm at the funeral of Julius and Ethel Rosenberg, executed as Soviet spies. Awarded International Peace Prize by the World Peace Council.

1954 Surprised by the Supreme Court decision in *Brown v. Topeka Board of Education*, which outlaws public school segregation, Du Bois declares "I have seen the impossible happen."

1955 Refused a U.S. passport to attend the World Youth Festival in Warsaw, Poland.

1956 Supports Reverend Martin Luther King Jr. during the Montgomery bus boycott. Refused a passport in order to lecture in the People's Republic of China.

1957 Publishes *The Ordeal of Mansart*, the first volume of the *Black Flame*, a trilogy of historical novels chronicling black life from Reconstruction to the mid-twentieth century. A bust of Du Bois is unveiled at the Schomburg Collection of the New York Public Library. Refused a passport to attend independence ceremonies in Ghana. His great-grandson Arthur Edward McFarlane II is born.

1958 A celebration for Du Bois's ninetieth birthday is held at the Roosevelt Hotel in New York City; 2,000 people attend. Begins writing *The Autobiography of W. E. B. Du Bois*, drawing largely from earlier work. A Supreme Court ruling allows Du Bois to obtain a passport. His subsequent world tour includes England, France, Belgium, Holland, Czechoslovakia, East Germany, and

	the Soviet Union. He receives an honorary doctorate from Humbolt University in East Berlin, known as Friedrich Wilhelm University when Du Bois attended in 1892–1894.
1959	Meets with Nikita Khrushchev. In Beijing, makes broadcast to Africa over Radio Beijing and meets with Mao Zedong and Zhou Enlai. Awarded the International Lenin Prize. Publishes the second volume of the *Black Flame* trilogy, *Mansart Builds a School*.
1960	Participates in the celebration of Ghana's establishment as a republic. Travels to Nigeria for the inauguration of its first African governor-general.
1961	Du Bois's daughter Yolande dies of a heart attack in March. *Worlds of Color*, the final book in the *Black Flame* trilogy, is published. Du Bois accepts the invitation of Kwame Nkrumah to move to Ghana and direct a revival of the *Encyclopedia Africana* project. Before leaving for Africa, Du Bois applies for membership in the Communist Party.
1962	Travels to China. His autobiography is published in the Soviet Union.
1963	Becomes a citizen of Ghana. Turns ninety-five in February. Dies in Accra, Ghana, on 27 August, on the eve of the civil rights march on Washington. W. E. B. Du Bois is buried in a state funeral in Accra on the 29th.
1968	*The Autobiography of W. E. B. Du Bois* is published in the United States.
1992	Honored by the United States Postal Service with a 29-cent commemorative stamp as part of the Black Heritage Series, and again in 1998, with a 32-cent commemorative stamp.
1999	Du Bois's efforts to produce alternately an encyclopedia of the Negro and of Africa and Africans are realized when *Encarta Africana* is published by Microsoft, and *Africana: The Encyclopedia of the African and African American Experience*, edited by Kwame Anthony Appiah and Henry Louis Gates Jr. is published by Basic Civitas Books. In 2005 a second much-expanded edition of *Africana* is published by Oxford University Press.

Selected Bibliography

WORKS OF W.E.B. DU BOIS

The Suppression of the African Slave-Trade to the United States of America, 1638–1870. New York: Longmans, Green, 1896.

Atlanta University Publications on the Study of Negro Problems. Publications of the Atlanta University Conferences, ed. Du Bois (1898–1913).

The Philadelphia Negro: A Social Study. Boston: Ginn and Company, 1899.

The Souls of Black Folk: Essays and Sketches. Chicago: A. C. McClurg, 1911.

John Brown. Philadelphia: George W. Jacobs, 1909.

The Quest of the Silver Fleece: A Novel. Chicago: A. C. McClurg, 1911.

The Negro. New York: Harcourt, Brace, 1928.

Darkwater: Voices from within the Veil. New York: Harcourt, Brace and Howe, 1920.

The Gift of Black Folk: Negroes in the Making of America. Boston: Stratford, 1924.

Dark Princess: A Romance. New York: Harcourt, Brace, 1928.

Africa—Its Place in Modern History. Girard, Kansas: Haldeman-Julius, 1930.

Africa, Its Geography, People, and Products. Girard, Kansas: Haldeman-Julius, 1930.

Black Reconstruction: An Essay toward a History of the Part Which Black Folk Played in the Attempt to Reconstruct Democracy in America, 1860–1880. New York: Harcourt, Brace, 1935.

Black Folk Then and Now: An Essay in the History and Sociology of the Negro Race. New York: Henry Holt, 1939.

Dusk of Dawn: An Essay toward an Autobiography of a Race Concept. New York: Harcourt, Brace, 1940.

Color and Democracy: Colonies and Peace. New York: Harcourt, Brace, 1945.

Du Bois, W. E. B., and Guy B. Johnson. *Encyclopedia of the Negro, Preparatory Volume with Reference Lists and Reports.* New York: Phelps-Stokes Fund, 1946.

The World and Africa: An Inquiry into the Part Which Africa Has Played in World History. New York: Masses & Mainstream, 1947.

I Take My Stand for Peace. New York: Masses & Mainstream, 1951.

The Ordeal of Mansart. New York: Mainstream, 1957.

In Battle for Peace: The Story of My 83rd Birthday. With Comment by Shirley Graham. New York: Masses & Mainstream, 1952.

Fourty-Two Years of the USSR [sic]. Chicago: Baan Books, 1959.

Worlds of Color. New York: Mainstream, 1961.

An ABC of Color: Selections from over a Half Century of the Writings of W. E. B. Du Bois. Berlin: Seven Seas, 1963.
The Autobiography of W. E. B. Du Bois: A Soliloquy on Viewing My Life from the Last Decade of Its First Century, ed. Herbert Aptheker. New York: International Publishers, 1968.

COLLECTIONS

Aptheker, Herbert, ed. *Creative Writings by W. E. B. Du Bois: A Pageant, Poems, Short Stories, and Playlets.* New York: Kraus-Thomson Organization, 1985.
Aptheker, Herbert, ed. *The Complete Published Works of W. E. B. Du Bois.* 35 vols. Millwood, NY: Kraus-Thomson, 1973.
Aptheker, Herbert, ed. *The Correspondence of W. E. B. Du Bois.* 3 vols. Amherst: University of Massachusetts Press, 1973–1978.
Aptheker, Herbert, ed. *Writings by W. E. B. Du Bois in periodicals Edited by Others.* 4 vols. Millwood, NY: Kraus-Thomson, 1982.
Foner, Philip S., ed. *W. E. B. Du Bois Speaks: Speeches and Addresses 1890–1919.* New York: Pathfinder, 1970.
Huggins, Nathan I., ed. *W. E. B. Du Bois: Writings.* New York: Library of America, 1986.
Lewis, David Levering, ed. *W. E. B. Du Bois: A Reader.* New York: Henry Holt, 1985.
Sundquist, Eric J., ed. *The Oxford W. E. B. Du Bois Reader.* New York: Oxford University Press, 1996.

BIBLIOGRAPHIES

Aphtheker, Herbert. *Annotated Bibliography of the Published Writings of W. E. B. Du Bois.* Millwood, NY: Kraus-Thomson, 1973.
McDonnell, Robert W., and Paul C. Partington. *W. E. B. Du Bois: A Bibliography of Writings About Him.* Whittier, CA: Paul C. Partington Book Publisher, 1989.
Partington, Paul C. *W. E. B. Du Bois: A Bibliography of His Published Writings.* Whittier, CA: Paul C. Partington Book Publisher, 1977.

BIOGRAPHIES

Broderick, Francis L. *W. E. B. Du Bois: A Negro Leader in Time of Crisis.* Stanford: Stanford University Press, 1959.
Du Bois, Shirley Graham. *His Day is Marching On: A Memoir of W. E. B. Du Bois.* Philadelphia: Lippincott, 1971.
Lewis, David Levering. *W. E. B. Du Bois: The Fight for Equality and the American Century, 1919–1963.* New York: Henry Holt, 2000.
Marable, Manning. *W. E. B. Du Bois: Black Radical Democrat.* Boston: Twayne, 986.
wick, Elliot M. *W. E. B. Du Bois: Propagandist of the Negro Protest.* 1960; reprint. w York: Atheneum, 1968.

CRITICAL WORKS

Appiah, Anthony. "The Uncompleted Argument: Du Bois and the Illusion of Race." *Critical Inquiry* 12 (Autumn 1985): 21–37.

Aptheker, Herbert. *The Literary Legacy of W. E. B. Du Bois.* Whit Plains, NY: Kraus International, 1989.

Ashton, Susanna. "Du Bois's 'Horizon': Documenting Movements of the Color Line." *MELUS* 26.4 (2001): 3–23.

Baker, Houston A., Jr. "The Black Man of Culture: W. E. B. Du bois and *The Souls of Black Folk.*" In *Long Black Song.* Charlottesville: University of Virginia Press, 1972.

Balfour, Lawrie. "Representative Women: Slavery, Citizenship, and Feminist Theory in Du Bois's 'Damnation of Women.'" *Hypatia: A Journal of Feminist Philosophy* 20.3 (2005): 127–148.

Bauerlein, Mark. "Booker T. Washington and W. E. B. Du Bois: The Origins of a Bitter Intellectual Battle." *Journal of Blacks in Higher Education* 46 (Winter 2004–2005): 106–114.

Bell, Bernard, Emily Grosholz, and James Stewart, eds. *W. E. B. Du Bois on Race and Culture: Philosophy, Politics, and Poetics.* New York: Routledge, Chapman, and Hall, 1996.

Bhabha, Homi K. "The Black Savant and the *Dark Princess.*" *ESQ: A Journal of the American Renaissance* 50.1–3 (2004): 137–155.

Blight, David W. "W. E. B. Du Bois and the Struggle for American Historical Memory." In *History and Memory in African-American Culture,* ed. Genevieve Fabre and Robert O'Meally. New York: Oxford University Press, 1994.

Bremen, Brian A. "Du Bois, Emerson, and the 'Fate' of Black Folk." *American Literary Realism* 24 (Spring 1992): 80–88.

Bruce, Dickson D., Jr. "W. E. B. Du Bois and the Idea of Double Consciousness." *American Literature: A Journal of Literary History, Criticism, and Bibliography* 64.2 (June 1992): 299–309.

Byerman, Keith. *Seizing the Word: History, Art, and the Self in the Work of W. E. B. Du Bois.* Athens: University of Georgia Press, 1994.

Castronovo, Russ. "Beauty along the Color Line: Lynching, Aesthetics and the *Crisis.*" *PMLA: Publications of the Modern Language Association of America* 36.2 (2006): 1443–1159.

Crouch, Stanley, and Playthell Benjamin. *Reconsidering the Souls of Black Folk: Thoughts on the Groundbreaking Classic Work of W. E. B. Du Bois.* Philadelphia: Running Press, 2002.

Early, Gerald, ed. *Lure and Loathing: Essays on Race, Identity, and the Ambivalence of Assimilation.* New York: Allen Lane, 1993.

Fisher, Rebecka Rutledge. "Cultural Artifacts and the Narrative of History: W. E. B. Du Bois and the Exhibiting of Culture at the 1900 Paris Exposition Universelle." *MFS: Modern Fiction Studies* 51.4 (2005): 741–774.

Fontenot, Chester J., Mary Alice Morgan, and Sarah Gardner, eds. *W. E. B. Du Bois and Race.* Macon, Georgia: Mercer University Press, 2001.

Frederickson, George. "The Double Life of W. E. B. Du Bois." *New York Review of Books* 48.2 (February 8, 2001): 34–36.

Frederickson, George. *The Black Image in the White Mind: The Debate on Afro-American Character and Destiny, 1817–1914.* New York: Harper and Row, 1971.

Gabiddon, Shaun L. "W. E. B. Du Bois: Pioneering American Criminologist." *Journal of Black Studies* 31.5 (2001): 581–599.

Gooding-Williams, Robert. "Du Bois's Counter-Sublime." *The Massachusetts Review: A Quarterly of Literature, the Arts and Public Affairs* 35.2 (Summer 1994): 202–224.

Herring, Scott. "Du Bois and the Minstrels." *MELUS* 22 (Summer 1997): 3–18.

Hubbard, Dolan, ed. *The Souls of Black Folk One Hundred Years Later.* Columbia, Missouri: University of Missouri Press, 2003.

Jones, Gavin. "'Whose Line Is It Anyway?' W. E. B. Du Bois and the Language of the Color-Line." In *Race Consciousness: African-American Studies for the New Century,* ed. Judith Jackson Fossett and Jeffrey A. Tucker. New York: New York University Press, 1997.

Judy, Ronald A. T., ed. "Sociology Hesitant: Thinking with W. E. B. Du Bois." Special Issue: *Boundary 2: An International Journal of Literature and Culture* 27.3 (2000).

Juguo, Zhang. *W. E. B. Du Bois and the Quest for the Abolition of the Color Line.* New York: Routledge, 2001.

Kirschke, Amy. "Du Bois, *The Crisis,* and Images of Africa and the Diaspora." In *African Diasporas in the New and Old Worlds: Consciousness and Imagination,* ed. Geneviève Fabre and Benesch Klaus. Amsterdam: Rodopi, 2004. 239–262.

Lemke, Sieglinde. "Transatlantic Relations: The German Du Bois." In *German? American? Literature? New Directions in German-American Studies,* ed. Winfried Fluck and Werner Sollors. New York: Peter Lang, 2002. 207–215.

McCaskill, Barbara, and Caroline Gebhard, eds. and introd. *Post-Bellum, Pre-Harlem: African American Literature and Culture.* New York: New York University Press, 2006.

McKay, Nellie. "W. E. B. Du Bois: The Black Women in His Writings—Selected Fictional and Autobiographical Portraits." In *Critical Essays on W. E. B. Du Bois,* ed. William L. Andrews. Boston: G. K. Hall, 1985.

Meier, August. "The Paradox of W. E. B. Du Bois." In *Negro Thought in America, 1880–1915; Radical Ideologies in the Age of Booker T. Washington.* Ann Arbor: University of Michigan Press, 1963.

Miller, Monica. "W. E. B. Du Bois and the Dandy as Diasporic Race Man." *Callaloo* 26.3 (2003): 738–765.

Mizrunchi, Susan. "Neighbors, Strangers, Corpses: Death and Sympathy in the Early Writings of W. E. B. Du Bois." In *Centuries' Ends, Narrative Means,* ed. Robert Newman. Stanford, CA: Stanford University Press, 1996.

Moses, Wilson Jeremiah. *Creative Conflict in African American Thought: Frederick Douglass, Alexander Crummell, Booker T. Washington, W. E. B. Du Bois, and Marcus Garvey.* Cambridge, England: Cambridge University Press, 2004.

Pauley, Garth E. "W. E. B. Du Bois on Woman Suffrage: A Critical Analysis of His *Crisis* Writings." *Journal of Black Studies* 30.3 (2000): 383–410.

Peterson, Dale. "Notes from the Underworld: Dostoyevsky, Du Bois, and the Discovery of the Ethnic Soul." *Massachusetts Review* 35 (Summer 1994): 225–247.

Posnock, Ross. "The Distinction of Du Bois: Aesthetics, Pragmatism, Politics." *American Literary History* 7 (Fall 1995): 500–524.

Rampersad, Arnold. *The Art and Imagination of W. E. B. Du Bois.* Cambridge, MA: Harvard University Press, 1976.

Rampersad, Arnold, and Deborah E. McDowell, eds. *Slavery and the Literary Imagination: Du Bois's* The Souls of Black Folk. Baltimore: Johns Hopkins University Press, 1989.

Rothberg, Michael. "W. E. B. Du Bois in Warsaw: Holocaust Memory and the Color Line, 1949–1952." *Yale Journal of Criticism* 14.1 (2001): 169–189.

Schneider, Ryan. "Sex and the Race Man: Imagining Interracial Relationships in W. E. B. Du Bois's *Darkwater.*" *Arizona Quarterly: A Journal of American Literature, Culture, and Theory* 59.2 (2003): 59–80.

Schrager, Cynthia D. "Both Sides of the Veil: Race, Science, and Mysticism in W. E. B. Du Bois." *American Quarterly* 48 (December 1996): 551–587.

Siemerling, Winfried. "W. E. B. Du Bois, Hegel, and the Staging of Alterity." *Callaloo* 24.1 (2001): 325–333.

Smith, Shawn Michelle. *Photography on the Color Line: W. E. B. Du Bois, Race, and Visual Culture.* Durham: Duke University Press, 2004.

Sundquist, Eric J. "Swing Low: *The Souls of Black Folk.*" In *To Wake the Nations.* Cambridge, MA: Harvard University Press, 1993.

Temperley, Howard, Michael B. Katz, and Thomas J. Sugrue. "W. E. B. Du Bois, Race, and the City." *The Times Literary Supplement.* No. 4996 (1999).

"The Study of African American Problems: W. E. B. Du Bois's Agenda, Then and Now." *Annals of the American Academy of Political and Social Science* 568 (March 2000): 1–313.

Warren, Kenneth W. "Troubled Black Humanity in *The Souls of Black Folk* and *The Autobiography of an Ex-Colored Man.*" In *The Cambridge Companion to American Realism and Naturalism: Howells to London,* ed. Donald Pizer. Cambridge: Cambridge University Press, 1995.

West, Cornel. "W. E. B. Du Bois: The Jamesian Organic Intellectual." In *The American Evasion of Philosophy: A Genealogy of Pragmatism.* Madison: University of Wisconsin Press, 1989.

Williamson, Joel. *The Crucible of Race: Black-White Relations in the American South Since Emancipation.* New York: Oxford University Press, 1984.

Wolters, Raymond. *Du Bois and His Rivals.* Columbia, Missouri: University of Missouri Press, 2002.

Zamir, Shamoon. *Dark Voices: W. E. B. Du Bois and American Thought, 1888–1903.* Chicago: University of Chicago Press, 1995.

Zamir, Shamoon. "'The Sorrow Songs'/'Song of Myself': Du Bois, the Crisis of Leadership, and Prophetic Imagination." In *The Black Columbiad: Defining Moments in African American Literature and Culture.* Cambridge, MA: Harvard University Press, 1994.

Zwarg, Christina. "Du Bois on Trauma: Psychoanalysis and the Would-Be Black Savant." *Cultural Critique* 51 (2002): 1–39.

Printed in the USA/Agawam, MA
March 13, 2015

610498.001